D0938462

WITHDRAWN
UTSA LIBRARIES

Strategies for Change in the South

**Thomas H. Naylor
and
James Clotfelter**

Foreword by Alan W. Steelman

The University of North Carolina Press
Chapel Hill

LIBRARY

University of Texas

At San Antonio

Copyright © 1975 by
The Twentieth Century Fund
All rights reserved
Manufactured in the United States of America
Library of Congress Catalog Card Number 74-16219
ISBN 0-8078-1236-6

Library of Congress Cataloging in Publication Data
Naylor, Thomas H 1936-
  Strategies for change in the South.
  Includes bibliographical references.
  1. Southern States—Economic conditions. 2. Education—
Southern States. 3. Southern States—Politics and government—
1951- 4. Southern States—Social conditions. I. Clotfelter, James,
joint author.
II. Title.
HC107.A13N36   309.2'5'0975   74-16219
ISBN 0-8078-1236-6

To Susanne Naylor
and Caroline and James Clotfelter, Sr.

Contents

Foreword by Alan W. Steelman xiii

Preface xv

1. Introduction 3

2. Out of the Quagmire and into the Economic Mainstream 10

3. Whither Public Education? 77

4. Adapting Higher Education to Changing Needs 129

5. Toward a Responsive Southern Politics 177

6. Controlling Urban Development 222

7. Agrarianism: Through a Different Looking Glass 264

8. Summary and Conclusions 281

Notes 285

Index 309

Tables

2.1. Per Capita Personal Income
for the United States and the South, 1900-1970   [10]

2.2. Per Capita Personal Income
for the Southern States, 1920-72   [11]

2.3. Manufacturing in the South, 1850-80   [21]

3.1. Estimated School-Age Population and Fall Enrollment in
Public Elementary and Secondary Day Schools, 1970-71   [78]

3.2. Estimated Average Daily Attendance in
Public Elementary and Secondary Day Schools, 1970-71   [79]

3.3. Estimated Populations
and Public High School Graduates, 1969   [80]

3.4. Southern Disqualifications on
Selective Service Mental Examination, 1971   [80]

3.5. Extent of Desegregation
in the South, 1970-71 and 1968-69   [82]

3.6. Estimated Number of Instructional Staff
Members in Public Elementary and
Secondary Day Schools, by Type of Position, 1970-71   [85]

3.7. Classroom Teachers, Estimates, 1970-71   [85]

3.8. Average Annual Salaries of Total
Instructional Staff and of Classroom Teachers, 1970-71   [86]

3.9. Teacher Characteristics: Selected Qualities   [87]

3.10. School Characteristics: Age and Capacity   [90]

3.11. School Characteristics: Selected Facilities   [91]

3.12. Estimated Number of Basic Administrative Units,
Board Members, and Superintendents, 1970-71   [94]

3.13. Student Characteristics: Selected Qualities   [95]

3.14. Student Enrollment, Fall 1970   [96]

3.15. Estimated Revenue Used for Education, 1970-71   [97]

3.16. Federal Grants to State and Local
Governments for Elementary and Secondary
Education Programs, by State: Fiscal Year 1969   [98]

3.17. Per Capita Income and Direct General
Expenditures of State and Local Governments, 1969   [99]

3.18. Annual Expenditure Per Pupil and Average Annual Salary of
Instructional Staff and Classroom Teachers, 1970-71   [100]

3.19. Average Annual Salary of Instructional Staff
in Full-Time Public Elementary and Secondary
Day Schools, by State: 1929-30 to 1969-70   [101]

3.20. Per Capita Income and Direct General
Expenditures of States with Approximately
the Same Per Capita Income as the South, 1969   [108]

3.21. Enrollment in Special Education
Classes in Southern States   [117]

4.1. Operational Appropriations for Higher Education   [130]

4.2. College Enrollment   [133]

4.3. College Enrollment as a
Percentage of College-Age Population   [133]

4.4. Lifetime and Mean Income of Males Twenty-five
Years Old and Over, by Years of School Completed   [135]

4.5. Level of Education and Racial Attitudes
of White Southerners   [136]

4.6. In- and Out-migration in Public
and Private Educational Institutions, 1968   [140]

4.7. Educational and General Funds Income
by Source, Public Insitutions, 1966-67   [141]

4.8. Educational and General Expenditures at
Institutions of Higher Education   [142]

4.9. Black Undergraduate Enrollment, by Institution, and as a Percentage of Black College-Age Population, Fall 1970   [164]

5.1. Voting Turnout as a Percentage of Voting-Age
Population, 1960 and 1968 Presidential Elections   [181]

5.2.   Ranking of Southern Legislatures by the
       Citizens Conference on State Legislatures, 1971   [184]

5.3.   Composition of State Legislatures,
       by Party Affiliation, 1970   [185]

6.1.   Population Living in Urban Areas, 1890-1970   [223]

6.2.   Metropolitan Population Growth,
       White and Nonwhite, 1960-70   [224]

6.3.   Percentage of South's Metropolitan Population,
       White and Nonwhite, in Central Cities and Suburban
       Rings of Ten Southern States, 1960-70   [226]

6.4.   Estimated Mean Annual Percentage Changes in
       Employment for the Central Cities and
       Suburban Rings of Forty Large SMSAs   [227]

6.5.   Percentage of Occupied Housing Lacking Complete
       Plumbing Facilities or Rated Dilapidated, 1968   [230]

6.6.   Metropolitan Housing Lacking Complete Plumbing
       Facilities or Rated Overcrowded, 1970   [231]

6.7.   Governments of All Types within SMSAs   [233]

6.8.   Number and Types of Governments within Southern
       SMSAs over 300,000 in Population   [234]

6.9.   Functional Classification of Cities
       over 10,000 Population, and SMSAs, 1963   [238]

6.10. SMSAs: Their Growth by Population Size, 1960-70   [239]

6.11. Blacks and Urban Growth in the South   [241]

6.12. Mean Annual Population
       Growth for Urbanized Areas Attaining
       Population Size of 100,000 by 2000   [243]

6.13. Property Tax, 1968-69   [248]

6.14. State Support of Public Education, 1968-69   [248]

7.1.   Rural and Urban Population, 1970   [264]

7.2.   White and Black Population, 1960 and 1970   [265]

The "South" is me, and I am it. For anyone who grew up there, it is difficult to think of the South in objective, impersonal terms. The region has its quota of lawyers, doctors, preachers, politicians, and loafers. It has its stores, mills, churches, schools, homes, banks, hotels, undertakers, Ford agencies, and Dairy Queens. But in a distinguishing sense, it is different. As was once said of one of my hometowns, Fordyce, Arkansas, it also has more flowers than weeds, more dogs than fleas, more homes than houses, more children than troubles, and more smiles than tears. Therefore, you will pardon, I hope, this bit of romantic musing; for you see, I am rooted as are most native-borns to its soil, its mores, its customs, its music, and its love for life and living.

Tom Naylor and Jim Clotfelter give us here an agenda for thought and action. Both are "thinkers," and to that extent, this is a work designed to raise our sights, to inspire us as Southerners to the kind of action that will preserve our regional "soul" as we build a structure whose change and growth will be at our direction.

For the first time since Reconstruction, we are in the driver's seat as far as national development is concerned, and we must realize that great responsibilities accompany this role of eminence. This agenda is meant to help us shoulder that burden. I do not endorse every proposal herein. Indeed, I strongly disagree with several. But I have been prompted to thought, and I for the first time have seen the interdependence of these problems and their solutions. I recommend its reading by all who feel for the South and who wish to be a part of its future. We as citizens and/or elected representatives must make the right decisions over the next several decades, and this work gives us some alternatives to choose from.

Alan W. Steelman

Washington, D.C.
27 February 1974

[xiii]

Preface

This book is the result of a project begun in the fall of 1970 that was co-sponsored by the Center for Southern Studies at Duke University and the L. Q. C. Lamar Society. The Twentieth Century Fund aided in financing the research for this work.

Since a study of Southern institutions and public policy is a major undertaking, a number of people have had a hand in shaping this book. Congressman Alan W. Steelman, who has written the foreword, played an important role in the initial formulation of the project. In the summer of 1971 a group of student interns from throughout the South gathered at Duke University to collect material for this project. Their contribution to this volume was substantial.

Three people played a major role in assembling this book—Katherine Savage, Susan Clubbe, and Sandra Köszegi. The authors also wish to thank the following people for their comments on sections of the book (with the usual waiver of any blame for errors): Charles Clotfelter, Horst Schauland, Robert Mosteller, Robert Clark, Albert Karnig, Lawrence Goodwyn, and Suze Carlson.

Part of James Clotfelter's work on this book was done while he was at the Duke University Center for the Study of Aging and Human Development on a research appointment supported by NICHD Grant HD00164. Professor Clotfelter also wishes to thank Lewis Bowman and Jack Hopkins for their general encouragement.

Thomas H. Naylor
James Clotfelter

The shopping centers and the housing developments, the new factories and football stadiums testify to the fact that the South is no longer in the backwaters of American prosperity. It may be economically under-developed, but it is developing. In 1972 *Business Week* ran a special report entitled "The New Rich South: Frontier for Growth."[1] And, indeed, in the 1970s the Southeast and Southwest have been outstrip-ping other areas in economic growth.

But what will growth bring with it? How will it affect the region's per-sistent racial, educational, and political problems? Will growth narrow or widen the region's disparity in income distribution? Will the South become a part of a homogenized nation—will it assume the virtues and embrace the mistakes of the rest of the country? Or will it follow a dif-ferent path of development? What kinds of choices must be made and what will the region get from and pay for alternative policies? In this book we will examine these and other questions. We will lay out an agenda for institutional and policy change in the region that we hope will be useful in stimulating and directing discussion and action.

Why a Regional Focus?

"The South" endures, and not just as an abstraction of the Department of Commerce. "The South has seemed to live inside its people like an instinct," it has been asserted. And even in the face of economic develop-ment and a pervasive mass media, Southern distinctiveness persists. John Shelton Reed shows that the South is a regional subculture, that it is a reference group for white Southerners particularly, that white South-erners feel a solidarity at least as great as that binding ethnic group members, and that Southerners have distinctive attitudes on a number of issues. [2] Southerners are more like non-Southern Americans than they are different, of course, and increasingly they are subject to similar eco-nomic, social, and political pressures.

[3]

This book will not attempt to make a case for Southern distinctiveness; rather, it will accept the evidence that there is enough distinctiveness to permit study of the problems and opportunities of the Southern states together. The book will attempt to do what one analyst has cited as the major need of research on the region: to bring order and systemization to regional studies, to overcome the prevailing fragmentation of research. [3]

Many excellent books have been written on the history, arts, education, politics, and economy of the South. For the analysis of institutional change and public policy problems, however, an interdisciplinary approach that emphasizes interdependence seems preferable. To understand the South one should view the region as an integrated system of economic, social, educational, and political subsystems. For example, one cannot understand the region by looking at its political system as if Southern politics were independent of the economy and the social structure.

This book is designed to be useful and to serve a variety of purposes. Specialists in one of these institutional or policy areas may be able to see how their areas are related to other institutions and policies in the South. Government, media, labor, academic, professional, and business people, and civic and interest-group leaders with knowledge of one of the Southern states might find this treatment of the region as a whole a spur to rethink their assumptions about their states. Students and others may find their understanding of the region and its institutions enhanced. We hope this book can help anyone who is interested in how best to direct change in the region. The book is ambitious in scope because the region's problems and opportunities do not admit of narrow disciplinary categorization.

The time is opportune for such a study because the South has passed the point at which we could ask ourselves whether we wanted change or no change. Rapid change—called progress and sometimes other names—is upon us, and there is no more time to waste. Hard decisions must be made in each of the areas examined here. Leaders within the region need to bring to the decision process a knowledge of the interrelationships of institutions and the intended and unintended impacts of policy decisions.

A Framework

This book uses a systems analytic framework to analyze the institutions of the region. Particular emphasis is placed on the interrelationships between the important economic, educational, and political subsystems.

This framework is general and may be applied to the analysis of a broad range of different types of social systems, including countries, regions, states, and cities. (We have previously used it to analyze a number of developing countries—Brazil, Chile, Nigeria, and Pakistan.) Our framework consists of three elements. First, we define a set of specific problems that block the South's progress (although the problems are not peculiar to the South). Second, we narrow the scope of the study by focusing on three institutional subsystems. Third, we analyze the institutions to determine what may be causing or aggravating the problems that have been defined.

Problem Definition

The approach here is pragmatic. Major problems of the region that different people might name would include the following: low per capita income; inequitable distribution of income; unemployment; stimulation and control of economic growth; insufficient control over working conditions by working people; an archaic welfare system; inadequate health care; racial discrimination; lack of responsiveness of the political system; population growth and geographic distribution; an inferior education system; and environmental pollution. In developing a set of strategies for change in the South we shall concentrate on increasing the level of per capita income, reducing the degree of racial discrimination, and improving the quality of education. We shall pay attention to the ways in which the political system can be made more responsive, because it is through that system that changes in regard to income, race relations, education, and other problems often can be affected. We will be concerned with the means to control growth.

The reasons for devoting special attention to per capita income are that the South still is the poorest region in the United States and the region with the most inequitable distribution of income. While the level of income and the distribution of income do not tell the whole story about a region, these are important measures of social well-being and quality of life.

Racial discrimination underlies most of the problems listed above. It is impossible to analyze the South's economic, political, and educational institutions without making race an integral part of the analysis.

There is considerable controversy as to whether education directly affects productivity and income levels. However, it appears that the South's inferior school system has done less than could be done to instill progressive attitudes in Southerners toward social responsibility, economic development, racial equality, and participatory democracy. As the largest expenditure item in the budgets of state and local governments in the South, education merits emphasis in this study. A primary objective will be to develop strategies to improve the effectiveness of public and higher education in the South.

Institutional Scope

The South can be viewed as a collection of four major types of institutions—economic, educational, political, and social. Each of these subsystems may be further subdivided. For example, the economy of the South consists of agriculture, commerce, industry, labor, and public finance. The social subsystem is something of a residual category: the family, religion, fraternal organizations, civic organizations, professional organizations, and the mass media might be included among the more important social institutions.

We shall focus our attention on the economic, educational, and political institutions in the South. We shall consider the effects that social institutions have on their behavior; that is, we will treat the outputs of social institutions as inputs into the economic, educational, and political institutions in the region. The urban South and the rural South are treated in the book as composites of economic, educational, political, and social institutions. Finally, we should mention one important subsystem of the South that is not an institution—the environment. It is treated in several places in the book. For example, in chapter 2 concern is expressed for the environmental implications of alternative economic development strategies. Environmental pollution also is closely associated with urban growth, treated in chapter 6.

ATTITUDES TOWARD INSTITUTIONS

Southerners do not express great confidence in the responsiveness of the institutions to be examined in this book. In attitudes toward economic, educational, or governmental institutions, and in attitudes toward "the system" generally, Southerners are even more skeptical than Americans generally. In public opinion surveys conducted between 1968 and 1973 in Southern states, the proportion of respondents agreeing with standard alienation items usually was three times the number disagreeing. On items that ask whether certain institutions or groups have treated them fairly or unfairly, respondents in several Southern states have rated their treatment from hospitals and insurance companies as the least fair, with more mixed evaluations of public utility companies, big business, labor unions, and the federal government, and more favorable evaluations of the police.[4] Harris poll results show that public confidence in *all* major institutions has declined in recent years.[5] This cynicism about institutional responsiveness is not restricted to the young, to minority groups, or to other groups singled out by the mass media; nor is it easy to argue that this cynicism is unjustified. We do not want to oversell the importance of the structural reforms proposed in this book, nor do we wish to ignore the practical problems to be faced in attempting to achieve the proposed substantive changes. But we do believe that these proposed changes would at least ameliorate the South's major problems and help develop institutions that could continue to deal with those problems in a responsive and responsible way.

Methodology

To analyze the institutions of the South we use a straightforward application of systems analysis called input-output analysis. For each subsystem we define the *output variables* relevant to our concerns. For example, for the economy of the South the output variables include per capita income, distribution of income, employment, investment, housing construction, and attitudes of employees. Next we identify four types of *input variables* that influence the behavior of the institution: (1) endowments, (2) external factors, (3) outputs from other institutions, and (4) policy decisions.

Having defined the relevant output variables for a given subsystem and having identified the more important input variables, we then analyze the subsystem components in light of the regional problems set forth above. We try to determine those characteristics of the institutions that are causing or adding to the problems. Finally, we develop policy recommendations aimed at ameliorating or solving the problems that have been identified.

ENDOWMENTS

To analyse the institutions and make policy recommendations, it is important that we consider the "state of the South" in the 1970s, that is, the given endowments of each of the South's major institutions at the time of this analysis. For example, the economy of the South has a given supply of natural resources, capital stock, and manpower, and a given transportation and communications system. The relative magnitudes of these endowments will affect the future behavior of the Southern economy.

EXTERNAL FACTORS

A second form of input into Southern institutions are inputs from outside the region that affect the South. Examples of external factors that have had important effects on the South include World War II and the Supreme Court desegregation decision of 1954. Federal policy decisions are treated as external factors. Although external factors are difficult to predict, they cannot be ignored.

OUTPUTS FROM OTHER INSTITUTIONS

This study focuses on the interdependence of the economic, educational, political, and social institutions in the South. With this in mind, we also consider the effects on a given subsystem of outputs from other subsystems. For example, outputs from the economy, the political system, and the social structure of the region many exert considerable influence on the South's public schools, colleges, and universities. Demographic and social characteristics and attitudes affect the economic, educational, and political institutions. Demographic characteristics would include the birth rate, death rate, and migration patterns of the region, for example, and social structure, racial composition, urban-rural mix, health conditions, and mobility are important social characteristics.

POLICY DECISIONS

Finally, the South's institutions are influenced by Southern policy decisions at the state and local levels.

A Reader's Guide

Chapter 2 examines the economy of the South. Chapters 3 and 4 deal with public and higher education. Southern governmental and political institutions are the subjects of chapter 5. Chapters 6 and 7 look at the urban and rural environments in which these institutions operate and at the developmental choices to be faced in those settings. Chapter 8 offers general conclusions.

Some of the government and other data used here employ different definitions of "the South," but for most purposes the South will mean the eleven states of the Confederacy (Virginia, North Carolina, South Carolina, Georgia, Florida, Tennessee, Alabama, Mississippi, Louisiana, Arkansas, and Texas) plus Oklahoma and Kentucky, or thirteen states in all.

Chapters are designed so that they may be read separately, or used separately in conferences, workshops, or courses, and yet convey the nature of the interdependent relationships of an institution or policy area. For this reason, some topics are mentioned in more than one chapter, although the overlap is minimal. In addition to being a book that can be read and argued about, this volume might have handbook or reference value since the same framework is used in each chapter.

In each chapter we begin by defining the problems associated with a set of institutions, or, in the case of chapters 6 and 7, the problems of the urban and rural South. We then include a historical summary of the evolution of the institutions, sometimes a quite brief one. Next we define the relevant inputs for that institution. We analyze selected subinstitutions. At the end of each chapter we present a list of policy recommendations. In other words, by viewing the South as an integrated system of economic, political, social, and educational institutions whose behavior is determined by endowments, external factors, policy decisions, and linkages between the institutions, we hope to gain insight into how the South is going about and can go about solving some of its major problems.

2. Out of the Quagmire and into the Economic Mainstream

The Setting

In 1938 President Franklin D. Roosevelt declared the South to be "the Nation's no. 1 economic problem." Although in terms of overall economic development, the gap between the South and the rest of the nation has certainly been reduced in the past thirty years, the South is still the nation's poorest region. A cursory glance at the voluminous statistical data is sufficient to convince even the most loyal Southern patriot that a considerable difference exists in the degree of economic development between the South and other regions of the country. Whatever the

TABLE 2.1. *Per Capita Personal Income for the United States and the South, 1900-1970*

Year	Per Capita Income			Per Capita Income as Percent of U.S. Total
	United States	South	Non-South	South
1900	$ 203	$ 103	$ 243	50.7
1920	655	399	755	60.9
1930	625	329	738	52.6
1940	596	358	690	60.1
1950	1,496	1,075	1,657	71.9
1960	2,215	1,687	2,412	76.1
1970	3,910	3,062	4,231	78.3

Sources: E. S. Lee, A. R. Miller, C. P. Brainard, and R. A. Easterlin, *Population Redistribution and Economic Growth: United States, 1870-1950* (Philadelphia: American Philosophical Society, 1957), for the years 1900-1920; *Personal Income by States since 1929: A Supplement to the Survey of Current Business, 1956,* for the years 1930-50; *Survey of Current Business* 41 (August 1961): 13, for the year 1960; *Survey of Current Business* 51 (August 1971): 29, for the year 1970.

measure of economic well-being, one cannot escape the conclusion that the South is still a relatively poor and underdeveloped region.

One measure of economic development in which economists place substantial faith (perhaps too much) is per capita personal income. In 1970 the South's average per capita personal income was $3,062, 78.3 percent of the $3,910 average for the nation as a whole, but up from 50.7 percent of the national average in 1900 and 60.1 percent in 1940. Although table 2.1 demonstrates that the South has indeed made substantial progress in playing the game of "economic catch-up," per capita income in the non-South was still 38.2 percent higher than that of the South as recently as 1970. The absolute difference in per capita income between the South and the non-South has been increasing and the percentage rate of "catch up" for the South has been decreasing. It is interesting to note the wide disparity in per capita income among the

TABLE 2.2. *Per Capita Personal Income*
for the Southern States, 1920-72

State	1920	1930	1940	1950	1960	1970	1972
Alabama	$313	$266	$282	$ 867	$1,487	$2,876	$3,333
Arkansas	329	223	256	805	1,379	2,864	3,357
Florida	437	464	513	1,288	1,954	3,664	4,188
Georgia	348	308	340	1,016	1,639	3,354	3,848
Kentucky	400	325	320	958	1,586	3,099	3,601
Louisiana	426	358	363	1,089	1,655	3,054	3,528
Mississippi	281	203	218	729	1,204	2,597	3,063
North Carolina	354	293	328	1,009	1,560	3,218	3,721
Oklahoma	504	368	373	1,133	1,867	3,332	3,802
South Carolina	336	241	307	881	1,379	2,933	3,448
Tennessee	361	325	339	995	1,545	3,075	3,640
Texas	539	411	432	1,340	1,927	3,573	4,045
Virginia	420	384	466	1,222	1,843	3,899	4,258

Sources: *Personal Income by States since 1929: A Supplement to the Survey of Current Business, 1956; Survey of Current Business* 53 (August 1973): 40.

Southern states for 1972 in table 2.2, ranging from a low of $3,063 in Mississippi to a high of $4,258 in Virginia. Not a single Southern state had an income level that reached the national average in 1972.

Although average per capita personal income provides us with a useful measure on which to base comparisons of the economy of the South with the economy of the rest of the nation, it by no means tells the complete story. If, for example, we want to know something about the distribution of income and the extent of poverty in the South, then we must consider other measures of income. The 1970 census figures showed that 14 percent of the families in the South in 1969 had incomes of less than $3,000 in comparison with 7 percent for the Northeast and 8 percent for the North Central and Western states of the country. [1] The definition of poverty that has been generally accepted is an income of $3,000 for a family of four plus increments of $500 for each additional member of the family when the family size exceeds four. In 1969, 11.2 million (46 percent) of the 24.3 million people in the United States living in poverty were located in the South. Equivalently, 18 percent of the people in the South were still living in poverty in 1969. Of the black families living in the South in 1969, 36 percent had incomes below the poverty level. [2]

Median family income for Southern whites in 1970 was $9,240. The corresponding figure for Southern blacks was $5,226. For the United States the median family income was $10,236 for whites and $6,279 for blacks. [3]

Other social indicators give further evidence of the extent to which poverty exists in the South. For the country as a whole there were 168 physicians and 56 dentists per 100,000 population in 1969. In the South there were only 113 physicians and 36 dentists per 100,000 population. The corresponding figures for the non-South were 189 physicians and 64 dentists. [4] In terms of hospital beds the South had 720 hospital beds per 100,000 population, contrasted with 832 for the United States and 876 for the non-South. [5] In 1970, 29.1 percent of the black housing units in the South lacked some or all plumbing facilities; [6] the comparable figure for blacks in the United States as a whole was 16.9 percent. [7]

Rather than belabor the point further that the South still lags behind the nation in terms of economic development, let us now turn to some of the historical reasons underlying the South's economic problems.

Historical Summary

Since the turn of the century economists and economic historians have argued that the principal reason for the South's lag in per capita income is attributable to its insufficient rate of industrial expansion. [8] For example, William H. Nicholls asserts that the South's lag in per capita income was caused by its "insufficient rate of industrial-urban development" and that this lag in industrial development was the result of its "stubborn adherence to a set of values inconsistent with a high rate of industrialization." [9] These values include (1) the persistence of agrarian values, (2) the rigidity of the social structure, (3) the undemocratic nature of the political structure, (4) the weakness of social responsibility, and (5) conformity of thought and behavior. We will have more to say about these values and their effects on the South later in this chapter.

In the remainder of this section we shall attempt to show that insufficient industrialization has indeed led to retarded economic growth in the South. We shall also argue that four basic factors have played a causal role in this phenomenon, that the forces underlying these four factors were approaching maturity during the thirty years preceding the Civil War (1830-60), and that they have to a great extent persisted for over a hundred years since the end of the Civil War. The four factors are (1) insufficient effective demand for goods and services, (2) insufficient supply of skilled nonagricultural labor, (3) insufficient supply of capital, and (4) insufficient investment in education and technology.

THE ANTEBELLUM SOUTH:
PRELUDE TO RETARDED ECONOMIC GROWTH (1830-60)

By the end of the American Revolution, the pattern of a landed aristocracy was already firmly established in the Tidewater areas of the Southern colonies. But the South was in need of a new crop, for cultivation of tobacco was declining because of worn-out soil, exhausted by the one-crop system, and because of the loss of a substantial part of the British market, which had sought other sources of supply during the war. Indigo was no longer profitable with the removal of the British bounty, and rice could be raised profitably only in certain areas.

But the major stimulus for a shift in production was the demand for cotton in England where the inventions in spinning and weaving had made the production of cotton cloth quite profitable. Furthermore, England's old sources of cotton supply, the Middle East and the West Indies, were incapable of further expansion. The increase in the demand for cotton was followed closely by the invention of the cotton gin in 1791 which made it economically feasible to separate short-staple lint from cotton seed. With the advent of the cotton gin, the cotton economy in the South could develop and prosper. "The resulting phenomenal expansion of cotton production not only revived the moribund institution of slavery (the South's answer to the problem of labor shortage) but gave new life to the plantation system in Southern agriculture."[10]

Even with the invention of the cotton gin, cotton production did not increase immediately. In 1880 the total production was only 35,000 bales, most of which was produced in South Carolina and Georgia. However, the most rapid era of expansion took place between 1820 and 1840 when the Southwestern lands including Alabama, Mississippi,

Louisiana, and Arkansas were thrown open to settlement.

Cotton production involved extensive exploitation of land and labor and a minimum use of capital. Cotton, like tobacco in colonial days, was produced on a particular plot of land until the fertility of that soil was practically exhausted, and then a new area would be planted. Individual planters owned plantations ranging from fewer than two hundred acres to twenty or thirty thousand acres, but the ownership of most of the better lands was concentrated in the hands of a small group of slave magnates.

In 1850 there were 1.25 million white families in the slaveholding states. Of these families, 347,000 held slaves. Nearly 250,000 of these slaveholders were yeoman farmers with less than ten slaves each. Fewer than 8,000 owned fifty or more slaves. The number of slaveholders with more than 100 slaves was less than 1,800. Eleven people owned more than 500 slaves. Nathaniel Heyward, the largest slaveholder in the South, owned 1,843 slaves when he died in 1851. [11]

The objective of the planters in accumulating a large estate, consisting of land and slaves, was essentially the combination of an economic objective with a noneconomic objective. Conrad and Meyers have pointed out that Southern planters enjoyed increasing returns to scale on slave breeding operations that provided a strong economic motive for increasing the scale of plantations. [12] On the other hand, a noneconomic objective, accumulation for the purpose of insuring and perpetuating the social prestige of the planter's family, played a significant role in determining the scale of Southern plantations. Even in the areas where the new planter aristocracies had emerged, small farmers continued to constitute the bulk of the population, but they increasingly came under the social and political domination of the new planter class. "Like Northern millionaires of a later generation, the planters controlled a disproportionate share of the income of their region. The annual income of 1,000 families of the Cotton Kingdom in 1850 has been estimated at $50,000,000; the remaining 666,000 families received only about $60,000,000." [13]

Let it never be said that the plantation system was not profitable in the South. [14] In fact, it was so profitable prior to 1830 that cotton production was almost doubled between 1824 and 1831. But this profitability proved to be a blessing of questionable value, for it led to increased cotton production and a specialized, one-crop economy between 1830 and 1860, which in turn drove prices and profits down. Between 1825 and 1831 the price of cotton fell from twenty cents to ten cents per pound, with prices reaching a minimum between 1840 and 1860.

Prior to 1830 "the plantation tended to find its center in itself: to be an independent social unit, a self-contained and largely self-sufficient little world of its own. In its beginnings, to be sure, it often required some degree of communal effort, particularly if the would-be planter had few or no slaves. But once the forest was cut and the stumps grubbed up, once the seed was in a few times and the harvest home a few times, once he had a Negro or two actually at work—once the plantation was properly carved out on its way, then the world might go hang." [15] The greater part of everything the plantation needed could be and was grown or manufactured on the place, and the rest could be imported from the North and West.

Although manufacturing activities were of comparable magnitudes in the North and the South in 1830, by 1850 there was active concern on the part of some Southerners over the widening gap between the occupational characteristics of the two regions. [16] In the 1840s when the South's per capita income relative to the rest of the nation was at its historic peak (89 percent of the national average), [17] a Mississippi political economist by the name of Nathaniel A. Ware expounded in 1844 that "it is our best and leading policy to encourage manufacturing." [18] This thesis was constantly reiterated during a series of commercial conventions held in the South between 1837 and 1859, but to little avail, for the South's "political leadership took the region into a war which demonstrated, if evidence were needed, the superior productivity of the Northern system over that of the South." [19]

As evidence of the disparity that already existed between the South and the North (the rest of the nation) in 1840 in terms of manufacturing activity, nonagricultural income in the South accounted for only 14 percent of total nonagricultural income in the United States in spite of the fact that 37 percent of the population of the nation was concentrated in the South. [20]

In the following pages we shall analyze the effects of four important factors on the extent of industrialization in the South between 1830 and 1860.

Insufficient Effective Demand

Fundamental to the operation of a market economy is the assumption that there exists a group of consumers who desire the goods produced by manufacturers and have the money to purchase them. Yet there is considerable evidence to support the hypothesis that there were relatively few people in the South between 1830 and 1860 who either wanted to purchase goods produced in the South or could afford to do so even if the will were there.

In analyzing the causes of insufficient effective demand during the antebellum period in the South it is convenient to view the problem in terms of the four major social classes of the period: planters, yeoman farmers, poor whites, and slaves.

We have previously indicated that most of the supplies required to maintain and operate a large plantation (including food for the entire plantation that included the planter and his family, the overseer and his family, and the slaves, as well as clothing for the slaves) were either produced on the place or purchased from the North and the Midwest. "Many of the planters spent their incomes by traveling with their families in the North or in Europe during the summer, and a large sum was required to pay the hog raiser in Ohio, the mule breeder in Kentucky, and above all, the Northern capitalists, who had vast sums of money on mortgage over the estates." [21]

There was also a substantial middle class of yeoman farmers within the South's agrarian society. This class of people also possessed a high degree of individualism and prided themselves on their self-sufficiency. Hence neither the planters nor the yeoman farmers provided a basis for a sound local market economy in the South. [22]

As for the poor whites (familiarly referred to as "crackers" and "white trash" by most Southerners), they simply did not have sufficient money incomes to exert any positive influence on the demand for consumer goods. But the poor whites tended to emulate the self-sufficiency of the plantation owners. The crackers and poor white farmers were fiercely independent and as "careful of their prerogatives of ownership, as jealous of their sway over their puny domains, as the grandest lord." [23]

The slaves whose real wages amounted to six cents per day (as compared to money wages of forty cents per day for free laborers in other parts of the country) could not have increased effective demand even if they had been paid money wages and permitted to make purchases outside of the plantation. [24]

Thus, with such an acute deficiency in local market demand in the antebellum South, there is little wonder that manufacturers did not flock to the South and that commercial (wholesale and retail) trade, as well as urban areas, showed few signs of rapid development. W. J. Cash expressed it this way: "Few towns grew up in the wake of the plantation's advance, and those which did were generally frowzy clumps of grocery-shacks and revolting grog shops." [25]

Insufficient Skilled Labor

Even before the Civil War, the South had a chronic shortage of skilled workers, caused primarily by the fact that the majority of skilled immigrants coming to America in the 1840s and 1850s settled in the North. Free labor has always feared competition from slave labor, and the distances between towns in the South limited the extent of the labor market. In 1840, 2,330,000 or 37 percent of the people living in the South were slaves. [26] In the states of Mississippi and South Carolina slaves constituted over one half of the population. A rumor that persisted in Europe that the climate in the South was unhealthy also contributed to the region's shortage of skilled labor. However, there was one exception to this pattern in the South. In the upland areas of the South (particularly East Tennessee) where it was not economically feasible to produce cash crops, the leadership had decided before the Civil War that their area's destiny lay in manufacturing rather than agriculture. As a result of this decision the upland areas of the South attracted considerably more immigrants than the lowland cotton-producing areas and developed a diversity of skills.

In 1844 Nathaniel A. Ware proposed that slaves be used in manufacturing. "Wherever the Negro slave has been put to, or entrusted with, manufactories, he has showed himself both trustworthy and efficient." [27] This point of view was a minority opinion, as most writers seem to have felt that slaves were unsuitable for manufacturing because of insufficient skill and the inherent problems involved in controlling them.

However, in spite of the shortage of skilled labor in the South, if there had been *sufficient* local and regional *effective demand*, risk capital for manufacturing probably would have been forthcoming from both Northern entrepreneurs and Southern planters (who held most of the South's capital), wages would have been bid up, and skilled labor would have been attracted to the region from the Northeast. Thus we have the elements of a vicious cycle in which insufficient effective demand is caused by the fact that relatively few wage earners are able to purchase goods produced in the South, and because few goods are manufactured in the South, skilled laborers who demand higher wages are not induced to migrate to the region. The cycle goes on and on.

Insufficient Capital

By 1860 technological inventions had already begun to revolutionize industry in the North, but such was not the case in the South, for both labor and capital were in short supply. As a result, the antebellum industries of the South were comprised of small local units such as old-fashioned mills, located on the bank of some stream and driven frequently by a lumbering waterwheel and occasionally by a steam engine. The average number of people employed in a manufacturing establishment was only six. Total capital and total number of laborers in industry in the South were only 9.5 percent and 8.4 percent, respectively, of those applied in industry in the United States.

Some economic historians have tended to attribute the shortage of risk capital for investment in manufacturing in the South to an "unsympathetic environment." However, Ernest Lander, discussing the situation in South Carolina between 1815 and 1860, contends that "the higher returns of agriculture, rather than the alleged but nonexistent hostility of the planters to industrialism, accounts for the subordination of manufacturing to agriculture in the economy of the state."[28]

Lander's argument appears to be the stronger of the two, at least during the period in question. Given the insufficient market demand in the South, the shortage of skilled labor, and the dearth of investment in education and technical research, plus the very favorable terms of trade that Southern cotton enjoyed with both England's and New England's manufacturers, it is not at all surprising that both Northern and Southern investors chose to invest in cotton production in the South rather than in Southern manufacturing. The expected profits were simply higher in cotton than in manufacturing of the region.

Insufficient Investment in Education and Technology

The cultural background of the antebellum South favored the development of a distinguished system of higher education. Thomas Jefferson and other Revolutionary leaders were trained in the only college existing in the area, the College of William and Mary, but a majority of them were educated in Europe and the colleges of the North. Plantation owners sent their sons to Eton, Oxford, and the Middle Temple. These same planters "strongly resisted measures to broaden the suffrage, to establish *ad valorem* taxation of land and slaves for the general welfare, and to provide free universal public-school education at a time when these democratizing influences were greatly strengthening the socioeconomic foundations of the more progressive Middle West. In the process, they effectively insulated themselves from social and political forces which might otherwise have been their undoing and continued to set goals to which lesser men aspired."[29]

The tendency of the South to invest its limited financial resources in higher education, rather than in public education at a lower level, is a pattern that first emerged in the eighteenth century. For example, Phi Beta Kappa originated in 1776 at the College of William and Mary in Virginia, and the University of North Carolina was the first state university to open its doors.

Public education was an altogether different story in the South. Although there were some schools in the South before the Civil War, support for universal education through taxation was not accepted as a responsibility of the states until the Reconstruction period. "The Southern states led in the establishment of state universities, but on the eve of the war there was about one elementary school per forty square miles in South Carolina, and Draconic laws forbade the education of Southern Negroes."[30] The pauper school was the typical antebellum school rather than the common or free school.

The development of public schools in Virginia was somewhat typical of the pattern for the entire South, for there the owners of the large plantations in the East opposed public schools while the yeoman farmers of the Western highlands were strongly in favor of public education. Public education became an important sectional issue culminating in the provision for increased support for Virginia's public schools in the constitution of 1851.

Douglass North has suggested a plausible explanation for the South's niggardly support for public education. "When extremely unequal income distribution is paralleled by unequal distribution of political power, the development of broadly based public education is less likely, since there are no obvious gains to those who must provide the bulk of the tax monies for such an investment."[31] This thesis may also serve to explain the differences in public education expenditures between the South and the North and Midwest. According to North, "Investment in public education is likely to be a larger proportion of income under conditions of more equal income distribution, since the broader distribution of costs will be matched by an equally expanded distribution of benefits."

Thus with this example we see the difficulty involved in attempting to analyze the South and its problems through the use of nice, neat compartments such as economics, education, and politics. To explain the region's lack of support for public education we have to examine social, political, and economic forces at work in the region.

Directly related to the South's minimal public education system were shortages of (1) technological inventions and research in agriculture and manufacturing, (2) "scientific" farming methods, and (3) competent farm and manufacturing managers, as well as entrepreneurs. In sharp contrast to the situation in the South was the Northwest where both the land and climate were less suitable to slave labor than that of the South, but where technological inventions were developed in part out of necessity and exploited by entrepreneurs much more readily than in the South. With the availability of slave labor, the South was deprived of any major incentive to develop labor-saving technologies.

Ironically, it was the invention of the mechanical reaper by a Southerner, Cyrus McCormick, which enhanced the agricultural prosperity of the Midwest considerably at that time. McCormick's invention was a commercial failure in Virginia because (1) it was not suitable for the hilly terrain in that region and (2) there was an abundant supply of slave labor in the area. Hence, McCormick moved to Chicago where his invention was a success and its exploitation by the Midwest virtually eliminated the South as a major competitor in the wheat market.

While many Americans were eagerly searching for new and improved mechanical techniques and improved farming methods, Southern agriculture had a high propensity to follow the system of the past.

We have shown that the South made little attempt to provide formal training to develop a class of successful entrepreneurs, industrial or farm managers, or inventors, who might in turn provide a point of departure for future industrial development. Furthermore, there were only limited opportunities for such individuals to receive on-the-job training in the South. Planters, who controlled the major supply of Southern capital, showed a very low propensity to invest or promote enterprises with a high degree of risk. Why should they, when cotton was a sure thing? As for sources of managerial talent, neither the plantation overseers nor the managers of the South's few isolated manufacturing facilities were noted for their managerial efficiency.

MILITARY DEFEAT, OCCUPATION, AND RECONSTRUCTION (1866-80)

In the preceding section we have shown that a combination of social, economic, and political forces had been set in motion in the South prior to 1860 that were sufficient to serve as a serious constraint on the region's economic development even if there had not been a Civil War. "The South had developed a regional philosophy, and social, political, and economic institutions which, despite the real but ephemeral agrarian prosperity of their own time, were unfavorable to the achievement of balanced and broadly based economic progress over a longer period."[32]

The Civil War had a devastating effect on the economy of the South, particularly on the agricultural sector. By decimating horses, cattle, and mules, the war destroyed a substantial portion of the South's agricultural production capacity and left farms at approximately 50 percent of their previous value.

It was agriculture, not manufacturing, which was dealt the more severe blow by the Civil War. The manufacturing labor force was not disorganized and the postwar demand for manufactured products was considerable. The increase in gross farm income made it possible for Southern manufacturers to serve an expanding farm market. Indeed, it can be argued that conditions during and after the Civil War were actually conducive to manufacturing capacity expanding faster than agricultural capacity in the South.[33]

The South did indeed expand its manufacturing capacity during the period between 1860 and 1870. In every case, the values of the manufacturing series in 1870 exceed their corresponding values for 1860. During this same ten-year period agriculture failed to regain its previous position.

But in the decade between 1870 and 1880 the South returned to the pattern, established before the Civil War, of agricultural output expanding at a faster rate than that of the United States while manufacturing output once again lagged behind the rest of the nation. By 1880 most measures of agricultural output in the South exceeded their previous values of 1860. Furthermore, despite the progress made in manufacturing during the 1860s, the South's position relative to the nation had slipped substantially by 1880. In 1880 the South, with 20 percent of the people in the United States, accounted for only 11.5 percent of the manufacturing establishments, 4.7 percent of the capital, 6.3 percent of the laborers, 3.9 percent of total wages, 4.5 percent of the cost of raw materials, and 4.5 percent of the value of manufactured prod-

TABLE 2.3. *Manufacturing in the South, 1850-80*

	1850	1860	1870	1880
No. of establishments	123,025	140,423	252,148	253,852
Percent of U.S. total	13.7	14.7	12.3	11.5
Capital (in millions)[a]	55.3	96.0	98.7	133.3
Percent of U.S. total	10.4	9.5	4.6	4.8
No of laborers[a]	88,390	110,721	144,252	171,674
Percent of U.S. total	9.2	8.4	7.0	6.3
Wages (in millions)	17.5	28.7	31.0	37.1
Percent of U.S. total	7.4	7.6	4.0	3.9
Cost of raw materials (in millions)	40.8	86.5	116.2	151.8
Percent of U.S. total	7.4	8.4	4.7	4.5
Value of products (in millions)	79.2	155.5	199.0	240.5
Percent of U.S. total	7.8	8.2	4.7	4.5

Source: Eugene M. Lerner, "Southern Output and Agricultural Income, 1860-1880," in *The Economic Impact of the American Civil War*, ed. Ralph Andreano (Cambridge, Mass.: Schenkman Publishing Co. 1962), p. 93, table 2.
Note: In this table the "South" includes the eleven states of the Confederacy only.
[a]Both series exclude slaves.

ucts (see table 2.3). Nonagricultural income in 1880 was 8 percent of that of the United States and per capita income had slipped from 89 per- cent of the national average of 1840 to 59 percent. [34]

Although the South suffered a major economic setback as a result of the Civil War, the sector that received the brunt of the destructive force of the war was the first to recover, while the industrial sector that suf- fered least once again lagged behind the rest of the nation. Thus one cannot place much credence in the view that pervaded the South for nearly one hundred years after the Civil War, that most of the South's economic ills were attributable to military defeat, occupation, and Re- construction. Indeed, there is substantial evidence that insufficient ef- fective demand, skilled labor, capital, and investment in education and technology continued to persist throughout the fifteen-year period following the war—factors that had been present at least thirty years before the war.

COLONIALISM IN THE NEW SOUTH (1880-1920)

Divisiveness and instability pervaded the South's economic, social, political, and educational institutions during the period 1880 through 1920. With the advent of the "Doctrine of White Supremacy," the dis- franchisement of blacks, and the enactment of a series of "Jim Crow" laws throughout the South in the 1890s, the groundwork was laid for the perpetuation (at least for another sixty years) of many of the socio- economic ills that had existed in the South since before the Civil War. Not even an upsurge in populism in response to a major depression in the 1870s or World War II had any appreciable effect on the South's social or political structure or the attitudes of white Southerners toward them- selves, blacks, or their own region. Despite a major agricultural depres- sion in the 1890s followed by a short upswing in agricultural prices during World War I and a disastrous collapse in agriculture after the war, the South remained predominantly rural and agricultural.

In 1900, for example, 60 percent of the South's total income was still derived from agriculture and 82 percent of the total labor force was agri- cultural in nature. Although the South contained 29 percent of the population of the United States in 1900, it accounted for only 10 percent of the nonagricultural income of the nation. [35] Even though the rate of growth of industrialization during the postbellum years of the nine- teenth century did manage to increase, this increase in industrial output was not sufficient to make more than a small dent in the overall economy of the region. Per capita personal income was $103 (50.7 percent of the national average) in 1900 and reached $399 (60.9 percent of the national average) by 1920 (see table 2.1).

The big news of the Southern economic frontiers in the 1880s and 1890s and continuing through the 1920s was the vision of the "New South"—an attempt on the part of Southern businessmen to emulate the industrial model of the Northeast. And there can be no doubt that during this period there was considerable expansion in the textile, lumber, railroad, tobacco, and petroleum industries. But all too often this expansion was financed by Northern capitalists seeking a short-term payoff without regard to the long-term effects on the South's human and natural resources. What evolved was a pattern of economic colonialism in which the South failed to develop a class of entrepreneurs of its own who might take a somewhat more long-range view toward the South's economic development. "The Morgans, Mellons, and Rockefellers sent their agents to take charge of the region's railroads, mine furnaces, and financial corporations, and eventually of many of its distributive institutions. The economy over which they presided was increasingly coming to be one of branch plants, branch banks, captive mines, and chain stores." [36]

The South seems to have had an almost fatal attraction for a specific type of industry—"low wage, low value-creating" industries. Most of these industries used as basic inputs the South's chief agricultural crops and natural resources—industries for which there were economies inherent in being located near the source of supply of raw materials. "Cotton yarns and coarse cloth, cane sugar, turpentine and rosin, polished rice, cottonseed oil fertilizers, wood-distillation products, liquors, lumber and timber, and tobacco products bulked large in the vaunted industrialization of the New South." [37]

Not only did the South fail to develop a pattern of industrialization that would lead it into the economic mainstream of America, but it also failed to develop the type of social, political, and educational infrastructure necessary for sustained economic growth. Much of the industry was exploitive in nature, utilizing child labor and sometimes even convict labor. State governments were controlled by coalitions of planters and leading industrialists. These men were both elitist and reactionary in their approaches to state government, taxation, public education, and race relations. They viewed themselves as champions of the property holders and landed gentry to the unpropertied masses. In many ways it was merely a continuation of an old philosophy based on expedient alliances and a new image called the "New South."

The concluding years of World War I gave Southern farmers a false sense of prosperity with an increased demand for the South's staples—a demand that collapsed shortly after the war, pulling the South into a period of deep depression while the rest of the nation moved ahead economically. This venture proved to be yet another reminder that Southern agriculture was not insulated from the laws of supply and demand and that the economy of the South was inextricably linked to the economy of the United States. It had finally become painfully apparent that the South had witnessed the end of an era and that it was time to begin the search for solutions to the South's economic problems.

BIG TOMORROWS ARE JUST AROUND THE CORNER:
THE GREAT DEPRESSION (1920-40)

Traveling through the South in 1927, a journalist made this observation: "Down in Dixie they tell you and always with cheerful pride that the South is the new frontier. . . . There is a feel in the air: Big tomorrows seem to be coming around the corner." Unfortunately for the South, that particular "big tomorrow" turned out to be the Great Depression of the 1930s. As historian C. Vann Woodward has observed, the many Southern converts to the gospel of progress and success could never carry a reluctant region with them. There were too many reminders of the Southern past—an experience that could not be shared with any other part of America.

Although per capita income in the South quadrupled during the first two decades of the twentieth century, the old problems of insufficient effective demand, skilled labor, capital, education, and technology continued to persist. Per capita personal income in the South stood at $399 in 1920 compared to $655 for the United States and $755 for the non-South. The South's position relative to the nation had improved from 50.7 percent of the national average in 1900 to 60.9 percent in 1920.

The two decades that followed brought forth a peculiar paradox of economic collapse and the beginnings of the South's first serious departure from agrarianism. The period was characterized by the search for a new rationale for the old system, for the causes of the South's predicament, for a new system, and for methods for accelerating the emergence of the New South. [38]

Although per capita personal income decreased throughout the nation between 1920 and 1930, the decline in the South exceeded that of the rest of the nation (table 2.1) and as always it was agriculture that led the way downward.

Agriculture continued to dominate the Southern scene in 1930 with 67.9 percent of the region's population living in rural areas and 42.8 percent of the work force working on the farm, at a per capita income of $189 in contrast to $484 for nonfarm occupations. [39] Low farm prices and heavy infestations of boll weevils gave the South a head start on the rest of the nation in terms of the effects of the Great Depression. Cotton prices, for example, after rising to a high of 41.75 cents per pound in 1920, drifted to 20.19 cents by 1927, then dropped to 16.78 cents in 1929, 9.46 cents in 1930, and 5.44 cents in 1931. [40] And once again the South had foregone the opportunity to accumulate capital and break the chain of farmers who "owe the merchants and the bankers who in turn owe the jobbers, the large city banks, and the Federal Reserve Bank." [41] Having received the brunt of the depression before the rest of the nation did, the economy bottomed out in the South more quickly than in other parts of the country, and from 1933 on, per capita income in the South was higher relative to 1929 than it was in other regions. Furthermore, after 1931 Southern manufacturing activity decreased proportionately less than it did in the rest of the country.

King Cotton was "down" and almost "out," and although a host of government farm programs inaugurated during Roosevelt's New Deal would eventually help revive Southern agriculture, the South would never be the same again.

To the problems of poverty and retarded economic development were added the problems of technological change. The tractor, the mechanical cotton picker, cattle grazing, and pulpwood-using industries, all based on changes in technology, emerged during this period. Among the direct effects of the tractor were (1) the consolidation of small tenant farms into large acreages, (2) the substitution of a wage system for the old sharecropping system, and (3) the displacement of the farm population. The advent of mechanical cotton pickers intensified these phenomena. All of these developments required fewer labor inputs per acre of land than the production of cotton and other row crops. [42]

And if all of this were not bad enough, things were even worse if one happened to be a Negro in the South. With few deviations from the doctrine of white supremacy in the 1930s, it was almost as if nearly 25 percent of the people of the region had been abstracted out of the economic system or, at best, relegated to a position of utter economic powerlessness. Racial segregation and inequality were strictly the rule, whether in education, employment, housing, or any other measurable criterion. In every case that mattered, Southern Negroes were forced into a position of second- and even third-class citizenship. Life was tough in the South in the 1930s—particularly if you were black.

Four alternative strategies were put forth during the 1930s to bring the South out of the depression and into the economic mainstream of America: (1) the revival of Agrarianism, (2) the modernization of agriculture, (3) out-migration, and (4) industrialization. Conspicuously absent were proposals to provide blacks with equality of opportunity in schools, jobs, housing, and politics.

Revival of Agrarianism

During the 1930s a view held by many Southern traditionalists was that the South should resist at all costs the pressures being brought on the region to urbanize and industrialize. Indeed, the South should return to self-sufficient agriculture and the virtues of rural life and cease the pattern of emulating Northern business and commercial practices to the detriment of Southern history and culture. This view was epitomized in a book by twelve Southerners that first appeared in 1930 entitled *I'll Take My Stand: The South and the Agrarian Tradition*. Fortunately for the South this approach, which ignored the inherent instability of an economy based entirely on agriculture, met with increasing opposition from those who had become increasingly conscious of the cyclical gyrations of Southern agriculture.

Modernization of Agriculture

A second approach sought to improve the welfare of Southern farmers by enlisting the support of the federal government to strengthen the markets for agricultural products and improve the technology of agricultural production. The former was achieved through the use of governmental price supports for agricultural commodities and the latter through government-sponsored research programs.

Southern congressmen were quick to embrace the farm programs of the New Deal and have continued to support them long after the depression conditions that provided their rationale ceased to be. It is only in recent years that economists and urban congressmen have begun to question these programs mainly on the grounds that their primary beneficiaries have been those farmers with large land holdings.

Finally, improvements in farm technology that resulted, in part, from increased federal expenditures for agricultural research greatly reduced farm labor requirements in the South and created severe problems of rural unemployment, dislocation, and out-migration.

Out-Migration

In every decade since Reconstruction, more people had emigrated from the South than had moved into the region, and the 1920s and 1930s were no exception. The net migration rate in the South during the 1920s was -5.2 percent. However, as the expectations of urban employment in the North were reduced in the 1930s, the net migration rate dropped to -2.8 percent. To some economists out-migration represented a rational solution to the South's economic problems. As agricultural jobs became increasingly scarce in the South, displaced farm workers and tenant farmers would migrate to the North, thus reducing the size of the total population to be supported in the South. The crucial question, of course, was, Who were these displaced farmers who left the South? Were they the more educated, more highly trained workers or were they the illiterate, undereducated types? There appears to be considerable evidence to support the hypothesis that the former alternative was frequently the case. That is, the South was exporting some of its most talented people to the North after going to the expense of educating and training them. And in many cases those who were left behind in the rural areas were those possessing the least amount of education and the smallest number of vocational skills.

Industrialization

Perhaps the most important long-range effect of the Great Depression on the South was that it finally convinced much of the Southern political leadership that agriculture alone could never solve the South's income gap problem and that the region had little choice but to embark on a strategy of increasing its rate of industrialization.

Many theories were espoused throughout the decade to explain the South's retarded rate of industrialization. Particularly popular among Southern demagogues was the conspiracy theory that held that the South's lack of industrialization was attributable to a deliberate conspiracy on the part of Northern corporations to thwart the South. The conspirators were alleged to have used four major weapons to hold the South down: (1) protective tariffs, (2) discriminatory freight rates, (3) monopolistic control of natural resources, and (4) absentee ownership. It was claimed that high protective tariffs on Northern-made manufactured goods and low tariffs on Southern agricultural products worked to the disadvantage of the South. Differential freight rates leading to higher transportation costs for goods shipped out of the South than for similar shipments originating in the North were said to create a major barrier to economic development in the South. Some concern arose that monopolistic control over the South's natural resources could result in rates of resource utilization that were lower than would be the case under competitive conditions. Finally, there was concern over the fact that most of the major industries in the South were controlled by absentee owners—Northern corporations—and that these absentee owners were frequently guilty of exploitation of the region and its resources. Although there was no doubt an element of truth underlying each of these assertions, studies by Hoover and Ratchford[43] and others have demonstrated that none of these four factors taken separately or in combination with any of the other three was a necessary or sufficient condition for the South's economic dilemma. They argued that fundamental to the future development of the economy of the South was a sound national economy operating at high levels of employment. They refuted the myth that Southern natural resources were available in abundant supplies but remained relatively underdeveloped. "Low per capita income in the South," they said, "stems from a low ratio of natural and capital resources to population." The need for greater selectivity in attracting industry to the South was also emphasized by Hoover and Ratchford—industries characterized by higher worker productivity and accompanying wage rates. The need for more entrepreneurs and individuals with managerial skills was given substantial emphasis by Hoover and Ratchford.

Although per capita income for the nation as a whole decreased from $625 in 1930 to $596 in 1940, per capita income in the South actually increased during this period, moving upward to $358 in 1940 from $329 in 1930. The reversal of the trend of the 1920s was "due largely to a higher rate of increase in the South than in the rest of the country in wage and salary payments by the Federal Government and increases in Southern incomes from manufacturing, construction, and mining." Furthermore, during the 1930s the rate of decrease in income from farming was greater in the South than in the rest of the nation. "By 1940 almost as large a proportion of labor income in the South came from manufacturing as from farming, while the proportion of incomes from wholesale and retail trade was higher than the proportion from farming."[44]

WAR AND PEACE (1940-60)

At the dawn of the 1940s, the South was on the threshold of its greatest economic growth, but the tragedy of it all was that it took another world war to drag the South back into the economic mainstream of the union. The most obvious impact of World War II on the economy of the South was the significant reduction in the gap between per capita personal income in the South and the nation. Per capita income in the South tripled during the 1940s, increasing from 60.1 percent of the national average to 71.9 percent. Expanded military facilities and payrolls, substantial out-migration, and rapid industrialization—all directly related to the nation's war effort—were the principal causes of the South's accelerated rate of economic growth. "Income originating in construction; manufacturing; communications and public utilities; wholesale and retail trade; and finance, insurance, and real estate rose quite rapidly in the South and at significantly higher rates than in the non-South."[45]

Employment in agriculture decreased sharply during the decade both in absolute terms and as a percentage of total employment in the region.

By 1950 only 22 percent of the people employed in the South were in agriculture—down from 35 percent in 1940. Employment in manufacturing in the South jumped from 15 percent of total employment in 1940 to 18 percent in 1950. Furthermore, the South's percentage of total employment in agriculture for the United States dropped from 50 percent in 1940 to 45 percent in 1950.

Both the income and employment patterns of the 1940s continued on into the 1950s long after the conclusion of World War II and the end of the fighting in Korea in the early 1950s. By 1960 the South's per capita personal income had reached 76.1 percent of that of the nation. Employment in agriculture in the South dropped to only 10 percent of total employment in the South in 1960 and employment in manufacturing increased to 21 percent of total employment. Manufacturing employment in the South accounted for 20 percent of manufacturing employment in the United States in 1960. At long last, the South was finally becoming industrialized.

There were also some interesting demographic changes in the South between 1940 and 1960, even though the South's share of the nation's total population changed only slightly from 28.1 percent in 1940 to 27.3 percent in 1960. During this period the South went through a rapid metamorphosis, changing from a predominantly rural region (65 percent rural) in 1940 to a predominantly urban region (58 percent urban) in 1960.

Both the 1940s and the 1950s were characterized by substantial out-migration from the South—particularly on the part of Negroes displaced by farm mechanization and attracted to Northern cities by the expectation of better-paying jobs. Between 1940 and 1950 there was a net out-migration of 2,242,000 people from the South of which 75.3 percent were nonwhite (predominantly blacks). Although the migration pattern for whites reversed itself in the 1950s with a new in-migration of 330,000 whites into the South, 1,512,000 more nonwhites left the South than entered it during the ten-year period.[46] As a result of the out-migration of Southern blacks during this twenty-year period, the percent Negro population in the South decreased from 24 percent in 1940 to 21 percent in 1960.[47]

Although the South achieved an unprecedented rate of economic growth between 1940 and 1960, it was still the poorest region in the nation and by a considerable margin. In 1947 the House Committee on Agriculture attempted to identify some of the forces causing low incomes and living standards in the cotton South. The list included the following reasons: (1) low productivity of manpower in Southern agriculture, (2) the exceptionally high rate of natural increase of the Southern farm population, (3) the past and continuous high rate of soil erosion and depletion, (4) lack of capital, (5) educational deficiencies, (6) health deficiencies, (7) lack of skills for nonfarm pursuits, (8) the South's infant industry status, (9) inadequate local market demand, and (10) adjustments required by increased rate of farm mechanization. Not unlike many other studies of the Southern economy, the House Committee on Agriculture conveniently overlooked the possible importance of racial discrimination, the rigidity of the social structure, and the essentially undemocratic nature of the South's political institutions in the economy of the South. And the policy recommendations proposed by the committee demonstrated a similar degree of ignorance or indifference on the part of the committee. At a time when the South had made substantial economic progress and solutions to some of the region's really difficult problems were within sight, the leadership of the South chose the path of the proverbial ostrich, burying its head in the sand and behaving as if the region's social and racial problems did not exist—a pattern of behavior that would come back to haunt the white leadership of the South in the 1960s.

PROSPERITY (1960-70)

While the sit-in movement, the civil rights movement, the Ku Klux Klan, the White Citizens Council, Martin Luther King, James Meredith, Ross Barnett, and George Wallace were capturing the national headlines during the divisive 1960s, the economy of the South was quietly grinding away at a record pace. When the books were closed for the decade of the 1960s, they showed that this was truly a period of remarkable socioeconomic progress in the South. Not only did many of the barriers to racial integration come tumbling down, but also per capita personal income increased by 82 percent from $1,687 in 1960 (76.1 percent of the national average) to $3,062 (78.3 percent of the national average). Using the census definition of the South, one finds that the median income of Southern white men and Southern black men increased by 61 percent and 178 percent, respectively, between 1959 and 1969, more rapidly than in any other region. Median family income increased by 48 percent in the census South between 1959 and 1969, in contrast to a 39 percent increase for the nation as a whole. Furthermore, there were spectacular increases on a statewide basis in nonfarm personal income during the decade in Florida, where it increased 145 percent; Georgia, 132 percent; and South Carolina and North Carolina, 131 percent and 130 percent, respectively.

For the first time since Reconstruction more people moved into the South than out of it and the immigration was heavy with people with college degrees, thus raising the average education level of the region. The rate of urbanization in the South was twice the rate of the North. Although all of the Southern states gained in population between 1960 and 1970, the South's percentage of the population of the United States remained relatively constant at 27.5 percent. The 1970 census also showed that Southern blacks streamed North during the 1960s at a rate nearly the same as the relatively high level of the 1940s and 1950s.

Two characteristics have differentiated the South from the rest of the nation since before the Civil War: (1) its dependence on agriculture and (2) its relatively high percentage of black people. Both of these characteristics appear to be coming to an end. The rapid rate of industrialization of the region in the 1960s and the continued out-migration of blacks to the North have tended to reduce the differences between the South and the rest of the nation.

By the end of the 1960s the South had indeed improved its position in the nation in terms of degree of industrialization. For example, the South's percentage of manufacturing employees in the nation increased from 20 percent in 1960 to 23 percent in 1967. [48] Value added by manufacture in the South in 1967 had reached 20 percent of the total for the United States, up from 18.5 percent in 1963 and 17.1 percent in 1958. Capital expenditures for new plant and equipment in manufacturing in the South accounted for 27.8 percent of the nation's capital expenditures in 1967, in comparison with 24.5 percent in 1963. [49]

Although industrialization has increased substantially in the South, personal income and earnings in manufacturing in the South still lag behind the rest of the nation. In 1969 personal income derived from manufacturing in the South was only 19 percent of the corresponding total for the United States. [50] Average weekly earnings in the South in 1969 were $108.71 in contrast to $129.51 for the entire United States. Average hourly wages in manufacturing were $2.66 in the South and $3.19 for the United States. [51]

At the beginning of this chapter we asserted that the South's retarded economic development was caused primarily by the region's lack of industrialization. We have attempted to show that although industrialization in the South has progressed substantially in the past one hundred years, the South still lags behind the nation in industrial employment and income. We also argued at the outset that the South's relatively slow progress in industrialization had been caused by four factors, each of which was present in the South before the Civil War: (1) insufficient effective demand, (2) insufficient supply of skilled nonagricultural labor, (3) insufficient supply of capital, and (4) insufficient investment in education and technology. Although we have made continual reference to each of these factors throughout our historical analysis, it may be useful to summarize the importance of each of them at the end of the decade of the 1960s. Have these factors persisted since the end of the Civil War? If so, to what extent are they still important now?

Insufficient Effective Demand

Insufficient market demand is both a reflection and a cause of low per capita income in the South. Insufficient demand has led to caution in business expansion in the South and has retarded business development. Estimates of effective demand are difficult to come by, since the Department of Commerce does not publish estimates of consumption by state or region. Although it would be difficult to prove, there is reason to believe that the average Southerner is somewhat less fiercely self-sufficient than the plantation owner and yeoman farmer of the antebellum South. To some extent what we have witnessed during the past one hundred years is the Americanization of the Southern economy necessarily implying a greater interdependence on the part of Southerners within the South and with the rest of the nation.

Of the four factors that have adversely affected the degree of industrialization in the South, insufficient effective demand is probably the most important factor today simply because as the South's income level approached the national average its buying power also increased, thus creating a strong source of demand for goods and services produced within the region as well as outside the South. As evidence that effective demand has been making rapid gains in the South, consider the following. Between 1960 and 1970 the percentage increases in the number of households in the South with one or more cars, with a washing machine, with a refrigerator or a freezer, and with a clothes dryer were all higher than the gains outside the South. Furthermore, new private housing starts in the South increased by 37 percent between 1960 and 1969 while they increased by only 7 percent outside the South. The number of new motor vehicle registrations in the South increased by 65 percent between 1960 and 1969. Outside the South motor vehicle registrations were up by only 36 percent.

One statistic, however, supports the hypothesis that this problem has not been completely eliminated: the South's share of personal income from retail and wholesale trade in 1969 amounted to only 23 percent of total income from retail and wholesale trade in the United States.

Insufficient Skilled Labor

From the preceding analysis it should be clear that the quantity of skilled nonagricultural labor in the South has increased significantly in the past thirty years, particularly in manufacturing. Employment in manufacturing in the South increased by 151 percent between 1940 and 1969 while manufacturing employment in the United States increased by only 90 percent. However, even with this impressive increase, manufacturing employment in the South in 1969 accounted for only about 23 percent of total manufacturing employment in the United States. In terms of nonagricultural employment, the South's share was 25 percent of total nonagricultural employment in the nation in 1969. Both percentages were clearly below 27.5, the percent of the nation's total population living in the South.

The equal employment provision of Title VII of the Civil Rights Act of 1964 has opened the door for the entry of blacks into many fields, including manufacturing, which were heretofore closed to them. Although the full impact of this legislation on the supply of skilled nonagricultural labor in the South is not completely known yet, it is expected to be substantial in the next few years.

Finally, in chapter 3 we will show that not only has the quantity of skilled labor increased significantly in the South during the past thirty years, but efforts have been made to improve the quality of the labor force with increased expenditures for public education and the advent of strong vocational and technical schools in the South.

Insufficient Capital

There can be little doubt that investment capital has also become more readily available in the South and that no longer are entrepreneurs primarily attracted to agriculture as the major recipient of investments from both Northern and Southern capitalists. As we have previously mentioned, in 1967, 28 percent of the capital expenditures for new plant and equipment for manufacturing in the United States were made in the South. Although it is impossible to get detailed breakdowns on the sources of this capital, it is safe to assume that a substantial portion of it originated outside of the South. That is, although the region is no longer seriously strapped by a lack of capital, sources indigenous to the region have by no means been sufficient to satisfy the South's capital needs.

Total assets of savings and loan associations in the South in 1968 accounted for only 20 percent of the assets of savings and loan associations in the nation. Savings and loan associations are an important source of investment capital for construction and related industries. [52]

On the other hand, since 1954 the level of capital expenditures in each of the divisions of the census South has risen more rapidly than in the United States as a whole. Capital expenditures in the South Atlantic states were $789 million in 1954 or 9.6 percent of the total capital expenditures in manufacturing in the United States. By 1967 they had risen to $2.8 billion or approximately 12 percent of the total for the United States. In the East South Central states, capital expenditures increased from 4.8 percent of the national total to 6.5 percent by 1967 and in the West South Central states from 8.8 percent to 11.0 percent.

As evidence that the South's financial institutions are not as fully developed as those of the rest of the nation, personal income from finance, insurance, and real estate accounted for only 21 percent of total personal income from these institutions in the United States in 1969. [53]

A study by Joe Floyd in 1965 provided optimism about the long-run future of Southern financial institutions, particularly with regard to narrowing the gap between interest rates on bank loans in the South and in the nation. "This narrowing gives support to the general thesis that with the growth of southern savings and the inflow of capital from other regions, rates of return on capital investment in the region are being brought into line with the rates of return that prevail elsewhere in the nation." [54]

Insufficient Investment in Education and Technology

The results of the 1970 census indicate significant progress in public education in the South during the 1960s. Expenditure per pupil in the South increased by 100 percent from $300 to $600 per pupil between the 1952-53 school year and the 1969-70 school year. Expenditure per pupil for the total United States increased by only 77 percent to $766 over the same period. Average salaries for elementary school teachers in the South increased by 60 percent, from $4,500 to $7,200 during this period, while the national average increased by only 49 percent to $8,300. On the other hand, average salaries for secondary school teaching in the South increased by 59 percent to $7,500 in contrast to the national average which increased by 48 percent to $8,800. [55]

Between 1959 and 1969 the proportion of five- and six-year-old children enrolled in schools in the South increased from 65 percent to 77 percent. The proportion of eighteen- to twenty-four-year-olds enrolled in school in the South increased from 20 percent in 1959 to 29 percent in 1969. But the South is still below the rest of the nation in the proportion of children attending school outside the ages for compulsory attendance.

The proportion of adults in the South who had completed at least a high school education increased from 33 percent in 1960 to 50 percent in 1970. The percent of Southern adults who had completed one or more years of college increased from 15 percent in 1960 to 20 percent in 1970. Southern adults are as likely to have completed some college as a Northern adult. Men living in the South who have a college degree are more likely to hold the Ph.D. or some other professional degree as their highest degree than are men with college degrees living in other parts of the country. [56]

And perhaps the most surprising development of all with regard to education in the South is the fact that by the fall of 1970, Southern schools had become the nation's most desegregated while racial isolation had worsened in many Northern, urban school districts. The percentage of blacks attending majority-white schools in the eleven states of the old Confederacy doubled from 18 percent in 1968 to 39 percent in the fall of 1970. This compares with 33 percent in the thirty-two Northern and Western states, and 32 percent in the six border states.

We have attempted to trace the economic history of the South between 1830 and 1970. We have also identified a number of factors that appear to have played a causal role in the South's slow rate of economic development and have shown that some of these factors can be traced back to the period before the Civil War. In recent years many of these factors have diminished in importance and the rate of economic growth has been greatly accelerated. Yet in spite of phenomenal economic development during the past thirty years, the South is still the poorest region in the United States by virtue of some factors that caused the South's previous economic problems.

In the words of Jon Nordheimer of the *New York Times*, "If the vices of the old economic system are simply replaced with the vices of the new—pollution, uprooted families and de facto segregation—the South will have missed an opportunity. But if it seizes every chance to improve its condition, it could very well emerge from the 1970s in a position to challenge the leadership of the North for the first time in more than a century—not to secede from the Union but to help salvage it. Wouldn't it be interesting if this time around it fell to the South to save the Union?"

Inputs to the Southern Economy

If one wishes to understand the economy of the South or any other major institution of the region, he must necessarily treat the institution in the broad context of its interrelationships with the other institutions of the region. That is, if we want to comprehend fully the economy of the South we must gain some insight into the interfaces between the Southern economy and the educational, political, and social institutions of the region.

As an initial step toward viewing the economy of the South from a somewhat more global perspective, the flow chart in figure 2.1 provides us with a useful conceptual framework. In this flow chart the South is

FIGURE 2.1. *The Economic System of the South*

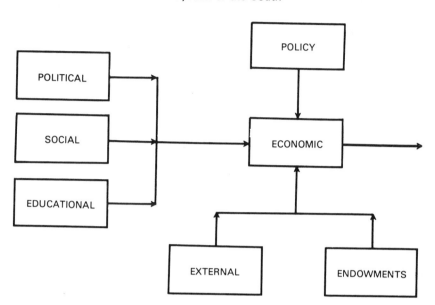

treated as a total system whose economy is affected by its educational, political, and social institutions. In addition, the economy of the South is influenced by its given endowments of capital, labor, natural resources, transportation, and managerial skills. In the language of systems analysts, the South is an open system whose behavior is affected by certain forces outside the region over which it has little or no control. We shall call these external factors. Finally, the Southern economy also responds to policy decisions made by local, state, and national policy makers.

Thus to analyze and understand what causes the outputs of the Southern economy to behave in the manner in which they do, we must examine *all* of the inputs into the economy. Although we are concerned primarily with per capita income as the principal output of the Southern economic system, we do recognize that employment, profits, savings, investment, and other outputs of the Southern economy are also important, particularly in terms of their effects on the other institutions of the region as well as the economy itself.

In the following pages we shall examine each of the inputs into the economy of the South in more detail so as to gain a broader insight into the inner workings of the South's economic institutions—agriculture, commerce, finance, industry, and labor.

ENDOWMENTS

Fundamental to the functioning of any economic system are the endowments of the system. Among the more important endowments of the economy of the South are capital, labor, natural resources, transportation, and managerial ability. For an understanding of how the Southern economy operates, one should start by examining the region's endowments. To some extent what follows represents merely a rearrangement of facts that were reported in our historical analysis, but the rearrangement is necessary for an appreciation of the extent to which the South's economic problems can be solved within the region, without resort to outside assistance.

Capital

The South throughout its history has suffered from a shortage of capital, particularly for industrial development. Our historical analysis has demonstrated that the South has been closing this gap at a rather rapid rate during the past twenty years. Although considerable evidence suggests that the South's financial institutions have become increasingly viable and responsive to the capital demands of the region, this sensitivity does not apply equally to blacks and whites. Sources of capital for black businesses in most of the South are restricted to a handful of black financial institutions (banks, insurance companies, and savings and loan associations), various programs of the federal government, and a small number of private foundations that specialize in grants to black businesses. Black-owned manufacturing plants are practically unheard-of in the South. The Congolese Steel Company in South Carolina and the Terry Manufacturing Company in Roanoke, Alabama, are among the few exceptions to this rule.

Although it is extremely difficult to establish the regional origin of capital flows within the United States, substantial evidence supports the hypothesis that the type of economic colonialism that developed in the South near the turn of the century is by no means a thing of the past. A recent study showed that about three-fifths of all funds used for industrial expansion in the Atlanta Federal Reserve District come from outside the South. [57]

Consider the case of Arkadelphia, Arkansas, a town of ten thousand people in southwest Arkansas. It has several department stores, a number of specialty shops, several drug stores, and six factories that employ over 20 percent of the town's population. Only one of the six factories was financed from sources within the state of Arkansas. Another, the Reynolds Aluminum Company, is owned by Virginia interests. The other four are owned by corporations located in New York, San Francisco, and other parts of the United States. Three Northern paper companies own 105,000 acres of land in Clark County where Arkadelphia is located. Only one of the department stores is locally owned. The only firms in the area that are locally owned are small retail and service enterprises that contribute relatively little to the town's economic base.

What really matters is not where capital invested in the South originates, but the contribution to regional resource development that results from income produced by the use of this capital in the South.

Labor

The South should have an ample supply of labor available for employment in manufacturing and service-producing industries during the 1970s as a result of (1) the continued pattern of in-migration into the South that began in the 1960s, (2) the natural rate of growth in the population of working age, and (3) further declines in employment in agriculture, sawmilling, mining, textile mill products, and personal services. Unfortunately, many of the available laborers in the South will be unskilled and inexperienced for work in the most rapidly expanding Southern industries: (1) electrical machinery manufacturing, (2) transportation equipment manufacturing, (3) rubber products manufacturing, (4) apparel products manufacturing, (5) nonelectrical machinery manufacturing, (6) paper and allied products, and (7) metal industry manufacturing. [58]

To meet the need for a more skilled, highly trained labor force during the 1970s, the South is going to have to increase substantially its investment in human resources through increased expenditures for education and vocational training.

Particularly acute is the situation facing the undereducated Southern black who lacks industrial experience and is still subjected to racial discrimination in employment. In spite of civil rights legislation in the 1960s, Southern blacks are still underrepresented in nonagricultural industries, managerial and professional positions, and sales and technical fields. Furthermore, employment in the sales, clerical, craftsman, and operative categories shows substantial underrepresentation of blacks while there is overrepresentation of blacks in the laborer and service categories.

In an extensive study of black employment patterns in the South, Ray Marshall and Virgil Christian found that blacks comprise a much larger proportion of the work force in declining industries in the South than in expanding industries. They further concluded that blacks are greatly underutilized in the South. "There is evidence that inadequate employment opportunities are causing the South to lose Negroes with higher levels of education and in the most productive age brackets." To the extent that better-educated whites move into the South, migration tends to widen the racial gap for it becomes an education and technological gap as well. [59]

Natural Resources

Although the South has failed to use its human resources, particularly blacks, to their full potential, this is certainly not true in the case of natural resources. The South is indeed well endowed with natural resources and these resources appear to have been developed rather extensively. In 1968 the South accounted for 53 percent of the value of the mineral resources produced in the United States. When one looks at the production of specific minerals, the South's record is even more impressive. In 1969, 69 percent of the crude oil produced in the United States came from the South and 70 percent of the country's proved crude oil reserves were located in the South. In the case of natural gas the corresponding figures for production and reserves for 1968 were 81 percent and 80 percent, respectively. The South is also a coal-producing region. It produced 29 percent of the coal in the United States in 1968. All of the sulfur and bauxite produced in this country is produced in the South. In addition, 49 percent of the nation's salt production in 1969 was in the South. Although the South produces small amounts of iron and zinc, its proportion of the supply of metals for the nation is relatively small and unimportant.

The South is also richly endowed with forest and timber resources. Of the commercial forest lands in the United States, 42 percent were located in the South in 1963. As recently as 1968, lumber production in the South was 31 percent of the total for the nation.

Another important resource in the South that is both a natural resource and a man-machine resource is the generation of electric energy. In 1968, of the installed electric generating capacity in the United States, 32 percent was in the South. Furthermore, 32 percent of the electric energy production in the United States in 1968 was in the South.

A particularly important quasi-natural resource in the South is the Tennessee Valley Authority which was created in 1933 to control the Tennessee River for rural electric power, flood control, navigation, and improved land use. Spanning the seven-state region of Alabama, Georgia, Kentucky, Mississippi, North Carolina, Tennessee, and Virginia, TVA has provided the region with some of the lowest electric rates in the world. In 1971 average home use of electricity by TVA customers cost 1¼ cents per kilowatt-hour, far below the national average of more than 2 cents per kilowatt-hour. Since 1936, when TVA's first project went into operation, TVA dams and reservoirs have averted nearly $400 million in potential flood damage and provided another $150 million in flood control benefits to the lower Ohio River and Mississippi River basins. Personal income in the Tennessee River Valley was 71 percent of the national average; thirty-seven years before it was only 45 percent of the national average.

Transportation and Communications Systems

A cursory glance at the data on transportation and communications in the South will provide substantial evidence that the South's transportation and communications systems compare favorably with those of the rest of the nation. Consider the example of highways. Surfaced rural highway mileage in the South in 1968 represented 32 percent of the national total. The South's share of the authorized Federal Interstate Highway System in 1968 was 30 percent. By 1968 the South had completed 60 percent of its authorized interstate mileage in comparison to 65 percent for the United States as a whole. In 1969 motor vehicle registrations in the South were 29 percent of the national total.

In terms of another form of transportation, railroads, the South had 30 percent of the country's railroad mileage in 1968. With regard to aviation, 28 percent of the active civil aircraft and 27 percent of the public airports in the country were located in the South in 1969. And in 1968, 35 percent of the tonnage that passed through the ports of the United States passed through Southern ports.

One obvious deficiency in the South's transportation system is the lack of rapid transit systems within or between the major cities in the region. Only the city of Atlanta has any explicit plans to develop a rapid transit system.

In 1968 there were 54 telephones per one hundred people in the United States and 46 per one hundred people in the South. Finally, 94 percent of the households in the South had a television set in 1969. This factor alone has played a considerable part in bringing the South back into the Union.

Management and Entrepreneurship

Whereas the South's natural resources and transportation and communications systems appear to be reasonably adequate for further economic development in the 1970s, management and entrepreneurship in the South reflect the region's propensity to underinvest in the development of its human resources. An inadequate supply of skilled, nonagricultural managers and entrepreneurs has persisted in the South for well over 140 years without any obvious signs of significant change. The scarcity of managerial and entrepreneurial talent is even more apparent among Southern blacks.

When one lists the major corporations in the United States that had their origins in the South, the list is quite short. It includes the Coca Cola Company of Atlanta and a few oil companies that originated in Texas by virtue of the source of crude oil.

With the possible exception of The University of North Carolina at Chapel Hill there is not a single first-rate graduate school of business in the South. Higher education alone, therefore, is not likely to lead to any quick solutions to the South's dearth of managers and entrepreneurs. However, there are some encouraging signs that the influx of Northern industry into the South is supplying the region with a new breed of managers who are trained in the more sophisticated tools of management science and computer technology. The phenomenal rise, in a very short period of time, of Southern business tycoons such as H. Ross Perot and Sam Wyly in Dallas, implies further that it is not impossible for the South to generate an indigenous breed of entrepreneurs of its own.

EXTERNAL FACTORS

Among those events that have had a significant impact on the economy of the South since the Civil War but have not been directly affected by the economy of the South are the period of Reconstruction, World War I, the Great Depression, World War II, the Korean War, and the Vietnam War.

Until 1940 the economy of the South was almost entirely at the mercy of price fluctuations in the world commodity market. But as we have previously mentioned, the combination of the Great Depression and World War II set loose forces that have tended to free the South from its heavy dependency on agriculture and the inherent risk associated with fluctuating agricultural commodity prices.

What has become equally clear during the past thirty years is the close relationship that exists between the economy of the South and the economy of the nation. The U.S. economy was characterized by rapid economic growth and full employment during the 1960s and the South generally outperformed other regions.

Federal government expenditures and employment also represent important external inputs into the Southern economy. In 1968, for example, 28 percent of the federal aid to state and local governments and individuals was expended in the South and in 1967 the South's share of federal government employment was also 28 percent. Given the hawk-ish tendencies of most Southern congressmen it is interesting to note that the South has not fared all that well in terms of defense contracts. Of the defense contracts awarded in the nation in 1969, only 20 percent of them were awarded to Southern states. The South does considerably better in military base employment and spending.

To fully analyze the impact of the aforementioned factors on the Southern economy one needs to utilize more sophisticated analytical tools—econometric models, for example—than have been applied in this book.[60]

OUTPUTS FROM OTHER INSTITUTIONS

The economy of the South is affected by a variety of forces in the South, including political, social, and educational institutions. In this section we describe some of the important relationships between the Southern economy and the political, social, and educational institutions of the region.

Political

Disfranchisement of blacks, states' rights ideology, racism, single-party politics, pure old-fashioned demagoguery, and unremitting opposition to the federal government have all been characteristics of Southern poli-tics at various times since the end of the Civil War—characteristics that have taken their toll on the economy of the South. Economists define the concept of cost in terms of foregone opportunities. The economic oppor-tunities foregone by the South as a result of its rigid, uncompromising political structure are enormous and include industries that did not come South, sources of employment that did not materialize, lost federal aid and contracts, scientists and engineers who refused to live in the South, and the out-migration of some of its brightest and most talented young people, particularly blacks.

Ideological polarization had become an established pattern in the South by the early 1960s. The political intransigency of Southern "liberals" and "conservatives" fostered an ideological isolationism that resulted in communication barriers on political, business, and social levels. The response of white conservatives to the Supreme Court de-cision of 1954, the Civil Rights acts of 1964 and 1965, and the entire civil rights movement has been one of reaction and negativism. The term "Southern conservative" came to represent a bastion for the status quo. In the name of "states' rights," "racial integrity," and "individual free-dom," Southern segregationists fought the civil rights movement every inch of the way, and the white South was swept again into an era of defensive introspection. While the decade cried for objectivity and critical self-analysis, Southern political rhetoric and Northern superciliousness only produced frustration, rationalization, and blatant hostility. It was not a new theme in Southern history; the tragedy was the frequency with which it recurred. The only issues were preservation of segregation and hostility to the federal government—issues kept alive by such politicians as Ross Barnett, Orval Faubus, John Bell Williams, George Wallace, and Strom Thurmond. The South has paid a high price for its undemocratic political structure and its race-oriented politics, not only in terms of economic and industrial development, but also in terms of the development of its human resources.

Social

Not unlike many other social phenomena, population growth and economic development are jointly determined. That is, population growth affects economic growth and economic growth affects population growth. In analyzing the effects of population growth on the economy of the South, we shall focus primarily on the birthrate and migration patterns.

As we have previously indicated, more people moved into the South during the 1960s than moved out. As a result of industrialization Northern whites flowed into the South at a rate that exceeded the rate of out-migration by Southern blacks. And we are beginning to see some signs of a slowdown in the black exodus and even reports of blacks returning to the South, having been frustrated by the deterioration in economic opportunities offered by Northern cities.

Although the birthrate is declining in the South, the rate of urbanization exceeds that of the rest of the nation. Many of the rural Southerners who once migrated to Northern cities are now moving to places like Atlanta, Birmingham, Charlotte, Dallas, and Memphis.

A major concern of this chapter will be that of evaluating the consequences of population growth on the South—particularly the urban South. Although a good supply of skilled labor is crucial for industrial development, an excessive rate of population growth can lead to substantial costs in terms of governmental social services including health, education, and welfare.

The one social characteristic that dominates all others in the South is race. Even though nearly twelve million blacks left the Census South during the 1960s, 53 percent of the blacks in the nation still live in the South. Blacks account for 19 percent of the population in the South in comparison to 11 percent for the United States. In a number of major

Southern cities the percent black population is close to 50 percent. For example, in 1970 the percent black population was 45 percent in New Orleans, 51 percent in Atlanta, 39 percent in Memphis, 42 percent in Birmingham, and 42 percent in Richmond.

That an entire political system and class structure centered on race and that racism evolved is well known to all and need not be described here. Suffice it to say that many of the social characteristics of the South had their origins in either the racial makeup of the region or the historical influence of agrarianism.

Long before the Civil War, a rigid social structure had evolved in the South. Neither the end of the Civil War, Reconstruction, the populist revolts of the 1890s, the Great Depression, nor World War II were sufficient to rid the South of a type of social rigor mortis characterized by the disfranchisement of blacks, the doctrine of white supremacy, states' rights ideology, and racial segregation. The absence of a strong middle class gave rise to a weakness of social responsibility reflected by blind individualism, indifference to public schools, hostility toward industrialization, opposition to change, a regional inferiority complex of major proportions, and the out-migration of the region's most promising prospective leaders.

Nicholls argues that the net effects of the South's rigid social structure on economic development were distinctly unfavorable for the following reasons:

> 1. The aristocratic ideal was seriously corrupted through its association with the positive defense of slavery before the Civil War and with white supremacy after the war. 2. The spirit of extreme individualism became increasingly dominant over *noblesse oblige*, so that the aristocrat increasingly held that his less fortunate neighbors were wholly responsible for themselves rather than being either his responsibility or a product of the social system. 3. There was an abnormal subordination of the Southern rural middle class, which was unable to contribute nearly as much to the democratization and economic development of its region as did its counterpart in the other American regions. 4. The South took on a backward-looking, pessimistic, and static outlook which was the natural product of its status society as the region emerged from the ordeal of military defeat. 5. The South's upper classes came to accept as normal and inevitable socio-economic arrangements based on a disproportionate number of low-income people, arrangements made tolerable to lower-income rural whites by a social structure which at least clearly supported their claims to superiority over the Negro race. 6. The relatively rigid, rural social substructure gave little ground to the development of Southern cities which, despite their more fluid social substructures and their growing urban

middle classes, were handicapped by inadequate growth rates and a discriminatory political structure. [61]

The weakness of social responsibility that has existed in the South since before the Civil War has provided another constraint to regional economic development:

1. It has kept the masses of Southern people, white and Negro, in relative ignorance in a world in which knowledge and skills are increasingly the key to both personal and social betterment. 2. It has led responsible political leaders to propose abolition of public schools as a solution to the school-integration controversy, without regard for the educational needs of the vast majority of their people or for the effects on concurrent industrialization campaigns. 3. It has caused large planters and managers of local low-wage industries to oppose measures to facilitate out-migration and local industrialization, despite the general community interest in such developments. 4. It has encouraged a continued belief that the South's low-income people are poor because they are innately inferior, rationalizing a policy of inaction toward the improvement of schools and other public services and the attainment of a more efficient and equitable social and economic organization. 5. It has resulted in a too-easy approval of the recent high out-migration rates by Southern Negroes, which, while undoubtedly contributing to an easing of racial tensions, must increasingly represent a substantial social loss—in terms of potential industrial labor force and prior public educational investments—to the states from which they migrate. [62]

Educational

We have previously attempted to establish the link between investment in education in the South and the productivity of the region's manpower resources. Inadequate investment in human resources is a principal cause of the South's retarded economic development.

In the heat of the school integration debate, we have all but lost sight of the more fundamental problem of quality education. Only recently many Southerners have become cognizant of the significant differences between the educational system of the South and educational systems in other parts of the country. Although these differences are partly attributable to the economic inefficiency of operating a dual school system, they also reflect a number of other factors, not the least of which is that the South is the poorest region in our nation. Long before the integration crisis in the South, teacher salaries and expenditures per pupil were lower than elsewhere. Compulsory education laws were not enforced, and dropout rates were noticeably high. Although it may be accurate to say that most Southerners were not really aware of the inadequacies of their educational system, it might also be argued that the region as a whole was not fully committed to the concept of a first-rate educational system for all its children.

Higher education, though sometimes unjustly stereotyped by those living outside the region, suffers from many of the same problems plaguing the public schools—lack of economic resources and a poorly defined concept of what quality education means on the college and university level. The latter can be explained in part by the earlier "in-breeding" within the educational institutions themselves and the strongly political overtones attached to the appropriations a state legislature makes to its colleges and universities. Higher education in the South suffers from a lack of imagination and innovation, poor economic policies, antiquated management techniques, and a frantic competition for funds and prestige—realities that taxpayers, alumni, and students are beginning to recognize.

POLICY DECISIONS

Policy decisions by federal, state, and local (city and county) governments have also played an important role in determining the nature and direction of Southern economic development. Policies that influence the Southern economy usually take on some combination of the following four forms: (1) constraints, (2) incentives, (3) taxation, and (4) public expenditures.

Federal

That the Southern economy is influenced considerably by the economy of the United States is now accepted by most economists. To the extent that federal monetary and fiscal policies are used to achieve such national goals as economic growth, full employment, and price stability, these same policies will also affect the economy of the South. Although a great deal is known about the effects of national monetary and fiscal policies on the behavior of the national economy, less is known about the differential regional effects of various national economic policies.

Other national policies that have influenced the Southern economy include the equal employment provision of Title VII of the Civil Rights Act of 1964, the farm subsidy program, protective tariffs, import restrictions, military expenditures, minimum-wage laws, open-housing laws, right-to-work laws, to mention only a few. In a book of this type we cannot possibly enumerate all of the federal policies that have affected the Southern states, much less elaborate on many of them. However, in the concluding two sections of this chapter we shall consider a relatively small number of federal policies that either already have considerable influence on the Southern economy or have the potential to influence the economy positively if they are either modified, expanded, or eliminated, depending on the particular case.

State

The fact that the economy of a state is what economists call an "open" economic system makes it somewhat more difficult to analyze the effects of state government policies on economies of the Southern states. The absence of any form of state income accounts frustrates matters even more. Nevertheless, we will be able to do at least some analysis on the effects of state tax and expenditure policies on the economies of the Southern states. It is possible to comment, for example, on the effects of state sales and income tax policies on income distribution in the South. That so-called right-to-work laws that ban the "union shop" in most Southern states serve as barriers to unionization and, therefore, attract low-income industries to the South can be easily demonstrated. Although it is beyond the scope of this book to come up with precise mathematical relationships relating state policy decisions to economic development in the South, a recent book by Thomas H. Naylor, John W. Wall, and Horst Schauland, SIMPLAN: *A Planning and Budgeting Language*, describes methodology for this type of quantitative analysis. [63]

Local

Since the economy of a city or a county is also a completely open system (much more so than a state or the region), the number of policies controlled by the local unit that will have any significant impact on the economy of the city or the county is likely to be rather small. In spite of this fact, one cannot deny the economic importance of such local policies as zoning, property taxes, land use policy, industrial development, as well as the collection of services provided by city and county governments. The manner in which these policies are administered in a particular local area may have substantial influence on the growth rate and distribution of income in the area. A policy of increasing importance is the merger of county and city governments, as in Nashville, Tennessee, and in Jacksonville, Florida, to reduce governmental operating costs. In many sparsely populated areas of the South, it may simply become financially impossible to continue separate county governments in all counties. The merger of county governments in multicounty regions may be the only way to improve or even maintain the present level of governmental services in some remote, rural areas. It is just possible that county governments may take on a new sense of importance in the South as we search for strategies to make the rural South more attractive and to stem the tide of rural-to-urban migration.

Analysis of Specific Economic Institutions

From the analysis of the preceding pages one can identify those aspects of the major economic institutions in the South that contributed most to the three problems of primary concern in this study: (1) low per capita income, (2) racial discrimination, and (3) poor quality education. We now examine what we consider to be the six most important economic institutions in the South: (1) agriculture, (2) commerce, (3) finance, (4) industry, (5) labor, and (6) public finance. In each case, we explicate those aspects of the institution in question that, if subjected to change by federal, state, or local policy decisions, could have significant impact on the solution of one or more of the three major problems of this study. Our purpose is to look for points in each of the aforementioned institutions where the application of specific policy decisions and strategies is likely to increase per capita income, reduce racial discrimination, and improve quality of education. The concluding section of the chapter makes some specific policy suggestions concerning each of the six major economic institutions.

AGRICULTURE

By 1969 the importance of agriculture to the economy of the South had diminished considerably and accounted for only 4 percent of personal income in the region. But the problems of Southern agriculture, particularly as they affect people, do not appear to have been greatly reduced. We shall argue in chapter 7 that problems such as widening racial income gaps and the displacement of farmers continue to persist in the South and that many of our federal agricultural policies actually contribute more to the cause of some of these problems than to their solution. Finally, we shall show that the solution to the economic problems of the rural South may be crucial to the solutions of the problems of the urban South in the 1970s, for if we continue to do nothing to stem the flow of displaced, poor, uneducated farmers from the farm to the city, our cities will soon become mirror images of New York, Chicago, and Los Angeles with their seemingly endless social and economic dilemmas.

These problems will be analyzed in detail and a set of specific agricultural policies proposed in chapter 7.

COMMERCE

In terms of their contribution to personal income, the South's commercial institutions (wholesale and retail firms) accounted for a larger percentage (13.5 percent) of personal income in 1969 than did the commercial institutions for the nation as a whole (13.2 percent). Although data on the relative performance of Southern businesses in comparison with those in other parts of the country are not available, there appears to be little evidence available to conclude a priori that there are any significant factors that differentiate Southern commerce from that of the rest of the nation.

However, there is at least one major problem of Southern business that is shared by commercial institutions throughout the entire nation—the conspicuous absence of minority-owned business enterprises of any significant size. The President's Advisory Council on Minority Business Enterprise reported the following findings on the extent of minority-owned business enterprise in this country:

> The 17 percent of the population who are American Indian, black, or of Spanish-speaking ancestry control only a tiny fraction of the productive resources of the nation. Current figures place minority-owned businesses variously between 55,000 and 165,000, from a total of more than 5.5 million, or between 1 and 3 percent of the total business community. Contributing to the picture is the nature of many of these minority-owned enterprises. In the main, these are small retail or service establishments, largely lacking in capital assets. As such, their control of capital is only a fractional amount of their 1 to 3 percent of business ownership. In fact, the combined assets of all minority banks is $350 million, less than 10 percent of the assets of any one of the twenty largest non-minority banks; the combined assets of all minority-owned insurance companies is less than 0.2 percent of the industry total. The continuing disparity of capital accumulation has significantly hampered the development of the minority community. [64]

Although the council did not disaggregate its report by regions, there is no reason to assume that the South represents an exception to the blank findings of their report. Indeed, with the exception of a few places like Atlanta and Durham, North Carolina, black businesses in the South rarely deviate from a well-established pattern of barbershops, funeral parlors, and "mom and pop" stores. Both Atlanta and Durham have a significant number of black businesses of a more substantial nature.

Among the obstacles to minority ownership are the following: (1) limited capital and high interest rates, (2) lack of management expertise and training, and (3) an inability to qualify for insurance at a reasonable cost, frequently at any cost. There is also an inability to get bonding, a high rate of vandalism and pilferage, and a lack of effective policy protection.

Another characteristic of black businesses both in the North and the South is the fact that they have traditionally operated in segregated markets and have tended to specialize in markets with relatively low growth potential such as personal services (barbershops and funeral homes) and retail trade. A recent survey conducted by the National Business League found that 30 percent of minority-owned enterprise marketed personal services, while only 7.4 percent of nonminority-owned enterprise centered on these services; correspondingly, only 1.2 percent of minority enterprise was in manufacturing as compared to 6.9 percent of nonminority enterprise.

If Southern blacks are to participate fully in the economic and social development of the South during the 1970s, then there is a definite need for expanded business ownership among blacks in the South. By expanded ownership we mean the promotion of ownership of an expanded share of the property and wealth of the South by blacks and other minorities in the region. Since blacks represent by far the largest minority group in the South, most of our comments in this section will be directed toward them. However, most of what we have to say about expanded business ownership is equally applicable to Indians, Chicanos, and other Southern minority groups.

Special emphasis needs to be placed on the expanded ownership by blacks of such economic enterprises as cooperatives, credit unions, savings and loan associations, and employee stock participation plans, as well as on the expansion of new and existing small businesses.

In a region in which until quite recently racial discrimination has been the rule rather than the exception, the implementation of the goal of expanded business ownership among blacks will not be easy to achieve. But if we are to achieve a type of postracial society in the South, expanded ownership among Southern blacks is an essential first step.

FINANCE

Earlier in this chapter we showed that in the past the South has indeed suffered from an insufficient supply of capital and a poorly developed financial market. Considerable evidence indicates that these deficiencies are no longer serious impediments to the future economic development of the region. Today the relevant question is not so much whether capital will be available for economic development in the South in the 1970s, but whether this capital will be provided by indigenous sources or from sources outside the region. In a decade of modern communications and financial institutions it is not nearly so important as it once was whether the capital required to build a new plant in southern Mississippi comes from Dallas or New York. The price is likely to be the same in either case, and the only relevant issue is one of control. We may argue that there are advantages in having local capital invested in local enterprises on the grounds that the owners will have a vested interest in the community as a whole. But surely New York or Chicago capital is better than no capital at all. Furthermore, it appears that it is only a matter of time before the South will develop its own financial institutions and will no longer have to go to the East in search of capital. Already, for example, Memphis, Tennessee, is showing signs that someday it may become the bond capital of the United States. Furthermore, in terms of the percent of personal income derived from financial institutions, the gap between the South and the rest of the nation does not appear to be unduly serious. In the South in 1969, 3.8 percent of personal income came from financial institutions in comparison to 4.2 percent for the United States.

In other words, although the South still lags behind the rest of the nation in producing its own indigenous capital and in the development of its own financial markets, the problem no longer appears to be particularly serious. However, just as there is a shortage of minority-owned business enterprises in the South, there is an acute shortage of minority financial institutions. Specifically, the limited number of black financial institutions in the South and the general scarcity of capital for the expansion and development of black businesses represents a serious financial obstacle to the development of the South.

INDUSTRY

For well over twenty years now the official policy of every state government in the South concerning industrialization has been to maximize the number of new firms that locate in the respective states. For the most part this policy has been administered without regard for the type of industry attracted to the region and without regard to the long-range consequences of an industrial mix that might actually impede the socioeconomic development of the region rather than accelerate it.

It is becoming increasingly clear that many of the industries that have come South during the past twenty years have had a detrimental effect on the environment of the region as well as on the sociopolitical structure of the South. The extent of the pollution of our streams, rivers, and more recently our coastal areas by the petrochemical and pulp and paper industries in particular, as well as the devastating effects of stripmining in eastern Kentucky and Tennessee, are well known.

If any one industry stands out as a symbol of the South's grievous errors in formulating a strategy for industrialization, it is the Southern textile industry. The Southern textile industry provides a major source of employment in the states of Alabama, Georgia, North Carolina, and South Carolina. In 1967, 639,300 people were employed in the Southern textile industry. Although this industry is best known for its low-wage policy and hard-line position against organized labor, some of its other policies may very well have had much more serious consequences for the region than these. For example, prior to the enactment of the Civil Rights Act of 1964 the textile industry engaged in blatant racial discrimination in its employment policies. The number of blacks employed by the Southern textile industry has increased substantially as a result of the Civil Rights Act of 1964. But even though it has become increasingly difficult to find whites who will work for the wages being offered by the industry, today it is virtually impossible to find any blacks holding positions of any significance in the management of Southern textile firms. Although a competitive labor market has forced the industry to drop its policy of using the threat of racial integration to stifle efforts at unionization, some of the industry's reactionary tendencies continue to persist.

A well-established pattern in textile mill towns throughout North Carolina and South Carolina illustrates that textile mills frequently do little or nothing to improve the quality of education in these areas on the grounds that better-trained workers are likely to demand higher wages and may even elect to abandon the careers chosen by their fathers in the textile mills. It is not at all uncommon to find textile firms openly opposing the entry of additional firms in a given location, especially if the firms in question are likely to employ more highly skilled and highly paid workers. Governor John West of South Carolina has run into this problem as a result of his highly successful program to attract foreign investment from outside the United States into South Carolina. South Carolina textile executives, on more than one occasion, have expressed their opposition to this program on the grounds that it will lead to increased wage rates in the state. Typical of the Southern textile industry's lack of concern for the welfare of its employees has been its reluctance to acknowledge the extent to which cotton textile workers are afflicted with byssinosis, a lung ailment commonly known as "brown lung disease." Dr. Arend Bouhuys of the Yale University Medical School has estimated that as many as 17,000 active textile workers now have byssinosis, and this figure does not include those cotton textile workers who have been forced to retire prematurely as a result of the disease.

The more recent policy of the Southern textile industry is one of advocating that the federal government place restrictions on the imports of textiles from foreign countries. The self-serving nature of this position seems blatant when viewed in the context of the industry's traditional position of staunchly defending the free enterprise system in this country and the fact that the Southern textile industry imports a substantial amount of its machinery and equipment from West Germany and Japan. The textile industry's present protectionist position is, in fact, the direct antithesis of the free enterprise system. Putting ideological arguments aside, let us examine some of the real effects of the Southern textile industry's protectionist policies in regard to the economy of the South. To be sure, some textile workers will no doubt lose their jobs as a result of foreign imports. The reality that some Southern textile mills will not be able to survive is merely a confirmation of the fact that they have been unable to adjust to changes in textile technology and to adjustments in the world textile market. There are indeed many textile firms in Asia, Latin America, and Europe that can produce textiles more efficiently (at a lower cost) than the textile industry in the United States. But why adopt a policy that may have the effect of penalizing the entire Southern economy in order to protect the interests of a few? Import restrictions on textiles and protective tariffs mean higher prices for textile products. Higher prices for clothes and other textile derivatives affect all Southerners, particularly the poor. Furthermore, there is a distinct possibility that the protectionist policies of the Southern textile industry could trigger an international trade war between the United States and the rest of the world. Such a trade war could result in the imposition of similar trade barriers by other countries, thus restricting the sale of tobacco, cotton, petroleum, timber, pulp and paper, and other products, the sale of which is vital to the entire economy of the South.

A more rational policy than import quotas to protect Southern textile workers would be for the federal government to provide assistance to displaced textile workers in the form of retraining, temporary subsistence allowances during the period of retraining, and finally moving allowances if in order to find a new job an individual worker must relocate. Protection of a relatively small special interest group at the expense of the rest of the South, the nation, and possibly even the rest of the world cannot be justified.

Certainly the textile industry is not the only villain in the industrial South. Racial discrimination has been widely practiced throughout Southern industry. Opposition to industrial development in local communities is by no means restricted to mill towns. Consider the case of Jackson, Mississippi, where until the election of Mayor Russell Davis in 1969 the city had experienced virtually no new industrial development during a twenty-year period. Business leadership, which was totally opposed to industrialization, and an incompetent city government virtually guaranteed that there would be no industrial expansion in Jackson.

To the extent that there has been any orderly planning for industrialization in the South, it has fallen without exception into the hands of the respective industry-hunting agencies in the Southern states. Whether it be the Agricultural and Industrial Board of Mississippi or the Conservation and Development Department in North Carolina, the name of the game has been how to attract an additional firm into the state. Industry-hunting boondoggles, special dispensations from the payment of state and local taxes, revenue bonds financed by state and local governments, and strong antiunion policies on the part of state governments are the devices used to industrialize the South. The state industry-hunting agencies have had little or no appreciation of the long-range consequences of their policies on the total economies of their respective states.

Although most Southern states have separate planning departments that are independent of their industrial development departments, the planning agencies are typically void of any real political power. Almost without exception, the existing planning agencies in the South were started with funds that were available from some agency of the federal government to establish a planning department. The money was relatively easy to obtain, and it mattered little whether the plans were used or whether they actually dealt with any relevant matters in terms of statewide economic development. In most cases the state planning agencies are not listened to either by the governor's office or by the state legislature and they are virtually powerless.

At the annual symposium of the L. Q. C. Lamar Society in Atlanta in May of 1971, Dallas industrialist H. Ross Perot said, "The problem of the South in the 1970s is not going to be how to attract one additional industrial firm to the region, for industry is going to come South whether we like it or not. The relevant question is, 'Will we be ready for the rapid industrialization which we are going to experience in the 1970s?' " While it is true that states such as Arkansas, Mississippi, and South Carolina are still in need of substantial increases in industrialization, industrial growth has lost some of its charm in states such as Florida and Virginia and in cities such as Atlanta, Dallas, Houston, and Miami. Since the 1890s the game plan for regional development in the South has essentially been the urban and industrial model. Throughout the South today many business, industrial, political, and academic leaders are having second thoughts about the urban industrial model. If we become entirely dependent upon industrialization as a strategy for economic development, particularly in our urban areas, then we may be well on our way to emulating the urban monoliths of the North, the Midwest, and the Far West. In order to avoid some of the urban mistakes of the North, we must find ways of controlling future industrialization of the South so that all of our industry is not concentrated in a relatively small number of extremely large cities such as Atlanta, Dallas, and Houston. We must seek ways of attracting industry to some of the smaller towns—the towns that have been steadily dying in many parts of the South for the past twenty years.

We are going to have to find alternatives to the urban industrial model. It is going to be necessary to explore rural industrial models and nonindustrial urban models, and in all cases to ask ourselves the question, What are the likely long-range consequences of any given industrial-development strategy on the total economy of the region and not merely on some special interest group whose stake in the economy may at best be temporary?

Finally, until recently the South has expended little effort in attracting foreign industries and investments into the region. (South Carolina is a notable exception.) Although it has recently become a fad to send state industrial development boards to Europe, Japan, and Latin America to promote the sale of Southern manufactured goods, the results of these forays are inconclusive at this point in time. In general, state and regional policies aimed at stimulating foreign trade between the South and the rest of the world should bode well for the future of the Southern economy.

LABOR

In our discussion of Southern labor we shall concentrate primarily on industrial labor. We shall begin by examining the wage differentials that still exist between the South and the rest of the nation. Following this analysis we shall consider the effects of unionization, right-to-work laws, minimum-wage laws, and racial discrimination in wages and employment patterns in the South.

Wage Differentials

As we have previously noted, in the case of average weekly earnings and average hourly wages in manufacturing there exists a significant differential between the South and the rest of the nation. There is no shortage of literature explaining wage differentials between the South and the United States as a whole; various economists have explained these differentials in terms of (1) racial discrimination, (2) an inadequate educational system, (3) an oversupply of unskilled labor, (4) insufficient capital equipment, (5) the relative weakness of labor unions in the South, (6) the fact that the South is less industrialized than the North, and (7) differences in the productivity of Southern workers compared to the rest of the nation, to mention only a few. No doubt there is some relevance in each of these factors. It is not our purpose in this study to attempt to pinpoint the exact cause of the wage differential in the South but rather to show how it is related to inadequacies in some of the South's major institutions. Most of the aforementioned reasons require little or no elaboration. The elimination of racial discrimination, the improvement of the quality of education in the South, and increased industrialization should all contribute to the reduction of this regional gap in wage levels.

Labor Unions

The South is the least unionized section of the country. Only 15.6 percent of the nonagricultural employees in the South are members of labor unions in comparison with 28.4 percent for the entire United States. Furthermore, only 13.3 percent of the nation's labor union members live in the South; however, statistics indicate that union membership has increased faster in the South since 1939 than it has in the remainder of the United States. Union membership as a proportion of nonagricultural employment is not increasing as fast in the South as it is in the non-South, although absolute membership in the South is increasing faster because of a more rapid increase in the region's nonagricultural employment.

Whether labor unions represent an appropriate strategy for reducing the South's wage and income gap is not an easy question to answer. On the one hand, it can be argued that to the extent that stronger labor unions imply higher wages, then clearly the South is better off with more labor unions rather than less. Unfortunately, though, a significant portion of the South's labor force is relatively unskilled. As a general rule, unskilled workers are at the mercy of the competitive market forces of the economic system in which they operate. When a Southern business firm is forced to raise its wage rate artificially through a union contract, then inevitably the firm will attempt to tighten its belt and eliminate workers either through automation, direct layoffs, or normal attrition. While those workers who are fortunate enough to be retained by the company have the benefit of a higher wage, those workers who are displaced may end up with absolutely nothing.

Another important question concerning organized labor in the South is, Does organized labor impede industrialization in the region? To the extent that the South's lower wage rate serves as an attraction to Northern industry to move South, then any device—whether it be a labor union or a minimum-wage law that artificially raises the wage rate above the market rate—may serve to reduce the incentive of Northern firms to move South. There are, of course, several counter-arguments to this position. Labor organizers would argue that, in the long run, higher wages in the South will raise the level of aggregate demand in the region and will ultimately lead to the creation of new industries and new jobs at a faster rate than if there were no unions at all. This argument also takes care of the marginal workers who become temporarily unemployed as a result of a union-induced wage increase. In other words, so the argument goes, these unemployed workers will eventually be employed again because those workers who did not lose their jobs will have greater buying power which will lead to increased demand for goods and services, the creation of new businesses and industries, and ultimately more jobs. The final argument in favor of the union position is that the types of firms that are attracted to the South solely because of the low wage rate are not the types of industries that the South should be attracting in the first place. They are, for the most part, apparel and garment firms, many of which employ unskilled women and contribute little or nothing to the improvement of the communitites in which they exist.

Statistics relating to whether labor unions help or hinder industrialization and in turn lead to higher or lower wages are inconclusive. It is our judgment that if the South wants to continue to increase its rate of industrialization and in turn increase its wage rate, the fewer obstacles placed in the path of industry—whether labor unions or minimum-wage laws—the better. Rather than attempting to use labor unions and minimum-wage laws to inflate artificially the wage rates of marginal, unskilled workers, we should either adopt a guaranteed income policy in this country or attempt to develop policies for upgrading the training and level of skills of these marginal workers. That is to say, we favor letting the market forces bid up the wage rates of the more highly skilled workers and using specific economic policies to solve the problems of the unskilled, marginal workers.

Although labor unions have a mixed effect, at best, on industrial development in the South, there are indeed some important social and political benefits to be derived from unionization in the South. Labor unions may frequently become a vehicle by which the views of working-class people can influence the political processes of the region. One of the reasons why George Wallace is so popular in the South is that he claims to speak for the "little man," "blue-collar workers," and the "working man." Given the ineffectiveness of labor unions in the political arena in the South, no one else does represent these people. Through the use of right-to-work laws and other antiunion devices, Southern political leaders have managed to render working-class people in the region politically ineffective.

Within the past five years a lot has been said about a phenomenon that has been observed throughout Northern industrial plants, as well as western Europe, called worker alienation. Worker alienation cannot be measured directly, but its effects take the form of increased absenteeism, decreased productivity, and high rates of labor turnover, alcoholism, and drug addiction on the part of blue-collar workers. Thus far the South has not experienced this phenomenon on the scale that other industrial regions have both in this country and in Europe. But there is no reason to believe that the South will be bypassed by this problem. Labor unions with strong support at the "grass roots" level provide an instrument for alleviating some aspects of worker alienation. Labor unions can provide a positive influence and source of pressure on management to introduce job democracy, job redesign, and other strategies aimed at giving blue-collar workers control over their working environment. In the long run, such strategies may be beneficial not only to working-class people, but to the entire economy of the South.

Right-to-Work Laws

Section 14(b) of the Taft-Hartley Act gives the states the right to pass so-called right-to-work laws banning the "union shop." All of the Southern states except Kentucky, Louisiana, and Oklahoma have right-to-work laws. The effect of these laws is as follows. In a right-to-work state, if a union holds an election in a particular plant and wins the election, it cannot force those workers in the firm who do not choose to belong to the union to pay union dues. Typically what happens is that even though the union may win an election by a substantial margin, it will gradually lose the financial support of its members simply because they are unwilling to continue paying dues for the same benefits that the nonunion members receive without paying any dues whatsoever. Under these circumstances union strength is soon eroded after an election. As a result of these right-to-work laws the relative strength of unions in the South by comparison to the rest of the country is even less than is implied by the figures that we cited previously.

The fact that there have been no serious threats to the right-to-work laws in the Southern state legislatures in the past ten years implies that union leaders are not likely to find their jobs any easier in the near future. Although some economists in the South have gone on record with forecasts of increased unionization in the South in the 1970s, this position hardly seems justified when one closely scrutinizes the current economic and political clout of labor unions in the South. Although we may see the day of increased cooperation between organized labor and blacks, the number of places where such coalitions presently exist in the South are few and far between. The South seems to be becoming much more progressive, but there is no evidence of any major shifts in attitudes in favor of organized labor in the South. For example, in a 1972 public opinion poll conducted by Social Systems, Inc., in North Carolina, the least unionized state in the nation, 60 percent of the people interviewed felt that labor unions were too powerful and 81 percent opposed requiring any working man to join a labor union if he went to work for a large corporation.

Minimum-Wage Laws

The economic consequences of minimum-wage laws are virtually identical to those of organized labor. In each case we have forces at work that raise the wage rate artificially above the prevailing market rate. The same arguments that we presented both for and against labor unions are equally applicable to minimum-wage laws. As was our position in the case of organized labor, we tend to favor alternatives other than minimum-wage laws to promote industrialization and to increase wages in the South—that is to say, we would rather see wages pushed up by increased industrial activity. And in the case of those people who because of health, education, or skill levels are not able to participate in the economic system, some version of guaranteed annual income is a more appropriate policy measure than a minimum-wage law.

Racial Discrimination

Little disagreement arises among economists that a significant portion of the South's income gap can be explained by the fact that until very recently racial discrimination in employment was the rule rather than the exception. Median family income, for example, for Southern blacks was only 57 percent of median family income for whites in 1970.[65] With the continued enforcement of the Equal Employment Provision of the Civil Rights Act of 1964 and with the elimination of racial discrimination in the public schools, the racial income gap in the South should begin to diminish rather significantly. As the racial income gap closes, the South's income gap with regard to the rest of the nation can also be expected to close correspondingly.

Revenue

Governmental units in the South, as in the rest of the country, are faced with the problem of raising revenues from a tax-weary public. Governments in the South are confronted with the additional disadvantage of having to draw their revenues from a below-average tax base that has tended to retard government services and programs within the South.

One way to measure the tax burden on state and local governments is through the computation of a tax sacrifice index. The tax sacrifice index is computed for each state by expressing state and local taxes as a percent of income and dividing by per capita income. In 1969 the tax sacrifice index for the United States was 3.01. Every Southern state had a tax sacrifice index higher than the national average except South Carolina, Florida, and Texas. Mississippi has the highest tax sacrifice index in the country.

In terms of per capita (state and local) taxes, the South lags behind the rest of the country. In 1969 the national average was $380. No Southern state came close to that figure, and the range varied from $221 for Arkansas to $330 for Florida.

Sales Tax / In 1970, the sales tax, both general and specific, was the primary source of revenues for all of the Southern states. As a percentage of all state tax revenues, the sales tax ranges from a low of 47.8 percent in Louisiana to a high of 80.8 percent in Florida with eight of the states deriving over 60 percent of their total revenues from this tax.

The use of the general sales tax began during the depression years when states were urgently seeking new means of obtaining revenues. The first permanent general sales tax was enacted in 1932 by Mississippi. The next year thirteen states followed suit and at present forty-five states, including all of the Southern states, levy general sales taxes.

General sales taxes are levied as a fixed proportion of consumer sales. Rates in the Southern states range from 2 percent in Oklahoma to 5 percent in Mississippi and Kentucky. The rates in the South are similar to those in other states, which range from 2 percent to a high in Pennsylvania of 6 percent.

Despite the proportional tax rate structure of the general and specific sales taxes, they are regressive in nature when personal income is used as the tax base. Thus the states tax low-income earners for proportionally more of their income than higher-income families are being taxed. Problems accumulate for the Southern states that have a high concentration of low-income families. An example of the regressiveness of the sales tax was found when income was used as the tax base in Georgia. The effective rate varied from 4.7 percent of income for families earning less than $1,000 to 1.8 percent for incomes of $15,000 and over.

It is ironic, yet consistent with Southern politics, that states that have the highest concentration of low-income earners in the nation rely most heavily on taxes that place the greatest burden on the poor. Mississippi, with the lowest per capita income in the nation, raised 46.9 percent of its taxes in 1970 through its general sales tax and another 29.2 percent by the use of selective sales taxes. The average state in the United States raises 29.5 percent of its revenues from the general sales tax and 27.3 percent from selective sales taxes. In Mississippi this practice resulted in an annual per capita tax expenditure of $102.81 for the general sales tax and $63.95 for the selective tax out of an annual per capita income of $2,192 in 1969. These compare to national figures of $70.04 and $64.59 per capita out of a per capita annual income of $3,680. In 1970, eight Southern states had a higher share of each $1,000 of income being paid in the form of general sales taxes than the national average.

The regressiveness of the general sales tax can be reduced by allowing exemptions for certain necessary commodities on which the poor spend a larger proportion of their income than do their richer neighbors. Specifically, certain states exempt food and medicines from the tax in an effort to ease the burden on the poor. Southern states have been slow to adopt exemptions, and only Texas and Florida exempt both food and medicine from their general sales tax. North Carolina and Virginia allow exemptions on the sale of medicine.

Personal Income Tax / Throughout the nation, states have traditionally placed less reliance on direct income taxes than on sales taxes, and the South is no exception. Only in the states of North Carolina, Virginia, and Georgia is the percentage of total tax revenues derived from the personal income tax higher than the national average.

Wisconsin adopted the first state income tax in 1911. In 1912, Mississippi became the second state to impose an income tax, and in 1915 Oklahoma became the third. With the depression providing strong impetus for states to find new taxes, the number of states levying income taxes by 1937 reached thirty-two, including all of the eleven Southern states that presently impose the tax.

Not only are most Southern states below the national average for raising revenues from income taxes, but they also make little use of progressive rate structures. For the United States as a whole, personal income tax rates ranged from a low of 1 percent to a high of 14 percent in 1970. For the South the typical range was 1 percent to 6 percent.

The income tax structure can be made more progressive by the use of personal exemptions. In general, Southern states allow higher-than-average exemptions. In 1970, Mississippi had the highest exemption, allowing a single taxpayer $4,000 and a total of $6,000 if a joint return was filed. Permitting deduction of the federal personal income tax from state personal income tax liabilities tends, however, to reduce the effective progressiveness of the state tax. Of the eighteen states that allow this deduction, only three (Alabama, Louisiana, and South Carolina) are in the South.

In 1968 the Advisory Commission on Intergovernmental Relations recommended that a state's income tax should produce at least 20 percent of the federal personal income tax collections in that state. In the South only North Carolina met this productivity standard in 1968.

Corporate Income Tax / In 1970 eleven of the thirteen Southern states levied a tax on corporate profits. Only Florida and Texas had no corporate income tax at that time. The corporate income tax rate in the South ranged from a low of 4.1 percent in Mississippi to a high of 9.4 percent in North Carolina. Florida has recently adopted a 5 percent corporate profits tax. The national average in 1970 was 7.8 percent.

Southern states have shown some reluctance to raise the corporate tax rate because of possible adverse effects on industrial development. Some Southern states have even offered tax exemptions to certain industries as incentives to locate in a particular state.

Property Tax / Throughout most of our nation's history the property tax has been the most important single source of tax revenue. In 1902 it provided over 51 percent of the total federal, state, and local tax collections. With the outbreak of World War II it dropped to only 9.4 percent of tax collections as the federal government vastly expanded income tax collections. During this period of the 1930s and 1940s states began to leave property taxation to the local governments. The property tax has now almost disappeared as a state tax measure, but local governments in 1970 still derived over 64 percent of their revenues from it.

All of the Southern states fell well below the $168 average per capita property tax for the United States in 1970 and ranged from a low of $39 for Alabama to a high of $128 for Texas. In terms of property tax per $1,000 of personal income, the national average in 1970 was $45. The range for the South varied from $15 for Alabama to $39 for Texas.

Property taxes are considered to be regressive largely because the value of a person's housing unit when compared to personal income tends to decline with increases in income. A flat rate on housing thus results in a heavier proportionate burden on low-income families. Instead of alleviating the regressive feature of the property tax, the granting of homestead exemptions tends to accentuate it. This results from lower-income groups being more likely to rent, where there is no exemption, than to own their own homes. Only nine states in the United States still allow homestead exemptions; seven of these are in the South.

Homestead exemption is only one of several ways the property tax base is being eroded. Other exemptions include those for veterans, the elderly, and business. As in the case of corporate income tax, business exemptions are used in an effort to entice new industry into states. In 1967 only eight states allowed local units to exempt certain types of industrial property, but five of these were in the South. Most of this erosion of the tax base has been determined by state legislatures, which have been subsidizing certain groups at the expense of the local governments. Exemption from the property tax is a poor substitute for adequate programs of aid to such groups as a state's elderly or its veterans.

Charges and Fees / With the exception of Virginia, in 1970 the Southern states relied much more heavily on the use of fees and charges for services at the local level than the national average. For the United States as a whole, 24 percent of all local revenues were derived from fees charged by local governments. In the South the percentage of local revenues derived from fees was as high as 52 percent in Alabama in 1970.

Federal Funds / Federal grants to the states began in the early 1800s but remained at modest levels until the depression years. They have continued to increase in importance as a source of revenue to the states, and in 1969 they totaled $20 billion of which $5.5 billion went to Southern states.

In 1970 the South, with 27.5 percent of the nation's population, received 28.4 percent of all federal grants to the states. For the United States in 1969, the average state received 19.3 percent of all its revenue (state and local) from federal grants, while in the South the corresponding figure ranged from a low of 15.5 percent for Florida to a high of 37.3 percent for Mississippi. On a per capita basis, the South has fared quite well in terms of federal grants. Seven of the thirteen Southern states received federal grants in 1969 that exceeded the national average of $98 per capita. Per capita federal grants in the South ranged from $69 in Florida to $141 for Kentucky and $147 for Oklahoma. In general, the Southern states have tended to benefit from the redistributive effects of federal grants.

Expenditures

With a tax base considerably smaller than the national average, it is not surprising to find that state governments in the South spend less than those in the rest of the country. Per capita expenditures by state in the United States were on the average $512 in 1968. This figure compares with a low of $340 in South Carolina for the South and a high of $506 in Oklahoma. However, if one views state government expenditures in relationship to personal income, then the story is quite different. In 1968 the average rate of state government expenditures per $1,000 of personal income was $164. Only Florida, North Carolina, South Carolina, Texas, and Virginia spent less than the national average.

Policy Recommendations

The economy of the South came much closer to the economic mainstream of the United States during the 1960s and early 1970s. But it is safe to say that the income gap that still exists between the South and the rest of the nation might be even greater if it were not for a number of major national policy decisions during the past forty years—the New Deal, military expenditures during World War II, the Supreme Court decision of 1954, the Great Society, and the Civil Rights acts of the 1960s.

In the remainder of this chapter we shall outline policies at the national, state, and local levels that could lead to a reduction in the income gap that exists in the South and make for a more equitable distribution of income. Recognizing that income is but one measure of social well-being or the quality of life, we also include policy recommendations in this and later chapters on health, housing, and welfare. Specifically, we include policy recommendations on (1) business and industry, (2) manpower and employment, (3) public finance, (4) health and population, and (5) planning. Policy recommendations on agriculture are made in chapter 7.

BUSINESS AND INDUSTRY

Expand Ownership of Business and Industry

In cooperation with the private sector and the affected people and communities of the South, the federal, state, and municipal governments can take several specific steps to expand ownership, economic participation, and economic independence in the South, particularly among minorities. Southerners must see the enemy for what it is—the lack of indigenous economic resources—and realize that it necessitates a joint effort by black and white to acquire a large-scale ownership. State industrial development commissions should be urged to reexamine their policies toward the location of outside-based companies in the South to assure that local development is getting priority treatment and that those outside interests that are locating in the South are serving the public good while pursuing their own private gain. State governments providing financial or tax incentives to firms outside the South to induce them to locate in their own particular state should insist on certain conditions, including employee stock participation plans, recruitment of local personnel as part of the management team, and adequate environmental protection agreements.

In the areas of management training and assistance, basic business and economic education should be made an option of public-school curricula. School facilities should be made available, when not in use, for compensatory economic education for adults. The President's Advisory Council on Minority Business Enterprise has recommended that federal assistance be granted to school systems to assist in curriculum development in this area.

Management training for prospective entrepreneurs should be made a high-priority program item for the private sector in the South. Local chambers of commerce and trade associations, in cooperation with colleges and universities, are probably the best channel for this training and are best equipped to provide it. In several Southern cities, including Atlanta, Dallas, and Houston, programs are already underway that could be used as pilot projects. The Dallas Alliance for Minority Enterprise is a good example of a public sector/private sector coalition of businessmen and government agencies whose objective is the promotion of business ownership through management education and assistance.

In addition, management assistance to existing businesses should be provided by other successful businessmen and trade associations. Local chambers of commerce are usually staffed professionally and thus could provide the coordination of management assistance.

Through the Small Business Administration and the proposed new Department of Rural Development the federal government should be urged to put more of its management and technical assistance monies into the South. [66] Those who are providing management training should seek federal and state funding for the program operating costs. The National Business League chapter in Atlanta and the Dallas Alliance for Minority Enterprise are both federally funded and have had a major influence in their respective cities. It is little known that much federal program money goes begging due to the public's unawareness of its existence.

As for financing, private corporations should be encouraged to form Small Business Investment Corporations and Minority Enterprise Small Business Investment Corporations to serve as sources of equity and debt for entrepreneurial development. The federal government through the Small Business Administration will match private funds two to one, the only requirement being minimum assets of $150,000 in the sponsoring corporation. The government share brings the initial capitalization to $450,000. Several successful SBICs are already operating in the South.

Second, commercial banks should be urged to adopt new lending priorities toward locally owned enterprises, giving preferential treatment to minorities where possible. Federal, state, and municipal governments should be requested to make deposits in those banks with demonstrated records of strong commitment to local and minority-ownership development.

Federal agencies, particularly the Small Business Administration, the proposed new Department of Rural Development, and the Office of Economic Opportunity, should be urged to organize extensive periodic "show-and-tell" visits to small towns and rural areas to acquaint the people with the federal financing programs available and to provide technical assistance in making application for such funding.

In addition, various informal steps can be taken. Government agencies and the private sector in the South should be encouraged to buy from local (especially minority-owned) suppliers, including cooperatives and community development corporations, since money used to purchase equipment or supplies from concerns outside the South is lost to the region and its people. Government agencies, private companies, foundations, and universities should be encouraged to deposit funds in local credit unions as a means of improving the viability of these important community institutions.

Expand International Trade between the South and the Rest of the World

At present, most agricultural commodities and manufactured goods produced in the South that are shipped abroad must pass through the port cities of Houston, New Orleans, Mobile, Miami, Charleston, Wilmington, or Norfolk. Although a few international flights go into Dallas, Houston, New Orleans, and Atlanta, for all practical purposes the Miami International Airport is the only international airport of any consequence in the South. In the day of high-speed jet aircraft there is absolutely no reason why Dallas, Houston, New Orleans, Memphis, Atlanta, and Charlotte could not all become major international airports. By expanding the number of international airports in the South, not only would the South benefit from increased trade flows and communications with the rest of the world but some of the traffic congestion at the Kennedy, O'Hare, and Los Angeles international airports could be diverted into the South, thus alleviating major air-traffic bottlenecks in these urban centers.

Not only would the South benefit economically by expanding the markets for its agricultural and industrial products, but such an outward-looking strategy might indirectly lead to solutions to some of the South's social problems. To some extent the South's racial problems are a result of the region's having created a type of "closed society" in which contact with "strangers" and foreign ideas was systematically discouraged.

Abandon All Protectionist Policies

If the South truly wishes to enter the mainstream of international trade and commerce, then it has no choice but to abandon its present support for import restrictions on textiles, apparel, and other manufactured products. A protectionist trade policy for the United States is incompatible with a vigorous expansionist policy for marketing Southern agricultural and industrial products. Southern congressmen should be informed that their persistent support for protectionist legislation in the Congress is myopic and working against the long-range interests of the South.

While it is true that the elimination of all import quotas, duties, and other restrictions may lead to the temporary displacement of Southern industrial workers, the solution to this problem does not lie in increased protection for the industries in question. Improved manpower programs specifically designed for workers displaced by foreign imports are a much more sensible long-run solution to this problem than the traditional approach of turning to the Congress for import restrictions.

Develop Coordinated Plans for Industrialization

Unfortunately, in most Southern states the goals, strategies, and policies of state industrial development commissions are determined quite independently of state planning agencies and without regard for their long-range effects on the state as a whole. Definite need exists for improved coordination between state industrial commissions and state planning agencies in designing strategies for industrial development. It is time to begin asking ourselves the questions: What kind of industrial mix is best for a given state or a given section of a state? Will the arrival of a particular kind of industry have an adverse effect in the long run on the manpower of a particular community? Will a new industry impose environmental costs on the state that exceed the short-term economic benefits it will provide? What effects will the introduction of industrial firms and business interests from outside the state have on the development of indigenous business and industries within the state? Should the South put more effort into attracting foreign-owned companies—as South Carolina has done—particularly from western Europe and Japan?

MANPOWER AND EMPLOYMENT

Establish Full Employment as a Regional Priority

Both the Democratic and the Republican parties on a national level appear to be committed to a full-employment policy for the economy of the United States. If the South is to continue to prosper economically, then the Southern congressional delegation should be encouraged to share this commitment to full employment for all of the people of the South who wish to be employed.

Adopt State Antidiscrimination Laws

Although the Civil Rights Act of 1964 represented a step forward in eliminating racial discrimination in employment, statewide antidiscrimination laws would shorten the time required to eradicate employment discrimination in the South. It is time for state legislatures in the South to face up to the economic irrationalities of tolerating discriminatory hiring practices. Racial discrimination in employment not only insults and deprives blacks; resultant low incomes for blacks mean reduced buying power, and reduced buying power means fewer jobs and lower wages for all of the people in the South—not just blacks.

Develop Financial Incentives for Firms
Employing and Training Minority Employees

With the increased registration of black voters in the South, the passage of antidiscrimination laws is becoming increasingly feasible. In some states an intermediate strategy may be almost as effective as antidiscrimination laws and may prove to be more palatable from a political standpoint. We recommend that both the federal government and the state governments in the South inaugurate programs that will provide financial incentives to firms and industries to employ and train minority employees. As with some of the other programs that we have proposed, this program should be of short-term duration—perhaps no longer than five years.

Expand Manpower Training Programs

Some economists have argued that since the advent of Henry Grady's "New South" movement in the 1890s the South has placed too much emphasis on developing factories and places and not enough emphasis on human resource development. The Economic Development Administration, the Appalachian Regional Commission, the Coastal Plains Regional Commission, and the Ozark Regional Commission are examples of economic development agencies that seem to have given higher priority to the development of Southern places rather than Southern people. This situation has been particularly acute in the rural South, where manpower education and training activities have generally been quite limited in nature. Those manpower programs that have evolved in the rural South have tended to be highly segregated and have focused on preparing people for existing employment patterns rather than for future employment patterns. Black vocational schools were oriented for black jobs and white vocational schools toward white jobs. Although the South has made substantial progress with vocational training and manpower programs in urban areas, manpower development in the rural South still leaves a great deal to be desired. Both the federal government and the Southern state governments should commit additional resources to rural manpower development programs. This activity could be funded jointly by the U.S. Labor Department and the proposed new U.S. Department of Rural Development.

Eliminate State and Federal Minimum-Wage Laws

Although the data are inconclusive, we believe that minimum-wage laws have served as impediments to the economic development of the South and should, therefore, be abolished both on the federal and state levels. We have previously argued that wage rates artificially inflated either through minimum-wage laws or through union contracts serve as a deterrent to industrial development in the South. We prefer to see wage rates bidded up through competitive market forces rather than through minimum-wage laws. To enable Southern workers who earn wages below the poverty level to subsist, we recommend some form of guaranteed annual income rather than the minimum wage.

Require Employee Participation in Corporate Policy-making

Alienation of employees of large corporations, exemplified by increased absenteeism, increased labor turnover rates, and decreased productivity, is not yet a Southern problem, but it soon will be. As an initial step in the direction of eliminating some of the conditions that give rise to alienation among blue-collar and white-collar employees alike, we recommend that Congress pass legislation requiring all corporations with more than one hundred employees to permit the employees to elect at least 25 percent of the directors of the corporation.

This idea is not new, for it has been in practice in West Germany for over twenty years and has recently been proposed for all of the Common Market countries in western Europe. In Germany this concept is called codetermination; we prefer to call it job democracy.

We also recommend that federal agencies provide sufficient funds for research to enable social scientists to carefully evaluate the impact of variations of job democracy on employee attitudes, absenteeism, labor turnover rates, and productivity.

PUBLIC FINANCE

Seek Alternatives to Local Property Taxes,
and Eliminate Exemptions

In spite of the fact that the United States Supreme Court has recently upheld the constitutionality of the use of local property taxes to support public schools, the property tax continues to be subjected to serious criticism. Critics argue that the use of the property tax to finance public schools is inequitable because the property tax makes the level of spending on a child (and possibly the quality of his education) dependent upon the value of the property of his parents and his neighbors in the school district rather than on the wealth of the state as a whole. We recommend that local communities throughout the South consider alternatives to the property tax as a primary source of revenue for local schools as well as other governmental services.

We recognize that local property taxes are likely to persist in the South for some time. If that is to be the case, then we recommend that local communities discontinue their present policy of exempting churches, private educational institutions, industries, and homeowners from the payment of local property taxes. Such exemptions are short-sighted and inequitable and disguise the fact that they represent explicit subsidies to special-interest groups in the community. If for any reason the local government decides that it wants to subsidize some special group for the long-range interest of the community as a whole, then the subsidy should be direct and open and not hidden in the form of a tax exemption.

Increase the Use of the Personal Income Tax and Make it More Progressive

Both state and local governments in the South should make greater use of the progressive personal income tax as an alternative to the sales tax and the local property tax, both of which are highly regressive. In addition, state and local personal income tax rates in the South should be made more progressive. Specifically, we recommend that state and local governments in the South collect a fixed percentage of each individual's federal income tax bill. This would enable state and local governments to take advantage of the more progressive nature of the federal personal income tax structure. It could also lead to significant savings in collection costs.

Use the Corporate Income Tax as a Policy Instrument to Control Industrial Growth

Since there is considerable evidence to support the hypothesis that the South may soon become even more industrialized than the rest of the nation, Southern states may want to give serious thought to the possibility of using the corporate income tax as a policy instrument for controlling corporate growth in the region. As the rate of industrial development in a given state or a given city appears to be reaching the point at which it is imposing excessive costs on the state or city in terms of environmental pollution, excessive crowding, and increased traffic congestion, then a flexible corporate income tax may become a useful policy instrument for controlling industrial growth.

Make State and Local Sales Taxes Less Regressive

State and local governments should attempt to render their sales taxes less regressive by allowing exemptions for food that is not consumed on the premises and for medicine.

Inaugurate Some Type of Federal Guaranteed Annual Income

The South being the poorest region in the nation, it would stand to derive substantial benefit from some type of guaranteed annual income. We recommend a guaranteed annual income as an alternative to the present welfare system, with incentives built in to motivate poor people to seek higher-paying jobs.

Eliminate Discriminatory Patterns in
the Disbursement of State and Local Funds

In 1971 a U.S. District Court ordered the city officials in Shaw, Mississippi, to discontinue their discriminatory practice of shortchanging the predominantly black neighborhoods in the city of Shaw in terms of paved streets, sewerage lines, and street lights. This court decision could have ramifications throughout the South. State and local governments in the South should begin to plan for the elimination of discriminatory expenditure patterns in public education and other public services. It is no longer acceptable for middle- and upper-income whites to be the primary beneficiaries of state and local governmental services.

HEALTH AND POPULATION

Establish the Concept that Every Southerner Has a Right to
Some Minimum Level of Health Care Regardless of His Income

Fundamental to increasing the per capita income in the South is an increase in the productivity of the Southern labor force. An unhealthy work force cannot possibly achieve significant increases in productivity. Yet as we have indicated, the South has fewer doctors, dentists, and hospitals per capita than any other region, and it also has the highest infant mortality rate. It is the only region where parasites and malnutrition are widespread among the rural poor. If all of the people in the South are to participate in its future prosperity, then we have reached the point at which the South must guarantee each of its citizens the right to some minimum level of health care regardless of his race or income. States should set minimum foundation programs for health comparable to their education programs, with the focus on health status and outcomes, not simply on expenditures.

Develop Alternatives to Present Health Care Delivery Systems

With the exorbitant increases in the cost of medical care during the past decade, serious doubts arise as to whether the South and the nation can continue to afford the luxury of the present form of free-enterprise medicine. An extended stay in a hospital can bankrupt an individual even if he possesses a modest amount of health insurance. Although in theory charity hospitals are available for the indigent, in fact these hospitals are extremely crowded and are simply not able to handle a massive number of charity cases. In our opinion, both the South and the nation will soon have no choice but to take a long, hard look at alternatives to free-enterprise medicine, such as national health insurance as well as other national health schemes like those in the Scandinavian countries. In Sweden, for example, every citizen in the country is entitled to free medical care, and the quality of this medical care may indeed equal or surpass the medical care of most private and public hospitals in the South today. The achievement of a healthy Southern economy and work force demand that we consider alternatives to the present health care delivery system.

Establish State Population Policies

During the 1960s, not only did the population of the South increase through a natural rate of growth, but for the first time in more than one hundred years more people moved into the South than left it. The region may soon face a population problem comparable to that of many of the large cities in the rest of the country. An increasing population in the South will lead to pollution of the land, air, and water. It has been estimated that every child born in the United States will use, for instance, thirty times more of the basic life-support systems of the earth than the average child born in India. (The basic life-support system includes all the necessary natural resources that are not replaceable or restorable, such as fossil fuels and metal ores.)

Both the federal government and the state governments should develop population policies. At the present time not a single state in the country has an explicit population policy. If the South is to avoid the population crises of cities like New York, Chicago, and Los Angeles, rational policies are needed for the control of population growth in the region. In the following recommendations we suggest two elements that might be included in statewide population policies.

Introduce Family Planning Services through the Public Health Departments of the Southern States / The public health departments should begin to distribute information on family planning and birth control throughout the respective states. Public health clinics should become distribution points for family planning services and supplies. No justification exists for the puritanical attitude taken by public health departments in many Southern states that has caused them to shy away from this extremely important form of health delivery service.

Make Abortions Available Free of Charge / With the recent U.S. Supreme Court decision legalizing abortion in this country, both the federal and state governments should take the initiative to make it possible for any woman who wants an abortion to have one. Congress should appropriate funds to cover at least half the cost of an abortion with the states being required to come up with a share as a condition for receiving the federal funds. This policy is justified on the grounds that the cost to the federal and state governments of providing health, education, and welfare services to an "unwanted" child are likely to exceed the cost of an abortion.

PLANNING

Reevaluate the Role of Regional Planning

The idea of some form of regional planning organization in the South goes back at least to the 1930s and the work of Howard Odum at the University of North Carolina. Southern history books are full of accounts of many fruitless attempts to create an effective regional planning organization in the South. The Appalachian, Coastal Plains, and Ozark commissions represent recent unsuccessful efforts on the part of the federal government to develop a regional planning capability in the South. Although the Appalachian Regional Commission has achieved some positive results, the Coastal Plains Regional Commission and the Ozark Regional Commission were failures—both involving large outlays of federal money with no tangible results.

In spite of the failures of the past, there is a definite need for coordinated regional planning in the South, particularly in the following areas: (1) economic growth and development, (2) population control, (3) urbanization, (4) land use planning, (5) transportation networks, and (6) environmental pollution. Without doubt the South is going to grow at an unprecedented rate during the next two decades. The real question is, Will this be carefully planned, orderly growth, or will it be the type of uncontrolled, unmanageable growth that overtook such cities as New York, Chicago, Detroit, and Los Angeles? The South may be able to avoid some of the growth problems of the North, but it will not do so by having each of the thirteen Southern States acting independently.

The recently established Southern Growth Policies Board shares our objective of planned, orderly growth for the region. It is too early to assess its chances for success.

Reorient State Planning Departments

The history of state planning departments in the South is not an impressive one. In most Southern states, state planning departments were organized not because of any commitment on the part of the governor to long-range planning, but because federal money was available to start a state planning department. Indeed, in many cases, having a state planning organization was a prerequisite to receiving additional federal grants. As a direct result of their historical origins, state planning departments have rarely been taken seriously by either the governor, the state legislature, or other state government officials. All too often, the only tangible results produced by state planners in the South have been irrelevant, esoteric studies read only by Washington bureaucrats.

If state planning is to be effective in the South, it must be tied to the political process. The state planning director should report directly to the governor. Although the planning department should have a professional staff consisting of planners, economists, engineers, and social scientists, the planning director must be an effective politician who has the governor's confidence. Unfortunately, an academic degree in planning does not guarantee that one will be an effective state planner.

In general, state planners can learn a lot from their counterparts in the private sector of the economy, namely corporate planners. Many of the concepts and analytical tools being used by corporate planners today are directly applicable to state planning. With the advent of revenue sharing and the current interest in land use planning, state planning and budgeting may be given higher priority by state government officials in the future. State planning departments may be be given a second chance to produce effective long-range plans for state government. It remains to be seen whether they will avail themselves of this opportunity.

Adopt Modern Approaches to State Planning

Effective state planning and budgeting in the 1970s requires a four-step methodology: (1) formulation of a conceptual model for state planning, (2) determination of goals and priorities for state planning, (3) development of a management information system and data base, and (4) formulation of a state planning model to evaluate the effects of alternative plans. [67]

Conceptual Framework / It is impossible to produce effective state plans without the development of a solid conceptual framework on which to base long-range plans. A conceptual framework for state planning is nothing more than a logical game-plan relating goals and priorities for state planning to historical data and an instrument for producing and evaluating alternative futures for the state.

Goals and Priorities / The point of departure for effective state planning is a set of goals and priorities on which to base alternative plans. But in determining goals and priorities for state planning a question arises. Whose goals and priorities should be incorporated into the state plan?

Clearly, several different constituencies—the governor, the state legislature, state government officials, and the people of the state—may be affected by the results of state planning and all may have an interest in goals and priorities for state planning. [68] An annual survey of public opinion in a state six months before the legislature convenes could be extremely useful in setting priorities for state planners as well as goals for the governor's legislative program.

Management Information System / Without adequate historical data, effective state planning is virtually impossible. What is needed is a management information system and data base that can be used to identify problems and evaluate the results of past policies and plans. Texas is the only Southern state that has developed a management information system.

State Planning Model / A number of states are now using computers to evaluate the effects of alternative state government policies on the economy of a state. Through the use of computer simulation models it is possible to simulate the effects of an increase in the sales tax rate or an increase in the education budget on per capita income, the distribution of income, employment, and other socioeconomic variables. With a state planning model it is possible to generate alternative scenarios for a state based on different assumptions about the national economy as well as different state government policies. For example, one could produce a rapid growth scenario, a slow rate of growth scenario, a scenario reflecting extensive industrialization, and one showing limited industrialization and an improved environment. With state planning models, the governor and state legislators can select those policies and those plans that yield scenarios compatible with their personal and political objectives.

3. Whither Public Education?

The Setting

DEFINITION OF THE PROBLEM

Education, defined by Charles Silberman as "the deliberate or purposeful creation or transmission of knowledge, abilities, skills, and values, " is not just an end in itself; it is related to all forms of human activity. [1] As a powerful agent of socialization, education does not simply mirror the values of the society of which it is a product, but possesses an independent force for social change. In the United States, as Gunnar Myrdal remarked, it has been assumed that "education has always been the great hope for both individual and society." [2]

In *An American Dilemma*, his epic work on American black-white relations, Myrdal analyzes the manner in which the American faith in education as a social engineer has drawn heavily upon the enlightenment ideals of liberty and equality. But this faith has been rooted in a belief that education increases the individual's lifetime earning potential. [3] To the extent that education is a tool by which the poor and disadvantaged can increase their per capita income, it is especially important for the South with its large share of the poorer people in the country. Education is also widely believed to lead to technological advances, thereby enabling people to increase the quality of their life as well as the quantity of material goods available. To the extent that education increases productivity and upgrades the credentials necessary to get given jobs, it also contributes to economic growth. [4]

Even more difficult to measure with certainty, but widely acknowledged, is the power of education to promote communication and understanding among members of a community. That education can assume this social and political function was noted by Alexis de Tocqueville during his visit to this country well over a century ago. Taking note of the danger that democracy, under the pressure of individualism, might give way to uncivilized anarchy, the Frenchman urged: "Educate

[77]

them, . . . for the age of implicit self-sacrifice and instinctive virtues is already fleeting far away from us, and the time is fast approaching when freedom, public peace, and social order itself will not be able to exist without education."[5] Confronted with the task of bringing the races to common understanding the South can hardly afford to ignore Tocqueville's admonition. The need is for an educational system that teaches not only spelling and ciphering, but also the vital lesson of social responsibility: that a man's "self-interest rightly understood" (as Tocqueville termed it) depends in the long run as much on the welfare of all the members of the community as it does on the achievement of his individual goals.

TABLE 3.1. *Estimated School-Age Population and Fall Enrollment in Public Elementary and Secondary Day Schools, 1970-71*

State	Population 5-17 Years of Age, 1 July 1970 (x1,000)	Percent Enrollment of Population 5-17 Years
United States	53,039	86.5
South	15,138	86.3
Alabama	962	83.5
Arkansas	525	88.3
Florida	1,602	89.1
Georgia	1,267	88.6
Kentucky	857	83.0
Louisiana	1,078	78.1
Mississippi	683	78.2
North Carolina	1,375	86.7
Oklahoma	643	99.5
South Carolina	762	84.8
Tennessee	1,028	87.5
Texas	3,131	86.3
Virginia	1,225	88.1

Source: National Education Association, Research Division, *Estimates of School Statistics, 1970-71* (Washington, D.C.: National Education Association, 1971), p. 27.

SPECIFICATION OF OUTPUTS

As Alexander Heard stated, "The adequacy of education in the South is inevitably a correlate of the adequacy of other aspects of our lives in the South."[6] To what degree does the Southern educational system produce outputs capable of satisfying the economic, political, and social needs of the region? The problem of measuring educational output is, of course, not a simple one. Measures of the impact of education on subsequent earning power and validated before-after tests of learning would be the best measures of public education output. However, most standardized tests used to measure educational attainment have been subject to serious criticisms in recent years. Counting enrollment and dollars spent is suggestive in the absence of ideal measures. Three yardsticks—the quantity of students and graduates, their performance on educational tests, and the nature of the racial and political attitudes that the educational system has confirmed or inculcated in them—will be used.

TABLE 3.2. *Estimated Average Daily Attendance in Public Elementary and Secondary Day Schools, 1970-71*

	Average Daily Attendance	Percent ADA of Cumulative Enrollment
United States	42,723,202	89.7
South	12,110,604	89.3

Source: National Education Association, Research Division, *Estimates of School Statistics, 1970-71* (Washington, D.C.: National Education Association, 1971), p. 29.

Tables 3.1 and 3.2 give statistics on the percentage of school-age population enrolled in public schools in the South and the average daily attendance in 1970-71: the South is only marginally behind the United States as a whole. Yet the lower percentage of children in public schools of the region is significant because a higher proportion of children in the South attend public schools than private or parochial schools. In the number of high school graduates it turns out annually, the South lags noticeably behind the rest of the nation. While the South comprised 27.8 percent of the nation's population, it was responsible for the production of only 27.2 percent of the nation's public secondary school graduates (see table 3.3). Since the South has a higher proportion of school-age youth than any other region, the 0.6 percent difference is worth attention. James Coleman's massive 1966 study of the nation's schools, *Equality of Educational Opportunity*, found that the nonenrollment rate in the South for persons sixteen and seventeen years of age was approximately 15 percent, nearly twice the rate for the rest of the country. [7]

There is no denying that the few standardized ability and achievement tests that have been administered throughout the country to meaningful samples of the population contain a degree of cultural bias. [8] But the test results are the closest approximations of valid indicators of quali-

TABLE 3.3. *Estimated Populations
and Public High School Graduates, 1969*

	1969 Population	High School Graduates	1960 Percent of Graduates in the Population
United States	201,921,000	2,522,345	1.24
South	56,164,000	686,830	1.22

Sources: U.S. Department of Commerce, Bureau of the Census, *Statistical Abstract of the United States, 1970,* p. 125, table 186; U.S. Department of Health, Education, and Welfare, Office of Education, National Center for Educational Statistics, *Digest of Educational Statistics, 1970,* p. 50, table 67.

tative school adequacy or educational attainment. The shockingly poor Southern performance on the Selective Service mental test suggests deficiencies in the Southern educational system as well as cultural depri-

TABLE 3.4. *Southern Disqualifications
on Selective Service Mental Examination, 1971*

State	Number Examined	Percentage Disqualified for Failure on Mental Test Only	Rank in United States High to Low
United States	589,700	3.9	
Alabama	9,400	8.8	6
Arkansas	5,100	7.7	8
Florida	17,800	6.3	11
Georgia	12,100	10.8	4
Kentucky	11,500	5.7	12
Louisiana	13,900	18.7	2
Mississippi	6,500	21.1	1
North Carolina	12,600	9.8	5
Oklahoma	6,100	....	...
South Carolina	7,100	16.6	3
Tennessee	10,800	8.2	7
Texas	34,800	3.9	15
Virginia	13,500	7.0	9

Source: U.S. Department of Commerce, Bureau of the Census, *Statistical Abstract of the United States, 1972.*

vations. In 1969, of the eleven states with highest rates of draftees' and volunteers' disqualification from military service exclusively because of failure on the mental test, ten were Southern (see table 3.4).

A more comprehensive and reliable measure of educational attainment emerges from the battery of tests administered as part of Coleman's survey. Not only did Coleman examine a more representative population sample than that of the Selective Service test,[9] but he also tested a wider variety of intellectual skills—verbal ability, reading comprehension, mathematics achievement, and general knowledge in the fields of practical arts, natural sciences, social sciences, and humanities. Yet his conclusion is the same: "The regional variation in achievement scores is rather consistent for both Negroes and whites. Consistently lowest for both groups is the nonmetropolitan South. Consistently highest is the metropolitan North. In general both whites and Negroes show higher achievement in the North and West than in the South and Southwest."[10] The Coleman study points out that, while the white student in the metropolitan South performed in 1965 at only slightly below the level of his Northeastern counterpart, other Southern student population groups fared worse. In verbal ability in grade twelve, for example, the metropolitan Southern black stood 3.1 grades behind his white urban classmates in the South, 1.1 grades behind his black counterpart in the urban Northeast, and 4.2 grades behind the average white metropolitan student in the Northeast. For the nonmetropolitan Southern black, the figures present an even bleaker portrait. He performed 5.2 grade levels behind the average Northeastern urban white in verbal ability and 6.2 grades behind in mathematics achievement. The nonmetropolitan white Southerner trailed the Northeastern urban white by 1.5 grades in verbal ability, 1.0 grades in reading comprehension, and 1.4 grades in mathematics achievement.[11] While the average Southern rural black graduates from high school with what amounts to eighth-grade training in the Northeast, no Southern student group (except perhaps urban whites) enters the world beyond the school with a record of educational achievement that approaches, much less matches, the level elsewhere.

More difficult yet to measure are the political and social attitudes that are shaped in and by the school. These attitudes are no less an educational output than are the scores on Coleman's achievement tests. Of particular interest are those attitudes connected with social change, especially race relations. A major study by the National Opinion Research Center indicated that, even among white Southerners, integrated education does produce a degree of tranquilization of racial attitudes. The U.S. Commission on Civil Rights concluded: "The racial attitudes and preferences of both Negroes and whites are influenced by the racial composition of the schools they attend. . . . Negro students are much more likely to prefer racially isolated schools if they have attended only isolated schools and are more likely to prefer desegregated schools if they have attended such schools. The same relationship holds for white students."[12] In the fall of 1970 "for the first time, school desegregation in one degree or another [was] the rule rather than the exception for the children of the South."[13] Table 3.5 shows a dramatic increase in Southern black students attending schools with white students, and the early 1970s saw further integration of the remaining all-black schools in the South.

TABLE 3.5. *Extent of Desegregation in the South, 1970-71 and 1968-69 (in Percentages)*

	1970-71	1968-69
Blacks in school population	27.2	26.6
Blacks in majority-white schools	39.1	18.4
Blacks in all-black schools	14.1	68.0

Source: *Race Relations Reporter,* 6 July 1971.

Quantitatively and qualitatively deficient, Southern elementary and secondary public education provides all-too-feeble inputs into other Southern institutions. Ill-prepared educationally, the South has been slow to adjust to the demands of technology in order to share the benefits of modern industry. In politics, Southern education has failed to provide the region with a participating and perceptive electorate. Finally, the educational system is only beginning to deal with inequities in social structure, especially in regard to race.

Historical Summary

Historians point to two warring threads of Southern thought to account for the way public education developed in the region: a sense of caste, which for many years restricted education to the children of the wealthy, and a spirit of individualism, which initially weakened conceptions of a general social welfare.[14] In the colonial era "the dominant idea of education was that it was a luxury for the rich, or a privilege of the well-born."[15] When "free schools" first developed, many Southerners were contemptuous of them because they "smacked of charity."[16]

The common-schools movement, which during the 1830s and 1840s transformed Northern education, failed to having a corrresponding impact on the South. White Southerners suspected, with good reason, that this movement drew on many of the same forces as the New England abolition movement. [17] Already linked with pauperism, public education then became associated with the slavery controversy, which tended to repress free inquiry throughout the region. [18]

The present system of public schools grew out of legislation by Congress and the post-Civil War Southern legislatures. This legislation provided for school officials and boards, tax support for schools, and the education of Negroes. However, after Reconstruction, the schools subsisted with minimal public financial support; indeed, Northern philanthropy was expected to maintain many black schools. The Populist platforms of the 1890s sounded a new note: demands for universal public education. With the elimination of blacks from Southern politics, and U.S. Supreme Court ratification of segregation in the 1896 case of *Plessy* v. *Ferguson*, ironically, public education gained new political supporters within the region. The general southwide movement for public education got under way in 1898 when Southern and Northern education supporters met in Capon Springs, West Virginia, for the first Conference for Education in the South. Its boards played a central role in channeling philanthropic funds to schools, and in advising legislatures and school officials on a wide range of policy matters. Negro education was not entirely neglected—either because of a belief that properly educated blacks were "always on the side of the law," [19] or because complete neglect would have too blatantly contradicted democratic ideals. Often, this meant "industrial education" for blacks.

In white education the decades after Capon Springs have witnessed extraordinary growth. The advent of motor transportation made possible the consolidated rural school, which helped to overcome the huge diseconomies of scale that had previously hindered the administration of education in the decentralized, agrarian South. The Great Depression and the New Deal put many Southerners, previously champions of rugged individualism, on the side of social engineering; education was increasingly praised as an important tool for regional progress. World War II, which brought about mass contact between Northerners and Southerners, spurred educational awareness in the South even more than had World War I. By the time of the Supreme Court *Brown* v. *Board of Education* decision of 1954, Southern devotion to public education seemed well established. However, a gap existed between appearance and reality. While most white Southerners had accepted the New South concept of education as a means to individual and regional economic growth, they had not yet accepted the American notion of education as a progressive political and social experience. Thus the response of Southern political leaders to the Brown case probably reflected the attitude of many whites toward education. They stood ready to accept whatever economic benefits the educational system spun off, but they wanted little else from it. When they received something else—the prospect of integrated education and the resulting threat to the Southern social structure—they rebelled not only against the authority of the Supreme Court, but also against the principle of public education itself. Indeed, there were times when the region became "essentially hostile to the intellectual process," just as had been the case in the last decades before the Civil War. [20]

In light of the initial resistance to court-ordered integration in the South, the extent of recent acceptance of desegregation is remarkable. In a Gallup poll in 1970 "only one white parent in six offered objection to sending his child to a school in which Negroes are enrolled; six out of ten objected in 1963. On the other hand, 69 percent objected to sending their children to schools where Negroes are in the majority, a decline from 86 percent who objected in 1963." [21]

The hard core of resistance that still exists in some areas of the South was responsible for the growth of "segregation academies," the all-white private schools often hastily thrown together to avoid integration. Although some of the segregation academies claim to offer education of a quality superior to that of public schools, none of the schools so classified was accredited by its state or regional accrediting board in 1971. During 1970-71 an estimated 450,000 to 500,000 white pupils attended segregation academies. However, significant drops in public school enrollments occurred in only three states—Mississippi, Alabama, and Louisiana. The story in most areas of the South today is one of unprecedented integration, and the South is now the most desegregated region in the nation. In 1960 only 0.2 percent of Southern blacks attended school with whites. Since then, the figures have been 2.3 percent in 1964; 15.9 percent in 1966; 32.0 percent in 1968; and 85.9 percent in 1970. [22] With the mixing of students of both races a fact, public education is now faced with the challenge of upgrading the lagging quality of the schools.

Inputs to Southern Education

ENDOWMENTS

Teachers and Staff

Table 3.6 indicates that in all categories except principals and supervisors, the South's share of instructional staff members is approxi-

TABLE 3.6. *Estimated Number of Instructional Staff Members in Public Elementary and Secondary Day Schools, by Type of Position, 1970-71*

	Classroom Teachers			Other Non-Supervisory Instructional Staff	Principals and Supervisors	Total Instructional Staff
	Elementary	Secondary	Total Classroom Teachers			
United States (including D.C.)	1,124,816	915,075	2,039,891	103,723	125,423	2,269,046
South	317,292	250,238	567,480	....	30,920	620,849
South as percentage of U.S. total	28.21%	27.35%	27.82%	....	24.56%	27.36%

Source: National Education Association, Research Division, *Estimates of School Statistics, 1970-71* (Washington, D.C.: National Education Association, 1971), p. 31.

TABLE 3.7. *Classroom Teachers, Estimates, 1970-71*

	Elementary Schools			Secondary Schools		
	Men	Women	Total	Men	Women	Total
United States	175,548	949,268	1,124,816	491,784	423,291	915,075
South	35,067	282,225	317,292	119,966	137,874	250,238
South as percentage of U.S. total	19.98%	29.73%	28.21%	24.39%	32.59%	27.35%

Source: National Education Association, Research Division, *Estimates of School Statistics, 1970-71* (Washington, D.C.: National Education Association, 1971), p. 31.

mately the same as its share of the population. However, it has a disproportionate share of women in classroom teaching, especially at the elementary level (see table 3.7). In 1970-71, 15.6 percent of the nation's elementary-school teachers were men, but only 11 percent of the South's elementary-school teachers were men. Similarly, although 53.7 percent of the nation's teachers in secondary schools were men, only 47.9 percent of male teachers were represented in Southern high schools. [23] One of the reasons that fewer men enter public-school teaching in the South is indicated in table 3.8; the vast majority of teachers in the South earned

TABLE 3.8. Average Annual Salaries of Total Instructional Staff and of Classroom Teachers, 1970-71

	Average Salary of Total Instructional Staff	Percent of United States Total	Average Salary of Classroom Teachers	Percent of All Classroom Teachers Whose Salaries Fall in Each of the Following Salary Groups							
				Below $5500	$5500 to 6499	$6500 to 7499	$7500 to 8499	$8500 to 9499	$9500 to 10499	$10500 to 11499	$11500 and Above
United States	$9,570		$9,210	1.5	7.2	15.6	18.4	16.7	14.9	11.3	14.5
South	7,865	82.18	7,622								
Alabama	7,525	78.63	7,376	0.0	4.5	65.0	14.0	11.0	5.0	0.5	0.0
Arkansas	6,790	70.95	6,634	12.3	37.1	34.6	7.2	3.3	2.5	0.7	2.3
Florida	9,206	96.20	8,805	1.1	0.6	19.3	27.9	23.9	14.0	9.3	3.9
Georgia	7,940	82.97	7,778	5.1	11.1	25.3	38.8	11.5	7.7	0.5	0.0
Kentucky	7,550	78.89	7,190	9.5	21.5	38.5	13.0	11.0	3.0	2.5	1.0
Louisiana	8,600	89.86	8,340	1.7	11.0	18.3	18.0	27.1	19.0	2.8	1.2
Mississippi	6,173	64.50	6,008	21.3	63.0	11.0	3.5	1.2	0.0	0.0	0.0
North Carolina	8,466	88.46	8,168	2.2	29.7	18.4	44.6	1.6	2.7	0.8	0.0
Oklahoma	7,650	79.94	7,360	0.0	10.0	51.9	17.9	9.8	8.5	1.9	0.0
South Carolina	7,150	74.71	7,000	6.0	26.0	33.0	31.0	3.5	0.5	0.0	0.0
Tennessee	7,550	78.89	7,400	2.2	25.4	34.1	17.2	11.2	5.2	3.7	1.0
Texas	8,646	90.34	8,325	3.6	16.4	20.8	11.0	20.8	18.1	6.5	2.8
Virginia	9,000	94.34	8,700	1.2	8.0	20.0	26.0	14.0	12.0	6.8	12.0

Sources: U.S. Department of Health, Education, and Welfare, Statistics of Public Schools, Fall 1970, p. 36; National Education Association, Research Division, Estimates of School Statistics, 1970-71 (Washington, D.C.: National Education Association, 1971), p. 33.

less in 1970-71 than $8,500 per year, while their counterparts in other regions averaged much higher salaries.

Pupil-teacher ratios are higher in the South than in the nation as a whole, particularly at the secondary level. The average number of pupils taught by an elementary-school teacher in the South in 1969 was 25.4, only fractionally higher than the national average of 24.8. However, four Southern states averaged 27 or more pupils per elementary-school teacher. In the United States as a whole, the pupil-teacher ratio in secondary schools is 20:1, whereas the Southern figure is 21.9 pupils per teacher. [24]

The Coleman report presents a rich portrait of the distribution of certain characteristics among teachers, as well as data on the percent of students instructed by teachers with certain characteristics. Except for metropolitan white teachers at the elementary level and nonmetropolitan white teachers at the secondary level, Southern classroom instructors average lower in verbal facility than the national norm (see table 3.9). On the other hand, in teaching experience all Southern groups except metropolitan white teachers averaged at least as many years in the profession as the national average.

TABLE 3.9. *Teacher Characteristics: Selected Qualities*

	U.S.	U.S.		Nonmetropolitan South		Metropolitan South	
	All	Negro	White	Negro	White	Negro	White
Elementary-school teachers							
Verbal facility scores	22.8	20.2	23.4	17.5	22.5	19.2	23.1
Years of teaching experience	12.0	13.0	12.0	14.0	16.0	14.0	10.0
Average number of hours per day in preparation for class	3.2	3.4	3.2	3.4	3.1	3.6	3.2
Average number of hours per day in classroom	5.8	5.9	5.8	6.1	6.2	6.1	6.0
Secondary-school teachers							
Verbal facility scores	22.9	21.2	23.2	19.4	23.2	20.6	22.6
Years of teaching experience	10.0	11.0	10.0	10.0	12.0	12.0	8.0
Average number of hours per day in preparation for class	3.2	3.4	3.2	3.5	3.3	3.5	3.2
Average number of hours per day in classroom	5.1	5.2	5.1	5.5	5.3	5.2	5.2

Source: U.S. Department of Health, Education, and Welfare, *Equality of Educational Opportunity,* by James S. Coleman et al., 2 vols. (Washington, D.C.: Government Printing Office, 1966). Compiled from volume 1, tables 2.32.1, 2.32.2, 2.32.3, 2.32.4, 2.32.5, 2.32.6, 2.32.7, 2.32.8.

The Coleman data indicate that Southern students in nonmetropolitan areas are more likely than the average national student to have a teacher who studied education as a college major and less likely to have one who concentrated in an academic field. Southern students are much less likely than their national counterparts to have teachers with appreciable college experience in integrated classrooms. [25]

Curriculum

Although some Southern school systems are attempting to broaden the curriculum, change in this area is slow. Elementary schools in the South typically do not have their own music, art, or physical education teachers; they are fortunate if they occasionally share the services of specially trained teachers with other schools in the system. Children study the same basic subjects as their parents did and only rarely are exposed to courses such as foreign languages which are more common in elementary schools in other sections.

At the high school level more attention has been given recently to the needs of students who will enter the job market immediately following graduation. Until the 1960s vocational education for students who were not college-bound consisted almost entirely of agriculture or home economics. Although vocational training has been greatly expanded at the secondary level and beyond, James Maddox could still write in 1967, ". . . it is still likely that two-thirds of the people of the South are engaged in occupations for which specialized education is seldom, if ever, available." [26]

A glance at recent Southern state requirements for high school graduation is revealing. Alabama has been granting a diploma without requiring mathematics or science in grades nine through twelve. However, it was the only state that specifically required instruction in basic economics, without which any high school graduate today is handicapped. At least four Southern states required the teaching of a subject called "Americanism versus Communism," either as part of the study of American government or as a separate course. The laws of those states spelled out the approach that teachers should take to the subject of communism—that it is a threat to the American "way of life."

Southern students have fewer options than students in other regions when selecting their high school courses. Courses in drama, speech, journalism, and other nonbasic subjects are often missing from the curriculum. This gap may be accounted for not only by a lack of regard for programs in enrichment, but also by the fact that many small, nonmetropolitan schools are financially unable to offer as extensive a curriculum as can their city counterparts. A recent phenomenon in

Southern schools is a heavier emphasis on black studies—a direct response to demands of newly integrated black students that their cultural heritage not be left out of the curriculum. Some schools have added separate courses in black history, literature, and the like, while others have incorporated black studies into existing courses to give a more balanced approach. In elementary schools as well, Negro contributions are beginning to receive attention. However, racial bias remains a problem in some textbooks.

Organization and Structure

No one pattern of organization exists among Southern schools. Although we have divided public education into preprimary, elementary, and secondary categories for subsequent analysis, many school systems do not conform to these categories.

Where kindergartens exist, they are usually attached to elementary schools. The number of grades included in an elementary school may vary from four to eight. Two common patterns of school organization are eight years of elementary school followed by four years of high school, or six years of elementary school followed by six years of secondary school. The secondary grades may be divided further into junior high school (usually grades seven through nine) and senior high school (grades ten through twelve). The newest innovation in educational organization is the middle school. Designed to serve the preadolescent or early adolescent, these schools commonly begin with the fifth or sixth grade and continue through the seventh or eighth. Systems with middle schools often have a "4-4-4" plan of organization, with elementary, middle, and high schools each encompassing four years of schooling. Proponents of the middle school claim that it deals more effectively with the peculiar needs of the early adolescent than does a junior high school, which is often an imitation of senior high school rather than a separate educational entity.

The structure within individual classrooms in the South is the same as in most schools in the nation: they are teacher-directed and teacher-motivated.[27] A few systems have begun restructuring their schools, chiefly through the open classroom approach that alters the roles of both teachers and pupils. Although pupils are given great freedom in pursuing their own interests, the teacher tries to structure the environment so as to create interest "in a whole range of subjects." The children are encouraged to "manipulate" elements in the environment and to interact with one another.[28]

Facilities

The South's share of school buildings is approximately the same as its share of the school population—27.2 percent. In 1970 there were 16,123 elementary schools in the South, or 25 percent of the nation's total, and 7,168 secondary schools, or 29.9 percent of the national sum. [29] The relatively higher proportion of secondary schools in the South reflects its more prevalent small-town and rural population.

TABLE 3.10. *School Characteristics: Age and Capacity*

	U.S.	U.S.		Nonmetropolitan South		Metropolitan South	
	All	Negro	White	Negro	White	Negro	White
Elementary schools							
Percent of students in school plants of specified age:							
less than 20 years	61	63	60	72	34	77	75
20-39 years	20	17	20	21	·43	11	20
more than 40 years	18	18	18	4	20	12	4
Average number of students per instructional room	30	32	29	34	30	30	31
Secondary schools							
Percent of students in school plants of specified age:							
less than 20 years	54	60	53	79	52	74	84
20-39 years	29	26	29	13	33	18	14
more than 40 years	17	12	18	3	15	3	0
Average number of students per instructional room	31	34	31	35	28	30	34

Source: U.S. Department of Health, Education, and Welfare, *Equality of Educational Opportunity,* by James S. Coleman et al., 2 vols. (Washington, D.C.: Government Printing Office, 1966). Compiled from volume 1, tables 2.21.1, 2.21.2, 2.21.3, 2.21.4.

In regard to the age of these schools and their physical capacity relative to the number of students served, the Coleman survey indicated that Southern schools generally equaled or, in some cases, surpassed national standards. Table 3.10 shows that, in 1965 at least, all groups of Southern students except nonmetropolitan whites attended schools that were generally newer than the schools attended by the average student in the country at large at the same level. And despite the relative antiquity of their buildings, nonmetropolitan whites suffered no overcrowding in comparison with other Southern student groups or with the average student nationally. On the other hand, nonmetropolitan Southern blacks at both levels and metropolitan whites at the secondary level were more likely to experience overcrowding than the average national student at the equivalent level. In any case, Southern deviations from national norms were not large. The average number of instruction rooms per school in the South in 1970 was 21.8, whereas the national figure was 20.5. Less than 7 percent of the one-teacher schools in the United States were located in the South; of the 149 such Southern schools, 103 were in Kentucky, presumably in remote Appalachian areas. [30]

In terms of special facilities, the Coleman data manifest a wide gap between the norms for schools in the rural South and for schools in the nation as a whole (see table 3.11). Nonmetropolitan blacks experienced the most serious shortages, especially in science and language labora-

TABLE 3.11. *School Characteristics: Selected Facilities*

	U.S.	U.S.		Nonmetropolitan South		Metropolitan South	
	All	Negro	White	Negro	White	Negro	White
Elementary schools							
Percent of students with:							
Auditorium (solely)	20	27	19	16	40	20	21
Cafeteria (solely)	37	38	37	46	64	34	32
Gymnasium (solely)	20	15	21	15	31	6	5
Infirmary or health room	67	71	68	49	44	81	76
Secondary schools							
Percent of students with:							
Auditorium (solely)	47	49	46	21	36	49	40
Cafeteria (solely)	67	72	65	65	78	77	97
Gymnasium (solely)	73	64	74	38	63	52	80
Shop with power tools	95	89	96	85	90	89	90
Biology lab	94	93	94	85	88	95	100
Chemistry lab	97	94	98	85	91	94	100
Physics lab	92	80	94	63	83	83	100
Foreign language lab	55	49	56	17	32	48	72
Baseball or football team	97	89	98	89	98	92	100
Typing room	90	88	91	70	92	89	99
Infirmary	74	70	75	53	45	83	83
Science lab facilities	94	89	94	78	86	91	99

Source: U.S. Department of Health, Education, and Welfare, *Equality of Educational Opportunity*, by James S. Coleman et al., 2 vols. (Washington, D.C.: Government Printing Office, 1966). Compiled from volume 1, tables 2.21.5, 2.21.6, 2.21.7, 2.21.8.

tories and other facilities related to academic growth. Rural Southern whites also experienced a shortage of academically related facilities. Southern urban blacks usually fared better in special facilities than the average black student in the nation, and often better than rural Southern whites. Faring best of all in the South, of course, were metropolitan whites.

Although the number of new schoolrooms completed and the number available for use in 1970 in the South are in line with figures for the United States as a whole, a disproportionate number of Southern instruction rooms were abandoned during 1969-70—46 percent of the rooms were abandoned nationwide. Furthermore, 74.4 percent of the rooms converted to instructional purposes during that year were in the South. [31] These figures reflect the demise of segregation in the South. As school boards implemented court orders to establish unitary school systems, all-black schools frequently were abandoned and vacant spaces in formerly white schools were converted into classrooms to facilitate integration.

Degree of Integration

The degree of integration achieved in the South, greater than in any other section, may not be sustained if antibusing sentiments prevail in Congress and the courts. The transporting of children beyond their own neighborhoods to attend integrated schools, found necessary in some areas because of housing patterns and past placement of schools, might never have exploded as a national issue if areas outside the South had not become threatened by busing in 1971-72. A Gallup poll in late 1971 "showed 76 percent of the American people against busing." [32]

Faculties also have been desegregated. But, in many instances, federal laws designed to end discrimination have had an ironic result. In 1970 the Race Relations Information Center surveyed eleven Southern states; the conclusion was that "the apparent effect of desegregation on black teachers across the South this year has been more negative than positive. Hundreds of them have been demoted, dismissed outright, denied new contracts or pressured into resigning, and the teachers hired to replace them include fewer and fewer blacks." [33] Demotion was found to be the most common weapon used against blacks; a major reason for the decreasing proportion of black teachers was failure to hire new ones when vacancies occurred; and the problems of displacement were most prevalent in rural, heavily black areas, particularly in the Deep South.

The most vulnerable position is that of the black principal. In North Carolina, for example, an Association of Educators official reported a decline in the number of black principals from 620 to less than 170 in a three-year period.[34] In few places are they fired; rather, they are stripped of authority and either demoted or given a high-sounding title to cover the fact that they have been given jobs of lesser importance.

"The demise of the black principal has ominous implications for the South and its black community," A. C. James pointed out.[35] "The black principal was for years the linchpin of his community—the link between the white and black communities, the idol of ambitious young blacks, the recruiter and hirer of new black teachers." Thus the black community sees its former leaders reduced to impotence. A similar fate has befallen many black athletic coaches, band directors, and guidance counselors. When black and white schools have merged, more often than not the positions of leadership have been given to whites while blacks have been made assistants or even assistants to assistants, in some cases regardless of qualifications or experience.[36]

Administration

In the South, as elsewhere, each state has a department of education and a superintendent responsible for the public schools as a whole. However, the basic administrative unit is the school district, governed by the local school board. "These are citizens elected or appointed to determine policy and to exercise general supervision over the operations of the local school systems."[37] The board employs a superintendent of schools who is responsible for the administration of the local system.

School districts vary enormously in size, both in the area they cover and in the number of pupils they include. In some states, districts correspond to county boundaries; in others each community may have its own system. "Primarily as a result of reorganization laws, which have facilitated the consolidation and annexation of school districts, the number of such units has declined steadily. The 1970-1971 total of 17,896 represents an 86.0 decrease from the 1931-1932 figures, a 52.2 percent decrease . . . since 1960-61, and a 5.7 percent decrease in the last year."[38] Generally, combining small districts into larger units makes for greater efficiency of operation.

Table 3.12 shows that the South has relatively fewer school districts than do other parts of the nation. Less than 20 percent of the school districts in the country are located in the South. And of the 3,556 districts in the region in 1970-71, more than half were in the Southwestern states of Texas and Oklahoma. While the average number of school districts per state is 351 for the United States, Southern states average only 274 districts.

TABLE 3.12. *Estimated Number of Basic Administrative Units, Board Members, and Superintendents, 1970-71*

	Total School Districts	Board Members	Superin- tendents
United States (inc. D.C.)	17,896	97,946	12,849
South	3,556	20,660	3,099
Alabama	124	627	124
Arkansas	389	2,021	359
Florida	67	343	67
Georgia	190	1,110	189
Kentucky	192	960	192
Louisiana	66	716	66
Mississippi	150	750	150
North Carolina	152	940	152
Oklahoma	665	2,607	459
South Carolina	93	653	93
Tennessee	147	970	147
Texas	1,187	8,253	976
Virginia	134	710	125

Source: National Education Association, Research Division, *Estimates of School Statistics, 1970-71* (Washington, D.C.: National Education Association, 1971), p. 26.

Students

Southern students entering elementary education are less likely to have had any formal preschool educational experience than their counterparts in other regions. Only 10 percent of the children attending public nursery schools or kindergartens are in the South. Other characteristics of the Southern student population are delineated in table 3.13. The Coleman report indicated that the average Southern student had a higher exposure than students in other regions to fellow students from economically and educationally deprived backgrounds. With the exception of metropolitan whites, Southern students went to school with more students whose mothers did not finish high school, whose parents had relatively low educational aspirations for them, and whose families possessed few material amenities—including those such as newspapers, encyclopedias, and books, which potentially relate to educational horizons—than their counterparts in the rest of the nation.

While the enrollment in public schools in the United States increased 0.6 percent from fall 1969 to fall 1970, enrollment in the South decreased 2.5 percent to 13.2 million. This is attributable to the rise of

TABLE 3.13. *Student Characteristics: Selected Qualities (in Percentages)*

	U.S.	U.S.		Nonmetropolitan South		Metropolitan South	
	All	Negro	White	Negro	White	Negro	White
Elementary-school students							
Mothers completed high school	45	33	48	24	38	33	44
Students read to often before entering school	17	19	17	17	17	19	19
Automobile in home	89	68	94	60	91	61	94
Daily newspaper in home	73	61	77	40	59	64	84
Encyclopedia in home	71	54	75	36	65	51	80
Telephone in home	80	63	84	40	68	57	86
100 books or more in home	...	...	...	...	...	...	...
Secondary-school students							
Fathers desire postschool technical training or less for students	31	28	31	33	35	23	29
Mothers desire postschool technical training or less for students	32	30	33	35	37	26	30
Automobile in home	93	79	95	75	94	71	95
Daily newspaper in home	85	77	86	60	74	80	93
Encyclopedia in home	80	69	82	52	75	67	88
Telephone in home	88	75	90	52	79	72	92
100 books or more in home	38	26	39	16	27	21	40

Source: U.S. Department of Health, Education, and Welfare, *Equality of Educational Opportunity,* by James S. Coleman et al., 2 vols. (Washington, D.C.: Government Printing Office, 1966). Compiled from volume 1, tables 2.42.1, 2.42.2, 2.42.3, 2.42.4.

private "segregation academies" in some areas; as table 3.14 shows, the Southern states experiencing enrollment decreases were those where the segregation academy movement was strongest. However, the 655,600 children estimated by the U.S. Office of Education to be enrolled in non-public schools in the South in 1970 made up only 11.7 percent of the private school enrollment in the country, much less than the South's proportion of public school enrollment. [39]

Finances

As table 3.15 indicates, every Southern state except Virginia deviates from the national pattern of sources of funds for public education. Whereas in the United States as a whole only 7 percent of the burden of support for public education is borne by the federal government, every

TABLE 3.14. *Student Enrollment, Fall 1970*

	Fall 1970			Percent Increase over 1969
	Total	Elementary	Secondary	
United States	45,903,371	27,496,754	18,406,617	0.6
South	13,164,777	7,852,988	5,311,789	-2.5
South as percentage of U.S. total	28.68%	28.56%	28.86%	
Alabama	805,205	426,209	378,996	-2.6
Arkansas	463,320	252,046	211,274	0.7
Florida	1,427,896	781,703	646,193	1.4
Georgia	1,098,901	705,347	393,554	-1.2
Kentucky	717,205	455,979	261,226	1.9
Louisiana	842,365	508,881	333,484	-1.3
Mississippi	534,395	312,093	222,302	-7.1
North Carolina	1,192,187	835,739	356,448	0.6
Oklahoma	626,956	350,004	276,952	2.4
South Carolina	637,800	393,319	244,481	-1.6
Tennessee	899,893	571,224	328,669	1.0
Texas	2,839,900	1,577,800	1,262,100	3.1
Virginia	1,078,754	682,644	396,110	0.2

Source: U.S. Department of Health, Education, and Welfare, *Statistics of Public Schools, Fall 1970,* p. 16.

Southern state has a greater proportion of its education budget provided by Washington, with states such as Mississippi greatly exceeding the national average.

Of the federal total going to elementary-secondary programs, 38.5 percent is earmarked for the South. Table 3.16 shows that a disproportionate share goes to the South in nearly every category. Although part of the reason for the South's greater share is its special needs brought on by massive desegregation, the South also does well in vocational education and aid to federally impacted areas (with large numbers of military and federal civilian personnel).

Southern public school systems receive a greater proportion of their budgets from the states than is true nationwide. Whereas schools in other regions must rely heavily on local revenue sources, primarily the local property tax, Southern schools are less dependent on the value of local taxable property. This should make it easier for the South to implement the recommendations of the President's Commission on School Finance, which called on the states to "take over the major burden of

TABLE 3.15. *Estimated Revenue Used for Education, 1970-71*

	Revenue Receipts	Percent of Revenue Receipts by Source		
	(x 1,000)	Federal	State	Local and Other
United States	$41,936,556	6.9	41.1	52.0
Alabama	443,431	15.8	62.8	21.4
Arkansas	261,813	18.4	44.5	37.1
Florida	1,179,534	9.1	56.0	34.8
Georgia	722,063	10.6	57.7	31.8
Kentucky	481,600	13.5	55.0	31.6
Louisiana	678,618	11.2	60.0	28.8
Mississippi	321,850	22.4	52.4	25.2
North Carolina	855,493	15.0	66.2	18.8
Oklahoma	372,000	9.8	43.5	46.7
South Carolina	454,040	13.0	61.7	25.4
Tennessee	567,900	12.6	47.0	40.3
Texas	2,004,015	10.0	49.3	40.7
Virginia	922,500	10.6	35.2	54.2

Source: National Education Association, Research Division, *Estimates of School Statistics, 1970-71* (Washington, D.C.: National Education Association, 1971), p. 35.

paying for public schools to eliminate the gap between the amounts spent per child in rich and poor districts."[40] (Of course, the regressive sales tax is a major source of state revenue.)

The effort made by a state to support public education may be expressed in several ways: as a per capita amount, as a percentage of the personal income of the state, and by comparing expenditures for education with expenditures for all functions of government. The first measure is the least valuable since there is such a wide variation in the wealth of states. Table 3.17 shows that in the United States as a whole the expenditure for public education in 1969 was $4.50 per $100 of personal income, and that Southern states approximated that amount. The table also indicates how much of total governmental expenditures is used for public education (based on per capita income percentages). Six Southern states match the national average, and seven fall short.

Just how far the South falls short in actual dollars spent per pupil in public schools and in the salaries it pays its school personnel is spelled out in table 3.18. The South resembles the rest of the nation in that more than two-thirds of its educational expenditure goes directly for instruction. Although Southern school personnel earn only about 82 percent of the mean salary for the United States as a whole, in recent years

TABLE 3.16. *Federal Grants to State and Local Governments for Elementary and Secondary Education Programs, by State: Fiscal Year 1969*

	Elementary and Secondary Education Programs				
	Total	Elementary, Secondary, and National Defense Education Acts[a]	Aid to Federally Affected Areas	Vocational Education	*Other Elementary and Secondary Programs*[b]
United States	$1,948,652	$1,251,006	$397,085	$253,199	$47,362
South	750,495	515,730	130,218	91,306	13,241
South as percentage of U.S. total	38.51%	41.23%	32.79%	36.06%	27.96%
Alabama	54,454	41,580	6,331	5,692	851
Arkansas	31,631	24,841	2,470	3,623	697
Florida	55,501	33,654	12,609	8,266	972
Georgia	62,744	40,825	13,482	7,364	1,073
Kentucky	47,228	33,578	7,177	5,695	778
Louisiana	42,489	32,411	5,142	4,616	320
Mississippi	51,598	45,058	1,537	4,217	786
North Carolina	79,604	58,732	10,168	9,073	1,631
Oklahoma	34,878	19,800	10,461	3,983	634
South Carolina	42,342	30,957	5,824	4,663	898
Tennessee	47,482	34,963	4,682	6,731	1,106
Texas	131,815	86,714	21,703	20,613	2,785
Virginia	68,729	32,617	28,632	6,770	710

Source: U.S. Department of Health, Education, and Welfare, Office of Education, National Center for Educational Statistics, *Digest of Educational Statistics, 1970,* p. 115.
[a]Includes $176,000 for the arts and humanities.
[b]Includes $26,265,000 for the handicapped, $19,358,000 for the Teacher Corps.

Southern states have put forth a greater effort than any other region to raise their teachers' pay. As table 3.19 shows, the difficulty has been that the South started from such a low base. Obviously, school financing is dependent on the condition of the Southern economy, which in turn would benefit from a greater input from the educational system.

Conclusion

To what degree do each of these endowments—school facilities, teacher characteristics, and student characteristics—influence the ultimate output of the educational process? With regard to attitudes, this question has never been systematically answered. But on one vital outcome of education, verbal achievement, work has been done. Here Coleman

TABLE 3.17. *Per Capita Income and Direct General Expenditures of State and Local Governments, 1969*

	Per Capita Income	Per Capita Total Expenditures of State and Local Governments	Percent of Per Capita Income	Per Capita Expenditures for Local Schools	Percent of Per Capita Income	Percent of Expenditures for All Purposes
United States	$3,687	$567.35	15.4	$167.15	4.5	29.4
South	3,001	445.38		129.62		
South's per capita income as % of U.S. per capita income	81.4%	79.0%		78.0%		
Alabama	2,582	420.48	16.6	112.95	4.4	29.9
Arkansas	2,488	395.55	15.9	110.55	4.5	28.0
Florida	3,525	496.84	14.1	160.07	4.5	32.2
Georgia	3,071	454.10	14.8	141.78	4.6	31.3
Kentucky	2,847	487.83	17.1	125.14	4.4	25.6
Louisiana	2,781	526.16	18.9	142.14	5.1	27.0
Mississippi	2,218	416.59	18.8	112.01	5.0	26.9
North Carolina	2,888	398.33	13.8	121.23	4.2	30.4
Oklahoma	3,047	521.52	17.1	128.70	4.2	24.7
South Carolina	2,607	359.18	13.8	122.38	4.7	34.0
Tennessee	2,808	408.39	14.5	116.38	4.1	28.4
Texas	3,259	443.39	13.6	145.85	4.5	32.9
Virginia	3,307	461.51	14.1	145.92	4.4.	31.6

Source: National Education Association, *Ranking of the States, 1971* (Washington, D.C.: National Education Association, 1971), pp. 30, 52, 62.

TABLE 3.18. *Annual Expenditure Per Pupil and Average Annual Salary of Instructional Staff and Classroom Teachers, 1970-71*

	Annual Expenditure Per Pupil In Average Daily Enrollment	Average Annual Salary	
		For Total Professional Instructional Staff	For Classroom Teachers
United States	$812	$9,570	$9,210
Alabama	463	7,525	7,376
Arkansas	549	6,790	6,634
Florida	728	9,206	8,805
Georgia	615	7,940	7,778
Kentucky	580	7,550	7,190
Louisiana	747	8,600	8,340
Mississippi	495	6,173	6,008
North Carolina	607	8,466	8,168
Oklahoma	659	7,650	7,360
South Carolina	615	7,150	7,000
Tennessee	571	7,550	7,400
Texas	599	8,646	8,325
Virginia	753	9,000	8,700

Source: U.S. Department of Health, Education, and Welfare, *Statistics of Public Schools, Fall 1970*, p. 36.
Note: Expenditures per pupil in average daily attendance are slightly higher.

concluded that, of the three basic endowments, "school characteristics are weakest," while "teacher characteristics are comparable to but slightly weaker than characteristics of student environment" in relative influence on verbal achievement. "Characteristics of facilities and curriculum are much less highly related to achievement than are attributes of a child's fellow students in school." While Coleman also found that "for both Negroes and whites, and for nearly all measures, more variance is accounted for by school differences in the South than by school differences in the North," the same general conclusion holds. [41] Coleman found that "schools are remarkably similar in the way they relate to achievement when the socioeconomic background of the students is taken into account. . . . The schools do differ, however, in their relation to the various racial and ethnic groups." Specifically, "the average white student's achievement seems to be less affected by the

TABLE 3.19. *Average Annual Salary of Instructional Staff in Full-Time Public Elementary and Secondary Day Schools, by State: 1929-30 to 1969-70*

	Adjusted Dollars (1969-70 Purchasing Power)[a]						Percent Increase in Salaries, 1929-30 to 1969-70 (in Adjusted Dollars)
	1929-30	1939-40	1949-50	1959-60	1967-68	1969-70	
United States	3,131	3,893	4,799	6,648	8,773	8,840	182
Alabama	1,746	2,010	3,365	5,142	6,548	6,954	298
Arkansas	1,484	1,578	2,871	4,234	6,351	6,445	334
Florida	1,932	2,734	4,716	6,527	8,324	8,600	345
Georgia	1,508	2,080	3,129	5,016	7,519	7,372	389
Kentucky	1,976	2,232	3,086	4,275	7,214	7,624	286
Louisiana	2,075	2,718	4,755	6,396	8,266	7,220	248
Mississippi	1,367	1,510	2,257	4,258	5,255	6,012	340
North Carolina	1,925	2,556	4,285	5,368	7,150	7,744	302
Oklahoma	2,359	2,740	4,362	5,986	6,884	7,139	203
South Carolina	1,738	2,007	3,015	4,433	6,381	7,000	303
Tennessee	1,989	2,329	3,670	5,048	6,847	7,290	267
Texas	2,038	2,915	4,977	6,049	7,408	7,503	268
Virginia	1,899	2,429	3,711	5,540	7,658	8,200	332

Source: U.S. Department of Health, Education, and Welfare, Office of Education, *Statistics of State School Systems, and Fall 1969 Statistics of Public Schools.*

Note: Instructional staff includes supervisors, principals, classroom teachers, and other personnel concerned with teaching.

[a]Based on Consumer Price Index published by the Bureau of Labor Statistics, U.S. Department of Labor.

strength or weakness of his school facilities, curriculums, and teachers than the average minority pupil's."[42]

To be sure, the Coleman conclusions cannot be regarded as unimpeachable. Indeed, they have been attacked by educational experts for a number of reasons; one is the sense that Coleman failed to measure fully the influence of school characteristics.[43] But the order of influence asserted by Coleman has not been challenged successfully.

The implications of the Coleman conclusions are significant for the South. The report indicates that for blacks the relative equality of Southern school facilities with those of the rest of the nation adds less to student achievement than the relative inferiority of the teachers in them subtracts (if teacher quality is justifiably indicated by the criterion of verbal ability). Second, since "in general, as the education aspirations and background of fellow students increase, the achievement of minority children increases," it appears that as long as isolation of different racial and socioeconomic groups continues, the South will not be receiving the maximal return, in terms of student verbal achievement at least, from the educational process.[44] The socioeconomic level of the South's students is a drawback no matter how these students are combined in the classroom, but when this combination results in economically and racially homogeneous groups, it will be an exaggerated negative factor.

EXTERNAL FACTORS

Federal Court Decisions

The most important exogenous input into the Southern educational process has been federal pressure for desegregation. Without the Supreme Court decision in 1954 in *Brown* v. *Board of Education*, there is no evidence that Southern schools, on their own initiative, would have integrated in the succeeding two decades. In the Brown decision Chief Justice Earl Warren asserted: "In these days, it is doubtful that any child may reasonably be expected to succeed in life if he is denied the opportunity of an education. Such an opportunity, where the state has undertaken to provide it, is a right which must be made available to all on equal terms." Defining "equal terms" thus became the crux of the matter, and Justice Warren took the first step toward a definition by declaring that separate is inherently unequal and that therefore, at least in the field of education, "the doctrine of 'separate but equal' has no place."[45]

The implementation of the Supreme Court's instruction to desegregate has continuously evolved since the first enforcement order in 1955, when "all deliberate speed" was judged to be fast enough. By 1969 this was found to be constitutionally unacceptable, and schools were ordered to desegregate without further delay. In 1971 in *Swann* v. *Charlotte-Mecklenburg*, Chief Justice Warren Burger, speaking for the Court, approved broad powers for federal district judges in the dismantling of the remainders of dual school systems. Among the approved tools to achieve desegregation was busing, except in cases in which, in the words of the Court, "the time or distance is so great as to risk either the health of the children or significantly impinge on the educational process." Racial quotas were also approved as tools. Burger noted that the existence of a few racially identifiable—i.e., all or nearly all black or white—schools within a given system does not itself represent a breach of the Constitution, but it does create a presumption of discrimination that is the burden of school officials to remove to the satisfaction of the courts. [46]

As this book was being completed, the U.S. Supreme Court's 4-4 tie vote on the Richmond desegregation case left unanswered the legal question of whether school district boundaries could be crossed for desegregation purposes. The federal district court had approved a merger of Richmond's predominantly black system with the school systems of neighboring counties, predominantly white in student enrollment. The counties opposed the consolidation effort, and the Fourth U.S. Circuit Court of Appeals blocked the merger. The Supreme Court's tie vote upheld the appeals court ruling, but left open the possibility of a different judgment next time.

The federal courts also were being asked to rule on various devices to provide direct and indirect government subsidies to private schools. In 1973 the U.S. Supreme Court rejected tuition reimbursement or tax relief plans for children attending parochial schools in two non-Southern states.

The federal courts' input into the educational process has both positive and negative aspects. On the negative side, court orders have intensified hostility to the schools in a region that has never embraced them fully, thereby running the risk of decreased community support. While white flight from the public schools has occurred with much publicity, a subtler erosion of support for school bonds and for taxes that go to the schools may threaten to damage even more lastingly the system in the South, as in other regions. [47] The switch from dual to unitary school systems has meant integration of faculties; as noted, this has had a devastating effect on black teachers and administrators.

The positive results of desegregation may have a chance to assert themselves over the long term. Not the least of these is potentially higher academic attainment for the population as a whole. The sample of integrated classrooms in the South has been too limited to allow for conclusive testing, but in other regions integration apparently has proved to have positive educational effects. [48] On further analysis of the Coleman findings (which declared that "although the differences are small . . . there is evident, even in the short run, an effect of school integration on the reading and mathematics achievement of Negro pupils"), the Commission of Civil Rights not only found black progress in integrated situations, but also discovered that "the achievement of white students in classes which are roughly half or more white is no different from that of similarly situated students in all-white classes." Though the commission found that desegregated schools reporting racial tension produce lower achievement scores for blacks than desegregated schools reporting little or no tension, even the former scores compare favorably with those produced in racially isolated, all-black situations. [49]

The Federal Executive Branch

The Department of Health, Education, and Welfare, with the authority to withhold certain federal funds, has influenced school desegregation. Through his public posture, the president also has a decisive influence not only on the pace but on the ultimate success or failure of desegregation. The confusion that can be created by presidential ambivalence was seen as Jackson, Mississippi, prepared to fully integrate its schools. Local school officials prepared a busing plan. Just as Jackson was ready to put its plan into effect, President Nixon withdrew his support from the whole concept of busing, leaving the city unsure of how to proceed, and threatening local school officials with political isolation.

OUTPUTS FROM OTHER INSTITUTIONS

Social

Group attitudes / The interest of business leaders in public education has had an impact on many Southerners who look to them for leadership. Noting that business concern for better schools stems from the need for skilled workers in industry, Harry Ashmore points out that "public education in the South has received increasingly effective support from industrial promotion campaigns." [50]

Regarding education as an investment capable of yielding high returns, businessmen played an important role in obtaining financial support. While Southern per capita expenditure for public education in

1969 lagged far behind the national figures of $167.15, the percent of personal income expended on schools in the South approximated and in a few cases exceeded the national rate of 4.5 percent.

Business interests also have insured the achievement of much non-violent if not wholly frictionless desegregation. Visiting Yazoo City, Mississippi, at the time of its adjustment to court-ordered integration in 1970, Willie Morris witnessed the reenactment in his old home town of a drama played in many communities. Faced with the possibility of a massive flight to private segregation academies and the subsequent virtual abandonment of the public-school system, the town held firm. Morris concluded that "the economic health of the town, its attractiveness to outside industry, was the most consistent argument of the pro-public school whites." Though he noted "feelings more subtle and significant, . . . on the whole it was pragmatic economics . . . which was playing the leading role."[51]

An occasional school reform campaign, such as Dallas's League for the Advancement of Education, partakes of a broader educational vision. Unlike many whites Southern blacks have generally looked upon education with high expectation; the school more than any other institution has seemed the most direct route to social and economic parity with the white majority. The social structure of the black community in the past has accorded to educated individuals, and teachers perhaps most of all, a higher status than does society in general to their white counterparts.[52] Federal authority has not created but rather has supported the black demands for equal education, a powerful force for change within Southern education.

Before 1954 blacks demanded at least equal funding—a demand that all-white school boards could not wholly ignore because of the Supreme Court's then-current requirement for "separate but equal" facilities. Since 1954, as demands for integration have been paramount, the racial composition of the schools has changed, and administrative arrangements that previously supported an officially dual system have disappeared. Desegregation has stimulated reconsideration of a variety of long-standing educational assumptions concerning not only race-related but *all* aspects of schooling. A study such as Coleman's, for instance, began with a focus on differences between black and white scholastic experiences, but ended with conclusions that challenge traditional notions of the relative influence of school-related and socioeconomically related factors on the academic achievement of all students. Integration has also raised questions about the educational validity, wholly apart from the racial validity, of the neighborhood school.

Family / The family competes with the school as a transmitter of cultural norms, although its influence has been on the wane during the industrial and postindustrial eras. Yet families still maintain a large responsibility for the training of the child, especially in the South.

Because "the Southern family has played a more important role in the socialization of the child than the non-Southern family," sociologist E. William Noland suggests that "the Southern school has played a less important socialization role than have schools elsewhere." [53] The Texas Governor's Committee on Public School Education, basing its conclusions on its 1968 opinion research survey, declared, "Most Texans recognize the role of public schools in building socially acceptable behavior among their students, but the majority still place more emphasis on the continuing responsibility of the home." [54] If divorce rates are any criterion, the Southern family is no more stable than families elsewhere. Nevertheless, in light of the agrarian, individualistic tradition of the South, and in light of the comparative absence from the Southern school curriculum of family-related subjects such as sex education, it seems probable that the Southern family has not surrendered as many functions to the school as have its counterparts in other regions. If so, the school may less readily become a center of community interest and activity.

Another family-related characteristic in the past has handicapped the development of good Southern public education: the greater proportion of children to adults in Southern population has made the burden of providing education heavier than in most other regions. At the turn of the century, for example, South Carolina had 61 adult males for every 100 schoolchildren, while New York State had 125 adult males for every 100 schoolchildren, a difference that appreciably affected the tax base. The South still has a disproportionate number of the nation's children. In 1969, of the estimated 70.8 million children under eighteen years old in the United States, 20.2 million lived in the South. Where 35.04 percent of the population of the country was under eighteen, the percentage in that category in the South was 35.94. [55] This difference becomes significant when considered in combination with the greater poverty of the region.

Religion / Popular Southern religion has traditionally been so homogeneous that it is not overgeneralizing to speak of a Southern Church. Its ethos is that of the two dominant white Protestant denominations in the region, Baptist and Methodist. Their revivalism and fundamentalism have permeated Southern culture and have left a legacy of anti-intellectualism that is inimical to the educational enterprise.

Southern churches have not encouraged a critical attitude toward the culture. Samuel S. Hill, Jr., describes this relationship:

> Despite the historical disinclination of all southern churches to make peace with their finite surroundings, they have blended in increasingly well with the general culture, imperceptibly espousing regional attitudes and beliefs which had little or no direct relation to the objective message which they hailed as their standard. This trend was continually being enhanced by the churches' driving compulsion to convert the entire society, a goal which encouraged a willingness to appeal to all the cultural thought-forms which might bring any individual over the line separating the unconverted from the saved. [56]

According to Wallace M. Alston, Jr., and Wayne Flynt, "The more firmly they established themselves in the social order, the more Southern churches tended to become defenders of the status quo in economic and political matters."[57] The church also has followed rather than led in the effort to bring educational opportunity to all the South's children.

In every period there have been Southern churchmen who dissented loudly from the church's position of accommodation to the status quo. But, as Alston and Flynt point out, "Radical Southern Protestantism usually met the same fate as radical Southern politics: it was buried beneath a conservative avalanche."[58] In the 1960s minority dissent became more evident; the churches were put to the test, and those that took the Social Gospel seriously emerged as champions of black causes.

Economy / Attempting to serve 27.5 percent of the nation's population, the Southern economy in 1970 generated only 22.6 percent of the nation's personal income, resulting in a per capita income for the region of $3,062, 78.3 percent of the national figure. Even though expenditures for public education per $1,000 of personal income are close to the national average, Southern per capita expenditure for public education still languishes far below that of the country as a whole. The economy may not be the insurmountable problem that it appears to be at first: as already noted, combined Southern local and state government expenditure rates for education approximate the national par. But table 3.20 reveals that Southern states as a whole are making less of a financial sacrifice for education than most of the non-Southern states in similarly poor economic positions. For example, South Dakota, with about the same per capita income as the Southern average, devotes substantially more of its resources to education than any one of the Southern states.

Perhaps, then, the most potent effect on education of the Southern

TABLE 3.20. *Per Capita Income and Direct General Expenditures of States with Approximately the Same Per Capita Income as the South, 1969*

	Per Capita Income	Per Capita Expenditures for All Purposes	Expenditures for All Purposes as Percent of Per Capita Income	Per Capita Expenditures for Public Education	Expenditures for Public Education as Percent of Per Capita Income	Expenditures for Public Education as Percent of Expenditures for All Purposes
Louisiana	$2,781	$526.16	18.9	$142.14	5.1	27.0
Idaho	2,953	517.85	17.5	134.05	4.5	25.9
New Mexico	2,897	658.98	22.7	190.42	6.6	28.8
North Dakota	3,012	640.80	21.3	165.58	5.5	25.9
South Dakota	3,027	592.77	19.6	189.11	6.2	31.9
Utah	2,997	566.62	18.9	193.92	6.5	34.2
West Virginia	2,603	458.65	17.6	126.73	4.9	27.7

Source: National Educational Association, *Ranking of the States, 1971* (Washington, D.C.: National Education Association, 1971), pp. 30, 52, 62. Also see table 3.17.
Note: In 1969 the per capita income for persons living in the South was $3,001. Louisiana was highest among the Southern states in percent of per capita income used for public education.

economy is a psychological one. Having apparently dwelt on its own poverty to the point of defeatism, could the South be underestimating its ability to pay for public education? In the manner of a self-fulfilling prophecy, those who regard themselves as poor remain poor. The South, in comparison to similarly impoverished areas, seems to suffer less from an inability to pay for education than it does from a lack of will.

The Southern economy is undergoing the transformation from primarily agrarian to primarily industrial modes of production. For the schools, the most profound consequence of this shift is the accompanying migration of population from rural to urban areas. To the present time this demographic flood seems to have positively influenced the educational output as the differential between urban and rural achievement scores suggests. Yet the South may be reaching the point at which the rural to urban shift will begin to produce diminishing and even negative returns to the educational process, especially if no solution is found to the problem of segregated housing in large cities. Before the relative prosperity of the post-World War II era, the migrating black from a rural area stopped in a Southern city on his way north only as long as necessary to change buses. Now, with jobs available in Southern urban areas, the black's migration sometimes terminates within his own region, with settlement in one of the enlarging ghettos at the core of Atlanta and other cities. The familiar reaction has been white flight to the city's outer rim or even beyond, hurting the tax base of the city proper while enriching surrounding counties. In such circumstances the Southern black will have gained little in educational opportunity with his move from the countryside.

Political

The preponderance of school board positions are held by the white middle and upper classes, in part because of the nonpartisan nature of school elections.[59] Considered to be too vital to be left to the alleged corruption and vagaries of the normal partisan political process, the governing of education was made into a virtually private affair by the white progressives of the early twentieth century. Ever since, it has been only the middle and upper classes that have been capable of fielding candidates with reasonable financial backing and of choosing among them without the help of party labels. In 1972, among the South's over 21,000 school board members, only 176 were blacks.[60]

Education is by no means an issue that limits itself to school board elections; rather, in the form of debates on busing in particular and integration in general, it is an issue that creeps into and often dominates many Southern political campaigns. Political actions in several sectors, such as those reinforcing segregated housing, also make school integration more difficult to achieve.

Higher Education

Higher education has a direct input to the public school system through the teachers it trains and retrains. Southern colleges and universities bear most of the responsibility for educating the elementary- and secondary-school teachers of the region, especially since the relatively lower salary scale for teachers in the South makes it less likely that teachers trained elsewhere would come South seeking jobs.

POLICY DECISIONS

Local

The major policy decision openly or implicitly made by Southern school boards in the area of desegregation has generally been to preserve the status quo as long as possible. Steps toward further desegregation than that required by court orders or by threats of withdrawal of federal funds are not unheard of, but they are rare. An example of the results of recalcitrance can be found in the Charlotte-Mecklenburg dispute, in which the school board's failure to submit a desegregation plan of its own to the federal court led to the imposition of an undoubtedly more severe one by the judge. By failing to cooperate and by failing to take the initiative and responsibility for desegregation, the board put the burden for school planning on a judicial body whose knowledge of the district was undoubtedly limited by comparison with that of the board. The board thus not only magnified the disruptive impact of a change that was virtually inevitable, but also increased the likelihood that hostility in the community to the resulting arrangement would do permanent damage to the school system.

A more common policy decision of school boards concerns the allocation of the school dollar. In Arkansas, Georgia, Louisiana, Mississippi, Tennessee, and Virginia, in which the ratio of expenditure for capital outlay to expenditure for instruction exceeds the national figure, the school dollar has been spent for the construction of new facilities at a questionable rate. If the South did not already have physically adequate schools, or if the physical plant had a large degree of influence over student achievement, then this pattern of allocation would make sense. However, the Coleman study casts doubt on the existence of either condition. The study did document a small lag in certain physical aspects of Southern schools, but overall it found the buildings and facilities to be near the national par, nearer in fact than any other aspect of Southern education. As for the existence of a strong relation between student achievement and physical features of schools, the report found none. Two education specialists explained: "The study set out to document the fact that for school children of minority groups school facilities are sharply unequal and that this inequality is related to student achievement. The data did not support either conclusion. What small differences in school facilities did exist had little or no discernible relationship to the level of student achievement."[61]

In public taxation state and local governments have pursued policies that are cautious in the amount of revenues they provide and regressive in the manner in which they fall on the taxable population. In 1968, for example, the estimated total residential property, sales, and income tax burden imposed by state and local governments on a family of four with a gross income of $10,000 living in the largest cities in each of the Southern states exceeded the equivalent fifty-state average of $676 only in the cases of Louisville ($862), Miami ($686), Charlotte ($695), and Jackson ($782). Norfolk ($573), Memphis ($567), Columbia, S.C. ($502), Atlanta ($538), Birmingham ($533), New Orleans ($442), Little Rock ($486), Oklahoma City ($547), and Houston ($414) all fell appreciably below the national total.[62] In most smaller cities and towns, where ties to the agrarian past are stronger, the tax burdens usually are even lighter.

At the same time that total taxation is generally low, there is a Southern propensity to rely on taxes, such as property and sales, which fall most heavily on lower income families, and to avoid those taxes, such as corporate and personal income, which might shift more of the burden to upper income units. In 1967, in a region in which total taxation is light, all of the states of the former Confederacy except Virginia and Texas had a higher share of personal income going to sales taxes than the national average. At the same time that general and selective sales levies accounted for 58 percent of all state tax revenues in the South, individual income, corporate income, and estate taxes were responsible for only 25 percent.[63]

State

The most important state-level decision affecting public education is the amount of state aid to be given to local school districts. The greater the share of responsibility the state assumes for raising and distributing funds to public schools, the greater is the likelihood that glaring inequities between school districts within a state will be eliminated, as states usually distribute money to school districts on an equal per pupil basis.

In the United States as a whole 41.1 percent of the revenue receipts for public education come from state sources. All but one of the Southern states contribute a substantially larger percentage of the revenue received by their public schools. The recent challenge to local property taxes as the basis for financing public schools resulted in court decisions in several states that "territorial uniformity in school finance is constitutionally required";[64] the Supreme Court did not agree. Southern states already meet this criterion for school financing better than most states.

Additional policy decisions are made by many states concerning the curriculum to be offered in elementary and secondary schools and the textbooks to be used. Although outside the region these matters are often decided locally, most Southern states exercise a measure of control over such decisions. The state generally designates certain core subjects that must be covered at each level, allowing the remainder of a school's program to be a local decision. School systems usually also have some choice among textbooks, although they may not be allowed to use books not included as alternatives on an approved state list. This restriction is especially prevalent in states that provide free textbooks.

Federal

Though the federal mandate for desegregation originated with the courts, it gained additional force with the congressional provision in Title VI of the Civil Rights Act of 1964 for the possible suspension of federal aid to school districts not in compliance with nondiscrimination guidelines set forth by the federal agency administering the funds. Having become increasingly dependent on federal funds, which generally represent a larger share of the revenue receipts in Southern school budgets than elsewhere, school systems began to feel a pressure for change more immediate and powerful than that exerted by the often slowly implemented decrees of the court.

Armed with this tool, Democratic and Republican administrations, mainly through guidelines laid down by the Department of Health, Education, and Welfare, have threatened and coaxed the schools into varying degrees of obedience to desegregation standards. This approach usually has been neither rigid nor lenient: neither so rigid that Southern schools might simply decide to do without federal funds altogether, in which case the education of blacks would suffer most, nor so lenient that no trend toward desegregation establishes itself.

Analysis of Specific Institutions

KINDERGARTENS

Although the South is the last region to adopt statewide public kindergarten programs, such programs now exist or are being developed in Oklahoma, Florida, Texas, North Carolina, Louisiana, Tennessee, and Virginia. Kindergartens are a subject of much discussion and can be expected to be provided for in the foundation program funds of each state as more money becomes available. Other preschool programs in many school districts have included federally funded Head Start projects designed for economically and culturally disadvantaged children. Head Start schools can serve as models and training centers for future state-run programs in the areas in which they are located.

The relative newness of public involvement in preschool education in the South makes it the area of education most amenable to innovation. Not only do kindergartens have the opportunity to structure the child's experiences in such a way as to improve his chances for success in elementary school, but they also can be catalysts for restructuring of the elementary schools themselves to make them "more responsive to the needs of the children."[65] Increasingly, the attention of educators is being focused on the prekindergarten years as crucial ones in the educational development of the young. However, few areas of the United States have added prekindergarten to the school system, and most Southern states are concentrating their efforts toward providing schooling for all five-year-olds; this will leave few, if any, resources for a three- and four-year-old program in the near future.

Economic benefits of early childhood education were suggested by the Education Commission of the States: "A 1967-68 financial study prepared by Moody's Investors Associates and Campus Facilities Associates for the State of South Carolina linked implementation of state kindergarten programs to the state's total manpower resources and the overall drive for economic growth. In addition to long-range development, the report estimated that the effect of pre-school and kindergarten programs would be to reduce the number of first grade repeaters and result in a savings of at least $2.5 million a year."[66] As a result of the report, South Carolina began a pilot kindergarten program in 1970.

ELEMENTARY SCHOOLS

The elementary schools of the South seem neither as open-ended and creative as the kindergartens nor as hidebound and reluctant to change as the high schools, in terms of structure and curriculum.

Many innovations in Southern elementary education today are the result of integration. As children of vastly different backgrounds and varied prior educational opportunities have come together in the same classrooms, traditional approaches have failed to work. The response of several districts in the Carolinas was described in the *Charlotte Observer*:

> All sorts of innovative approaches have emerged to improve the quality of instruction, bolster public support for the integrated schools, and ease problems of adjustment as youngsters of widely varied backgrounds found themselves in classrooms together for the first time.
>
> Many of these techniques originated in superintendents' offices, but many others have sprung from a public which has visibly become more involved in the operation of its children's newly desegregated schools. [67]

The most commonly employed innovations are nongradedness and individualized instruction, designed to allow students to progress at their own rates. Open classrooms are also being tried, particularly in recently constructed elementary schools. Generally, teams of teachers operate in the open situation, allowing for faculty integration in the most painless way. Federal funds dispensed through various federal programs, inclucluding the Emergency School Assistance Program designed to ease integration, have enabled many districts to employ extra personnel as classroom aides, guidance counselors, and special tutors.

Throughout the United States the vast majority of elementary-school teachers are women, a condition reflecting the traditional bias that work with young children is neither important nor challenging enough to attract men. Elementary schools would benefit from a greater number of male teachers, who could serve as role models for young schoolboys. In the last several years more men have turned to elementary-school teaching because of the tight job market.

SECONDARY SCHOOLS

Many secondary schools are faced with the problem of negative student attitudes, which often give rise to disciplinary difficulties. Racial tensions are frequently cited as the cause of infractions of school discipline, but that is only part of the story. Students of both races often react to their high schools as " 'prisons,' places where they serve their required time." [68] They resent the arbitrary rules, usually set by school administrators without student input and often dealing with trivia. They also resent the failure of high school to prepare them adequately for the future, particularly if they do not intend to go on to college.

School administrators are grappling with these problems in a variety of ways. Some are attempting to bring out the best in students by trusting them to take part responsibly in decision making; many individual teachers are working to make their approach to their subject matter more "relevant" to the students. Most Southern states also have acknowledged the need to broaden the curriculum to include more opportunities for job training.

Vocational Education

Until the 1960s vocational education in the South usually meant home economics for girls and agriculture for boys, perhaps with a "shop" course thrown in for good measure. However, as more high school graduates encountered difficulties finding jobs because of their lack of training, the need for a wider range of vocational courses became clear.

The response of some Southern states, such as Alabama, was to begin a crash program of setting up vocational and technical schools geared to students who had completed or dropped out of secondary school. Some states, such as Georgia, Kentucky, and Louisiana, allowed upper-level secondary students to attend area vocational-technical schools on a part-time basis or in lieu of their regular high school classes.

The South is just beginning to develop high schools designed specifically for students interested in vocational programs. Virginia is in the midst of building area vocational schools throughout the state. Two types of vocational schools are available in Virginia: "a vocational education center, serving one or more school divisions, for high school students and adults, and the wing of a large comprehensive high school serving students and adults in one school division."[69] These offer a greater range of courses than do the regular high schools and middle schools of the state. Georgia is also trying to provide comprehensive high schools, in addition to twenty-five tuition-free area vocational-technical schools. "The comprehensive high school is a traditional high school with a distinct department offering vocational training to high school students."[70] In 1970 Georgia had nineteen such schools and hoped eventually to make one available to every school system. Kentucky already has a standard for vocational schools that places one within twenty-five miles of any school in the state.

Further development of specialized high schools, and introduction of students to vocational courses at an earlier age, can be expected.

Adult Education

Adult education as part of the public school system is by no means universal in the South. Most states do not include it as part of their foundation program, but school districts may decide to offer some adult programs, depending on their estimates of the needs and interests in their communities.

Oklahoma has perhaps the best-conceived Southern plan for adult education. Through thirty-seven adult learning centers it offers programs of enrichment, reinforcement, and remedial training for all interested adults. Students may work toward an adult elementary school certificate, a high school equivalency certificate, an adult high school diploma—or they may simply take courses for self-improvement. [71]

In some states, such as Georgia and Alabama, adult education courses are heavily dependent on federal funds. Where the state offers no aid, a fee may be charged or some community group may underwrite the costs of adult programs—poor substitutes for the state's assuming responsibility for the continuing education of its citizens.

Some educators predict that adult education, broadly defined, will be one of the most important functions of public schools of the future. This will be particularly true if birth rates continue low; the proportion of the population over sixty-five is expected to grow at a rapid rate. Even if basic literacy courses and programs leading to diplomas for those who prematurely ended their formal schooling cease to be needed, adult and continuing education can add to many aspects of life by teaching "more about home and parental responsibilities . . . satisfying a vocational interest . . . developing competence in community activities . . . providing appealing activities for senior citizens . . . fulfilling individual desire for cultural enrichment; and . . . enabling employed individuals to acquire additional knowledge and ability related to their work." [72]

SPECIAL EDUCATION

The most neglected school-age group in the South is the one that includes those children with abnormalities that require different or additional educational services from the normal child. Included in this category are the mentally and physically handicapped, those who cannot cope with the normal classroom situations because of emotional problems, and the unusually gifted children. The idea that education at public expense is a right for these children, too, has only been accepted recently. The special training needed by teachers of the exceptional child is now offered at many Southern universities, but the supply of such teachers still falls short of the need.

TABLE 3.21. Enrollment in Special Education Classes in Southern States

	Enrollment by Categories												
	Educable Mentally Retarded	Trainable Mentally Retarded	Brain Damaged	Physically Handicapped	Specific Learning Disabilities	Speech and Hearing Problems	Deaf or Hard-of-Hearing	Visually Impaired	Emotionally Disturbed	Homebound and Hospitalized	Gifted	Other Special Programs	Total
Alabama	11,206	1,508		252	85	4,890	1,103	767	70	396	24	20	18,451
Florida	22,932	3,003		1,168	5,000	36,145			2,750	4,495	10,160	2,125	90,065
Georgia	27,021	1,270	550		1,615	18,840	496	370		752	1,640	210	52,764
Mississippi													11,560
North Carolina	26,208	2,495		245	........a	32,548	151	173	........a	........a	22,249	733	84,802
Oklahoma	6,914	936	9	137	1,180	10,023	180	29	135		21	20,125	39,689
South Carolina	17,616	1,816		542	5,284	14,000	813	1,557	1,443				43,071
Tennessee	12,928	2,235			2,210	19,222	416	266	256	6,977		1,389	45,899
Texas	42,911[b]		7,860	3,054		83,882	1,882	1,027	280				140,896
Virginia	15,680[b]			887	1,358	19,860	1,093	721	2,182	6,988		921	46,690

Source: State departments of education, correspondence with the authors, 1971.
[a]Served on an interim basis, thus no figures are available.
[b]Not divided into educable and trainable.

Table 3.21 gives some idea of the status of special education in the South. What it does not tell is how many students in need of special education are not getting it. In Florida in 1971 programs for exceptional children had a waiting list of 21,466. Alabama estimated that 150,000 students needed special education who did not receive it; Georgia, 111,170; Louisiana, 77,288; Mississippi, 100,000; Oklahoma, 30,000. [73]

Some new fields of special education are beginning to be covered by the schools. For example, learning disabilities that were not even recognized a few years ago are now being diagnosed and treated. The two types of handicaps that have the longest history of treatment programs, visual and hearing impairment, are inadequately provided for. Since there is no excuse of "newness" for programs for the blind and deaf, explanation for their inadequacy probably lies in the expense of such treatment, which commonly takes place at special institutions—the most costly method.

The handicap that seems to receive the most attention is speech impairment. Again, cost is probably a major factor: one speech therapist can work with a large number of children, taking them from their regular classroom for brief but intensive periods of individual therapy and then sending them back again. If other exceptional children could remain a part of the classroom whenever possible, the special education teacher could act as a resource person, working with the child and his regular teacher to establish a program to meet his special needs. Gifted children would particularly stand to gain from this approach.

PRIVATE SCHOOLS

Somewhat more than 500,000 children attended private schools in the states of the old Confederacy in the early 1970s. Almost all were in all-white schools in 1971; they represented "only slightly more than 5 percent of the white pupils in 11 Southern states. [The figure] also includes older private schools not deliberately founded for the purpose of maintaining segregation, but still without black pupils." [74] Parochial schools and private preparatory schools have long existed in the South, although in much smaller numbers than in the rest of the country. However, a recent phenomenon unique to the region is the hasty founding of private schools for whites only—the so-called segregation academies—in countless Southern communities faced with integration of the public school systems.

Segregation Academies

To maintain segregation most parents of children in segregation academies are willing to tolerate deficiencies in educational plant or program. The basic problem encountered by the academies is that of financial support. If tuition is set too high, the potential student body will shrink to a size that cannot maintain the school for long. In the absence of substantial outside support, "most segregation academies simply scrimp in the name of quality education, slighting such needs as libraries, athletics, music, and art."[75] The buildings in which the schools are housed often do not comply with health and safety regulations. Salaries of private-school teachers are typically much lower than those paid by public schools; thus, teachers are frequently of low caliber, and curriculum offerings are limited. These deficiencies usually mean that segregation academies cannot gain accreditation, either from the states in which they operate or from the Southern Association of Colleges and Schools.[76]

The Internal Revenue Service dealt a blow to segregation academies when in 1970 it declared that any school practicing a discriminatory admissions policy would lose its tax exempt status. "However, the IRS, in accepting the 'good faith' statements of the schools themselves as to whether they discriminate, has not been very effective in enforcing its own ruling."[77]

On the other side of the coin are the problems that segregation academies cause for the public schools. In some areas teachers and administrators have chosen to leave public schools for jobs in private ones. An even greater loss is the loss of community support for public education, reflected in its failure to adequately fund its public schools. In Sumter County, Georgia, the school board was controlled by people active in the private school movement; a group of local citizens sued to have them removed from the board in light of their apparent conflict of interest.

Policy Recommendations

Much has been expected of public education in the past, perhaps too much. The Coleman and Christopher Jencks reports, together with skepticism about the abilities of all institutions to change and to foster change, have led to new questioning of the propriety of heavy investments in education.[78] Our approach in this chapter, and to some extent in the following chapter on higher education, is pragmatic. Given the heavy investments already made in education and the vested interests involved, it is probably politically unrealistic to propose a major downgrading of education even if the data to support such a decision were available and agreed upon. And the data from Coleman and Jencks that would suggest a reduced investment in education, although persuasive at points, are certainly not conclusive regarding the socializing or more purely educational aspects. Under these circumstances, we believe that the best approach for the South is to continue spending for education at the same or somewhat higher levels, but to direct that spending in ways that will prove most fruitful, while reducing or ending investments in education where payoffs in student achievement or future earning power are most in doubt. Jencks's proposals on income redistribution, with which some of our proposals in the previous chapter deal, are not likely to be embraced overnight, and in the interim the impact that education does have can be maximized. Southern schools are the least likely to have reached the point of diminishing returns on investment in education.

PRIORITIES

Consider Means to Equalize the Amount of Money Spent on Each Child

Insuring that the child who drops out of high school and needs vocational training receives the same support from the state as the child who goes to graduate school, for example, would be difficult to carry out in practice, given the varying costs of different types of training. However, states should see that students who are not going on to higher education should not have to pay an unwarranted amount in taxes to support those who do.

Devote More Resources to Vocational Training

Businessmen throughout the South complain of poor vocational education in most high schools. Businesses need skilled workers; students who are not going to college need skills to insure them well-paying jobs. Given the increasing difficulties college graduates have had in finding employment, it is possible that good vocational programs would be of value to a large proportion of high school students. Vocational training should not be geared so closely to a particular firm's needs that trainees will be without usable skills if the company closes or moves away. However, opportunities for vocational training should be brought into line with the realities of the job market, so that the skills acquired will be marketable. Adequate counseling is also essential if each student is to assess realistically his own abilities and match them to the available training and occupations. It is crucial that career counselors keep up with current trends in the job market, and make information readily accessible to students. Ideally, each student should have the opportunity within the framework of the public schools to acquire the skills necessary for his chosen vocation, except for those vocations requiring college work.

Devote More Resources to Early Childhood Development

Education now takes a large share of public resources. Decreasing enrollments, which are occurring in the early grades already because of demographic changes, might permit school systems to keep their share of public resources and to increase per-pupil spending. However, it is also possible that decreasing enrollments will lead to demands for stabilized education budgets (in absolute dollar terms, amounting to a reduction in share over a period of years). If this occurs, with the hard choices it will force, we believe that the highest priority should be accorded to early childhood development—kindergarten and the early elementary grades—because of the importance of these years in shaping character, socializing children, and establishing their orientation to the educational process. Good education in the early years is particularly important for children from so-called deprived backgrounds.

The gap between the South and other regions in public support for kindergarten should be closed as quickly as possible. Support for prekindergarten also should be considered seriously.

Devote Fewer Resources to Capital Investment

Although the South laudably spends more of its budget for instruction and less of it for construction than the nation as a whole, this fact should not make it smug. All budgets should be closely analyzed to determine whether the items in them are justified by educational returns. The Coleman report should give pause to those school boards in the South that have poured resources into capital investment at above the national rate when these same resources could be devoted to the strengthening of factors found to influence student achievement more directly. Only in those localities where repeated bond issue failures led to serious overcrowding should capital expansion be considered.

TEACHERS AND STAFF

Establish the Principle of Educational Accountability

The concept that school officials—teachers and administrators—should be held accountable for whether or not children learn is basic and should be established as a fundamental principle of public education.

Develop Criteria and Methods
for Evaluating Student Performance

A major difficulty in assessing the effectiveness of public education and in holding it accountable is what criteria and methods to use for evaluating student performance. No agreement is yet in sight. To give meaningful results, methods of evaluation must take into account the physical, psychological, and cultural differences between children that affect their performance on mental tests. Noteworthy among recent efforts to determine ability levels in specific areas is the National Assessment of Educational Progress, begun in 1970 with a series of examinations the results of which will provide a base against which to compare the results of subsequent tests. [79]

Provide for Teacher Participation in Policy Making

Good teachers share one characteristic: concern for their students. Many teachers are no longer content to have a voice only in decisions about their own working conditions, but they have also begun to demand a voice in decisions that affect student welfare. To encourage a professional attitude among teachers, policy makers should provide for teachers to be heard.

Make Greater Use of Teacher's Aides

A standard measure of quality in a school system—although not supported by the Coleman study—is the pupil-teacher ratio. Teachers often proclaim that if the pupil-teacher ratio were only brought low enough, their accomplishments in the classroom would soar. There is an economic limit to the number of fully trained teachers who can be hired to teach a given number of students. However, recent experiences, particularly in open classrooms, indicate that teachers may in fact be able to teach more rather than fewer students, if they are provided with teacher's aides. Although parent volunteers may be a good source of aides in financially pinched school districts, it is preferable that paid aides be employed. Teacher's aides would require neither the training nor the salary of a certified teacher. They could handle nonteaching chores, working with children individually and in small groups, or oversee the classroom while the teacher gave individual attention to students.

Evaluate Teacher-Education
Programs to Determine Restructuring Needs

One of the many proposals being made for changing teacher-education programs is that college students be required to take two or three years of general subject matter before entering schools of education or preeducation. Then, if they have shown sufficient ability and still desire careers as teachers, they would be eligible for admission to education programs. There may be better proposals; the important thing is to reopen the question of the adequacy of teacher training in the South's colleges and universities.

No amount of preparation can equal the experience of classroom teaching. Throughout the South practice-teaching under supervision is a prerequisite for professional certification. The first half of practice-teaching generally consists of observation and preparation of lesson plans, followed by perhaps two months of responsibility for directing a class. This is enough to whet the appetite of the prospective teacher but falls short of giving him sufficient experience to proceed on his own without supervision. Therefore, it is proposed that a year's internship be required for teacher certification. It should be done in the classroom of an experienced teacher who has been selected because of his competence as well as his willingness to work with aspiring teachers.

CURRICULUM

Adopt Individualized Instruction at
Every Level, and Be Open to Research Findings

The practice of grouping students according to their ability in various subject areas has been so misused that it should be employed only with great caution, if at all. The desired result—teaching the child at his level—could be achieved through individualized instruction. Individualized instruction recognizes that each child is an individual who may differ in various ways from the norms for his age group. Consequently, futile attempts to teach entire classrooms of children the same things at the same rate are avoided. Instead, the teacher plans a series of learning tasks for each child according to his level. This practice will require that a teacher spend a much greater proportion of his time planning and evaluating; indeed he may only spend a few minutes a day with each child. The child thus becomes primarily responsible for his own learning, receiving help and encouragement as he needs it. If the process works as intended, the fact that his schooling is now geared to him as an individual should increase both his motivation and his sense of mastery as he is able to accomplish each task at his own rate.

When team teaching is combined with an open classroom, it means that a teacher may be free to work with children individually while his teammates are conducting group activities. The greatest advantage of team teaching for a child is that it gives him more than one teacher to whom to relate.

Research in child development has revised downward the estimates of the age at which children can be taught various subjects. In the 1960s many elementary schools added foreign language study after it was discovered that young children could master a new language more easily than older children. Now the traditional notion that small children are not capable of abstract mathematical thinking is being seriously challenged. The most important thing that can be taught a student is *how* to think. The ability to gather and evaluate information is developed gradually; all schooling should seek to increase and refine this ability.

Provide Adult Education
through the Public School Systems

Adult education may include everything from basic literacy courses to high school-level courses necessary to receive a diploma for those adults whose schooling was interrupted, vocational training, and continuing education. The public schools should provide all of these important programs, set up in such a way that the maximum number of adults may benefit from them. With their relatively high illiteracy rates and their underemployment, Southern states have a demonstrated need for adult education.

Represent All Ethnic Groups in the Curriculum

Textbooks chosen for the public schools should give a balanced view of the contributions made by all ethnic groups to a particular subject area. This means that many Southern school systems will have to replace the traditional textbooks in such courses as history and literature with texts that give a fair share of attention to blacks and other minority groups. Now that attention has been focused on textbooks, most textbook companies have revised their offerings.

Offering special courses in black studies—such as black literature, music, history, and sociology—does not guarantee that the majority of students will be exposed to this perspective. Most of the students enrolling in such courses are black, and the general lack of interest is causing some schools to curtail their offerings. A better approach would be to integrate black studies (and Indian and Chicano studies) into the regular curriculum as a part of other courses.

ORGANIZATION AND STRUCTURE

Institute Nongradedness in Presecondary Schools

The old lock-step progression from one grade to the next should be abolished. Assigning children to grade levels does not take into account the fact that an eight-year-old, for example, may be reading at fourth-grade level but working math at second-grade level. Grade assignments often hold back bright children who are ready for more advanced work than the curriculum of their grade provides. Children who are slow to learn, or whose learning rates do not conform to the norms for their grade, experience failure when they are not promoted to the next grade level. Each child would still have to acquire a set of prescribed skills ultimately. School integration need not mean that black children fail at first or that white children are kept from advancing, if nongradedness and individualized instruction are instituted.

FACILITIES

Increase the Utilization of School Facilities and Equipment

Ideally, school buildings should be open day and night, every day of the week. After school hours the facilities should be utilized for activities by other community groups. Proponents of the "lighted school" point out that public funds build and operate the schools, thus the public is entitled to make use of them for a variety of purposes. School boards should enlist the aid of the community; supervision might be carried on by volunteers. A proprietary attitude toward the school and school property such as buses is inappropriate for school officials. Summer school should be available in every community. Not only should remedial and accelerated work be offered in summer school, but it should include an enrichment program to encourage children to make educational use of their summer. Florida, a pioneer in such a program, offers "day camping, theater, field trips, library services, music, swimming, driver education and special events."[80]

Explore the Uses of Educational Television

Educational innovations that make use of advances in technology promise to go beyond the limits of what a teacher alone can offer. With every state now having access to educational television channels, the possibilities of employing this tool should continue to be explored.

ADMINISTRATION

Work for Meaningful, Long-Term Integration

What might become the second Atlanta Compromise—the first was Booker T. Washington's 1895 speech—developed in 1973, when the local NAACP branch agreed to a settlement of the city's fifteen-year-old school desegregation suit that minimized busing in favor of administrative jobs for blacks. In 1968, 75 percent of the city system's pupils were white. In 1973, although the population of the city was only 52 percent black, the schools were 80 percent black. "There are not enough white children in Atlanta schools now to make a dent, if you're talking about meaningful integration, and not token," local branch president Lonnie King, Jr., said.[81] The national NAACP opposed this plan, and it still was being debated at the time this book was being completed.

The Atlanta situation raises difficult questions relating to methods to achieve racial balance in the short term. Busing faces serious obstacles, quite apart from the value of neighborhood schools and bus rides: (1) the U.S. Supreme Court seems unlikely to mandate large-scale busing to achieve racial balance in the near future; (2) even if ordered, it leads to serious political problems for probusing political leaders and for the school systems; and (3) forcibly hauling back enough whites from outlying county systems would be difficult. In many localities busing makes sense and will continue to make sense; the South has had much busing in the past, and should continue to bus children for a number of purposes. However, there also are circumstances, particularly in the largest cities, where it might be wiser to pursue other goals in the short term, such as black control over school policy-making procedures. For the longer term, in situations such as exist in Atlanta, vigorous enforcement of open-housing laws, and state requirements that zoning policies encourage dispersement of low-income housing, together with federal action described in the urban development chapter, offer the best chance for desegregated schools to stay desegregated. In the meantime, the public school system can be directed and strengthened by those whose children attend its schools.

It must be acknowledged, however, that to date desegregation of public schools has increased segregation in metropolitan areas, particularly in the South. [82] If large-scale busing is not attempted, and if one is serious about integration, governmental powers related to housing patterns must be used much more aggressively than in the past.

Merge City and County School Systems

Separate city and county school systems mean redundant administrative and financial efforts. A problem additional to smaller school districts is that of achieving a meaningful racial balance in the schools when a predominantly black city system is surrounded by an overwhelmingly white suburban county district. Merger of city and county systems would provide greater efficiency and economy and would afford a basis for better distribution of white and black students.

One of the greatest fears of school-district merger stems from concern of parents in higher-tax districts that the level of financial support for schools will go down when they are merged with a district that is less willing to tax itself. The variance in quality between city and county systems is often large, due to differences both in financial resources and in citizen interest and demands. New systems of financing would help to deal with this problem.

Give Local Districts
Control over Nonfinancial Affairs

If the responsibility for financing schools passes from the local to the state and federal levels, as we recommend and as seems to be the trend, control of all aspects of the schools may follow financial control. This needs to be avoided, lest American public education come to resemble too closely the regimented European models. Local control should cover " 'educational affairs'—what books will be used, what teachers hired, what programs carried on." A special study commission in New York State has pointed out that "once districts are freed from the necessity to raise revenues, they will have more time for academic matters." [83] Local control should not be the special province of the school board and its paid employees; officials should promote community involvement in educational matters.

FINANCIAL

Discontinue Reliance on Local Property Taxes

The quality of a child's education should not be conditional on his place of residence; in many areas there is insufficient taxable property, or property of insufficient value, to support quality public education through the local property tax. This tax should be replaced by state support from general tax revenues.

Explore the Possibilities of the Voucher System

One method being discussed to channel education funds from the state (or federal) government is the voucher system. A major weakness of this plan is that it could facilitate resegregation of schools. Controls might have to be exercised over the admissions policies of schools, so that minority-group children would be allocated as many spaces in a student body as the proportion of applicants from their group, as well as controls over tuition charges to prevent the charging of fees beyond the value of the vouchers.

Basically, a voucher plan would work as follows: parents of school-age children would be given vouchers that they would take to the school where they wanted to enroll their children. The school would then exchange the vouchers for cash payments from the government that cover the school's operating expenses and the amortization of capital costs. Such a scheme could greatly enlarge the range of choices open to families, as they gained the freedom to select a school on the basis of what and how it was teaching rather than accepting a school assignment simply because of location. Private as well as public schools might be allowed to receive vouchers.

Allocate Additional Funds
to Meet Special Educational Needs

Children who are mentally or physically handicapped, emotionally disturbed, and culturally deprived, and those with learning disabilities, have special educational needs. Any condition that makes learning more difficult for a child than for the average student must be dealt with if he is to have an equal educational opportunity. Meeting special education needs requires a greater outlay of money per pupil than does educating the normal child. Therefore, in addition to the basic per pupil allocations, additional funds should be allotted for special education based on the number of children that require special services and the cost of providing those services.

4. Adapting Higher Education to Changing Needs

The Setting

DEFINITION OF THE PROBLEM

Higher education across the nation is in trouble. Rising costs and a lag in productivity place the higher education establishment in a management crisis. The rising costs faced by universities are due in part to general inflationary forces, but they are also related to increasing numbers of specialized programs with few students. Although tuition and fees have gone up, the teaching productivity of professors has not. Whereas in 1960 a normal teaching load in the better universities was nine to twelve hours, it has now been reduced to six hours per week. Sometimes, but not always, this is justifiable because of professors' research and community service efforts. Relatively little research has been done on ways to increase the productivity of faculty through unconventional techniques such as television and gaming.

Universities have made many contributions to improving the life of Americans and of Southerners; yet, many universities have been poorly managed and their money has been spent unwisely. Administrators usually have been unwilling to close down programs when they become obsolete. When subjected to an analysis of their benefits and costs to their states, many programs do not seem justified. For example, engineering schools offer an expensive type of education with heavy emphasis on equipment. Yet some Southern states still do not have the industrial capacity to employ all engineering school graduates. In effect, then, these states finance the training of technicians for jobs in the North and West, with some graduates coming from outside of the state in the first place.

Costs have been increasing faster than available funds. While this problem is faced by virtually all institutions, it is especially acute for private schools, where tuition must meet a much higher proportion of the cost of an education than at state-supported colleges. Private school officials believe there is an upper limit to which they may raise tuition before pricing themselves out of the market. Some institutions are being forced to draw on endowment principal to cover operational costs—a short-term practice that spells long-term disaster. Some policies adopted during the affluent fifties and sixties, such as expansion in tenured faculty and increased aid to students, are now too expensive. Clark Kerr, who was president of the University of California during the early days of student demonstrations at Berkeley, suggested other factors that affected financial support for colleges:

> First, as campus dissent has turned to campus violence, people have been extremely dissatisfied with higher education and its seeming role in such improper lines of expression; second, there is increasing concern that higher education is the source of change, scientific and nonscientific, and people are tired of having their lives changed so rapidly; and third, there is a . . . feeling that the training of "experts" by colleges and universities is contrary to the idea of democracy where every man's opinion is worth as much as that of anybody else. [1]

To date the South has shown a greater willingness to support higher education than it has public education. Southern expenditures per capita and per pupil for higher education, though varying widely from state to state, are on the average equal to the expenditures of the nation as a whole (see table 4.1). Although the South is ahead of the nation as a whole in spending as a proportion of personal income, because the South is poorer, appropriations to higher education are lower than in other areas. On the other hand, support for public education in the South lags considerably behind that of the rest of the nation in both per capita and per pupil expenditures. The region's heavier emphasis on higher education may not have been the wisest course. To correct twelve years of

TABLE 4.1. *Operational Appropriations for Higher Education*

	Per Capita	Per Full-Time Equivalent Student	Per $1,000 of Personal Income
United States	$30.16 (1969-70)	$1,245 (1969-70)	$8.25 (1969)
South	30.77 (1970-71)	1,248 (1969-70)	9.00 (1969)

Source: Southern Regional Education Board, *Fact Book on Higher Education in the South, 1970* (Atlanta: Southern Regional Education Board, 1970), pp. 3-16, 53.

educational deficiency after a student reaches college is difficult, if not impossible. Increased expenditures for public education would achieve a beneficial balance, perhaps eliminating the need for college remedial programs.

Other problems are exclusive to the South. For example, one of the educational institutions in greatest danger today is the predominantly black college. Of 111 predominantly black colleges in the nation, 104 are in the South. A second problem is the regional "brain drain" that has robbed the South of some of its best students, teachers, and scholars. In a 1961 survey of doctoral candidates' preference for teaching positions, the majority of students at non-Southern universities ranked the South last of five regions; even students in Southern universities ranked the South next to last. [2] At the time, beliefs about racial prejudice critically affected responses; hopefully that problem has diminished somewhat. Nonetheless, the South still has a way to go to provide intellectual environments that are attractive to prospective students and faculty.

The methods of ranking higher education in the regions can only be accepted with qualification; but, without exception, the studies show "a sizeable and regrettable gap between the South and the rest of the nation." [3] In the 1960s Alexander Heard, chancellor of Vanderbilt University, found that of 50 American Nobel Prize winners in science, none was educated at a Southern university; of 599 members of the National Academy of Science, only 3 percent were from Southern universities; and of 481 members of the American Philosophical Society, the oldest learned society in the country, only 15 were from Southern institutions. [4] A 1964 survey of quality of graduate faculty found 21 departments in seven universities in the South to have "strong" or "distinguished" faculty. By 1969, 56 departments in the region were ranked among the top 25 in the nation in their respective disciplines. However, 43 of these departments were located in three universities (North Carolina, Texas, and Duke). [5]

Many factors have contributed to the situation in which Southern education occupies the bottom rung of the educational ladder. Nationally, education has been viewed in the past not only idealistically as a right, but also pragmatically as an investment in the economic future. In the South, however, education was a privilege of the elite, a luxury for the "gentleman" whose life was one of ease and independence. Southern higher education, mostly church-related, was romantic in nature, steeped in classics, history, and literature. It was conservative in outlook, serving to rationalize and to reinforce the hierarchical social structure. Most of the population developed the notion, which persists to a lesser extent today, that higher education was not only unattainable but unnecessary.

Otis Singletary, president of the University of Kentucky, classifies the fundamental causes for the plight of Southern higher education as poverty, prejudice, piety, and politics. Although these are not exclusively Southern phenomena, their interaction in the South has had a peculiar effect on higher education. Poverty, a result of the relative weakness of the region's economy for many years, yields an inadequate tax base for legislative appropriations. Racial prejudice has inhibited faculty recruitment and has in the past imposed a barrier to admission to universities. The influence of Southern religion on higher education is seen not only in the number of church-related institutions, but in the effect of fundamentalism and orthodoxy of religion, which have contributed to the region's traditional anti-intellectualism and conservatism. Political meddling has included direct interference in university affairs. The activities of Governor George Wallace at the University of Alabama and Governor Ross Barnett at the University of Mississippi in the early sixties, and Governor Eugene Talmadge in Georgia in the forties, are cases in point. Singletary concludes that political "violations of institutional autonomy and academic freedom have helped create an atmosphere that is fundamentally hostile to the development of institutions of quality."[6]

In the South, as throughout the nation, university administrators and faculty have been challenged to assume their responsibilities to their students and their region. Some university faculties have been torn apart in battles between the "academic purists" with their perverse sense of objectivity and the generally younger "relativists" with their overt disdain for professionalism and their naive subjectivity. It is not apparent why relevance should be inconsistent with high academic endeavor and professionalism.

SPECIFICATION OF OUTPUTS

The best measures of higher education output would be validated before-after tests of learning, measures of the impact of education on subsequent earning power, and hard measures of the "civilizing" effects of such education. In the absence of perfect measures, we also must rely on less satisfactory measures such as enrollment figures. The South's 721 colleges and universities (of which 72 percent are accredited) enroll about 22 percent of the students attending higher education institutions across the nation, a figure that has remained fairly constant over the past twenty years (see tables 4.2 and 4.3). Although the South is slowly gaining on the nation in terms of college enrollment as a percent of college-age population, the region's 41.7 percent (in 1969-70) ranks considerably below the 57.6 percent for the nation as a whole.[7] Almost 50 percent of all students in the South finish their college education within four years of matriculating, a figure that is comparable to the United States as a whole.[8]

TABLE 4.2. *College Enrollment*

	1950-51	1961-62	1969-70	1975-76 Projection
United States	2,296,592	3,891,000	7,976,834	9,957,000
South	501,229	855,093	1,758,716	2,310,000
South as percentage of U.S. total	21.8%	22.0%	22.1%	23.2%

Sources: Southern Regional Education Board, *Statistics for the Sixties: Higher Education in the South* (Atlanta: Southern Regional Education Board, 1963), p. 24; Southern Regional Education Board, *Fact Book on Higher Education in the South, 1970* (Atlanta: Southern Regional Education Board, 1970), p. 30.

TABLE 4.3. *College Enrollment as a Percentage of College-Age Population*

	1950-51	1960-61	1965-66	1969-70	1975-76 Projection
United States	27.3	39.2	49.9	57.6	62.6
South	17.7	28.1	35.2	41.7	48.4
Alabama	14.2	24.9	28.6	38.5	47.9
Arkansas	14.8	26.6	34.1	38.0	44.4
Florida	21.6	27.5	40.9	51.4	60.3
Georgia	15.7	21.5	26.1	32.6	38.4
Kentucky	15.4	27.6	36.2	41.5	47.7
Louisiana	18.8	31.8	38.4	43.0	46.2
Mississippi	13.0	27.3	34.9	37.2	41.7
North Carolina	15.4	24.0	30.8	39.9	48.8
Oklahoma	27.9	45.5	56.6	60.2	65.1
South Carolina	14.8	20.1	22.1	28.7	35.3
Tennessee	17.5	30.6	39.1	45.1	52.8
Texas	25.4	34.7	42.2	49.6	55.7
Virginia	15.5	23.5	27.8	36.8	45.6

Sources: Southern Regional Education Board, *Statistics for the Sixties: Higher Education in the South* (Atlanta: Southern Regional Education Board, 1963), p. 24; Southern Regional Education Board, *Fact Book on Higher Education in the South, 1970* (Atlanta: Southern Regional Education Board, 1970), p. 31.

A factor in the relatively low enrollment statistics is black enrollment. In 1966, for example, while 46 percent of Southern college-age whites enrolled in institutions of higher learning, only 17 percent of Southern college-age blacks did so. [9] And the Carnegie Commission on the Future of Higher Education points out that "although college enrollment of blacks increased 85 percent between 1964 and 1968, the proportion of college-age blacks enrolled was still only half that of whites." [10]

A second factor is income. The Carnegie Commission found that a family with an annual income of over $15,000 and including at least one college-age student was five times as likely to include a full-time college student as a family with an income of less than $3,000. [11] More than half the college students in the country come from families with incomes in the top 25 percent. Families in the bottom 25 percent produce only 7 percent of all college students. [12] Thus the region's poverty has affected college attendance. The relationship of level of education attained to a person's income and racial attitudes is shown in tables 4.4 and 4.5. The figures suggest that an emphasis on higher education for the South's people might positively affect both their per capita income and tolerance level, although the causal linkages are unclear.

The South is responsible for a decreasing percentage of the total degree production in the United States at each successively higher level. Thus, while the region produces 23.6 percent of the nation's graduates at the bachelor's level, it produces 23 percent of first professional degrees, 18.3 percent of the total number of master's degrees, and 16.9 percent of the nation's doctoral graduates. [13] While the proportion of bachelor's degree production has remained fairly constant over the past decade, doctoral production has increased—an indicator with mixed meanings given the currently glutted job market in some fields.

Universities have two major functions, that of providing graduate and undergraduate education, and that of providing centers for scientific, intellectual, and cultural development, the latter including research and service. In 1961 the Southern Regional Education Board postulated these goals:

1. To provide every individual with opportunity for maximum development of his abilities
2. To produce citizens responsive to the social, economic, and political needs of their time
3. To achieve excellence in teaching, scholarship, and research
4. To accelerate the economic progress of the Southern region through education and research
5. To guide the region in solving social problems created by popula-

TABLE 4.4. *Lifetime and Mean Income of Males Twenty-five Years Old and Over, by Years of School Completed*

	Elementary School		High School		College	
	0-7 Years	*8 Years*	*1-3 Years*	*4 Years*	*1-3 Years*	*4 Years or More*
Lifetime income (in thousands of dollars)						
1949	91	123	142	175	202	287
1956[a]	122	166	189	228	268	359
1961[a]	142	192	223	257	325	437
1967:						
Computed from grouped data[a]	183	246	283	338	401	558
Computed from ungrouped data[b]	177	240	275	325	383	529
1968, computed from ungrouped data[b]	196	258	294	350	411	586
Annual mean income (in dollars)						
1949	2,062	2,829	3,226	3,784	4,423	6,179
1956[a]	2,574	3,631	4,367	5,183	5,997	7,877
1961[a]	2,998	4,206	5,161	5,946	7,348	9,817
1967:						
Computed from grouped data[a]	3,715	5,280	6,529	7,907	9,229	12,532
Computed from ungrouped data[b]	3,606	5,189	6,335	7,629	8,843	11,924
1968, computed from ungrouped data[b]	3,981	5,467	6,769	8,148	9,397	12,938

Source: U.S. Department of Commerce, Bureau of the Census, *Statistical Abstract of the United States, 1970*, p. 111.

[a]Estimates based on series of estimated mean values for specific income class intervals.

[b]Improved methodology introduced in 1967 permits the computation of data based on actual reported amounts.

tion changes, racial differences, urbanization, and technological growth. [14]

Stated succinctly, the goals are quality and equality, and their realization depends on the region's willingness to commit itself to improving its human resources.

TABLE 4.5. *Level of Education and Racial Attitudes of White Southerners (in Percentages)*

| Amount of Schooling | Racial Attitude | | | |
	For Strict Segregation	In Between	For Integration	Don't Know, Refusal to Answer, No Answer
0-6 years	89	9	0	2
Junior high school	75	19	3	3
Incomplete high school	70	26	1	3
Complete high school	66	30	3	1
Complete high school plus other (noncollege) training	54	36	8	2
Some college	50	36	14	0
Complete college	41	45	14	0
College and post-graduate education	11	47	42	0

Source: Donald R. Matthews and James W. Prothro, *Negroes and the New Southern Politics* (New York: Harcourt, Brace & World, 1966), p. 343.
Note: Interviews were conducted with a sample of 694 whites in the eleven states of the former Confederacy.

Historical Summary

An agricultural economy neither demanded nor encouraged the education of large numbers of people. This factor combined with the region's relative poverty and antibooklearning attitudes [15] to prevent the region's respectable higher education system of the late eighteenth century— including the College of William and Mary and the first two state universities (Georgia and North Carolina)—from flowering. The Civil War closed most Southern universities, and it was years later before they recovered. Also, too little money was divided among far too many colleges. [16] At the close of the nineteenth century, only Thomas Jefferson's University of Virginia in the South was recognized as a major institution. Of forty-eight schools in the nation with as much as a $1 million endowment, only Tulane and Vanderbilt were in the South. [17] The Morrill Land-Grant Act of 1862 became a major source of income for Southern schools after World War I.

Educational reform in the South promoted two ideas: the value of utilitarian training, and the value of mass education (although separate) for Negroes. Not until the 1920s was there a significant increase in state appropriations for higher education. In 1930 the South's enrollment in higher education was still less than one-sixth of the United States total. And the region still lacked a first-rank university and an atmosphere of free inquiry. [18] Negro institutions grew largely out of support from Northern foundations and churches. [19]

1940–

Not until the 1940s did the South begin to come to terms with the depressing educational situation, and efforts were made to allocate the limited available funds more effectively. [20] The status of higher education improved markedly in the next two decades. The emphasis began to shift from athletics and physical expansion to improving instructional quality, particularly in the sciences. Southern educators cooperated with business, industry, and government to promote development. While the immigration of industry to the South initially inhibited educational progress because of the demand for low-wage, unskilled labor, in recent years industrialization, in combination with improved transportation and communications facilities, has influenced the South's efforts to improve its higher educational resources.

Appropriations for higher education in the late 1960s were a slightly higher percentage of the tax revenues of the Southern states than they were of the United States as a whole. Just as states sometimes have been less than judicious in their allocation of these funds, individual institutions have been guilty of unwise spending—in the South, as in the rest of the nation. The 1960s saw relative prosperity for higher education; everything went up—enrollments, tuition, state appropriations, faculty salaries. In the ensuing competition for prestige, some departments and programs were established for which there was little real need or demand, and these have siphoned funds from more worthwhile programs. And there is the problem of athletic expenditures, summarized thus by Cartter in 1965: "Few state universities in the South spend as much each year on acquisitions for their libraries as they do putting their football teams on the field." [21] In 1970, when the need for student aid was approaching an all-time high, it was announced that 80 percent of a $5 million bequest to the University of South Carolina would be applied to expansion of the university's stadium. [22] Only in varsity athletics have most Southern universities met or surpassed national standards.

Admissions selection is a problem in Southern universities. Many state universities set low standards of admission, contingent on the quality of public elementary and secondary education, and assume a large—often as high as 50 percent—initial attrition rate, with consequent indifference to student failure. This wasteful practice hurts the talented but educationally and socially disadvantaged student. "Student attrition is viewed less as a problem than as a solution to a problem." [23]

Another problem that has contributed to the region's educational inferiority has been the poor quality and relative unavailability of higher education for blacks. In 1966 46 percent of the Southern white college-age population was enrolled in higher education institutions as compared with only 17 percent of Southern blacks of college age. Of this 17 percent more than four-fifths attended predominantly black colleges, where (a) the undergraduate curriculum generally is weak and often obsolete; (b) the faculty carry heavy teaching loads and are paid on the average $1,500 less than faculty of comparable rank and experience in white institutions; and (c) library and laboratory facilities are usually well below established standards. [24]

Although a college degree no longer is believed to guarantee a job, the demand for people with specialized training continues. The opportunities for farmers and unskilled workers continue to decline although this is not true for students with modern agricultural training. A great deal has been done to improve the quality and availability of Southern educational facilities. State appropriations have been increasing. Twenty-nine Southern institutions reported average faculty compensation of $13,500 or above in 1969-70. Federally funded research increased 200 percent between 1963 and 1968. Library facilities are improving: of thirty university libraries in the country holding more than 1.25 million volumes in 1967, six were in the South. [25] And there has been an extension of educational opportunity in the region. Cartter wrote in 1965:

> There will be five or six private universities and an equal number of public universities vying for a place on the national scene. It is a tribute to this new spirit that the best of Southern colleges and universities have taken desegregation in stride with hardly a ripple. There remain a few "closed societies," but these are islands in the South, no longer the mainland. In most states the foundations of higher education are now firmly enough implanted not only to withstand the buffeting of immediate social pressures, but to provide the precept and example for the constructive resolution of such problems. [26]

Inputs to Higher Education

ENDOWMENTS

Physical Plant

In 1968 institutions of higher education in the South had physical plant assets of $7.6 billion—21.8 percent of the value of all college physical plant assets in the United States. The South's share in increased value of physical plants that year was 24.1 percent. In 1969-70 only four Southern universities budgeted as much as a million dollars for new books, periodicals, and bindings. The average library holdings of fifty Southern schools surveyed by Louisiana State University were slightly more than 800,000 volumes as of 1970.

Faculty

In 1969 only 43 percent of Southern faculty members had received a doctorate, compared with 54 percent for the West-Southwest and the North Atlantic regions and a national average of 50 percent. Twenty percent of Southern teaching faculty have not taken more than their first professional degree, compared to 17 percent for the entire nation. [27] In light of the differential between the compensation received by faculty in the South and the United States, it is not surprising that Southern faculty members are less qualified. In 1969-70 the median faculty salary at four-year institutions in the South (including West Virginia but excluding Texas and Oklahoma) was $11,133, the lowest average for any region and $600 below the national average. [28] The South is not competitive in any of the ranks.

The student-faculty ratio in the South in 1951-52 was 13:1, compared with the national norm of 14:1. The increased demand for higher education, exacerbated by a teacher shortage, increased this ratio to nearly 20:1 for the South and 18:1 for the nation in 1966-67. The quality of education in the South, insofar as it was reflected in student-faculty ratios, was not significantly worse than that of the nation. There were exceptions: Oklahoma's ratio doubled from 17:1 in 1951-52 to 34:1 in 1966-67. Only three states in the South—Georgia, South Carolina, and Tennessee—were able to hold their ratio increases down to the national increase level between 1951 and 1967. [29]

The professional organization that has traditionally been the major voice of the college faculty is the American Association of University Professors. It is facing competition today from two organizations that represent teachers at all levels—the National Education Association, and the

American Federation of Teachers, AFL-CIO. The issue currently confronting all of these groups is unionization of college faculties. Although collective bargaining has not yet reached campuses in the South, at least two Southern states in 1971 had faculty groups that had begun to explore the possibilities of unionization. If the idea catches hold, the professional organizations chosen to act as bargaining agents will assume new influence as they negotiate with university administrators.

Students

In 1969 the South had 1.39 million students in public institutions of higher learning, and 370,000 in private institutions. In 1972 the thirteen states of the region had a total of 2.11 million students in higher education institutions. [30] In the South in 1968 1.14 million undergraduate students were enrolled in their home states and 159,000 were enrolled out of state. Also, 225,000 nonresidents were enrolled in Southern institutions. The net migration of students across state lines in the South relative to the rest of the nation is summarized in table 4.6.

TABLE 4.6. *In- and Out-migration in Public and Private Educational Institutions, 1968*

| | Net Migration, Public Institutions Only | | Migration, Public and Private Institutions Combined | | | |
| | | | Percent of Residents Going Out of State | | Percent of Nonresidents in Institutional Enrollments | |
	Undergrad.	Grad. and Prof.	Undergrad.	Grad. and Prof.	Undergrad.	Grad. and Prof.
United States	31,305	29,587	16.0	24.5	16.7	28.5
Alabama	2,495	154	11.0	30.2	14.4	23.6
Arkansas	329	-393	13.1	45.5	14.5	27.4
Florida	-3,332	-286	16.3	27.4	15.3	18.3
Georgia	3,364	561	15.9	27.8	19.6	37.7
Kentucky	5,808	330	13.6	30.6	22.6	34.6
Louisiana	1,953	-251	6.9	18.6	10.3	26.7
Mississippi	2,536	37	8.9	34.6	12.0	23.7
North Carolina	6,712	2,342	10.5	28.2	26.8	45.0
Oklahoma	4,427	1,053	8.4	22.4	15.0	24.4
South Carolina	1,613	-2	22.6	40.5	23.8	30.4
Tennessee	5,494	905	12.1	24.6	27.3	36.2
Texas	6,489	1,770	5.3	14.8	8.7	11.0
Virginia	-2,126	467	12.7	35.9	30.1	33.5

Source: Southern Regional Education Board, *Fact Book on Higher Education in the South, 1970* (Atlanta: Southern Regional Education Board, 1970), p. 35.

Organization

Florida, Georgia, Mississippi, and North Carolina have statewide agencies with power to govern as well as to coordinate four-year graduate public institutions. However, only in Georgia does the board control junior colleges as well; the other three states have separate agencies for community colleges. The other Southern states have agencies for higher education with coordinating functions only; however, they encompass junior as well as senior institutions, and thus can attempt to plan for all levels of higher education. [31] Private colleges and state institutions not governed by state agencies are governed by their separate boards of trustees. Where private schools are church-related, they are usually answerable to some denominational board as well in making policy decisions.

Finance

State appropriations, already discussed, are the major source of funding for public education. Table 4.7 gives a breakdown of all sources of

TABLE 4.7. *Educational and General Funds Income by Source, Public Institutions, 1966-67 (in Thousands of Dollars)*

	Total Revenue	Student Charges	Endowments and Gifts	Federal Government	State Governments	Local Governments
United States	7,133,946	997,419	102,041	1,585,062	3,286,511	413,994
South	1,630,276	245,598	27,517	287,695	824,609	35,697
South as a percent of U.S. total	22.8%	24.6%	26.8%	18.1%	25.0%	8.6%

Source: Southern Regional Education Board, *Fact Book on Higher Education in the South, 1970* (Atlanta: Southern Regional Education Board, 1970), p. 59; U.S. Department of Health, Education, and Welfare, National Center for Educational Statistics, *Financial Statistics of Institutions of Higher Education: Current Funds, Revenues and Expenditures, 1966-67,* table 5.

income for 1966-67. Private institutions must rely mainly on sources of income other than governmental aid. The increasing expense of educating a college student is illustrated in table 4.8, showing cost figures at a seven-year interval.

TABLE 4.8. *Educational and General Expenditures at Institutions of Higher Education*

	1961-62		1968-69	
	Total (x1,000)	Per Student	Total (x1,000)	Per Student
United States	$5,768,243	$1,482	$12,469,127	$1,647
Alabama	57,108	1,191	165,603	1,746
Arkansas	31,962	1,153	69,137	1,366
Florida	97,624	1,226	328,397	1,626
Georgia	79,854	1,537	210,399	1,934
Kentucky	58,130	1,123	159,034	1,691
Louisiana	81,123	1,302	170,168	1,475
Mississippi	41,483	1,075	102,194	1,488
North Carolina	123,305	1,591	302,075	2,036
Oklahoma	58,199	976	....	....
South Carolina	36,445	1,113	100,929	1,798
Tennessee	84,931	1,315	216,739	1,771
Texas	196,199	987	478,197	1,284
Virginia	92,288	1,491	193,790	1,520

Source: Southern Regional Education Board, *Fact Book on Higher Education in the South, 1970* (Atlanta: Southern Regional Education Board, 1970), p. 58.

The Southern Regional Education Board pointed out that the federal government assumed an increasing proportion of the cost of supporting higher education in the 1960s. "The obvious inelasticity of other sources of support in relation to the expansion of the educational task ahead explains this steadily increasing reliance upon federal aid."[32] However, the board's belief that the trend would continue has not been supported.

Constituency

The groups that make up the constituency of higher education influence policy decisions and are affected by them. The groups include those within the walls of the university—students, faculty, and administrators—and parents, alumni, and boards of trustees of institutions. In addition, public institutions must consider as part of their constituency the governor, state legislature, state governing board of higher education, and the general public.

EXTERNAL FACTORS

Higher education is influenced by many outside factors, including gifts from foundations, the market mechanism, population growth, such events as the Vietnam War, and conditions affecting faculty recruitment.

Philanthropy from Foundations

Since the mid-nineteenth century, gifts from foundations have played an important role in the shaping of Southern institutions of higher education, especially black colleges. Such early educational foundations as the Slater Fund and Peabody Fund, and later the Rockefeller Foundation and the Ford Foundation, have left their mark on black higher education.

Certain drawbacks are inherent in dependence on foundation grants. First, institutions often begin to define their needs in terms of the money available. Instead of examining themselves closely for problems and opportunities and then exploring avenues for funding, institutions scrutinize available funds and then look for problems to match the categories in which funds are available. This procedure allows the foundations, completely exogenous units, to set the list of priorities. Institutional autonomy is further compromised by the conditions attached to many grants. Foundations are paternalistic in the manner in which they disburse funds, requiring that the utilization of such funds be made in a precisely described manner. Thus, colleges may be required to subvert long-term goals to the exigencies of acquiring and keeping funds. Finally, foundations tend to prefer publicity-laden breakthrough projects rather than the more mundane follow-through projects. Emphasis is often placed upon quick and spectacular results, such as three-month summer remedial precollege programs designed to eradicate the effects of twelve years of educational privation. Yet few of these much-heralded experiments are truly innovative; foundations shy away from bolder programs as "too risky."

Since conventional methods of remediation have proven impractical when dealing with large numbers of students, foundations must make an investment in new and radical experiments if they want their money to achieve lasting results. Generally, the role of philanthropy in Southern higher education should be a supportive one. Foundations should supply money to Southern colleges and universities with as few conditional strings as possible, with minimal guidance and red tape.

The Market Mechanism

Colleges and universities offer training in skills in relationship to the demand for such skills in the job market. For example, when the demand for medical doctors is at a high level and the supply is relatively low, the fees for doctors' services remain high. This high income in turn makes the profession more attractive, leading to a rise in demand for entrance to medical schools.

Unfortunately, lengthy periods of time are necessary for the academic market to adjust itself to a changed supply or demand, and the government has sometimes found it necessary to act as an equilibrator. The launching of the Russian sputnik precipitated a tremendous demand for aerospace scientists and technicians. Since it felt that vital time would be wasted if reliance were placed upon the market, the federal government initiated crash programs to rapidly increase the supply of such people. Higher education responded to the government incentives, expanding existing programs and forming new departments in fields related to aerospace, until the point was reached that the supply of graduates exceeded demand. In the early 1970s, with jobs in aerospace engineering scarce because of drastic cutbacks in federal spending in that area, the government did not assume responsibility for the consequences of its earlier educational investment (e.g., by retraining aeronautics and space workers).

The effect of the job market was also apparent until recently in the course offerings of black colleges. Historically, the only professional opportunity open to blacks was that of teaching. Black higher education institutions responded by offering a preponderance of degree programs in education. It made no sense for students to demand training in areas where little or no employment was available. Women comprised a large majority of black college students because teaching (particularly in elementary and secondary education) has traditionally been a female occupation.

Population Trends

The tremendous increase in college enrollments—108 percent between 1960 and 1969 [33]—caused by the post-World War II baby boom is expected to continue to level off in the future because of the decreasing birth rate. The actual number of births per year in the United States has dropped steadily in the last several years. If we take as constant the percentage of the college-age population that will enter colleges and universities, the statistics would point to a decreasing enrollment. However, if the opportunity for higher education is expanded to everyone who wants it, then the percentage of the population enrolled should increase. Another factor is the recent emphasis on education as a continuing process, with adults reentering institutions of higher learning several times during their lives.

Student Unrest

The Vietnam War jarred the consciousness of Americans as few events have done. College students were particularly affected. The war contributed to a cynicism toward authority so pervasive that university administrations were forced to alter their role vis-à-vis students.

Protest against the war was joined by other types of student unrest on many campuses during the 1960s. The violent eruptions of Berkeley, Columbia, and Madison were largely absent in the South; nevertheless, they influenced higher education in the region. More cosmopolitan Southern schools such as The University of North Carolina at Chapel Hill and Duke University had their share of less violent student protests. There was bloodshed at Jackson State and Orangeburg. Southern legislatures, like their counterparts in other regions, have been extremely sensitive to student unrest, even that occurring outside of the South. They have sometimes sought to punish or to gain greater control over institutions of higher education in an attempt to curb student rebellion. However, the recent diminution of protest activity seems less a reaction to the pressures from legislatures than a natural ebb in the flow of activism.

Factors Influencing Faculty Recruitment

The South has benefited from exogenous conditions limiting the range of choices of job-seeking faculty. As Northern cities have begun to be perceived as less attractive places to live, the task of attracting good faculty to Southern colleges has become easier. Because of the tight job market in most fields of college teaching, professors who five years ago would not consider coming to the South now find it attractive. More positive incentive is offered by the larger starting salaries resulting from increased legislative appropriations in some states. Southern schools that still have funds for new faculty can, if they spend their money wisely, get some of the outstanding young doctoral graduates of the best universities in the country.

Economic

The South's traditional agricultural economy and the poverty that in large part results from it directly influence the quality of the educational institutions of the region. The most immediate cause-and-effect relationship is between the inadequate tax base and financial support for education. Although the South in 1967-68 allocated 12.5 percent of its tax revenues to higher education, compared to a national average of 12.1 percent, the relatively poorer Southern tax base results in below-average state appropriations. For 1969-70 only two Southern states, North Carolina and Florida, exceeded the national average of $423 per college-age person in state-appropriated operational funds. [34]

Second, an agricultural economy does not demand highly educated workers. The few industries that traditionally located in the South—textiles, for example—did not require highly skilled workers or high levels of research and development; [35] in fact, a major attraction for such industries was the low level of education and aspiration in the region and the consequent availability of cheap, unskilled labor. Such demand as did exist for more highly skilled workers and managers could usually be met by importation from outside the region. This is not to make non-Southern industrial interests the scapegoat for the poor quality of Southern education, since Southern legislatures encouraged exploitation through such measures as the granting of liberalized tax treatments. Spengler has pointed out:

> The general shortcomings of the Southern economy are fourfold. Most important is the lag in education, for not only is the day past when an abundant supply of cheap, unskilled labor can draw industry to the South; the day is at hand when automation is beginning to convert the underskilled into the chronically idle and hence potential inner barbarians. Until the education of the South's population, together with provisions for education, is on a par with that found (for example) in the urban Middle West or in California, the South will not be able to share as it might in the development of growing industries; for these are based upon modern technology and cannot flourish in areas where both scientific and technological education is underdeveloped at all levels. [36]

However, recognition of the value of improved higher education opportunities has coincided with growing demands on the public budget for improvements in other social services—health and welfare, for example. In combination with reemergent popular skepticism, stemming from the inconsistency between the publicized goals and the actual achievements of higher education, the prospects for greatly increased appropriations to higher education are slim.

Education and the economy are interdependent in that education stimulates economic development, which, in turn, produces affluence sufficient for the improvement of the educational system.

Political

Inputs from the political sector traditionally have been more relevant to public institutions than to private ones. As recently as the middle 1960s, Salisbury could write that "public and private universities are intellectually indistinguishable from one another . . . [and are] functionally . . . closely linked. But politically the differences are major, indeed." [37] Now, with increasing pressures for public support for floundering private institutions and the inclusion of private institutions in statewide planning, this is becoming less the case.

Political interference with the operation of schools is as old as public education. The rationalization is simple: the taxpayer should have a say in the operation of the institutions his money supports. This can have beneficial effects, as Maddox points out: "Southern political leaders have 'discovered' education. Many of them have found in education a political program which appeals to nearly all of the diverse and competing segments of the electorate. . . . Upon assuming office most governors find they have no choice but to underwrite a sizeable increase in state appropriations for education. . . . The results have been especially beneficial to a number of Southern states." [38] Yet, too often, and particularly under current conditions of increasing operating and construction costs in combination with a near-critical shortage of funds, the power to allocate resources can be misused. The response of Southern state legislatures to campus turmoil in the late 1960s was to hold the line on appropriations to higher education for several years. And the occasional suppression of academic freedom in the name of order is hardly attractive to the good teachers and researchers the South needs, nor does it ultimately serve society's broader interests.

The atypical economic and political history of the region created an atmosphere that was sometimes hostile to the intellectual process. That this attitude persists is not surprising: attitudes are perpetuated long after the conditions that fostered them have ended. This attitude remains a barrier to the development of the South's educational resources. A continuing problem for the region has been the loss of many of its most talented natives. In the late sixties the Southern Regional Education Board noted, "The drain of talent from the South at the graduate level results in a disproportionately small return of scholars to the region, at least in the field of college teaching." [39] In addition to lack of economic opportunities compared to other regions, political interference with the universities has helped to encourage this drain.

The South's reputation for suppression of academic freedom and intellectual inquiry generally has taken its toll as well on the recruitment of non-Southern faculty. Middleton's 1961 survey (cited earlier) indicated that the threat of constraint upon freedom of expression was a significant factor in the reluctance of prospective faculty to accept Southern posts. [40] Southern state legislatures have made periodic attempts to protect students in their states' colleges from exposure to alien ideas. The 1963 Speaker Ban Law in North Carolina sought "to prevent communist rabble rousers and their kind from using the campuses of North Carolina as a forum for their evil activities." [41] The act forbade the use of "facilities of such college or university for speaking purposes" to any individual "who (1) is a known member of the Communist Party; (2) is known to advocate the overthrow of the United States or the State of North Carolina; and (3) has pleaded the Fifth Amendment of the Constitution of the United States in refusing to answer any question." [42] The threat of loss of accreditation of its state institutions forced the legislature to amend the law, but not before gaining for the state a reputation for parochialism that caused a temporary drawback in recruiting faculty even for its excellent university system.

Statewide coordinating agencies for higher education should promote statewide planning and reduce the degree to which individual institutions are subject to the year-by-year shifts in political fortunes. Such systems are far from perfected, however. Cox and Harrell note:

> Interposed between the state's general governing agencies and the institutions, the coordinating agency has been subject to pressures from both sides. Institutions have regarded its authority and its exercise of that authority as an encroachment upon institutional autonomy, and the state officials who brought about its creation have been reluctant to accept its performance in the role which they established. Unlike the statewide governing agencies which were established and had their relationships developed in a period of relative educational tranquility, the coordinating agencies were created to try to bring order and planning to rather chaotic educational growth and expansion. . . . An appropriate role . . . has yet to evolve. [43]

Again there is a chicken-and-egg problem in the interaction between politics and education. On the one hand, planning for higher education must involve a recognition of the partial autonomy of individual institutions within the framework of overall state and regional planning for the development of human resources. And the institutions, for their part, must develop new methods of accountability and service to their constituencies.

Social

With improved transportation and communications facilities and the resulting increase in interstate migration by students, education is becoming "nationalized." Many undergraduates enrolled in Southern colleges are nonresidents. And as McKinney and Bourque suggest:

> Education . . . is a *generalizing* medium. Physics is physics, and mathematics is mathematics, whether you study them in New Orleans or Chicago. As a much larger proportion of the Southern populace attends schools for longer periods of time—approximating national norms—it is in effect sharing in a national (in many respects international) culture. . . . By increasingly sharing in that sector of national culture, the region is inevitably divorcing itself from those values, attitudes, and folkways attached to the status and outlook of being "uneducated."[44]

Public Education

The inferior quality of primary and secondary public education directly influences the quality of higher education. Excluding Florida, Georgia, and Virginia, in 1963 only 30 percent of the region's high schools were fully accredited.[45] The standards of admission at state universities cannot be inconsistent with the standards required for high school graduation. In addition, "The absence of social pressure for diligent work in high school underlies the scarcity of first-rank universities or colleges in the South, for the college years are too late to inculcate zeal for intellectual work."[46]

The effects of segregation exacerbate these problems. Even as integration is becoming a fact in the South, young black students finishing high school today have been as segregated and as subject to inferior education during the major part of their schooling as were their brothers and sisters before them. This factor has resulted in many black students being ill-equipped to handle university work; yet to refuse to admit them to universities would continue the discrimination responsible for the present educational gap between the races.

POLICY DECISIONS

Federal

The aid-to-education amendments of 1972 included major innovations in federal aid to higher education. [47] For the first time, federal funds were authorized for general operating expenses of institutions of higher education. Aid to institutions was to be dependent on the number of students receiving basic grants and the total amount of other federal student aid distributed at each school; however, two years later no funds had been appropriated for this purpose. The legislation provided that every undergraduate student would be entitled to a Basic Educational Opportunity Grant toward the cost of his education: $1,400, minus his expected family contribution (the total not to exceed by half the cost of attending the institution). This could encourage institutions to actively seek poorer students eligible for federal aid.

The amounts provided to students in the first two years were not large, but it was important that it be established as a national policy that students who could not afford the cost of education would get some federal assistance.

Two major problems exist in programs of federal funding, generally. The government often attaches unrealistic conditions to its appropriations. For example, in September 1970 the Nixon administration earmarked $20 million to provide low-cost construction loans to predominantly black colleges. However, the colleges were required to raise 30 percent of the costs on their own and were unable to do so because of dwindling alumni support and the difficulty of obtaining private loans. As of January 1971 less than 10 percent of the appropriated funds had actually been allocated, and these funds went to only three schools. [48]

Second, "the federal government originally implied permanent federal funding of certain types of activities, especially graduate education, research, and facilities construction, and now is threatening to renege. . . . The states will have to pick up the tab." [49] This underlies the necessity of maintaining a mix of revenues to prevent heavy reliance on a single source of funds.

The federal government is involved in a wide range of other higher education decisions. For example, federal agencies such as the National Science Foundation, in choosing recipients of research grants, make decisions daily that determine how and where many faculty members will invest their resources.

State

Policy decisions affecting higher education are made by state legislatures, boards of higher education, and boards of trustees of state-run colleges. The primary decision of legislatures is the amount of money to appropriate for educational expenditures. Southern states also are beginning to recognize that private colleges are an educational resource and to look for ways to subsidize their operations. North Carolina and Georgia in 1971 passed acts authorizing payments to subsidize private institutions, directly or indirectly, for every in-state resident they enroll.

All Southern states now have central coordinating or control boards to oversee long-range planning and coordination of higher educational resources. The strengths of statewide planning are (1) regulation of the development of new institutions and expansion of old ones; (2) the promotion of institutional differentiation; and (3) the improvement of interinstitutional communication and minimization of competition between institutions. The possible pitfalls in statewide planning are somewhat less apparent. The tendency is to concentrate on public institutions to the neglect of integrating the private sector, and to give insufficient attention to the quality of education. Furthermore, statewide planning inevitably results in some loss of autonomy for the institutions, and the coordinating board may become too distant from the schools. And, as noted earlier, too frequently the central board is limited in its authority and acts only in an advisory capacity.

In most Southern states public colleges are governed by their own boards of trustees. Selection of members for these boards is the responsibility of the legislature in some states; of the governors, with legislative approval, in others; and occasionally a board is self-perpetuating, choosing its own new members. Trustees in all cases have far-ranging powers to set the policies under which their institutions operate; college administrators are accountable to them.

University

University administrators allocate resources within the institution. Although the source of funds is outside of the college, the decisions as to which items to include in the budget and what proportion of funds to assign them is made within the administration. Every aspect of university operations, from the size of faculty and number of course offerings in a discipline to the amount of scholarship aid available to needy students, is dependent upon resource allocation decisions.

Also important is the power to set admissions policies. For years colleges and universities throughout the South have relied heavily on preadmission tests in determining a candidate's acceptability. In September 1961 the Southern Association of Colleges and Schools determined that 65 percent of the accredited four-year colleges in the association's region required some form of preadmission test (predominantly the Scholastic Aptitude Test), while an additional 14 percent recommended some form of test for admission. Of accredited junior colleges, 29 percent required the tests and 33 percent recommended them. [50]

Two major criticisms of intelligence tests are generally recognized as valid: (1) tests are couched in culturally related terms, which gives an individual intimately related to the culture an advantage over the one who is new to the culture; (2) tests do not take into consideration the mood of the subject being tested. On the second point, Peter Watson performed an experiment on West Indies blacks in England. His results indicated that when the subjects were told that they were taking an I.Q. test, they performed at a level ten points below that at which they performed when told that the test was merely an aid in curriculum planning. When told that the test was an I.Q. test, the subjects scored higher when the test monitor was black than when he was white. The hypothesis supported by these results is that blacks are keenly aware of white attitudes toward them, and realizing that there is little hope of overcoming the attitudes, their motivation is low. [51] To the extent that conventional means of testing for admission to colleges are culturally related, it is unfair to use these indicators for people of different cultural backgrounds. Recognizing this, college administrators are becoming increasingly reliant on a diversity of criteria for determining whom to accept.

At least eleven states have required that all graduates of state high schools should be guaranteed admission to an institution of higher education. Often this open-admissions policy is restricted to two-year community colleges, which were created to relieve the strain on four-year institutions and provide relatively quick and economical means of expanding educational opportunity.

Personnel policies generally are made at the university level to be carried out by each department. Such decisions as minimum qualifications for faculty, conditions to be met for the granting of tenure, and the number of faculty positions at each rank allotted to a department determine who obtains or keeps teaching jobs. Often departments are allowed a great deal of leeway in making personnel decisions under general administration guidelines.

Curriculum planning affects the quality of instruction. The balance between providing "relevant" courses while insuring that the essentials are met by the curriculum is delicate. In the scramble to institute courses in black studies, environmental engineering, and other new fields, colleges are tempted to overreach themselves rather than risk the accusation of not being up to date. This may lead to hastily conceived courses taught at superifical levels by instructors whose grasp of the subject is tenuous. Wasteful duplication of course offerings among universities is a more serious problem. Each school feels it must have its own department in a discipline, regardless of whether it is equipped to provide a comprehensive curriculum in that area. State governing boards of higher education need to be given some control over curriculum if competitiveness is to be replaced by cooperative planning, with each institution offering degrees in those areas in which it can maintain adequate teaching quality as well as level of demand. [52]

Analysis of Specific Institutions

PRIVATE COLLEGES

A study by the Southern Regional Education Board in the mid-sixties revealed that private colleges are generally strongest in the humanities and traditional liberal arts curriculum, whereas public universities have been developing in the direction of technical and vocation-oriented subjects. [53] Since the early fifties the expansion and improvement of state systems of higher education has been remarkable. They have grown not only in size but in diversity and quality as well. By contrast, most private colleges and universities of the South have changed little in the last twenty years, and as a result they now find themselves unable to define and realize their educational goals. Nearly half of all Southern four-year institutions of higher learning are private, yet they enroll only 21 percent of all students attending college in the region, and that percentage is declining. [54]

Finance

The most serious problem facing private colleges is a financial one. They are small and cannot realize the economies of scale available to larger institutions. One result is that while student-faculty ratios closely parallel those of the public institutions, faculty salaries at private colleges are generally considerably lower. [55] In addition, private colleges have less diversified sources of revenue: they must rely in large part on tuition and student fee charges often three to four times higher than those of public institutions. [56] These costs are prohibitive for the vast majority of potential students, and enrollments have been dropping seriously in the last few years. In fall 1970, for example, despite extensive recruiting campaigns, eighteen of the twenty-nine private senior institutions in North Carolina experienced a drop in enrollment, the largest of which was almost 25 percent. [57]

In the past private institutions have been considered more or less incidental to the educational goals of the states in which they were located. Today the states and their private colleges are becoming increasingly interdependent. Private colleges are in need of public financial support, and the states over the long term can use the additional enrollment capacity of the urban private colleges (as well as their research and service capabilities). And as William F. McFarlane notes, "With the task [of providing ready access to the state's institutions of higher education for larger segments of the population] only partially completed, the capacities of state systems appear to be reaching a saturation point: commitments to equality of opportunity, especially for the underprivileged, and state goals for truly adequate higher educational resources are still far from being fulfilled." [58]

Short of direct public support of private institutions, which raises serious issues of constitutionality, there are indirect measures that could enhance the solvency of private schools. Most educational institutions already enjoy tax exemptions. A second possibility is to grant parents of college students a tax deduction for each enrolled student in the family. A third, which came under legal challenge in Texas in 1974, is state subsidization to private colleges for each in-state student enrolled. The North Carolina program not only pays private colleges a per-student amount for each North Carolinian enrolled each year, but it also gives an additional amount for each in-state student in excess of the number of such students enrolled as of 1970, the base year. [59]

Church-related Colleges

One genre of private institution should be singled out for special mention: church-related colleges. There are 261 church-related institutions of higher education in the South, which in 1969 enrolled 239,000 students, or about one-seventh of the total number of college students in the region. [60]

The quality of education a student receives in many church-related institutions is suspect. Faculty salaries are among the worst offered in higher education. In 1962 faculty members in church-related senior institutions were paid $1,700 less than their counterparts in nonreligious private institutions, and $2,000 less than the average for faculty of public schools. [61] Low salaries rarely attract highly competent faculty. Furthermore, a main source of faculty for church schools is their own alumni, leaving them open to the criticism of inbreeding. The parochialism of some church-school administrations and faculty is antithetical to the pursuit of higher learning.

Many problems of the church-related school are those of the small school. In 1970 only four church-related schools had student bodies of over 5,000 and most had student populations of well under 1,000. Although there may be advantages in smallness, efficient operation is not one: each dollar does not produce the same effect as in the large school. A library collection is a relatively fixed cost regardless of whether 1,000 or 5,000 students are using it.

In determining aid to private colleges, states should take a close look at the church-related schools to decide which have the potential for providing quality education and which are too weak to offer hope of a significant return on state investment in them. Not every institution of higher learning deserves to survive. Ultimately, the need is for state-wide planning and coordination for all colleges and universities, with public subsidization of many private colleges. The effect would be a better distribution of enrollment for various educational purposes. [62]

PUBLIC COLLEGES

Public institutions of higher education are not afflicted with the same ills as private institutions. Public colleges tend to be larger: although only about half the region's colleges are public, they enroll more than three-fourths of all the students attending Southern institutions. By 1975 this figure may reach nearly 85 percent. [63] As a result of their larger size, the public schools can realize greater economies of scale. In addition, greater financial resources allow for higher faculty salaries.

However, public institutions are by no means immune to the hard times that beset higher education today. In addition to the general problems associated with decreased funding and growing public skepticism, the public institutions have difficulties of their own.

Finance

The solvency of public institutions is heavily dependent on state support. With this support public colleges and universities have traditionally been able to maintain relatively low tuition and student charges. As long as sufficient state funds are forthcoming, public universities and their students do not face severe financial problems. The condition, of course, is "sufficient."

As noted, state appropriations in the South have increased rapidly during the last twenty years; recently, however, the rate of increase in appropriations has not kept pace with the rate of increase in enrollments and in the basic cost of education. A survey in 1970 of 78 of the 99 major state-supported universities revealed that 14 incurred operating deficits during the 1969-70 school year. Seven of these are located in the South. [64] McFarlane notes that "to offset shortages of funds many public institutions are resorting to restrictive economies (e.g., tuition increases, enrollment limitations, delays in vital facilities and programs, and under-financing of costs to improve quality)."[65]

States finance their public institutions of higher learning through annual or biennial appropriations. These include funds for the physical plant, instruction, and student aid. Students pay a small portion of the cost through tuition, which is usually less than the instructional cost. Objections to this system can be raised on at least two grounds: (1) the state is subsidizing the college rather than the student, and (2) in application, the rich are being subsidized by the poor and the middle class.

When the state appropriates funds directly to the colleges and not to the students, this practice may result in colleges being self-oriented rather than student-oriented. The state is then financing institutions that organize themselves after their own interests. If students want the benefit of state subsidization, they must attend these schools, whether or not the academic program is to their liking. Adam Smith wrote: "Whatever forces a certain number of students to any college or university, independent of the merit or reputation of the teachers, tends more or less to diminish the necessity of that merit or reputation."[66]

A study of the California college system revealed that the average income of parents of students in that state was above the average for the state. With most state taxes tending to be regressive or proportional, this situation suggests that families in the lower- and middle-income brackets are subsidizing the college education of the children of higher-income families.

Out-of-state students who attend public institutions of higher learning have their educations subsidized, in effect, by the taxpayers of the state in which the institution is located. The policy adopted by the Southern states in the 1950s and 1960s of charging only a modest tuition differential for out-of-state students raised questions regarding the states' best interests. Although it is desirable for students to have interaction with students from other states, the states should not have to pay for this. Perhaps the federal government will ultimately devise a formula of aid to students attending out-of-state universities. Perhaps Southern states can work out a transfer system for students attending schools in other states within the region. Meanwhile, some schools such as The University of North Carolina have greatly increased out-of-state tuition; this temptation is powerful, but in the long run it may discourage inter-Southern cooperation and encourage construction of unnecessary facilities. In addition, the U.S. Supreme Court in 1973 found Connecticut regulations on resident status to be unconstitutional.[67] This decision might lead to elimination of higher charges for any but freshmen, and could reduce university revenues by several hundred million dollars annually; the implications for resident tuition levels are serious.

With the exception of state and local government appropriations and support from auxiliary enterprises income, public institutions are out-ranked by private ones in nearly all sources of income. Only about 10 percent of the total endowment funds held by the nation's institutions of higher learning are in public universities. The public colleges receive only about one-quarter as much income from private gifts and grants as private universitites. As a result, decreases in state support can be disas-trous. Southern public institutions are beginning to rely heavily on loans for building construction, a measure that will inevitably be felt in future tuition increases. [68]

Enrollment

Increased enrollment at public institutions is an encouraging indicator of expanded educational opportunity in the region. Enrollment expan-sion has its drawbacks as well, however. An increase in the number of students is desirable only if facilities expand to accommodate them; otherwise, as is the case in many Southern colleges, a larger student body only compounds already existing problems of inadequate facili-ties, crowded classrooms, and substandard quality of education. As a result, high attrition rates do not elicit the concern they deserve; "ex-panded opportunity" is illusory if it merely means that more students are admitted and allowed to fail.

There are solutions to the problems of expanding enrollments and fi-nancial hardship other than enrollment limitation, which is antithetical to the goal of providing equal access to all who have the ability and mo-tivation. Very few institutions make full use of their existing space. A 1965 study of space utilization by the Southern Association of Colleges and Schools noted that "the range of utilization of buildings varied from five-day morning classes only to institutions which utilized their build-ings from seven in the morning to ten at night for five and one-half days each week." [69] The trend in recent years has been toward the elimination of early morning and Saturday classes. In light of increasing reliance on loans to cover construction costs, requests for new buildings should be accompanied by proof of efficient use of currently available space. The practice of operating colleges at full tilt only eight or nine months each year also is questionable. [70]

Institutions should also experiment with the size of classes. Small classes are not equally necessary, or even desirable, for all courses. Many basic and advanced undergraduate courses can be taught as successfully through a combination of large lecture sections and smaller seminars led by junior professors or graduate teaching assistants. Freshmen and sophomores need some exposure to a university's best teachers in a seminar setting. Much greater use also should be made of television, teaching machines, and other technological aids.

Administration

In planning and decision making, universities lag far behind the business world. By and large, higher education has not taken advantage of modern management techniques and systems analysis. Even campuses with outstanding business schools do not take advantage of the available expertise.

One reason universities are not managed better is that there is no way of systematically training college administrators. An academic background is not necessarily adequate, yet administrators are often chosen from the ranks of the faculty on the basis of their competence in an academic discipline.

Intercollegiate Athletics

Intercollegiate athletic programs in football and basketball receive considerable emphasis on most Southern campuses. The Atlantic Coast, Southeastern, Southwest, and Big Eight conferences are known for the professional effort that is devoted to recruiting and coaching successful teams, especially at the large state universities. The cost of intercollegiate athletics varies from school to school; at some, the major spectator sports are so successful that they support other athletic programs as well, but at others the major programs are hard-pressed to break even. It is debatable whether funds devoted to building new stadiums and supporting the teams would go otherwise to educational programs.

Accountability

The concept of accountability in education must be vitalized. For far too long service to the student has been among the last concerns of university administrations. Clearly, a few students will not succeed, despite compensatory, remedial, and cultural enrichment programs; but, as Timothy Healy noted, "Standards ought to refer to what a university does for its students, rather than to their opening handicap. An older way of putting it would be to say that the Lord God gave them their brains, while we as educators stand or fall on what we help those brains to accomplish. Standards must clearly be tied to the kind of degrees a university awards, not to the batting average of its dean of admissions."[71] Both the student and the university are responsible for what the student accomplishes educationally; the university cannot place the sole blame for failure on inferior gifts or preparation of its students.

COMMUNITY COLLEGES

One of the most dramatic changes in higher education in recent decades is the proliferation of two-year community colleges and technical education institutes. The need for vocational training is especially pressing in the South, where native Southerners have frequently found themselves restricted to unskilled laboring positions because of lack of education, while more highly trained Northerners were imported for managerial and skilled positions. Specialized education beyond the high school level is imperative for the great majority of new jobs; the growth of community colleges to meet this need has been noteworthy. North Carolina enrollments, for example, increased from 11,000 to over 200,000 in ten years. [72]

"The community college in the United States has been described as the only educational institution that can truly be considered an American social institution." [73] This phenomenon, spurred by the post-World War II G.I. Bill, has its roots in the late nineteenth century, when the incipient industrialism of the region began to create demands for specialized training that could not be met by the traditional institutions. Although the land-grant colleges founded in the Reconstruction era were designed in part to meet this need, the majority of four-year colleges continued to offer a classical curriculum.

The College and the Community

The community college is a democratizing institution. It has been argued that, "while the universities continue to cater to a relatively homogeneous group from a dominant stratum of society, the community college embraces a heterogeneous group that represents a cross-section of the total population. . . . Community colleges have become the primary vehicle for social and economic advancement for the lower two-thirds of the population. The typical student body is often drawn from backgrounds characterized by low economic and social status, low educational achievement, marginal employment, and limited participation in community organizations." [74] The philosophy of the community college is to provide more equal educational opportunity for all members of society, and to provide services to the community that supports it. The community college is a local enterprise. In North Carolina, for example, the funds for establishment of a community college are split evenly between state and local revenues, and 40 percent of the operational funds are derived from local revenues. [75]

In the South, community colleges in 1968 accounted for approximately 16 percent of the region's college enrollment, with a high in Florida of 46 percent and a low of 3 percent in Louisiana. The community colleges enrolled 13 percent of all degree-credit students and three-fourths of all occupational program students in the region. [76] The majority enroll 500 to 5000 students, although a few vastly exceed this number. [77]

Curriculum

Of the Southern states, Florida has the most highly developed program of open-door community colleges. So far there have been no enrollment restrictions, but the system will eventually have to expand even further or redefine its admissions policies. In addition to offering freshman and sophomore parallel courses and vocational and technical training, the system has extensive programs in adult occupational education, especially in technical and health-related fields. The major universities can now concentrate on upper level and graduate education; furthermore, "there appears to be evidence . . . to indicate that the development of community colleges has increased in great measure the college attendance patterns." [78]

Student achievement is the most accurate measure of the success of the community college program, and the statistics indicate that the two-year colleges are falling short of their goals. "Unless student needs are met, the open door only creates a traffic problem." [79] Annual attrition rates are about 50 percent, and 75 percent of the low achievers withdraw within the first year. [80] Remedial and compensatory courses are often poorly designed and poorly taught and often are not evaluated carefully. The typical faculty member is "not in accord with the generally acknowledged purposes or with the principles of admission." [81]

The two-year institutions need to design programs that include college parallel, occupational, and general education courses to provide students with the maximum number of educational options. Programs must make allowances for individual rates of progress, and remedial programs and extracurricular cultural enrichment programs should be available (pending further evaluation of their effectiveness).

Access

Geographic location of community colleges has a significant influence on college attendance. The Carnegie Commission on the Future of Higher Education recommends the following: "If economies of scale are not a significant consideration, there is a strong case for discouraging community colleges from growing too large. State resources can be used more effectively to achieve the goal of a community college within relatively easy commuting distance of all students if plans call for increasing the number of institutions of moderate size rather than for a more restricted number of very large institutions."[82] However, Cross has noted than "even if all geographical and financial barriers could be eliminated, racial minorities, women, and children from low socioeconomic classes would still be sparsely represented."[83] Community colleges, if they are serious about their role, need to intensify their recruiting efforts; career and financial counseling should be available to all students, and work-study programs for summer and part-time employment should be available.

The community colleges are an important resource for providing educational opportunity for blacks. The open-door colleges generally have been integrated, at least in theory, from the beginning. Many of the characteristics of community colleges—low costs, geographical proximity, specialized programs—make them potentially attractive to disadvantaged students. Yet blacks are frequently reluctant to enroll in the predominantly white institutions and are often less than enthusiastic about their communtiy college experiences. The stigma of inferior status is an inhabiting factor on black enrollment,[84] and the educational programs are often unfortunately reminiscent of the vocation-oriented educational pigeonhole into which blacks have been directed since Reconstruction. Despite the relatively low costs of attending community colleges, particularly for day students, lack of money is the most frequently cited reason for dropping out.[85] Tuition and fee charges in some two-year colleges have doubled in less than five years in the 1960s.[86]

PREDOMINANTLY BLACK COLLEGES

Of the South's higher education institutions, the predominantly black colleges are in the most serious trouble. Their role in the education of Southern blacks cannot be overstated: three-quarters of the South's blacks enrolled in higher education institutions attend the 35 public and 69 private predominantly black colleges.[87] Nor can the potential of these institutions for providing educational opportunity for black youth in the future be dismissed lightly. As Goldman has noted:

> However paradoxical it may seem to look to colleges established expressly to serve a segregated Negro community as the central institution to lead the educational movement for integration, it is a fact of life . . . that the Negro community "for as long as any of us will be alive" will have to rely on those colleges for most of its educational needs. . . . Thus, while it is expected that the process of de-

segregation of both the white and Negro colleges will continue, the major burden of responsibility for the educational implementation of the transition to integration and a good society for Negro southerners will remain on the school predominantly serving Negroes. [88]

The Problems

Nearly every factor that spells potential disaster for higher education institutions is present among the traditionally black colleges. More than a quarter of them are not accredited, and of those that are, the available education is by nearly all standards inferior to that in the South's white institutions. [89] There are exceptions, of course: Fisk and the Atlanta University schools, Hampton, Dillard, and Tuskegee (private), and Texas Southern (public).

In expenditures per student the black schools spend only two-thirds of the national average. The salary level for professors is approximately 75 percent that of white schools. [90] Attrition runs from 40 to 70 percent due often not to academic failure, but to boredom and frustration. [91] The curriculum in the black colleges is one cause of the high attrition rate. The late sixties saw the introduction of black studies on campuses throughout the nation; surprisingly, the black colleges have been the last to establish courses and departments in black studies. In fact, innovation of any kind is rare. Course offerings frequently do not reflect employment opportunities. Graduate and professional degrees are available at twenty-one of the predominantly black schools, the doctorate at Atlanta University only. [92]

Another problem is relatively small enrollment, which results in both financial inefficiency and inadequate diversity of course offerings. In 1966-67, 65 of these schools enrolled fewer than 1,000 students, and 35 enrolled fewer than 500. At present the most critical problem is financing. Public black colleges rely on the state for three-fourths of their educational and operational budgets. Less than 1 percent of their income is derived from endowments (a median of $936,000 in 1964, as opposed to $8 million median endowment for white colleges); tuition and fees are low; alumni giving, which has never been substantial, is now seriously lagging. [93] With the exception of perhaps a dozen, the predominantly black colleges "have no endowment whatever, no alumni capable of supporting them more than at a token level, little time or imagination to develop programs which get federal or foundation support, few contacts with men who distribute such funds, and no obvious appeal to white philanthropy, faculty, or students." [94]

In their early days the black colleges were elementary schools, serving a student body of newly freed slaves. In the intervening years the dual school system in the South has insured that this situation would not improve a great deal. Unfortunately, many of the colleges have refused to come to terms with the inadequate preparation of their students. In 1964 only fifteen black institutions had compensatory programs of any sort, and only six had comprehensive programs. [95] "The fact that Negro colleges recruit students, most of whom are of very limited academic promise, is not necessarily an indictment of either the students or the colleges. We have the impression, however, supported by fragmentary statistics, that these colleges do even less to remedy their students' academic inadequacies than comparable white colleges. As a result each new generation of Negro professionals, and especially teachers, perpetuates the cycle of deprivation." [96]

Seemingly, this situation should have improved since desegregation of the public schools began. However, the best black students are being heavily recruited by white institutions. Nonblack enrollment at black colleges is very small and is not likely to get much larger. Black colleges are left with students with little preparation for college and Scholastic Aptitude Test scores averaging in the 300s (the bottom 5 to 10 percent of those taking the test). [97] The poor quality of the faculty, encouraged by lower salary levels, has been made worse by the nonreciprocal migration of younger, better-trained black professors to white institutions. And the black colleges have not been helped by the lack of foresight and imagination of many of their administrators. [94]

Alternatives

Black schools have kept tuition low enough so that over 60 percent of the families with one or more students enrolled have an annual income of less that $6,000 per year. [99] In terms of social desirability, Riesman notes that many black youths, especially from small towns and rural areas, "prefer an evil they know (segregation) to a promise they only half believe (integration)." [100] Many black students who do choose to attend white institutions transfer to black colleges, not only for academic and financial reasons, but because of the loneliness and discomfort they experience at the white institutions.

The argument against black colleges is that the education they provide prepares their students for neither skilled employment nor further education. Perhaps the best reason for salvaging and improving as many of these schools as possible is that a poor education is better than none. Negro-college enrollments have doubled since 1964 and may double again by 1980. [101] Enrollment by state is shown in table 4.9. If the marginal black colleges fold, thousands of potential students may have nowhere to go.

TABLE 4.9. *Black Undergraduate Enrollment, by Institution, and as a Percentage of Black College-Age Population, Fall 1970*

	In All Institutions	In Traditionally Black Institutions		In Traditionally White Institutions		Percent of 18-21 Age Group
		Public	Private	Public	Private	
United States	356,138	95,758	51,544	178,331	30,505	21.0
Alabama	14,519	6,183	6,036	2,117	183	21.2
Arkansas	5,899	2,955	1,211	1,513	220	23.0
Florida	13,940	3,841	2,715	7,177	213	18.5
Georgia	14,915	6,192	6,256	2,102	365	16.1
Kentucky	3,193	913	....	1,954	326	16.6
Louisiana	21,327	15,397	2,229	3,562	139	25.1
Mississippi	15,334	10,417	2,654	2,104	159	24.2
North Carolina	20,015	9,554	5,359	4,481	621	19.9
South Carolina	8,160	1,703	4,387	1,486	584	11.8
Tennessee	11,859	3,774	4,314	3,421	530	24.4
Texas	21,878	6,881	4,576	8,982	1,439	20.4
Virginia	12,499	6,233	3,780	2,255	231	18.3

Source: Southern Regional Education Board, *Fact Book on Higher Education in the South, 1971-72* (Atlanta: Southern Regional Education Board, 1972), p. 42.
Note: Data for Oklahoma are not available.

Interinstitutional cooperation holds promise for many weaker black colleges. Permanent arrangements of this sort raise fears of loss of identity; for this reason, except for colleges with very small enrollments, the most productive cooperative programs are short-term programs with specific purposes. Many benefits could be derived from cooperation among institutions. Extensive overlapping of course offerings is a severe drain on limited resources. For example, at predominantly black colleges "there are now 20 fields other than teacher-training in which the M.A. is offered," all of which are also offered at major state universities that now admit blacks. [102] By concentrating on their stronger fields and phasing out inadequate, overly expensive or duplicative programs, the black colleges would raise the quality of their overall educational program. The other side of the interinstitutional approach is that the predominantly white colleges must be willing to accept more black students, and to provide remedial programs to enable them to compete with educationally advantaged students. [103]

Individual institutions should give more attention to the development of compensatory programs for the freshman year and the summer. The majority of the students need remedial work in at least one subject area. [104] Furthermore, black colleges should extend their services into the larger black community by offering adult vocational training and retraining programs.

The most critical needs are financial: for "(1) basic operating income which is stable, recurring, and sufficient to permit dramatically increased faculty salaries, and (2) supplementary funds which will support the upgrading of curriculum and instruction, a full battery of remedial and compensatory programs, and the expansion of administrative services." [105] The Carnegie Commission recommended that the federal government triple its appropriations to black colleges. It further advocated the establishment of a new federal agency, with a budget of $40 million a year, to study methods of curriculum improvement. [106] The colleges, for their part, should make every effort to enroll at least a thousand students, to realize economies of scale.

A more radical recommendation was made by Riesman and Jencks: the future development of the nonelite Negro college should be in the direction of becoming an authentic community college. [107] Such a college would offer many types of teaching services for the rural black communities in which they are located. They could also serve as a means of channeling to local community federal funds that local public agencies would not handle. Riesman and Jencks also suggest that some black colleges could become intermediate schools where inadequate secondary school education could be remedied. Hopefully, larger white universities then would cooperate by accepting the black student even if he lacked the ordinary credentials for admission.

GRADUATE EDUCATION

The phenomenal expansion of doctoral training in the United States in the 1960s was precipitated by the launching of Sputnik in 1957. Following that event the federal government undertook reassessments of manpower needs and concluded with projections of a drastic shortage of highly trained specialists, particularly in the sciences, but to some extent in nearly all fields. The government responded to this unnerving prospect with massive grants in support of advanced work, first in the sciences and later in the social sciences and humanities. "Federal funds stimulated, but state funds largely underwrote, the numerous new doctoral institutions which came into existence in the 1960's. . . . State coordinating and planning boards, aware of the disproportionate funding required of the states, nevertheless were unable to resist the lure of creating a 'great university' or a 'center of excellence.' " [108]

In the South, graduate enrollment more than tripled between 1957 and 1967. Between 1949-50 and 1968-69 doctorate production at Southern universities increased more than ninefold, compared with an increase of slightly more than threefold for the United States as a whole. [109] In 1965 the Southern Regional Education Board noted: "The region's growth (between 1956 and 1965) has been unusually high at the doctoral level (106.9%) and rather low at the master's level (42.4%). Actually, the South has increased its doctorate production at about the same rate as the nation in disciplines other than education, but a heavy increase in the number of education doctorates caused the overall growth of Southern doctorates markedly to exceed the national rate." [110]

In a 1960 study of graduate education in the United States, no Southern university graduate program was ranked in the top two categories, although 10 out of the next group of 27 were Southern. [111] By contrast, a 1970 survey of graduate programs commented: "Particularly notable is the South, where, in 1969, 256, or 73 percent of the faculties . . . merited a rating of 'adequate plus' or above. In 1964, only 207, or 59 percent, had such ratings." Forty percent of the South's graduate programs showed a net increase in "quality of graduate faculty" of more than .2 on a five-point scale. The South showed the greatest percentage increase (34 percent) in programs in the top score category. Still, "in the highest score category . . . the South accounts for only 11 percent, less than half its share of all the programs surveyed." [112]

Impressive as the figures on the expansion in the number of graduate programs may be, this is not necessarily an indication of improved quality. The fragmentation that results may lower the quality of not only graduate education but undergraduate education as well. As Miller commented in 1970, "it appears that we face the strong likelihood that we have already authorized more doctoral programs than are desirable, at least in most states. Careful state-level control over the establishment of additional programs must be exercised to prevent further proliferation, to weed out unsuccessful programs, and to nurture the healthy growth of doctoral education in the institutions where it is properly located." [113] One Southern state authorized five doctoral-level institutions and another authorized four between 1965 and 1970. [114] As for the productivity of many of these institutions, Governor Robert Scott of North Carolina noted in 1970 that 40 of North Carolina's 105 doctoral programs produced no graduates in 1968-69, and 75 percent produced four or fewer each. Only 14 programs produced as many as 10 graduates. On the master's degree level, 85 of the state's 300 programs produced no graduates. About half produced fewer than 10 graduates each. [115]

The problem of the rapid proliferation of graduate programs was made more acute by the cutbacks in federal support during the late 1960s and early 1970s. Institutions that were highly dependent on federal funding were forced to cut graduate enrollments and to turn to state governments to take up the slack. The money required to produce a doctorate may reduce funds available for other levels of education; allowing for the student attrition factor, the average cost of a science doctorate has been estimated at $62,000, [116] an amount sufficient for the undergraduate education of six or eight students.

States should undertake immediate reevaluation of manpower supply and demand. Planning must be done with an eye to the long-range implications of the measures that are recommended. Immediate and drastic cutbacks in doctoral programs could conceivably prove to be as calamitous as the careless expansion of the past decade. The anticipated shortage of funds in the near future probably will require some radical alterations in graduate education in the region. Graduate programs that are weak, too costly, or underproductive should be eliminated. At the very least, rigid standards should be set for the authorization of any further doctoral programs or institutions, and long-range planning should aim to reduce the number of public institutions offering the doctorate in any field to one or two per state. "Individual states and regions now lacking adequate graduate quality in selected fields can hope to arrive at the threshold of quality only by making the hard decision to specialize in particular areas and share their programs." [117] There should be specialization by university, by school within universities, and by department. Schools and departments should not try to be all things to all people. Above all, graduate education for a few should not hinder the improvement of undergraduate education for the many.

Policy Recommendations

Much money has been invested in higher education in recent years, and some has been invested unwisely. Yet higher education is a vital tool in the South's development of its human resources, and will require continued investments of federal, state, and local government and private resources. To insure that higher education will play its necessary role at a tolerable cost, a number of changes should be made at the state, institutional, and sub-institutional levels.

ORGANIZATION AND STRUCTURE

Establish Single Board of Higher Education at State Level

Statewide planning and coordination is essential to the orderly development of all components of the South's higher education system. Thought must be given not only to the immediate task of allocating funds more efficiently among the state's programs, but also to the ultimate goal of fully coordinating the assignment of educational tasks and responsibilities among the state's institutions. This can be best accomplished by a single board at the state level. The board should be particularly attentive to the role of community colleges, predominantly black schools, and private institutions. To insure that they have political influence as well as formal authority, state legislators should be kept closely informed of the board's work. With the expansion of higher education opportunity, and with the growth of community colleges, the rationale for rigidly segregating "public" from "higher" education is weakening. The two need to be more closely integrated, with consultation between the state board and public education officials on how changes in one sector will affect the other.

Adopt "Academic Common Market" Plan

The Southern Regional Education Board in 1973 approved a plan in which public universities with "uncommon" graduate programs would agree to admit out-of-state students to those programs without charging nonresident tuition. The states should adopt a plan of this type and should extend it to undergraduate programs. [118]

Reduce Disciplinary Isolationism within Universities

Too often there is no communication among professors in different disciplines. Restructuring the university along interdisciplinary lines wherever possible would alleviate this problem. Disciplines such as political science, economics, and sociology have a common methodology and differ only in the practical problems of the institutions they focus on. Departmental lines should be dropped in selected universities and the three disciplines combined as social science; this also might facilitate the marshaling of social science skills to deal with social problems, perhaps through problem-oriented research institutes.

ADMINISTRATION

Introduce New Selection Criteria for College Administrators

The experience of businessmen and politicians may equip them to run a college campus better than some of the men who are currently trying to do the job. Appointments might be made from the ranks of business and politics or, alternatively, people interested in careers in university administration should be required to have training in such areas as management techniques.

Change Faculty Tenure and Salary Systems

Professors' salaries should be based on productivity, not longevity. Not only contributions in research and publishing but also superior class-room teaching should be rewarded by higher pay. Universities should experiment with long-range contracts for professors as a prelude to phasing out the tenure system. Tenure, defended as a bulwark of academic freedom, currently is more significant for the financial burdens it places on universities and for its discouragement of curriculum revision. Universities need to be free to adapt their curriculum and faculty more rapidly than the tenure system permits.

Some universities also could better utilize their instructional staffs by setting more realistic and less uniform teaching loads. During the 1960s increased financial resources often led to reduction of the number of courses and students assigned to an individual professor. This practice was good to a point, but that point has been passed in the myriad cases of nonpublishing professors teaching no more than four courses a year to a total of sixty students or fewer.

Abolish Inadequate Academic Programs

Any department should be able to justify its existence within the university community on some basis other than the fact that it has been around for years. This could lead to abolishing departments that are obsolete or have students and faculty below the caliber of the rest of the university. If the subject matter and teaching methods of a department no longer satisfy the needs of the university and the society it serves, money spent maintaining that department should be reallocated to another department that fulfills its own function. All universities do not need to have all types of departments.

Require Policy Makers to Formulate Explicit Goals

College presidents should set up goals committees with representation from all of the constituencies that have an interest in higher education—students, parents, faculty, alumni, administrators, boards of trustees, and, in the case of public institutions, the legislature, the governor, and the public. Federal and state policy-makers as well should explicitly articulate the goals they are pursuing in higher education.

Establish Long-Range Budgeting and Planning Procedures

Budgeting and planning procedures comparable to those of corporations should be established. University planners should approach the university as an open system, identifying and defining the subsystems within it (people, physical plant, financial resources, curriculum). Computers and higher education policy models may be used to simulate the effects of alternative plans on the university. Part of the ongoing planning process of the university should be a provision for institutional self-evaluation beyond what is required for accreditation purposes. Self-assessment of an institution's effectiveness in achieving its goals would be aided by the development of computerized systems of relevant information.

Southern schools should concentrate not only on the problem of acquiring additional funds, but also on developing programs and policies that make more efficient use of the funds currently available. Inter-institutional cooperation in teaching, research, and fund-raising can help.

Adopt Rational Criteria for Resource Allocation Decisions

Resources of the universities must be allocated in a manner consistent with stated goals. Many current practices of resource allocation are not subjected to cost-benefit analysis. For example, college libraries often develop the habit of buying large numbers of books, especially old manuscripts, at the wish of a single faculty member. Such allocations should be scrutinized for their value to the entire university community. More libraries should be developed jointly by more than one college. More universities might experiment with what University of Pennsylvania president Martin Meyerson called "responsibility centers" (similar to corporate "profit centers"), where financial decisions and responsibility for living with the consequences are partially decentralized.

FINANCE

Adopt as Fundamental Policy that Ability to Pay Shall Not be a Criterion for Admission

Every Southern state should commit itself to the principle that ability to pay for a college education should not be a qualification for attending one of the state's institutions of higher learning. Ability and motivation should be the only requirements.

Keep Direct Institutional Support to a Minimum

The 1972 Federal Education Act authorized payments of the direct financial aid for which institutions had lobbied. However, even if massive doses of federal money did begin to flow into higher education, its problems would not be solved. What is needed is not subsidies for the status quo, but incentives for higher education institutions to upgrade quality and to extend opportunity.

Consider Alternative Schemes for Financing Higher Education

States should consider alternative financing schemes. Two types of student aid, deferred tuition and guaranteed loans, are available at some institutions. Although these programs do enable more people to attend college, they do not meet the basic objections to the present system of financing higher education through state subsidization of institutions. The following plans represent several alternatives to the present system.

Voucher Plan / This method would entail the state's giving direct grants to students in the form of vouchers, which could be used to pay for an education at any public or private institution in the state. The extent of aid that the state would grant to students under this plan might range from instructional costs alone to the full cost of a college education. The amount of the voucher could vary with the income of the student's parents.

A voucher plan using the instructional cost of colleges as the maximum payment to students is little different from the present financing system. It would still force the state to finance the remainder of the cost to the institution. If students are required to pay the full cost of their education and are given assistance through a graduated voucher system based on family income, the objections to present methods of financing would be answered. All state aid for instruction would go to students and none to the institutions. This would force the state colleges to become comparatively student-oriented. It would also insure that more affluent students would bear more of the cost of their education, freeing aid for poorer students.

A major objection to the full-cost voucher system is its impact on middle-income students. If the graduation of aid to students is too rapid over middle-income brackets, these families will be priced out of educational institutions. On the other hand, if the graduation is slower and extends into the higher-income brackets, the cost of the voucher system soon becomes exorbitant.

Full-Cost Pricing and Guaranteed Loans / A combination of approaches comes closest to meeting our criteria for a financing scheme (aid directly to students, according to need). The student would pay the full cost of his educational program. States would not fund any institution but would guarantee loans to all students. The amount that could be borrowed would depend on the family's income. Lower-income families could borrow the full cost of the program plus the amount of income foregone by the student by going to college rather than immediately taking a job. Repayments and interest rates would vary with postgraduation earnings. A variation of this scheme would be tuition based on family income; Beloit College in Wisconsin has announced charges based on a sliding scale.

Continuation of Small Grants for Specific Projects / The merit of granting funds directly to students is that the fulcrum of power might be shifted from the faculty and administration to the prospective students. This alteration might force colleges to provide what students think they need, not recruit students for what the college has to offer. However, colleges with small student bodies or large extension programs might suffer financially under this system. Therefore, states might continue to subsidize directly certain research and extension projects.

ADMISSIONS

Maintain Open-Door Admissions Policy at Community Colleges

Southern states have increased the number of junior or community colleges, bringing closer the time when every citizen will be within commuting distance of one of these institutions. They should offer both academic and occupational courses, and they should be open to anyone who has the equivalent of a high school education.

Recruit Minority-Group Students and Encourage Their Entry into New Fields

If the goal of a more fully integrated society is to be attained, minority-group students must not only be recruited and equipped for university participation but should also be encouraged through financial incentives to go into fields they are not presently entering.

CURRICULUM

Involve Students in Planning Their Own Curricula

A goal of curriculum reform should be greater student participation in their own education. Students are more than passive consumers of knowledge. The wise professor recognizes that mutual exploration of his subject with his students is the most valid learning experience. Some colleges have begun experimenting with such approaches; for example, an undergraduate student in Program II at Duke University designs his own course of study suited to his individual needs and abilities. The student must have exhibited unusual interest or talent in his chosen field and must present a well-thought-out study plan approved by a faculty committee. Academic credit can be given for off-campus projects.

Students also deserve input into decisions affecting them less directly. There should be voting student members on all administrative committees, on most faculty committees, and on boards of trustees. Preferably, students should select from their own ranks whom they want to represent them. Students should be included on selection committees for deans and college presidents, and they should have a part in decisions on hiring and retaining faculty.

Provide Opportunities for Lifelong Education

Adult education should be a major responsibility of higher education institutions—for vocational, avocational, and general education purposes. Education should no longer be thought of as a process that is continuous to a given age and then ends; rather, people should be able to enter and leave institutions of higher education when they choose, regardless of their life stage. Colleges have particular community responsibilities to older people who have left or will soon leave gainful employment. [119] Courses should be offered where adults want to take them, which in many cases will mean off campus.

Promote Student Internships, and Expand
Advanced Placement and Compensatory Programs

Student public service internships offer an excellent opportunity for learning. Schools also should offer plans whereby students alternate a semester on campus with a semester of work related to their career choice. The practical experience and study are likely to be mutually reinforcing. [120]

Most educational researchers agree that in many cases the first two years of college are more appropriate to high school education, both in scope and content. Advanced placement tests administered to freshmen have been used for a number of years to allow students to skip the first year of certain courses. Usually advanced placement is restricted to one or two fields, however, and frequently no credit is given for courses skipped. Advanced placement should be extended to cover all freshmen and sophomore courses, with credit for the bypassed courses. The result would be reduction in the time required to complete a degree, and a consequent reduction in the cost of the student's education.

The other side of the coin is the student who brings to college a history of economic, social, and educational deficiency—and the number of such students will increase as efforts are made to expand educational opportunity to all who desire it. An optional "foundation year" [121] with intensive instruction and counseling in all basic subjects would help to prepare the disadvantaged student to compete in college-level studies. The community college would be the appropriate place to offer a foundation year. Then, minimum-load requirements might have to be reduced to enable the student to proceed at his own rate. Although this could result in some cases in increasing the time required to earn a degree, it is less costly in the long run than the money lost due to attrition.

ATHLETICS

Deemphasize Intercollegiate Sports

Southern universities should take a page from the manual of Ivy League schools that have maintained large sports programs without letting the images the institutions project be based upon the success of their teams.

STUDENTS

In Loco Parentis

An increasing number of institutions of higher education are conceding that students have a legitimate grievance in regard to the university's acting in loco parentis. The doctrine that the university student is not yet mature enough to be responsible for his actions outside the classroom is obsolete. The function of the university is to teach, not to police its students' personal lives.

Universities should get out of the business of providing nonteaching facilities, especially housing. Dormitory regulations have been a major source of friction between students and college administrators. If it is not economically feasible in the short run for the university to divest itself of its dormitories, it should at least assume the role of a normal landlord rather than a parent. Dormitories should be converted into university office buildings, or sold or leased for private interests to operate.

The university's propensity for behaving as a judging parent surfaces whenever one of its students finds himself in trouble with civil authorities. Not content to let the law courts mete out justice, some universities try students in their own courts and pronounce sentences ranging from a reprimand to expulsion. Since this is an apparent violation of the Fourth Amendment prohibition of "double jeopardy," the practice has begun to be successfully challenged.

Improve Counseling Procedures

Too many students in large and not-so-large universities feel that they have no place to turn for individualized counseling in regard to their academic programs and career prospects. Universities should regard counseling not as a minor part of teaching and student services, but as a vital component of higher education, and they should devote significant manpower resources to the task.

THE UNIVERSITY AND SOCIETY

Change Focus of Universities to a More Outward-Looking One

Unless universities are serving the larger community outside of their walls, they are not performing adequately their role in contemporary society. The motto on the seal of Auburn University lists "Research, Instruction, Extension" as the three goals for the university. Too often universities do a good job of the first two while neglecting the third. Yet reasearch is of limited benefit to society unless its findings are widely disseminated. Agriculture is one of the few areas in which the results of research (usually at agriculture experiment stations) are made available on a systematic basis (through a network of extension service agents).

Direct Energies of Universities toward Societal Problem-Solving

In choosing the areas to emphasize in its teaching and research, universities should look at the problems and opportunities of the cities, states, and regions they serve, and direct their energies accordingly. The university is equipped to help in dealing with complex problems requiring expertise in many areas. For example, if land-grant colleges would give more attention to rural, nonfarm development, they would be performing a needed service that they are best equipped to provide. Universities do not have any magic answers to the problems of society, but many people within universities have the training and interests to help other institutions deal effectively with these problems.

5. Toward a Responsive Southern Politics

The Setting

The framers of the Constitution and the framers of the constitutions of the individual states were unanimous on one point: the system of government should be democratic, or a "government by the people." In a democracy, government should be representative, responsive, and accountable to the people, and should be judged by how closely it approximates this goal.

To determine how the South has measured up in these terms, we will examine (1) the effects of one-partyism, (2) the extension of the right of political participation to blacks, (3) the extent of unequal justice and unequal representation, and (4) who benefits from existing forms of governmental structures. Then we will examine approaches that attempt to invest more people with more power.

DEFINITION OF THE PROBLEM

One-Party Domination

The politics of the South through most of the last century has been the politics of the Democratic party, or more precisely, of the Democratic parties of the individual states. Other characteristics that distinguish the political profile of the South have been low voter-registration and a low percentage of participation by those who were registered. The figures are especially depressed by the large-scale, long-term exclusion of blacks from political participation until recently in many areas of the South.

Although the trend in recent years has been for voter participation in the South to approach the national average, low levels of registration and voting remain a problem. Lewis A. Froman, Jr., found six factors influencing voter turnout for congressional elections: (1) the greater the percentage of nonwhite population, the smaller the voting turnout, (2) the smaller the percentage of owner-occupied dwelling units, the smaller the voting turnout, (3) the smaller the percentage of urban population, the smaller the voting turnout, (4) the lower the population per square mile, the lower the voting turnout, (5) the less competitive the district, the lower the voting turnout, and (6) Democratic districts have smaller voting turnouts than do Republican districts. [1] Southern states tend to rank poorly on five of the six factors associated with voting turnout; in owner-occupied dwellings, Froman found no significant differences between the regions. The factor of special significance in the South has been the lack of party competition.

The most important reason for the dominance of the Democratic party is the common historical experience of the Southern states. "The Civil War and its aftermath, the racial composition of Southern states and the determination of the South to keep its Negro population from exercising political power, all contribute independently to one-partyism in the South," Thomas Dye wrote. [2] The Republican party, as the party of the Reconstruction, was anathema to several generations of Southerners who saw Democratic unity as the way to guarantee white supremacy. Although Reconstruction is now one hundred years in the past, the rank and file of the Democratic party tends to perpetuate itself. [3]

The political domination of Southern states by elements of state Democratic parties was virtually unbroken through the first half of the twentieth century. In only two instances were there deviations in presidential voting: the 1928 revolt against Al Smith, whom many Southerners saw as the epitome of the Yankee-Catholic-Wet and Big-City menace, and the Dixiecrat revolt of 1948. The Dixiecrats carried only the Southern states in which they ran as Democrats, having won over the state conventions and replaced the Truman-Barkley ticket on the ballot. In states where they ran under the Dixiecrat label, they did badly.

Thus for years—George Tindall dates it from 1880 to the election of 1948—the South was indeed "solid." As Tindall observes:

> Almost from the birth of the Solid South, reports of its death flew on every shifting breeze of politics. "I am looking every year for a break-up of the Solid South," Henry Watterson of the Louisville *Courier-Journal* wrote in 1887. The third nomination of Grover Cleveland "snapped the last cord which binds freemen to the Democratic party," said Robert Beverly, Jr., of Virginia, in 1892. Different southerners reacted in the same way to William Jennings Bryan. In 1908, Walter Hines Page welcomed "the impending and inevitable breaking of the Solid South" when he introduced William Howard Taft to the North Carolina Society of New York. In 1909 Enoch M. Banks foresaw "The Passing of the Solid South" in

the *South Atlantic Quarterly*. In 1910, James W. Garner predicted a "New Politics for the South" in the *Annals of the American Academy*. . . . The rise of Populism in the 1890's, the bolt of the Hoovercrats in 1928, reaction against the New Deal in the 1930's and 1940's, all gave rise to predictions of imminent breakup. [4]

Although allegiance to the national Democratic party began to disintegrate after 1948, state and in particular local elections have in many areas of the South not yet had genuine two-party competition. [5] The Republican party has become active in some Southern states, and indeed in Texas, Florida, Tennessee, North Carolina, and Virginia there is organized strength; yet by the early 1970s the great majority of voters in the South were still registered as Democrats. Not all of these voters vote Democratic, of course. The point is that in spite of Republican gains in some elections, these gains have not been reflected in large-scale switching of party registration. A 1967 published study of Mississippi voters found that although there had been some switching from the Democratic party in response to positions on racial integration and social problems taken by the national party, 90 percent of those who switched from the Democratic party considered themselves "Independent" rather than Republican. The analyst remarked, "Though the Republican image was probably better in 1967 than it had been for 100 years, it was still not a very positive one. Thus the Republican Party had still not overcome a century of loyalty to the Democratic Party." [6]

Although the Democratic party is the majority party nationally, national opinion surveys have shown that the South continues to be the region with highest levels of Democratic party self-identification. (This is a psychological, rather than a formal identification; survey respondents are asked if they think of themselves as members of the Democratic or Republican parties, or as Independents). State studies have shown the same result: in five Southern and border states in September 1968 the percentage of voters identifying themselves as Democrats ranged from a low of 53 percent in Georgia to a high of 66 percent in North Carolina. Those who identify themselves as Republicans usually are a fourth of the electorate or less, and in 1968 and 1970 in Georgia only 13-14 percent of the respondents said they considered themselves Republicans. When questions refer directly to *state* party identification, Republicans do little better; in Florida in 1970, 64 percent said they considered themselves Florida Democrats and 23 percent called themselves Florida Republicans, and in Georgia the percentages were 67 percent Democrat and 10 percent Republican. A panel survey in North Carolina and Florida showed no increase in Republican self-identification between

1968 and 1972, and showed no greater Republican self-identification in general versus state party terms. [7]

Discrimination

The central theme of Southern history, as stated by U. B. Phillips, has been the place of the black man and the corollary determination of whites to keep their region a "white man's country." Thus whites have attempted to enshrine permanently in their laws the idea of their racial superiority even after Negro slavery was abolished. The black man in the South has been the primary reason for the development of many political institutions, and in fact a regional way of life, but he has had little active role in his region's destiny until recently.

Following the Civil War, the Southern Redeemers wasted no time rewriting the constitutions of their Southern states. One of the first devices written into the constitutions to allow most white men to vote but to exclude almost all blacks was the "grandfather clause," which stated that any applicant who had a father or grandfather registered to vote before 1865 could be registered. This, of course, eliminated all those whose parents were slaves.

The grandfather clause was struck down in 1915 by the U.S. Supreme Court. Many Southern states then moved to the adoption of an "understanding clause" for qualification for voting. It required that an applicant interpret a clause of the state or federal constitution to the satisfaction of the registrar. With black applicants the registrar's standards were high indeed. Southern lawmakers were not afraid to adopt evasions that were rejected by their forebears. Judge John Minor Wisdom in 1965 found that in 1898 the constitutional convention in Louisiana "rejected an understanding clause as too obnoxiously a fraud and adopted instead a grandfather clause." Only after the Supreme Court found the grandfather clause unconstitutional did Louisiana hold a convention, without minutes, and adopt an understanding clause. And this was not used until the demise of the next great evasion, the white primary. [8]

The white primary excluded Negroes from voting in the Democratic primary and thus from voting in the election that counted most. It was declared unconstitutional in 1944, when the U.S. Supreme Court in *Smith* v. *Allright* ruled that although a political party was a private organization, in the performance of state elective functions it lost its private character, and therefore its exclusion of people on account of race violated the Fifteenth Amendment.

With the loss of the white primary, reliance was placed on the poll tax already in existence. Many of the devices used to keep blacks from participating in the political system also served to minimize the participation of the poorer, less-educated (and often rural) whites. The tax was usually cumulative and the deadline for payment was either not announced or difficult to determine. It took an amendment to the United States Constitution to terminate the use of the poll tax to deny any citizen the right to vote for federal officials. Literacy tests came into vogue after other methods of defeating registration efforts were disallowed. A major provision of the 1965 Civil Rights Act was aimed at the suspension of literacy tests in many of the Southern states.

It is ironic that the best examples of innovation within the political system and of the effective and rapid functioning of state government have come in support of racial segregation. If the time and energy spent in that cause can be refocused, perhaps they can positively affect the outputs of state and local government.

SPECIFICATION OF INSTITUTIONAL CHARACTERISTICS

Electoral Politics

In the presidential election of 1960, when a record 63.1 percent of American voters of voting age voted, only Oklahoma and Kentucky of the Southern states approached the national average (see table 5.1). The

TABLE 5.1. *Voting Turnout as a Percentage of Voting-Age Population, 1960 and 1968 Presidential Elections*

	1960	1968		1960	1968
United States	63.1	60.7	Mississippi	25.3	53.2
			North Carolina	52.9	54.3
Alabama	30.8	52.7	Oklahoma	63.1	61.2
Arkansas	40.8	53.3	South Carolina	30.4	46.7
Florida	48.6	53.0	Tennessee	49.8	53.7
Georgia	29.2	43.4	Texas	41.2	48.7
Kentucky	57.6	51.2	Virginia	32.8	50.1
Louisiana	44.6	54.8			

Source: U.S. Department of Commerce, Bureau of the Census, *Statistical Abstract of the United States, 1972,* p. 375.

average for the thirteen states of the South was 40.7 percent. Presidential voting always brings out more voters than elections in nonpresidential years. Yet in 1962, while 46.7 percent of the nation was voting in electing its United States representatives, the South mustered a vote of only 23.9 percent of the voting-age population. In the one-party states of the South, most state and local elections were decided in the Democratic primary; before the Voting Rights Act of 1965, many blacks had no chance to participate: both practices worked to depress participation rates.

While the percentage of participation did not increase significantly in the nation as a whole from 1960 to 1968, participation in the Southern states did increase significantly. By 1968, when the nation voted 60.7 percent, the South was less than ten percentage points behind, and only three states (Georgia, South Carolina, and Texas) has less than 50 percent of their voting-age population participating in the presidential election. In 1972, 63 percent of those of voting age in the nation reported that they voted, compared with 55.4 percent (and 47.8 percent of blacks) in the South. [9]

The dominance of the Democrats has left a legacy of political structures and distinctive political style that has come to be widely accepted as characteristic of the South. A system that depressed voting registration and participation obviously leads to control of political processes by those who do vote and who do contest and win offices. Virginia provides a striking example: the Byrd machine, built and managed by the late Senator Harry F. Byrd, Sr. The voting population of Virginia was so small between 1925 and 1945 that control of between 4 and 6 percent of the electorate often assured victory in the state Democratic primary— which was, in the words of the old cliché, tantamount to election. [10] It was not until the mid-1960s that the Byrd machine finally lost control of the state in the wake of the defeats of Senator Willis Robertson and Congressman Howard W. Smith.

Louisiana and Texas are unusual in the one-party South in that each contains party factions that have remained largely unchanged over time. In Louisiana, the factions are a result of the history of the Long family and its opponents; in Texas, economic interests and the special interests of labor and Mexican-Americans come into play. The factionalism of Louisiana is near death as memories of the "Kingfish" and his brother Earl fade in the public mind; the remaining Long, Senator Russell Long, has been reelected every six years with little opposition. [11] Political factions in Texas suggest a "modern" division based on socioeconomic differences. Arrayed against each other are what have been known as the Yarborough wing and the Connally wing. The former, named for the former senator Ralph Yarborough, is composed of liberals, organized labor, blacks, and Mexican-Americans. The latter, named for the former governor and secretary of the treasury John Connally, contains middle-class whites, farmers, cattlemen, and the oil interest. So far neither wing has found life impossible in the Democratic party, although Connally himself has. Not unlike the national Democratic party, which has tolerated diverse ideological positions, Democrats in Texas demonstrate the potential strength and the recurrent fragility of attempts to broaden the scope of the party.

In part of the South, then, in state and local elections, the Democratic party has served the function of a two-party system. In spite of general Southern dislike of many positions taken by the national party, Democrats in most Southern states have thus far survived challenges to their control of a broad position on the liberal-to-conservative spectrum.

To the extent that "left-right" is a useful distinction, the forces of the right that have moved against the Democrats have usually been mustered by the region's fledgling Republican party. Alexander Heard predicted in 1952, "In the long run southern conservatives will find neither in a separatist group nor in the Democratic party an adequate vehicle of political expression. If this is true, they must turn to the Republican party."[12] In the 1964 Johnson-Goldwater election "antagonism toward the national Democratic party was of such a high intensity in the Deep South that a number of Democratic candidates at the grassroots level were hurt by it. Seven of the ten new seats won by the Republican congressional party were added by Deep South electorates, and in addition, impressive numbers of local Republicans were elected."[13] Republican victories were repeated in some places in 1968, and Republicans did better in the Upper South. In 1972 President Nixon swept the South.

Yet the Republicans in the South are far from being on a firm footing, for their inroads between 1964 and 1972 may reflect Southern dissatisfaction with national Democratic stands on racial issues more than an embracing of Republican political tenets. Matthews and Prothro found that "economic conservatism and racial prejudice do not tend to go together in the South. Among white Democrats in the South, in fact, economic liberals are much more likely to be strict segregationists than are avowed opponents of the welfare state."[14] Clotfelter and Hamilton found that Wallace supporters and Republicans were "different kinds of people," and that continued alliance might be difficult.[15] From its inception the Republican party has been affected by the one-party culture of the South. Its great problem has been to say something other than "me, too" and still say something that voters want to hear. For state and local offices, Republicans have succeeded in this effort in only a few states.

Government

State / The national Citizens Conference on State Legislatures completed in 1971 a ranking of state legislatures of the fifty states using these criteria: functional ability, or structural and organizational capacity to make laws intelligently; accountability, primarily to the constituency; information-handling capability, or access to information about bills, laws, and other informational resources; independence from the other branches of government and from special interests; and representativeness of constituents. Table 5.2 shows that by these criteria, Southern

TABLE 5.2. *Ranking of Southern Legislatures by the Citizens Conference on State Legislatures, 1971*

	Overall	Functional	Accountable	Informed	Independent	Representative
Florida	4	5	8	4	1	30
Oklahoma	14	9	27	24	22	8
Tennessee	26	30	44	11	9	26
Kentucky	31	49	2	48	44	7
Louisiana	33	47	39	33	13	14
Virginia	34	25	19	27	26	48
Texas	38	45	36	43	45	17
Mississippi	42	46	43	45	20	28
South Carolina	44	50	45	39	10	46
Georgia	45	40	49	36	33	38
Arkansas	46	41	40	46	34	33
North Carolina	47	24	37	44	47	44
Alabama	50	48	50	49	50	41

Source: *New York Times,* 4 February, 1971.

states fared badly when compared to the rest of the nation. Only Florida, where a new constitution went into effect in 1969, is listed in the top ten states, ranking fourth. The next Southern state is Oklahoma, ranking fourteenth, followed by Tennessee, ranking twenty-sixth. Four ranked in the thirties and the rest of the southern states ranked in the forties, with Alabama ranking fiftieth. Although the Citizens Conference does not pretend that its survey is the final word, it seems clear that, as deficient as legislatures are nationally, those in the Southern states manage to be a little worse.

All Southern legislatures have been reappointed since the *Baker* v. *Carr* and *Reynolds* v. *Simms*[16] decisions, and the present representation is very close to the ideal of one-man, one-vote. Reapportionment overwhelmed the legislatures neither with new Republicans nor with new liberals. Although some argue that the state legislative process itself is not conducive to liberal action,[17] Florida combined its court-ordered reapportionment with a new constitution and made great strides toward developing a legislature that included representatives with a diversity of perspectives.

Reapportionment has had some effect in increasing the number of Republican legislators, but the legislatures of most Southern states are still dominated by the Democratic party. Table 5.3 shows the party

TABLE 5.3. *Composition of State Legislatures,*
by Party Affiliation, 1970

	Lower House		Upper House	
	Dem.	Rep.	Dem.	Rep.
United States	3,345	2,139	1,100	760
Alabama	104	2	35	.....
Arkansas	98	2	34	1
Florida	81	38	33	15
Georgia	173	22	50	6
Kentucky	72	28	23	15
Louisiana	104	1	38	1
Mississippi	120	1	49	3
North Carolina	96	24	43	7
Oklahoma	78	21	39	9
South Carolina	113	11	42	2
Tennessee	56	43	19	13
Texas	140	10	29	2
Virginia	76	24	33	7

Source: U.S. Department of Commerce, Bureau of the Census, *Statistical Abstract of the United States, 1972*, p. 371.
Note: Excludes one Independent each for Mississippi and Virginia in the lower houses, and two vacancies for South Carolina and one Independent for Tennessee in the upper houses.

composition of Southern legislatures in 1970. Of the legislatures as composed in 1968, only the Houses of Representatives of Tennessee and Kentucky were truly competitive by party, and in both cases the Republicans suffered major losses between 1968 and 1970. Significant GOP minorities exist in Florida, North Carolina, and Oklahoma. All the Senates are controlled by the Democrats, with those of Kentucky and Tennessee being the only ones with majorities of less than two to one.

As a rule Southern legislatures are overworked, underpaid, and usually lacking in adequate staff, office space, or time to legislate (much less prepare to legislate). Their position is complicated by that of the Southern governor.

The North Carolina Governor's Committee on State Government Reorganization in its 1971 report to the General Assembly found the organization of the executive "unresponsive, uncoordinated, unwieldy and impossible for the average citizen to understand." [18] The governor is in the illogical position of having little control over the executive branch, some of the leaders of which are elected and many of the departments of which are controlled by boards over which he has only limited appointive power. Governors must then "assert their influence, not in the executive branch, but over the legislature." [19] Malcolm Jewell points out that "the governor is not so much usurping the power of the legislature (although he does gain a measure of control over their considerations) as he fills a void in leadership where there is no party organization or discipline." [20]

The system of justice in the South has been frequently indicted as racist in enforcement and administration. [21] There is much evidence of racial prejudice in jury selection, admission of testimony, and criminal penalties, and even occasional resistance or outright refusals by Southern Federal District judges to carry out mandates from higher courts. [22] State judges in the past have been deft in "avoiding as much of federal rulings on desegregation as possible." (Of course, state and lower federal court judges in other regions have done the same on other issues.) One method is for the judges to write an opinion based on state (i.e., non-federal) grounds. As a rule, unless there is a clear constitutional issue the federal court will not review the case. "A state appellate judge who is a skillful opinion writer can, when so minded, do much to prevent Supreme Court review even of a federal question." [23]

A recent survey of sheriff's departments in the South found that although some offices in the largest counties were large, employed reasonably skilled personnel, and had at least some modern equipment, many—particularly in poorer rural counties—were undermanned. Their employees worked long hours for low pay and used only the most basic equipment. The study characterized the Southern sheriff as "male, white and a member of the Democratic party."[24]

Police department offices are often understaffed and underequipped, and salaries are far below the national average. As enforcers of segregation laws, Southern police in the past found themselves the objects of black criticism. Therefore many departments have developed community relations projects to try to restore respect for law enforcement officers.

County / Counties are the primary units of state administration, particularly in the South. Cities are incorporated by the legislature at the request of their residents, but counties are created by the legislature as administrative units whether the residents want them or not. County administrative organizations can be tightly limited by statute or by the constitution. Legislative time is frequently taken up with local bills necessary to allow counties to function and assume duties and responsibilities not foreseen or provided for when the county was created. For example, most of the 236,000 words of the Louisiana constitution are given to local amendments.

Two types of counties in the South have particular problems. The first type is the small, rural county that is losing population to the cities and watching its most productive citizens leave, its tax base fall, and its staple agriculture replaced, reduced, or terminated. These factors create a condition reported by the President's Commission on Rural Poverty: "Important as local government is, candor impels the conclusion that it is marked in rural areas by inadequate resources, unprofessional administration, undersized jurisdiction and lack of real interest in the problems of poor people."[25]

The second type of problem county is the new metropolitan county in and around the growing cities of the South. Its problem is its own growth and abundance with which it is often unequipped to cope because it lacks the authority and jurisdiction to regulate, direct, or control that growth. Whereas the counties that are dying find themselves unable to perform the most basic services due to lack of funds or expertise, the growing counties find themselves limited by statutory and constitutional restraints on such important functions as borrowing, taxing, zoning, and other types of regulation. Metropolitan areas have turned to the use of special districts, heretofore not widely used in the South, to meet their rapid growth and expansion.

The traditional functions of counties in the South include law enforcement, judicial administration, construction and maintenance of roads, recording of legal documents, relief of the poor, and some school administration. [26] Of these, the most politically sensitive function may be that of judicial administration. Virtually all the judges and sheriffs in Southern counties are elected. One critic has observed, "Like legislators and many other elected officials, state judges in Louisiana are selected according to the principle of localism: they are born in and socialized in the districts they serve. . . . Possibly, the judge views the whole political panorama in his court cases from the perspective of local political values." [27]

Although county government's inadequacies are properly included as Southern problems, Paul M. Wager commented, "All in all, county government in the South has perhaps made more progress and is more receptive to new ideas than in any other part of the country. Everywhere county government is conservative, but in the South it has always been close to the people." [28]

Selected Outputs

The three central problems under study all are affected by the political system. Racial discrimination has not only been built into the practice of Southern politics but has been codified and made legitimate by Southern legislatures and courts. This output also is amenable to change through the influence of a growing black electorate.

Chapter 2 discussed the inhibiting effects of Southern politics on the economy and consequently on per capita income. Neither badly needed industries nor talented individuals have been eager to make their homes in a section that talked and voted as if it had never really rejoined the Union. It is no accident of fate that the boom town of the Southeast, Atlanta, has been the regional model of progressive leadership. A succession of forward-looking mayors has encouraged both races to work together harmoniously, and has simultaneously attracted jobs and people. Atlanta's example indicates that political climate affects economic opportunity, and is affected by it.

Quality of education is again largely dependent on political structures, for both the direction and support of public schools are decided in the political arena. Although the South has had fewer resources with which to work than some other sections, the allocation of these scarce resources has not reflected a sufficient commitment to education as a key to improving the region's economic standing. Other states with the same per capita income as the South tax themselves more heavily for education.

Southern education has also suffered from the dual school systems of the past, which produced inferior education for blacks, and from the intransigence of many of the South's political leaders in the face of desegregation. For a time the attitude that no education was better than integrated education threatened to overwhelm the pro-education sentiments of the region. Although public schools have returned in the areas where they were disbanded, many have only shaky community support.

Historical Summary

Because the history of Southern politics is discussed widely in the literature,[29] no extended historical analysis will be included here. The major events since the Civil War have been Reconstruction and the region's response to it, the Populist phenomenon, the imposition of "Jim Crow" laws, the New Deal's impact, and the civil rights controversies of the 1950s and 1960s.

Inputs to the Southern Political System

ENDOWMENTS

Constitutions

Much of what is reprehensible about Southern state government is enshrined in the state constitutions. Most state constitutions are inferior when compared to the United States Constitution with its brief, well-stated, and broad principles of government.[30] Even so, constitutions of many Southern states are among the worst.

The most frequent indictment of these documents is that they are inflexible, too long, and involve too many specific details best left to statutes. Southern states have amended their constitutions almost twice as often as the rest of the country, averaging 178.9 amendments per constitution compared to 97.7 for non-Southern constitutions. Yet, on the average, constitutions of the Southern states are not as old as those of the rest of the nation. Including amendments, Southern state constitutions average over 50,000 words, while the rest of the states average 30,000 words per document.[31]

Most Southern constitutions owe their inadequacies and irrelevancies to the time and manner of their adoption. Following the Civil War, all of the Southern states adopted new constitutions. The effective dates of all but three of the states' present documents lie between 1868 and 1905, a period when legislative morals both in state capitals and in Washington were at perhaps the lowest point in history. For this and other reasons, state constitutions adopted during those years tended to keep as much power out of the hands of the legislators as possible. Local government units were likewise restricted both in the form that they could take and in their activities. To escape such limitations, amendments were added.

While many provisions in Southern state constitutions are simply outdated, unconstitutional under federal law, repetitious, or else border on the absurd (Georgia offers $250,000 to the first person striking oil in the state), some provide inefficient government. Many problems of legislative organization could be cured by revising the constitution. The constitutional limitation that evokes the most debate in nine Southern states is that which prevents the governor from succeeding himself. Only five states outside the South have such a limitation. Arkansas (and, until 1974, Texas) sets the governor's term at only two years, although he can succeed himself. The demand for amendments to deal with local matters also is widely criticized.

Urban-Rural Balance

Through most of its history, the South's political structure has been dominated by a conservative rural minority that sought to advance its self-interests through policies such as the perpetuation of a ready supply of cheap labor. Because of the South's rigid social structure the rural middle class was abnormally subordinated to the planter class. The urban middle class was likewise handicapped by the slow rate of Southern urbanization and by the legislative malapportionment that prevented redistribution of political power. Although blacks until recently were disfranchised, they were counted in the population of legislative districts. More important was the failure to reapportion legislative seats, even after years of farm-to-city migration shifted the center of population. Urbanization was regarded suspiciously by rural interests because it encouraged greater political activism by an expanded middle class. It also created an environment in which barriers to political participation by blacks and low-income whites were more easily circumvented. Rural interests frequently crippled governmental ability to deal with the problems associated with urbanization and industrialization through constitutional provisions limiting the power wielded by legislatures, governors, and local governments. The grip of rural interests upon state government was finally broken in the 1960s when two federal court decisions, *Baker* v. *Carr* and *Reynolds* v. *Simms*, forced the states to reapportion seats in their legislatures to insure that all citizens would have equal representation.

Growth of Black Influence

Although whites support blacks in some campaigns and vice versa, it is clear that an expanded black electorate is responsible for the election of more blacks to political office. Before the Voting Rights Act of 1965 was passed, fewer than 100 elected officials in the South were black. By November 1972 that number had climbed to 1,144. [32] That year 598 of 1,276 black candidates were elected to office, including two to Congress.

While pointing out that this is still a small percentage of the 79,000 state and local elected positions in the region, John Lewis, executive director of the Voter Education Project, nevertheless concludes, "The continued upswing in the total number of blacks in public office over the past six years is an indication that blacks are beginning to acquire the kind of political sophistication which will enable them to begin to control their own destinies." [33] To aid in the political education of black elected officials, the Voter Education Project and other groups have sponsored workshops to provide black officials with assistance to enhance their effectiveness in office and their responsiveness to their constituencies.

EXTERNAL FACTORS

To be a Southerner is to know Yankees. The great events that have effected change in all the institutions of the South—the economic developments of England and New England that produced a market for Southern cotton, the Civil War invasion, the Reconstruction amendments to the Constitution and the laws and decisions that began to implement them one hundred years later—have come from outside the South. Much of the genius and energy of the political institutions of the South has been spent opposing change; when change has come, it has been implemented by extraregional entities, primarily the national government. The injection of national issues and political personalities has contributed to the undermining of the South's one-party system, as have the benefits of an expanding economy. The nationalization of policy debates has provided an alternative level of decision making to those who are frustrated at the state and local levels. The federal stimulus to regional economic growth through direct expenditures, e.g., defense contracts, military payrolls, and farm subsidies, has supplied additional momentum to political as well as economic change.

It is widely believed that "the most painful experience for the South since Appomattox and Reconstruction was the aftermath of the Supreme Court Decision of 1954."[34] The Supreme Court had acted against the most blatant forms of racial discrimination in the political sphere before 1954. In the Brown case of 1954 the Court overruled an 1896 case, *Plessy* v. *Ferguson*, which had sanctioned the doctrine of "separate but equal."[35] Ordered to dismantle segregated schools with "all deliberate speed," Southern states deliberated. But after nine years no state could continue to boast of total noncompliance with the desegregation mandate. The school decisions were the first in a long series that greatly altered the political, social, economic, and educational institutions of the South.

Ten years later Congress passed the comprehensive Civil Rights Act of 1964, which moved to eliminate discrimination in public accommodations. The bill evoked in the Senate a 93-day filibuster before it passed overwhelmingly. Title VI of the bill called for the termination of federal funds to noncomplying (i.e., segregated) institutions. The law that most affected the political structure of the South was the Voting Rights Act of 1965. It provided for the suspension of literacy tests and "other devices used to deny citizens the right to vote because of their race or color," and allowed for the appointment of federal registrars where registration practices had been discriminatory.[36] The act covered states that had a literacy test before November 1964, and in which less than 50 percent of the potential voters voted or were registered in 1964: Alabama, Alaska, Georgia, Louisiana, Mississippi, South Carolina, Virginia, and twenty-six counties in North Carolina.

The result of this law was the registration of thousands of blacks in every Southern state. Not only did they register, often in the face of physical and economic threats from whites, but they voted and even ran for office. Matthews and Prothro found that "the Southern Negro becomes more politically active the longer his experience at participation, regardless of the age at which he first officially enters the political world."[37] The impact of black voting, noticeable in the moderated tone of many Southern white politicians, probably has not yet reached its highest point.

Where the desegregation decisions and civil rights laws attacked the South's problems of racial discrimination and low educational level, other decisions struck at the heart of the decision-making structure of the states. These were the reapportionment decisions of the 1960s. The legislatures of the South were not the only ones improperly apportioned;

that the two landmark cases in legislative apportionment arose from Southern states is more a matter of chance than it is of malapportionment being a uniquely Southern tradition. [38] Between 1960 and 1967 all but three state legislatures were reapportioned following Supreme Court decisions in *Baker* v. *Carr* and *Reynolds* v. *Simms*. There were only four states in the nation, and none in the South, whose redistricting had not been subjected to or actually accomplished by court action. [39]

Prior to the 1960s, most states did not have plans to reapportion after each census report, and those that did seldom complied with their own regulations. What resulted was legislatures with disproportionate rural influence, particularly in the South with its dying agricultural counties and fast-growing metropolitan ones. Alabama had been apportioned in 1901, Tennessee in 1903, Louisiana in 1921, and Mississippi in 1916. [40] Rural legislators usually had the least competition, [41] lasted the longest in the legislature, and were directed to positions of power in the committees by their senior rural colleagues.

States adopted different methods of complying with the one-man, one-vote decisions. Alabama adopted a system that included "legislative agents" who watched out for the interests of counties denied an individual representative by the new reapportionment. [42] Many states, when a county or district was allowed more than one legislator, opted not to divide the area into single-member districts but required each man to run at large. When this system was challenged before the Supreme Court, the Court held that "equal protection does not necessarily require formation of all single-member districts in a state's legislative apportionment scheme." [43]

Some argue that the apportionment of a legislature makes no difference in its policy output. However, it is hoped by many that the new representative constituencies of the legislatures will orient them toward problems of growing municipalities and urbanizing counties, largely neglected by past legislative sessions, and will generally make the legislatures more responsive to all groups in the population.

Another significant development has been the vast expansion of federal grant-in-aid programs in response to a growing catalogue of perceived domestic needs since the depression. The "inadequacy of state and local revenue systems to meet the financial crisis created by the depression" [44] contributed to the increased scope of federal government activity. The South has failed to capitalize on, indeed has bitterly opposed, "the development of a partnership between the nation and the states and their subordinate units of government for the most effective handling of the nation's public business."[45] There are indications that this position is changing, as state and local politicians actively seek out, announce, and applaud federal funding for projects geared to some problem of their constituency. Ironically, this trend was occurring when many federal categorical grant programs were being cut back by the Nixon administration, with its revenue-sharing emphasis.

Although major changes are necessary if state governments are to assume a full partnership role in any scheme of "cooperative federalism," the expansion of grant programs has not reduced the states to mere administrative agencies for the national government. State governments have been strengthened by increases in the number and quality of personnel and by the greater visibility of their operations. The pre-1973 increases in the percentage of state-local revenue supplied by national grants meant that state governments had been given some relief from the insistent demands of their citizens for added services in the face of state tax structures that sent revenues up at a considerably lower rate than the growth of the gross national product.[46] Despite the restrictions often accompanying federal funds, significant operating autonomy and reciprocal power remain with the states and localities.

Significant disadvantages have accrued from the multiplication of grant programs. The focus of the national government on urban problems neglected by state governments meant that project grants began flowing directly from Washington to the cities. Such a course, if continued, could seriously alter the nature of the federal system. Also, the needs of all states are now so pressing that despite equalizing formulas and the greater tax effort by low-income states to meet federal matching requirements, grant programs minimize the redistribution that could aid the South.[47] Part of federalism's fiscal crisis has been generated by the very grants-in-aid designed to assist the states. If state officials ignore the inducement of federal funds for new activities, they appear blind to the need for such activities. If they accept the funds, they find themselves in a tighter financial squeeze as they lock in their generally inflexible budgets for the necessary matching funds.[48]

OUTPUTS FROM OTHER INSTITUTIONS

Economic

Personal income, migration trends caused by economic aspirations and necessities, the development of the labor movement, and taxation structures are economic factors that affect the politics of the South and are in turn affected by it.

Studies have established that voter participation varies directly with economic well-being, increasing as personal income increases. [49] Therefore, even without the structural political factors that militate against voter participation, economics would suggest that it would not be as high as in the richer states. In the past, registration and voting in the lowest-income classes, specifically among blacks, has been depressed by threats of economic reprisals from whites. Perhaps the greatest stimulus to voter registration and participation in the future will be rising per capita income, if it is spread widely throughout the population.

The one-party tradition in the South presents an exception to the general finding that the upper classes are primarily Republicans. [50] Southern Democrats draw significant support from all economic levels in most areas. So far there has been only a modest tendency for local party units to drift toward the economic composition and positions of the national parties. If this movement occurred, blacks, liberals, organized labor, and other lower-income whites would form a coalition; but the low level of union organization is a deterrent. In the census South only 25.8 percent of the blue-collar workers are organized, compared to close to 50 percent in the rest of the country. The Department of Labor shows 14.7 percent of the total Southern work force unionized. [51]

Coupled with court-ordered reapportionment of legislative and congressional districts, migration patterns have greatly affected Southern politics. Migration to the cities, both in the South and in other regions, is made up of two kinds of people: "those coming for more opportunity, and those coming for any opportunity." [52] While the loss of the former further depresses rural areas, the loss of the poor and uneducated is not greatly mourned since some potential welfare problems are shifted to the cities. In many places the black migration from farm to city has eliminated the possibility of the takeover of local government by blacks.

Political institutions are also affected by industrialization. Most of the Southern states have governmental agencies that solicit industry. At least three grant tax exemptions to new industries. Alabama allows local governments to lend money to new industries to get their building started. South Carolina voted funds in 1961 for a program to train workers for industries that would locate in the state. [53] Less explicitly, the politically popular vocational education programs do the same thing in every state.

There is scarcely a more accurate indicator of whom a governmental unit responds to than how it raises its revenue. Taxation is both an economic and a political question, and affects both how the political unit is organized and what it can do. Although state and local taxes in all regions are regressive compared to the federal tax structure, the taxes of Southern states are the most regressive. All the Southern states have general and selective sales taxes, which hit poor people harder than the wealthy. In 1967 all Southern states except Texas and Virginia collected more in sales taxes from their citizens per $1,000 income than the national average. Texas and Virginia have increased their sales tax percentages since then. [54] The most progressive type of tax commonly used is the personal income tax. Only North Carolina and Virginia match the national average in percentage of state income collected by this tax and in the revenue from the tax per $1,000 of personal income. The progressivity of Southern income taxes is unusually modest: rates stop at 7 percent or less, and progression ends at fairly low income levels.

Sixty-six percent of local revenue in the United States in 1967 was collected through property taxes. The average tax per capita was $32.81. Southern states fell far below the national average in both collections per capita and in collections per $1,000 of personal income. Only Georgia and Texas approached the national figure. [55] Even with a lower cost for services in the South, the lower tax revenue in the region limits the provision and development of state and local services.

State and local taxes reflect the economic interests of the politically influential; the people hurt most seriously by the regressive nature of taxes, poor whites and blacks, are those least likely to vote. Enjoying the greatest advantages from the tax structure have been the favored industries, e.g., the extractive industries in Louisiana, the oil and cattle barons in Texas, or the banking and utility interests in other states. However, a taxpayers' revolt may be in the making. Florida governor Reubin Askew was elected in 1970 with a promise to impose the state's first corporate income tax. He carried out his campaign promise and, contrary to dire warnings by special interest groups, there has been no mass exodus of industry from booming Florida.

Educational

The 1954 Supreme Court school desegregation decision [56] provoked retaliation: "interposition," "massive resistance," school closings. Such efforts consumed untold time and energy of Southern policy-makers through the 1950s and 1960s. Now that school integration has finally arrived and has been supplemented by increasing amounts of schooling for the average Southerner, many observers are hopeful that education will help to liberate the mind of the South from parochialism and prejudice. Studies indicate that political participation is directly related to the degree of education attained, but the relation of education to racial understanding is less consistent. Matthews and Prothro found that "when the average education of whites in a county increases, Negro voter registration in the county tends to go down." They found that education among whites did not significantly increase racial tolerance *until the college graduate level.* "Education may be the secular road to salvation in America, but it must come in large quantities to make any positive difference in the average Southern county."[57]

The education of blacks has tremendous potential for influencing the political system. Already, as the number of educated blacks in the United States has increased—from 39 percent with a high school degree in 1960 to 58 percent in 1968[58]—black aspirations for meaningful participation in the political system have risen.

Social

Following Reconstruction, Southerners at the top of the socioeconomic ladder regained control of government. Then, to maintain dominance in the face of a Populist threat, they resorted to racial appeals and violence to drive a wedge between poor whites and blacks. White supremacy was enshrined in law as blacks were disfranchised. "Many Black Belt sponsors of disenfranchisement 'saw in it an opportunity to establish in power "the intelligence and wealth of the South. . . ." ' "[59] The complete success of the planter class in gathering unto itself all the prerequisites of leadership had far-reaching implications. William Nicholls noted that "by removing the threat of insurgency by lower-class whites, disenfranchisement at last gave to the planter class the whip-hand it had previously lacked in its increasingly distasteful alliance with Southern industrialists. . . . The planters were much freer than before to fall back upon the more ancient anti-industrial, anti-urban, and (as the principal embodiment of these) anti-Northern biases of the more comfortable tradition. In sum, it was finally safe for them to accept a little of the old Populist spirit themselves so long as they could keep it fully under control."[60]

The planters were astute in perceiving the urban and industrial movements as threats to their power. Increasing urbanization produced a middle class both active politically and more progressive than the Southern elite. But the effectiveness of this middle class in bringing about change was hampered as long as rural interests dominated the legislatures. Only with reapportionment in the last decade did the urban middle class finally gain a voice proportionate to its numerical strength. Until then, the observation held that the political South "is far more conservative than are Southerners themselves,"[61] for the elite perennially lagged behind the majority of the people in readiness for change.

POLICY DECISIONS

Party organization in the United States is decentralized. And the Southern one-party system has meant that party policy decisions, rather than coming from the state level, are even more often made at local or factional levels. A candidate in the Democratic primary might decide to court the black vote to the chagrin of or in direct opposition to the wishes of the leaders of the party organization. But they have no control over his positions. If nominated, the candidate has his own organization and advisers and often neither needs nor wants association with the official party structure. The size and inclusiveness of the Democratic party accommodate candidates who espouse widely varying philosophies.

The Republicans, on the other hand, made a decision in 1964 that may affect the nature of the party in the South for some time. The party of Lincoln, in an attempt to outflank the "party of rebellion" on the racial right, altered its stance and accepted the almost complete withdrawal of Negroes from the Republican presidential party. The strategy depended on racial considerations overwhelming all others. Although the GOP did gain votes in the Deep South that year, it did less well in the Upper South, where the party had been slowly gaining strength. In 1968, the traditionally Democratic counties of eastern North Carolina, for example, although voting heavily for George Wallace (presidential nominee of the American Independent party), returned to the Democratic column the rest of the way down the ticket. [62]

Several old Dixiecrats have found themselves receiving black votes because their Republican opponents have been so objectionable to blacks. Democrats have not had to court blacks overtly; they have gotten them by default.

In the early 1970s it appeared that the Democrats would dominate state and local governments in most Southern states in the future. (It seemed that the exception would be Tennessee, and perhaps North Carolina, Virginia, and Florida.) Even the Nixon landslide of 1972 did not dramatically improve the picture for the Republicans, except in North Carolina.

Southern state legislatures have been notoriously poor policy-making bodies. Part of the blame lies with antiquated state constitutions that cause much of the typical legislature's time to be taken up with consideration of constitutional amendments.

In many instances Southern counties cannot make their own policy decisions. "The city is what the legislature chooses to make it, but the county is what the constitution makes it, and the legislature is limited to deal with the organization written into the constitution." [63] The inability of some counties to borrow money for capital improvements dates back to constitutional limitations of the last century. Counties are also restricted in setting their own tax rates. Where the demographic make-up of counties differs substantially, the result is often that "to the extent that the states must deal with the counties uniformly, state law and policy often tend to be shaped by the limitations of the weak rather than the competences of the strong." [64] The local services provided by counties vary in quality, fairness, and equality of administration from outstanding to very bad, with variation among county administrators being an important factor.

Analysis of Specific Political Institutions

POLITICAL PARTIES AND PRIMARIES

"I am a member of no organized political party," Will Rogers used to say. "I am a Democrat." That is a particularly apt description of the Democratic party in the South, which is composed of most registered voters in the region, often with nothing more in common than nominal membership in the same party. Because most Southerners identify themselves and are registered as Democrats, the fortunes of the party and the region are intricately woven together. The reasons for the continued dominance of the party reinforce each other; for example, the history of the region influences the process of socialization into politics, and as long as the great majority of voters are socialized into the Democratic party, the individual who registers as Republican does so with the knowledge that he is eliminating himself from voting influence in many cases.

One hundred years ago the Republican party in the South was the party of the black man, and the Democratic party was that of the white. As Southern whites secured control of their states following Reconstruction, they began through party organizational rules and through laws to provide for the exclusion of blacks from the party. It took the events of the Great Depression and the Roosevelt reaction to it, the authority of the U.S. Supreme Court in ruling the devices used by Southern Democrats unconstitutional, and Republicans' ostensible abandonment of the cause of civil rights to move most black voters from the Republican to the Democratic party. In the fifties the majority of black votes often went to Republicans, on both the national and state levels. The sixties were the turning point. Although 20.6 percent of the black vote in the South in 1960 had gone to Richard Nixon, 1964 Republican nominee and Civil

Rights Act opponent Barry Goldwater captured only 1.7 percent of that vote. [65]

Most electoral decisions in the South are made in the Democratic primaries. In addition to other roles, the Democratic party exists as the party organization and as the arena in which candidates compete for office.

Party structure is pyramidal, with the lowest level being the precinct organization. Delegates from precinct organizations gather every other year in county conventions. Although they may adopt resolutions and hear partisan speeches and appeals for funds, their main task is to elect the party's county officers, and choose delegates to district and state conventions. While the county convention has the atmosphere of a local baking contest, the state convention has the dignity and excitement of a county fair. The conventions must handle funds, select their officers, recognize and reward the faithful, and on occasion mitigate local feuds. The state conventions (which choose delegates to the national party convention every four years) have an impact on the selection of their party's candidates for president and vice-president. However, they seldom have much impact on the selection of candidates for state or local offices; the reason is the system of the direct primary.

The direct primary was part of the Progressive reform package of the early twentieth century. In the South it was adopted as a democratizing device to remove nominee selection, at that time synonymous with election, from the hands of a few. The result is that virtually any self-starting candidate can get on the ballot. It also means that time and money must be spent and issues debated in the spring of every election year as well as in the fall.

Each primary candidate is left to his own devices to put together an organization. In theory and usually in fact, the party does not campaign for or materially aid any of the candidates until the voters have decided on the nominee. Some states even have laws that forbid a party official from campaigning for any candidate in a primary. [66] The result is that many candidates who build their own organizations have neither need nor desire to work with—or even, at times, to associate with—the official party. Political coalitions and groups often arise, last for the duration of the campaign, then disappear. The direct primary does not foster continuity. It is a system in which virtually any officeholder may be challenged, and in which the official party structure, such as it may be, is unable to help. Through the first half of the twentieth century Southern congressmen were much more likely than others to be defeated in their bids for reelection by members of their own party. (Of course, Southerners were much less likely to lose their seats in general elections.)

A party organization that cannot force ideological or demonstrated "party responsibility"[67] from its incumbents and challengers cannot expect it from rank and file voters. The primary-equals-election formula, or "tantamountcy," has fostered an attitude among party members that allows them to ignore their nominees with impunity. Typical is the case of a Democratic precinct chairman in Durham, North Carolina, who maintained his position even after serving as a local campaign manager for Barry Goldwater, a Republican, and George Wallace, at the time an American Independent. The Democratic party in the South has been so large and amorphous that it has been able to tolerate such defections without penalty. Like the great dinosaurs of old, the Democratic party has dominated the landscape of the South more by its size than its cunning. The Democrats have managed to extend their ideological flanks far enough to both the left and the right so as to leave the Republican party little firm ground.

After the Civil War, Republicans cast their lot with the newly enfranchised black voters in the South. Soon afterward, however, the GOP abandoned the Southern states to the Redeemers in exchange for four more years in the White House.[68] Excluding 1928, the Republicans looked South next in the 1950s. By 1964 Goldwater could claim a majority of the white votes in every state of the South except Texas.[69] The Southern GOP will continue to grow; it will contest and sometimes win elections in traditional and new areas. It may, in time, make real inroads in Democratic control of some of the states. But as long as the Southern Democrats can continue to keep their image separate from that of the national party, and as long as the national party allows them to do so without sanction, the politics of the South will remain—although with more frequent interruptions—primarily Democratic.

LEGISLATURES

Most campaigns for the state legislatures are not issue-oriented, and since most elections are decided in the Democratic primary, there is no real party platform to which the legislators are bound or to which they may look for guidance. Legislators are oriented to their own areas and to the special interests therein.

Some new Southern legislators will arrive at the capital several days before the session opens for an orientation period and some will not. (Georgia, for example, has a good orientation session through its Institute of Government.) Some will arrive at an office, while others will find themselves conducting business from a desk on the chamber floor, from the corner of a corridor, or from a hotel room. Some of the legislators will be provided with staff and secretarial assistance; most will not. All will be faced with the virtually insurmountable task of dealing with thousands of bills, many of local character, in a few weeks with little assistance in understanding them. The legislatures of the South have a problem inherent in one-party states: without organization of parties in the legislature, the members, who could not possibly be familiar with every bill, have no party leadership to whom to turn for cues on how to vote. [70]

Since there is little party organization or discipline in the process of election to the legislature or within the body itself, the presentation or enactment of a comprehensive program of laws is scarcely possible. It is at this point that the governor makes his weight most strongly felt. Voters have come to expect the governor to attempt to carry out his campaign promises, and the governor in most cases makes such an attempt; he is successful a surprisingly large percentage of the time. [71] The groups that form in the legislature tend to orient around support or opposition to a measure proposed by the governor.

Many of the bills introduced by individual legislators into the long process of committee consideration are either local bills or bills that are proposals of or for special interests. Local bills usually are for the purpose of allowing cities or counties to act on borrowing, capital improvements, construction, city-county cooperation, or annexation. As recently as 1969 in North Carolina, "Anywhere from ONE HALF to THREE FOURTHS of the laws enacted and about two thirds of the bills introduced by a typical General Assembly involve local affairs." [72] (North Carolina has since cut down on the number of local bills considered on the floor.) Cooperation with special interest groups can help legislators in several ways. Interests provide legislators with information and expertise often not available elsewhere. They can also help out in other ways to make a lawmaker's stay in the capital more enjoyable. One champion of the Texas lobbying process identified the "three B's that control the legislature—Bourbon, Beefsteak and Blondes." [73] Of course, all lobbyists do not deal in the three B's. Many are helpful in other ways, honest, and even necessary. Whether in committee or on the floor, if a bill gets as far as consideration, the pressures of the system will peak. The governor, committee chairmen, members of executive agencies, and the interests have a chance to influence the individual legislator. Each holds favors that the legislator wants or needs for himself or his constituents.

Southern legislatures have a limited time in which to consider bills. The last weeks of a session are filled with hyperactivity. In most of the South committees are not allowed to meet when the legislature is not in session, and bills not disposed of by the end of the session die with the final rap of the speaker's gavel. Few legislators in the South choose to make a career of the legislature, [74] a circumstance that does not improve these bodies' performances.

Reapportionment is no longer a problem now that Southern legislatures conform to the one-man, one-vote principle. States have greatly reduced the power if not the personnel of their respective "Pork Chop Gangs." Many states have made periodic reapportionment automatic by adding to their constitutions an amendment that requires it after each census. The multimember district is the remaining structural problem associated with numerical representation.

In multimember districts, prevalent throughout the South, candidates for the seats allotted to a district or county all run at large, and those that capture the greatest total vote are elected. The appellants who brought the multimember district before the Supreme Court (arguing that it was a violation of the Fourteenth Amendment) tried to demonstrate that a definable political group or unit in a large district could cast all its votes for a candidate who would still lose, although the vote for the candidate would have been enough to elect in a single-member district. The group or entity was effectively disfranchised, they argued. In 1965 the Supreme Court found that "it might well be that, designedly or otherwise, a multimember constituency apportionment scheme, under the circumstances of a particular case, would operate to minimize or cancel out the voting strength of racial or political elements in the voting population. When this is demonstrated, it will be time enough to consider whether this system still passes constitutional muster." [75] Large multimember districts allow the whites and the Democrats to maintain control of the legislatures over the new political elements, the blacks and the Republicans. "The Republican minority is usually concentrated in the suburban sections of a metropolitan area, and the use of [single member] districts would make it possible to elect legislators from these areas." [76]

Will reapportionment make any difference in the policy outputs of the legislatures, particularly regarding racial discrimination, low per capita income, and low level of educational accomplishment? Malcolm Jewell suggests that formal plans to revitalize state legislatures cannot be expected to revolutionize state politics or grossly change the output of state political systems. [77] Thomas Dye found economic and social variables the controlling factors in legislative performance in spite of reapportionment. [78] Frank Trippitt even suggests that since people are not the "true constituency" of the legislators anyway, reapportionment will not greatly affect policy output. [79]

Nevertheless, the combination of reapportionment and structural and constitutional reorganization of the legislature can be significant. Flor-

ida has made such significant improvement in its legislative organization and in its total governmental structure that it might serve as a model
for other Southern states.

At the time of *Baker* v. *Carr* Florida probably had the most malap-
portioned legislature in the country, with representatives of 12 percent
of the state's population able to control both houses. The body suffered
from most of the inadequacies discussed above: short biennial sessions,
low pay, committees with ineffective or nonexistent staffs. No service
was available to print and circulate the bills that the legislatures voted
into law. The legislature served as a specimen for muckrakers.

Reapportionment and the new constitution of 1968 changed all of
that. The Citizens Conference on State Legislatures ranked Florida's
legislature fourth in the country behind California, New York, and Il-
linois. The commission executive director said in 1969, "In the past few
years Florida's legislature has made the most dramatic and impressive
progress of any in the country. They have literally transformed the legislative system in that state, and as a result, in some aspects, the Florida
legislature heads the country, and I mean including California." [80]

Legislators were granted annual sessions, a procedure that allowed
bills to be "prefiled" before the session, and the right to set their own
salaries, which they exercised in 1969 (raising annual compensation
from $1,200 to $12,000 per year.) One benefit of the new constitution is
what it did *not* say concerning legislative organization. As a result, the
legislature could set many of its operational rules by statute, which
could be altered by statute as necessity dictated. The Florida legislature
is not without its lingering inadequacies. Sessions are limited to sixty
days, committee structure is still bulky, and bills do not extend over from
one session to the next. Nevertheless, Florida has taken great steps
toward the establishment of a policy-making body equipped to consider
and decide on the real problems of the state.

GOVERNORS

As elsewhere, behavioral characteristics are vital in analyzing the
governor's role. But much of the literature on the governor stresses the
advantages of a strong legal position commensurate with his responsibilities, and these formal matters are more amenable to policy decision.
Important in determining whether the governor really is the state's chief
executive or merely "the first among many executives" are his powers of
appointment and removal, his control over preparation and execution
of the state budget, and his term of office or tenure potential. [81]

The power to appoint officials is one means of exercising control over
them and the executive branch. With the notable exceptions of Tennes-

see and Virginia, ranked as among the "strongest" in the nation on Schlesinger's index of formal powers, most Southern states are ranked as "weak." This results from the diversity of ways in which executive officials are selected: popular election, appointment by an agency or individual other than the governor, appointment by a board or commission of which the governor is merely a member, and appointment by the governor requiring the concurrence of one or both houses of the legislature. [82] Whatever control most Southern governors exercise over the executive branch must arise from their ability to appeal to legislators and the public.

In most Southern states there is some form of executive authority to prepare the budget that grants the governor some control over administrative agencies through the power to grant or deny their operating-fund requests. However, this control is diffuse in Florida, Mississippi, South Carolina, and Texas, where the governor shares budget-making authority with others. A further restriction on the governor's control over funds is the common practice of earmarking, or setting aside funds for particular purposes. Even when the governor appears to have strong budget powers, his control may be diminished when the budget director is protected from removal by civil service regulations. [83]

Granting governors a more sophisticated, well-structured administrative machinery that can compete with the multiplicity of special interests for control of state government has been resisted, especially in more rural states. "Through the fragmentation of administration by autonomous agencies, each held effectively responsible only to narrow constituencies, and through a variety of devices precisely designed to block coordination and control by the governor, he is often reduced to impotence." [84] Recently, however, the frustration of being unable to bring concerted state action to bear on critical problems has supplied much of the impetus for administrative reform in several Southern states.

All Southern governors are rated weak in terms of tenure potential, as measured by length of term and stipulations concerning reelection. Such restraints result in weakened influence over executive personnel who may outlast a governor and over the legislature in the session meeting during his last two "lame-duck" years. In the absence of cohesive parties a governor is usually unable to transfer support to a like-minded candidate to perpetuate his policies. The limitation to one term militates against long-range planning and a sustained focus of effort to deal with social problems.

Another index of the governor's formal strength is his power to veto bills passed by the legislature. Where the governor has had this power, he can interject himself into legislative debates. He can also check administrators from appealing over his head for legislative support for their desired appropriations, especially when he can veto a particular item without rejecting the entire bill. In all but two Southern states the governor's veto power is rated strong, as measured by whether he can exercise an item veto, the length of time he has to consider a measure, and the number of votes required to override his veto. However, the governor of North Carolina, who has no veto powers, is generally thought to be at least as strong in his legislative relationships as other Southern governors, and the governor of Tennessee, whose veto powers are weak, frequently chooses the legislative leaders. [85]

Despite their overall weakness in formal powers, Southern governors usually dominate the shaping of public policy because archaic legislatures possess so little capacity for effective oversight of administration. It remains for the governor to provide focus for the legislative process through his powers of initiation; his legislative program sets the main outlines of the legislative agenda. Despite few formal legislative powers, the governor often can steer his program over the legislative and special-interest shoals by exploiting his visibility, his prestige as the representative of all interests, his personal resourcefulness, the party influence, the control of much patronage, and the threat of veto, or by calling a special session for consideration of his proposals. [86] Malcolm Jewell asserted that, in the South, "perhaps more than in most other states," legislative leadership has come from the governor. [87]

As a result of the factionalized politics of the South, its governors have lacked cohesive, disciplined legislative parties through which to work in securing desired legislation. Governors must rely upon personal organization or factional support. But the coalition that elected the governor usually has little carry-over effect with legislators elected independently of him. The governor "is the leader of his party in only the most nominal sense," and he must negotiate with factions and individual legislators "on an issue-by-issue basis." [88] Again the governor is hindered by the constitutional prohibition of succeeding himself, so that whatever influence he amasses dissipates during the final legislative session of his term as individuals begin jockeying for position in the next election. The influence derived from patronage—a valuable source of power in the past with the South's rural economy, poor education, and low income levels—is no longer commensurate with the governor's needs. [89]

However, this lack of a disciplined legislative party can cut both ways. While legislators with independent bases of electoral support have little political stake in the success of the governor's program, neither do they have a particular stake in its failure. In the absence of serious party competition, many Southern governors "do not have to deal with any group having the organizational structure or the motivation to constitute an 'opposition party.' " In most Southern states there is an "identity of interest between the governor and the dominant legislative forces" that encourages passage of much of the governor's program. [90]

COURTS AND LAW ENFORCEMENT

The North Carolina Bar Association's Committee on Court Improvement summarized the problems of state courts in 1957 thus: ". . . extreme decentralization; considerable duplication of work; overlapping, conflicting and confusing jurisdiction; wide diversity of local courts with marked lack of uniformity among courts of the same general purpose; a high degree of autonomy in individual courts; lower courts characterized by incompetence, dishonesty or both; and a virtually total absence of authoritative supervision from any competent source." [91] North Carolina has begun reforming its court system, but many other Southern states have done little toward making justice available in the same measure in all parts of the state. The worst culprits are the local courts of special jurisdiction. In the absence of enforceable guidelines, how justice is administered can depend on whether the accused has crossed a county line.

The method of selecting state judges, from the State Supreme Court to traffic courts, allows men to acquire and hold office who sometimes act to inhibit directives from higher state and federal courts. Most Southern states elect their judges and solicitors, or state attorneys. All elect their attorney general, the chief legal official in the state. The process of election produces judges who reflect the dominant feelings and prejudices of the community. Even federal judges have been obstinate in the carrying out of orders, particularly those dealing with desegregation issues. [92] Federal district judges are appointed by the president upon the recommendation of the senators of the state in which the judges are to sit. This judge, too, is likely to reflect the political culture of his state.

Although it is not unique to the South, civil and criminal justice can often be bought with money, the comparative social position of the combatants before the bar, or both. And there is the factor of years of institutionalized racism enforced by many judges still on the bench today.

The size and effectiveness of the law enforcement units of localities vary with the size and the wealth of the areas they serve. Generally law enforcement units, particularly in rural areas and smaller towns, lack modern training and equipment, another example of the inability of many localities in the South to generate enough revenue to pay for necessary services. Many units are understaffed, and those officers must work long hours, sometimes for no extra compensation. Police units in large cities generally can afford to pay and employ their officers for a forty-hour week, although few localities allow pay for policemen while they are in court following arrests they have made.

Recently police departments have started programs in community relations. Although no major city in the South reflects its racial make-up within the police department, many have black officers, something practically unheard-of in past years. Several Deep South counties have even elected black sheriffs.

Law enforcement agencies reflect the political decisions made around them, as a study of the Wilmington, North Carolina, police department concluded. [93] Second, as a report of the sheriff's department in Union County, North Carolina, put it, "the personality of an office holder casts, to a great degree, the mold and direction of the operation of the office." [94] The lawmen of the South are a mixed lot, reflecting the social mores of their local cities.

COUNTIES

As creatures of the states, counties are imbued with the infirmities and inefficiencies of the states, as well as their own problems. John Sanders has written:

> Increasingly the county is being looked to, not only for more and better services of the traditional kinds, but as the agency for providing a host of urban type services—water supply, sewage disposal, fire protection, recreation, land use regulation, airports, mass transportation, poverty eradication programs, economic development leadership and the like. These demands are being heard not only in the metropolitan counties; some of them are being heard in the less populated areas as well. Yet their fulfillment is being increasingly complicated by the counties' lack of the necessary money, authority, and trained manpower to make prompt and adequate response. [95]

With the exceptions of special grants to specific counties in Florida, Tennessee, and Louisiana, a Texas provision that allows some home rule to local units with a population over 62,500, and a North Carolina constitutional provision that lets counties choose their governmental structure from a list of acceptable alternatives, the administration of county government is strictly spelled out in statute, the constitution, or both. [96] So-called home rule grants to counties are sometimes misleading. Defined most strictly, home rule means the right of a local unit to select the structure of its own government; so defined, it does not apply to many administrative decisions that may be subject to state approval in spite of provision for home rule. Home rule grants to municipalities are often broader than those made to counties.

Local county decisions are usually made by elected boards of three to five members. Some states allow administrative boards of as many as fifty members. It is typical of the problematical relations between legislatures and counties that North Carolina's constitution provides for county boards of three members, but includes countless local amendments that allow specific counties to have five members. [97] In a minority of Southern states the governing board is composed of members of the judiciary, both judges and justices of the peace (a provision left over from the days when the justices of the peace were all-purpose officials). Terms vary in length according to the state.

Also varying from state to state and within the states is the method of administration. Some Southern counties do not have one individual in whom administrative authority and responsibility lie. In these counties each member of the board has responsibility for certain county functions. Elsewhere authority has gravitated to one person whose position gives him the equivalent of executive authority. In still others one elected official is charged with executive duties. Finally, some counties, when allowed to do so by the states, have adopted a system of government that calls for a county manager (a professionally trained, full-time executive) to oversee and direct administration. He is usually employed at the pleasure of the policy-making board. At one time three-fourths of all county managers in the country were working in the South. [98]

As administrative units charged with many state functions, counties receive substantial funds from state agencies. Counties also often receive funds for federally sponsored programs. Until revenue-sharing, federal programs seldom granted money to local units without restrictions or guidelines as to its use. Ira Sharkansky suggests that this method of finance may have helped to "nationalize" the policies of the receiving units. [99] One example was the threatened or actual withdrawal of federal school grants from county school districts to force them to comply with desegregation guidelines. Counties must also pay for their own activities, primarily through the collection of a property tax. This tax is limited by the states, often in the constitution. County activities are also restricted by archaic state limits on borrowing and financing of projects.

As V. O. Key has noted, to speak with precision of the structure and content of Southern counties is "not unlike coming to grips with the Holy Ghost." [100] The South, like other regions, has counties containing and contained by great metropolitan centers, and counties that are small, poor, and practically empty of people. The problem of local governments is not that they are so varied but that they need to have the ability to adapt their structures to their own changing needs, whether these needs are expanding or shrinking.

Policy Recommendations

The recommendations that follow are intended to suggest ways in which the South can move toward a more responsive political system. But changes in electoral and government institutions are not enough to bring a more humane politics to flower. Adjustments in government structure do not automatically mean that better people enter government service and govern more wisely, with greater attentiveness to and concern for all their constituents. The reforms of the Progressive era and some of the changes associated with the civil service reform and public administration professionalization trends have succeeded in inhibiting the old kinds of corruption and unresponsiveness. But new problems arise, and no institutional structures should be above recurrent tinkering. A clean bureaucratic flow-chart is not the highest goal, and continued public caution about "experts" is healthy. Ultimately, the quality of a county's, a state's, or a region's politics is determined by what is done by voters and leaders. Institutional improvements help make good leaders and good policies more likely; that is all, but that is a great deal.

Many of the problems of Southern state executives, legislatures, and counties grew out of the desire, for various motives, to hamstring these bodies. Given the level of expertise, honesty, and representativeness of these bodies in much of the past, it was not such a bad idea. But when formal governmental bodies were unable to govern, informal power groups governed. The South no longer can afford government by economic interests unaccountable to the people. State executives, legislatures, and counties need to be empowered to plan for comprehensive action, and to act, with the risks thereby entailed. The state executive is the proper place to lodge most planning and budgetary responsibilities, but the much-maligned legislatures are in particular need of strengthening. Legislatures can be forums to make humane and far-sighted policies; Florida, for example, has shown that, in part, the old model can be broken.

The judicial branch does not need strengthening so much as it needs redirecting, in ways suggested below. The party system is particularly important because it embraces government agencies as well as its own electoral mechanisms; however, parties are not always amenable to change through institutional adjustments because of the looseness of their organizations. The key need here—to provide meaningful alternatives—is met when effective political groups organize around contrasting positions on real issues.

Strengthen the Two-Party System in the South

Partisanship is not a weed to be uprooted, but a plant to be nurtured; partisanship helps voters make decisions that are rational for them. The major political parties need to become truly competitive if voters are to have policy alternatives. Increased party competition might encourage candidates to adopt varying issue-oriented platforms. States with high levels of party competition tend to have higher levels of legislative party responsibility, which may strengthen a voter's ability to choose between alternative programs as well as alternative candidates. [101]

Two-party politics would not, of course, create instant policy alternatives. The greatest competition arises over voters closest to the middle of the political spectrum—to the extent that "left," "right," and "center" retain any meaning. This accommodation moderates the ideologies of both parties nationally. In the South, where most voters still see themselves as conservative in some sense, the initial policy differences between the two parties may be even more modest.

The Republican party in the South reflects the ideology and style of the national Republican party to an extent that the Democratic party in the South does not. To accomplish the nationalization of the Democratic party in the South, as is sometimes advocated, would require extensive organization of "liberal" groups and enforceable national sanctions against those bolting the party during election years. Close examination of credentials and party loyalty oaths of allegiance from delegates and candidates, denial of seniority in the U.S. Congress, the refusal to honor recommendations of governors and senators for federal appointments, even threats to the granting of political pork to states or districts might encourage party regularity. But to what effect? In most of the South the liberal-national Democrats are a distinct minority; ideologically pure parties would give them the psychic benefits of party control, but governmental control would be beyond their grasp. Ideologically pure parties might even be impossible (given the voters' nonideological bent). Policy alternatives, however, can be offered in the absence of ideological purity.

Restrict Campaign Costs and Expenditures

The costs of running for state office have risen so astronomically that they surpass the expense of seeking national office a generation ago.

Thus the candidate who is backed by the most "big money" has a head start and candidates of modest means are handicapped. (There are exceptions, such as Florida's U.S. Senator Lawton Chiles, who gained much free media time by walking across the state during his 1970 primary campaign.) The cost of seeking office must be put within the reach of anyone who can pay the filing fee, which should be set low enough to be met by anyone with a nucleus of followers who could donate small amounts.

The biggest campaign expense is advertising, especially on commercial television. Therefore, we recommend laws that would eliminate or severely restrict the purchase of television time for political advertising. Instead, a certain amount of television time should be required to be donated as a public service, to be equally divided among the candidates; or, states might choose to experiment with their own versions of recent federal legislation to provide public monies to the parties for general election campaigns.

Conduct Drives to Register and Organize Voters

Those people most affected by the problems focused on in this study— racial discrimination, low level of educational attainment, and low per capita income—are those most likely *not* to participate in the political system. If the poor, the less educated, and the minorities are encouraged to participate, and if they are properly organized, they may substantially improve their own circumstances. Federal laws and court decisions have set the stage for this effort, and continued vigorous court action is needed. Local organization of the newly enfranchised voters should be conducted within the existing party system to maximize the effect on policy. Holding elections on Saturdays and keeping the polls open later also would permit more widespread voting participation.

Institute Training for Nonprofessional Political Participation

Training should not be restricted to civil servants or already-elected legislators. Each state needs a program to encourage people from a wide range of backgrounds to become politically active by showing them how. Such a program was started in Louisiana in 1968, and similar programs have been initiated in three other Southern states; in Georgia the Chambers of Commerce sponsor such a program.

GOVERNMENTAL

Hold Constitutional Conventions to Rewrite Constitutions That Have Not Been Rewritten in the Last Three Decades

Drastic alteration in Southern state constitutions is needed. In particular, state legislatures must be given greater flexibility to govern themselves and the states. Structural change is not a panacea for substantive problems, but it will help to make change possible. Resistance to constitutional revision will be powerful, but new constitutions can be voted in, as Louisiana showed in 1974.

Make Changes in the Legislature

Increase the Time Available to Legislatures / Legislatures can no longer accomplish the work demanded of them in biennial sessions. States that have not yet done so should provide for annual sessions. Legislatures, often circumscribed by constitutional or statutory limits on the number of days in session, should have the power to extend sessions or to hold special sessions when necessary.

Improve Committee Procedure / Since, as the Citizens Conference on State Legislatures points out, legislative committee procedures have a "bearing on the accountability and representativeness of state legislatures," committees should move toward "on-the-record votes, . . . adequate notice of meetings and hearings, . . . [regularized] meeting schedules, and . . . more openness and less secrecy in committee procedure." [102] Committee staffs should be strengthened.

Raise Legislators' Pay to Realistic Levels / Southern states are among the worst in refusing to pay legislators enough salary and compensation for expenses to allow them to devote their time to legislative duties. A Southern legislator must either be independently wealthy or must compromise between the demands of earning a living and serving in the legislature.

Provide a Research Arm for the Legislature / To act intelligently in writing and voting upon proposals, legislators need more information than they or their immediate staffs can provide. Therefore, legislatures should establish research agencies, such as the Public Affairs Research Council in Louisiana, to provide information on state needs and possible solutions. An alternative is to increase support for institutes of government or university public affairs bureaus, where good ones exist.

Update Facilities / Attention should be given to updating legislative facilities, ultimately to include private offices for all legislators, adequate quarters for staff, and access to adequate information-processing equipment.

Ascertain the Effect of Multimember Districts on Representation of Minority Interests / We know that multimember legislative districts may cancel out the influence of sizable minorities living within those districts. If data is collected to show that multimember districts actually discriminate against minority interests, they should be replaced by smaller single-member districts. Particularly in larger cities, one would expect single-member districts to permit more blacks and possibly more Republicans to be elected to the legislatures.

Discourage Conflicts of Interest / Legislative ethics has always been a touchy subject, with legislatures loath to police the business and financial dealings of their members. A full financial disclosure of the income and assets of all legislators should be required. If the legislators are lawyers, realtors, insurers, or bank officers, they should be required to list their major clients or customers. Stricter prohibitions are needed against using public office for personal gain or privilege.

Make Changes in the Executive Branch

Remove Bars to Gubernatorial Self-Succession / Aside from the impact on executive leadership and planning, restrictions on a governor's succeeding himself limit the voters' right to choose whomever they want to be governor.

Reduce the Number of Elective Offices / Chief executives need authority sufficient to match their responsibilities. A consequence of balkanization of the executive branch of state government, as Richard H. Leach has noted, is that "responsibility is confused, policy decisions are difficult to reach, and if reached, to enforce, and effective executive leadership is rendered impossible."[103]

Executive leadership is limited by the fragmentation written into the constitution or adopted in legislation at the behest of interest groups because of the advantages to them of disorganized administration. The large number of elected officials in administrative positions in Southern states results in their obscurity and diminished public concern. The effective constituencies of many elected administrators become the groups immediately affected by their policy decisions. To these interest groups "the prospect of a centralization of authority in the governor's office through powers of appointment and removal is a serious threat. The multiplicity of elective offices . . . is a guarantee of the governor's impotence to require conformity with his own policy, . . . an obstacle to coordination, . . . [and] a limitation on the ability of the whole public to influence policy."[104]

Relatively obscure elected officials should have their independent authority curbed, and the governor should be allowed to appoint and remove them. Examples of such officials are the treasurer and the labor commissioner.

Restructure State Agencies with the Governor Having More Authority / The multiplicity of governmental agencies poses problems of accountability to the governor and to the coordination of programs, and makes for waste of scarce resources through duplication of effort. For example: "Earmarking of public funds . . . goes far to render some boards and commissions impervious to any requirement of coordination of public policy or effective consideration other than clientele needs." [105] Recent reorganizations in Arkansas, Georgia, Florida, North Carolina, and other states have dealt with some of these problems.

If the resources and energies of a state are to be constructively focused on solving its problems, strengthened gubernatorial control over a moderately rationalized administrative structure probably is necessary. The administrative structure should be organized along broad functional lines for more effective coordination, perhaps by grouping functionally related agencies together in departments with lines of authority to governors empowered to appoint and remove agency heads. Following the initial restructuring (which in most states will require constitutional revision), the governor should have the authority to reorganize executive agencies in the future, subject to a legislative veto within a limited time. [106]

Operate State Government "in the Sunshine" / Voters have a right to know how policies are made as well as what the policies are; all meetings of state agencies—except those truly dealing with quasi-judicial matters—should be open to the press and public. Several Southern states have passed such "government-in-the-sunshine" laws. Political leaders who see the importance of leveling with the people as a means of reducing cynicism about governmental institutions should be particularly concerned to promote this practice.

Use Polls to Help Find Out What the Public Wants / Periodic public opinion surveys should be conducted with state samples to determine the public's attitudes toward various issues and classes (although not particular pieces) of legislation. The results would be available to all executive agencies, to legislators, and to the press. Polls should supplement direct contacts through hearings and agency requests for interest-group comments on regulations.

Make the Governor the Chief Budget Officer for the State / Critical impediments to a governor's meeting his responsibilities are the frequent constitutional and statutory failures to make him the responsible budget officer and the chief planner for state government. The budget-making process "involves bringing together the requests of all existing state agencies, calculating the cost of new state programs, estimating the probable income of the state, and evaluating these costs and income estimates in the light of program and policy objectives." [107] Concretely, of course, it occasions intense competition among groups to shape the budget to suit their policy preferences.

The governors of Arkansas, Florida, Mississippi, and South Carolina have been given only weak formal authority, since actual preparation has been carried out by a budget commission. Instituting an executive budget will not, however, be the final solution. Other factors that circumscribe the governor's ability to exert fiscal control and relate expenditures to perceived state needs include (1) the political nature of budgeting, which finds virtually autonomous agencies and their clientele groups importuning the legislature to support their requests; (2) the conservative nature of budgeting, which generally results in funding an agency at last year's level, plus an incremental increase for good (or safe) behavior; (3) federal limitation of alternatives by the interjection of grant availability into the decision-making process; (4) the constitutional imposition of unrealistic tax ceilings and "earmarking" of funds; and (5) the constraint of revenues imposed by the underdeveloped Southern economy. [108]

Planning and budget control need to be professionally staffed, their activities closely meshed, and the governor given ultimate responsibility for them. Improved budgeting procedures are necessary if programs are to ameliorate the problems that presumably gave rise to them. "Programmatic budgeting (PPBS) might change the conservative nature of the budgetary process, and undermine the pattern of cozy familiarity between legislators, agencies, and their clientele. If maximum value is to be gained from scarce revenues, a better budget could be drawn up by annually reconsidering the value of at least a majority of existing programs. This approach would be politically controversial and intellectually difficult. Ideally, it could lead to timely curtailment of irrelevant or ineffective programs and could illuminate the changed emphases or new programs that could better attack social problems.

Make the Governor Responsible for State Planning / A strong central planning agency should be organized principally as a staff arm of the governor, to assist him in formulating long-range policies and designing programs to carry them out. Such an agency could be augmented by planning mechanisms in the operating executive departments. [109] The budget office thereby could better fit requests into a coherent pattern and compare it to projected revenues, enabling policy makers to assess the implications of a proposed budget for identified long-term goals. State planning should not, however, have an exclusively executive focus. Since separate legislative planning probably would be wasteful at present, information generated by planning agencies should be made accessible to legislative committees and should be supplemented by periodic legislative review of planning activities.

There will be resistance. "State planning means changing the behavior of state officials and institutions in many fundamental [ways]." [110] Planning must be sold on the basis of its contribution to the ability of government to respond meaningfully to citizens' needs. The planning staff can assist in identifying present and future public needs, assess the adequacy of existing policies and programs in meeting those needs, and formulate and evaluate alternative courses of action. Planning can assist the governor in his role as legislative leader, and can help to exert direction over a fragmented executive structure.

Create Departments of Administration / The governor's role as political leader militates against consistent administrative supervision; "the practical realities of the operation of the governor's office are not those of the reorganizer's theory: the governor does not know what is going on until there is some reason to have to pay attention to a trouble spot." [111] Departments of Administration, if instituted where they do not yet exist, could serve as staff control units, assisting the governor in planning, budgeting, accounting, and personnel oversight. The department could be headed by an official directly responsible to the governor who would assume authority for the day-to-day management of the executive branch. [112] To the governor such a staff inevitably presents dangers of self-arrogation of power, and it would have to be itself kept under surveillance by the governor and legislative leaders.

Employ More Blacks in State and Local Governments / Under the leadership of governors Linwood Holton and John West, the states of Virginia and South Carolina, respectively, made significant progress toward the employment of blacks in state government positions. As recently as September 1970 only one black was in attendance at the Southern Governors Conference in Biloxi, Mississippi, and he was from a border state. The South still has a long way to go in the employment of minority employees in state and local governments. The time has come for Southern governors and mayors to move energetically to employ more qualified blacks as well as Chicanos and Indians.

Change Judicial and Law Enforcement Practices

Adopt Unified Court Systems / The system of justice should be restructured to centralize administration and standardize the rules and substance of justice dispensed by the state. Without this, justice can be, and often is, a commodity to be bartered or sold, dispensed under local rules without supervision from higher authorities and often, in effect, without appeal. Each state should adopt a flexible unified court system "in which judicial power is conserved, the administrative activities of tribunals are systematized and provision is made for expert and responsible supervision." [113]

North Carolina has adopted a unified court system that might serve as a model. Implementation for all its one hundred counties was completed in 1970. [114] All lower courts—city or county recorder's court, domestic relations court, juvenile court, mayor's court, justice of the peace court, and others—were replaced with district and superior courts. The appellate process includes a new Court of Appeals and the State Supreme Court. Justices of the Peace were replaced by magistrates paid by the state, and a uniform system of fees and charges was established. All judicial personnel are paid by a central office. Juries are drawn from a list composed by an independent jury commission and all occupational excuses have been abolished. The centralization of the system and the standardization of procedure and fees create a judicial product that is potentially fairer to all than an intricate system of specific courts of highly limited jurisdiction. The need for flexibility within a logical structure, seen in the legislative and local government settings, is also present in court systems.

Adopt the Missouri Plan for Selecting Judges / The majority of Southern states elect their judges. The Missouri Plan, which sets out a three-step process for the selection of judges, is preferable. First, a judicial commission of lawyers and laymen recommends three candidates to the governor, who chooses one. The appointee then runs in a general election unopposed, with the public given the right to vote "Yes" or "No" on his candidacy. If he is approved, he has the office subject to periodic reapproval by the electorate. [115] This form of selection would not put the power of appointment in any single person or body, but would remove the office from its present brand of electoral politics.

Subsidize Public Interest Law Firms / The growth of the consumer movement has given rise to advocacy, or representation, of groups hitherto unorganized and without spokesmen. Public interest law firms are dedicated to representing the public by bringing class action suits against corporate or governmental abuses. Such litigation is costly. States should subsidize public interest law firms in cases in which they represent citizens attempting to redress grievances, up to a reasonable dollar maximum; this would reduce the extent to which lack of money hinders the exercising of the right to seek redress.

Make Legal Aid Available to All / Wealth has always been a factor in American courts. As long as great diversity in personal wealth exists, this influence cannot be entirely eliminated. It can be tempered, however, if Southern states adopt programs of state-paid public defenders to act in criminal trials, to replace court-appointed attorneys. Legal aid also should be available from private firms, perhaps through a state incentive program to provide legal aid to the poor in civil proceedings.

Appoint and Promote Lower Court Officials through a Merit System / To encourage impartiality and competence of lower-court officials, they should be appointed and promoted through a merit system with standards set by the state. More emphasis also needs to be placed on management training for judicial administrators.

Establish State Training Centers for Law Enforcement Officials / The most visible representative of the power of the state is the policeman or the sheriff and his deputies. The Southern states should each, or as a group, establish central training centers for law enforcement officials and require that officers meet minimum standards of competence.

Encourage Police Forces to Reflect Racial Composition of the Community / The distrust that many blacks and other minorities feel for law enforcement officials is the consequence of years of uneven justice meted out on the basis of race. To gain the support of the black community for their local police force, not only must justice be dispensed evenhandedly, but some blacks must be included in the force. Localities should be urged, perhaps with state assistance for training expenses, to develop a police force that approaches in its racial composition that of the community.

Make Changes on the County Level

Grant Home Rule to Counties / Legislatures should grant home rule to counties (in most cases through constitutional amendment). Home rule is defined here as the opportunity for a county to make decisions affecting the structure of its government. Counties, like cities, should be permitted to vote into being charter-type governments with broad powers—as in the proposed Texas constitutional revisions of 1973.

Minimize State Limitations on Counties / Many states have strict and often archaic limitations on county fiscal policy. Although some guidelines on borrowing and spending are necessary for the financial integrity of the state and counties, these guidelines must be adapted to reflect modern monetary practices and economic theory. State limitations on county activities should be minimized as much as possible, and limitations that are believed necessary should be kept as statutes and not in the constitution.

Consolidate Counties, or Cities and Counties, Where Beneficial / Even with liberal grants of new authority, many Southern counties are either too small, underpopulated, or poor, to provide minimal services. As population shifts continue from rural to urban centers, governmental activities will be an increasing strain on those counties losing population and tax base. The problem is obvious, as one farm organization saw it: "The governmental structure of rural America must be modernized. The piecemeal fractionated planning programs of the present will not suffice in coping with the problems of low income areas." [116] The solution to the problem is not so obvious.

An answer to the problem of inadequate service in an inadequate area is the consolidation of local units of government, both within and among counties. Problems could be more efficiently addressed on regional lines adapted to demographic realities and human needs rather than on lines surveyed and adopted by legislatures over the last three centuries. County consolidation also might break up "courthouse gang" politics in some rural regions.

General revenue-sharing funds could encourage archaic units of government to remain independent, and could stimulate incorporation of new communities with inadequate tax bases. This is one reason that federal revenue-sharing should be scrutinized for its effects, intended and unintended, after several years of operation.

Develop Interlocal Cooperation / Although consolidation of counties offers a long-term solution to area-wide administrative problems, more immediate needs might best be solved by less drastic structural change. When allowed by appropriate legislation, county and city units could enter into pacts of cooperation in the solution of specified area problems that they could not handle alone. Interlocal cooperation could handle services with economies of scale and not alter the structure of existing governmental units. Conceivably, the cooperation could become so broad-based and the administration so integrated that it would amount to functional if not official county consolidation. [117]

In rural law enforcement, where there is often inadequate manpower, equipment, and money, all law enforcement units in a county or region should cooperate and combine as many functions as possible. Counties containing reasonably large towns might consolidate the sheriff's office with the police and create a metropolitan police force.

Where cooperation and consolidation of counties, or even the creation of "regional area development districts" (proposed by the President's Commission on Rural Poverty), [118] are necessary in rural areas, in the metropolitan counties the emphasis should be on planning for growth. Metropolitan area also need area cooperation, not only to provide services, but also to regulate growth to insure orderly development of the land.

Avoid Creating Special Districts / Largely because of its lack of special service districts and special school districts, the South has less of the layering of government than other areas have. Other areas have begun to find that special districts often make administration of services uneven and separate people from the political process. Southern local governments should keep their administrative units as centrally organized as possible, not diffusing authority, administration, or responsibility by the creation of special districts. Southern municipalities should be given substantial extraterritorial zoning authority, and local and regional planning should be integrated and so tied to zoning (perhaps on a regional basis) that it is legally enforceable.

The recently formed multipurpose planning districts in Florida, North Carolina, Virginia, and other states, and older districts, should be strengthened.

6. Controlling Urban Development

The Setting

INTRODUCTION

Cities are relatively dense concentrations of people and their political, economic, social, and educational institutions. According to figures from the 1970 census the South remained, as it had been since the first census, the least urbanized region in the nation. At 64 percent urban, however, it stood much closer to the national level than at any time in recent history, closing a 1960 gap of 12.2 percent between the region's and the nation's percentages to 9.5 percent in 1970 (see table 6.1). For the first time, more than half of the South's population resided in a Standard Metropolitan Statistical Area (SMSA): 54 percent compared with 74 percent of the non-Southern population. [1] The region's SMSAs grew 22.5 percent during the 1960s while those of the non-South grew only 15 percent; only the West's SMSAs grew more quickly. [2] Thus differences between the South and the rest of the nation in degree of urbanization and urban growth are being reduced. The problems of Southern cities also are those of the cities in the rest of the nation. There are no fundamental ways in which the cities of the region are unique. The differences that exist are only the product of the age and the stage of development of Southern cities. [3] Given a little time, inattention, and inaction, the differences will vanish, along with the advantages these differences might have provided the South. Even without such inattention and inaction, the tools necessary to avoid great urban problems may not exist.

Just as urban growth closes a gap that once separated the South from the rest of the nation, this same growth is undermining the unity of the region. [4] On the basis of metropolitan growth rates in the 1960s (see table 6.2), three Southern subregions can be identified. They are (1) the five states of the rapidly growing Atlantic seaboard, which experienced 29.4 percent metropolitan growth, with all five states in the subregion exceeding the national average and four rising above that of the South (Florida, 37.2 percent; Virginia, 28.4 percent; Georgia, 25.7 percent;

TABLE 6.1. *Population Living in Urban Areas, 1890-1970 (in Percentages)*

	1890	1900	1910	1920	1930	1940	Old Defn.[a] 1950	New Defn.[b] 1950	1960	1970
South	13.4	15.2	20.1	25.4	32.1	34.8	43.3	47.1	57.7	64.0
Non-South	43.7	49.6	.55.9	61.3	65.2	65.0	65.8	70.4	74.4	77.1
United States	35.1	39.7	45.7	51.2	56.1	56.5	59.6	64.0	69.9	73.5
Urbanization change in South (by decade)		1.8	4.9	5.3	6.7	2.7	8.5	12.3	10.6	6.3
Urbanization change in non-South (by decade)		5.9	6.3	5.4	3.9	-.2	0.8	5.4	4.0	2.7
Urbanization change in U.S. (by decade)		4.6	6.0	5.5	4.9	0.4	3.1	7.5	5.9	3.6
Alabama	10.1	11.9	17.3	21.7	28.1	30.2	40.1	43.8	54.8	58.4
Arkansas	6.5	8.5	12.9	16.6	20.6	22.2	32.3	33.3	42.8	50.0
Florida	10.0	20.3	29.1	36.5	51.7	55.1	56.5	65.5	73.9	80.5
Georgia	14.0	15.6	20.6	25.1	30.8	34.4	41.4	45.3	55.3	60.3
Kentucky	19.2	21.8	24.3	26.2	30.6	29.8	33.5	36.8	45.5	52.3
Louisiana	25.4	26.5	30.0	34.9	39.7	41.5	51.4	54.8	63.3	66.1
Mississippi	5.4	7.7	11.5	13.4	16.9	19.8	27.6	27.9	37.7	44.5
North Carolina	7.2	9.9	14.4	19.2	25.5	27.3	30.5	33.7	39.5	45.0
Oklahoma	3.7	7.4	19.2	26.5	34.3	37.6	49.6	51.0	62.9	68.0
South Carolina	10.1	12.8	14.8	17.5	21.3	24.5	30.8	36.7	41.2	47.6
Tennessee	13.5	16.2	20.2	26.1	34.3	35.2	38.4	44.1	52.3	58.7
Texas	15.6	17.1	24.1	32.4	41.0	45.4	59.8	62.7	75.0	79.3
Virginia	17.1	18.3	23.1	29.2	32.4	35.3	41.4	47.0	55.6	63.1

Sources: U.S. Department of Commerce, Bureau of the Census, *Census of Population, 1960,* vol. 1, *Characteristics of the Population,* part 1, U.S. Summary, tables 9 and 20; U.S. Department of Commerce, Bureau of the Census, *Census of Population, 1970,* vol. 2, *General Population Characteristics,* Advance Reports, Series PC (V2); T. Lynn Smith, "The Emergence of Cities," in *The Urban South,* ed. Rupert B. Vance and Nicholas J. Demerath (Chapel Hill: University of North Carolina Press, 1954), p. 33, table 4.

[a]"Old definition" refers to the definition used prior to 1950 when a number of large and densely settled places were not included as urban because they were not incorporated. In 1950, the U.S. Bureau of the Census adopted the concept of the urbanized area and delineated boundaries for unincorporated places.

[b]The population residing in urban-fringe areas and in unincorporated places of 2,500 or more is classified as urban according to the "new definition."

North Carolina, 23.8 percent; South Carolina, 19.4 percent;[4] (2) the slow-growing six states of the middle South, which had metropolitan growth of only 12.2 percent and of which only one exceeded the non-South average (Mississippi, 15.4 percent; Arkansas, 14.3 percent; Kentucky, 14.2 percent; Louisiana, 14.1 percent; Tennessee, 13.1 percent; Alabama, 6.5 percent); and (3) the expanding Southern Southwest with a subregional growth of 23.2 percent, both states of which (Texas,

23.7 percent; Oklahoma, 19.8 percent) exceeded the non-South average and one the average for the South as a whole.[5] Developing subregional alignments comprised of entire states may be old-fashioned. Urban growth is tending to shift toward clusters of large cities; as Southern centers of regional growth become more clearly identifiable, state lines will tend to lose their meaning in talk about urban growth, as is already the case in other areas. Some of the configurations suggested are the Gulf Coast conurbation (Houston to Pensacola), the Atlantic Coast conurbation (Miami to Charleston), the Carolinas conurbation (Roanoke to Augusta);[6] and/or the Texas-Louisiana urban region (Houston to Lake Charles), the Central Gulf Coast urban region (New Orleans to Pensacola), the Southern Piedmont urban region (Lynchburg to Anderson), the North Central Georgia urban region (Rome to Athens), and the North Central Texas urban region (Dallas to Fort Worth).[7] In 1972 the Presidential Commission on Population Growth and the American Future anticipated these Southern regional constellations by the year 2000: Atlantic Seaboard (Virginia), Mid-South, Florida Peninsula, Gulf Coast, and Central Oklahoma-East Central Texas. These alignments promise further fragmentation of Southern urban identity.

In spite of these qualifications, there are advantages in the South's

TABLE 6.2. *Metropolitan Population Growth, White and Nonwhite, 1960-70 (in Percentages)*

	Metropolitan Area			Central City			Suburban Ring		
	Total	White	Nonwhite	Total	White	Nonwhite	Total	White	Nonwhite
South	22.0	22.0	21.7	11.2	6.9	24.1	35.6	38.5	15.6
Alabama	6.5	10.6	-2.6	1.1	2.3	-1.3	12.3	18.7	-4.4
Arkansas	14.3	18.4	2.0	18.3	18.4	17.9	9.6	18.5	-14.3
Florida	37.2	39.4	26.2	15.5	14.9	17.7	56.5	59.2	38.5
Georgia	25.7	26.7	-2.8	7.9	-4.1	28.0	45.3	51.0	6.2
Kentucky	14.2[a]	13.6	18.8	4.2	0.5	21.7	22.9	23.4	6.7
Louisiana	14.1[a]	14.9	12.0	4.0	-1.8	15.0	31.0	38.8	4.3
Mississippi	15.4	16.8	12.5	11.2	8.0	19.2	23.0	34.1	2.7
North Carolina	23.8	25.0	19.7	16.9	14.5	22.8	31.8	35.4	13.3
Oklahoma	19.8[a]	17.2	45.4	19.3	15.0	52.1	20.9	20.5	25.9
South Carolina	19.4	24.6	5.8	5.3	7.2	1.9	24.5	30.0	7.9
Tennessee	13.1	12.6	14.4	19.8	18.7	22.7	0.9	2.7	-29.1
Texas	23.7	22.0	35.5	15.8	11.7	40.1	42.3	44.5	16.2
Virginia	28.4	31.2	17.5	8.0	4.6	15.8	46.4	49.8	21.4

Source: U.S. Department of Commerce, Bureau of the Census, *Census of Population and Housing, 1970,* Final Reports, Series PHC (2), pp. 25-27, tables 2-4.
[a]Corrected figures using U.S. Department of Commerce, Bureau of the Census, "Rank by Population Size of Many U.S. Metro Areas Changed as a Result of 1970 Census," 23 March 1971 news release. Percentages not corrected otherwise.

looking at itself as a region. Though parts of the South will continue to grow in different directions and at different rates, most of the region's cities share a common stage of development. The South's subregions may be able to cooperate to avoid the problems that have grown to crisis proportions elsewhere.

DEFINITION OF THE PROBLEM

Three basic problems will be discussed here: (1) residential segregation, the concentration of blacks and the poor in central cities, and the suburbanization of middle-class whites and newly created employment; (2) substandard housing; (3) the consequences of rapid growth, urban sprawl, and governmental clutter and misfit.

Residential Segregation and Suburbanization of Jobs

In a study based on 1960 census data, Southern cities were found to be more segregated than cities outside the South,[8] though the differences were not great. Special census results for 1964-67 in five Southern cities indicated that the problem was growing worse. In each case, the percentage of urban blacks living in census tracts that were 75 percent or more black increased: from 65 to 78 percent in Memphis; from 57 to 67 percent in Louisville; from 79 to 90 percent in Shreveport, Louisiana; from 33 to 41 percent in Little Rock; and from 86 to 88 percent in Raleigh.[9] Southern cities, once less segregated in housing,[10] had become centers for the most rapid increase in segregation.

With regard to the concentration of blacks in the central incorporated city of the SMSA and whites in the suburban outer ring, there is some population dispersal in the South. Of the region's central city population, 29 percent is nonwhite, while the comparable figures are 20 percent for the Northeast, 22 percent for the North Central, and 10 percent for the West.[11] However, while only 3 percent of the population of the Northeast residing in outer rings is black, almost 14 percent of the South's outer-ring population is black[12] (see table 6.3). Regional differences in the nature of outer-ring populations reduce the significance of the latter figures. Blacks living in outer rings of non-South SMSAs are likely to be suburban residents in a sense similar to whites who predominate in those areas. Southern SMSAs are more likely to have expanded and encompassed black rural populations. Although represented in the census figures as part of the outer ring, in reality these blacks, as remnants of a past agricultural age, could hardly be more separate.[13] The South was the only region where the outer-ring black increase, as a percentage of previous black population, was less than such increases for whites during the 1960s.[14] But one-third as much black population growth in the South was sustained in the suburbs as in the central cities, with heavy losses occurring in rural areas.

Little of general residential segregation or segregation by metropolitan subareas can be explained by income. [15] On the basis of income differentiation alone one would have difficulty explaining why in 1969 only 52.8 percent of whites below the poverty line lived in central cities of Southern SMSAs while these cities contained 80.8 percent of poor blacks. In 1959 the corresponding figures were 53.4 percent and 77.6 percent, respectively. [16]

As a result of housing discrimination, blacks receive less for their rental housing dollar. [17] But discrimination has other costs, too. "When a minority group is physically isolated, differential treatment follows almost as a matter of course." [18] The dimensions that this discrimination can take were brought to light in Shaw, Mississippi, where 97 percent of the homes on unpaved streets were in black neighborhoods; storm sewers and drainage were limited almost entirely to white sections of the city; and 99 percent of white homes had sanitary sewers as compared to only 80 percent of black homes. [19] Inadequate public facilities are part of what the National Commission on Urban Problems called a dwelling's "living environment," which any home buyer freed from racial discrimination and severe economic restrictions scrupulously examines before choosing a home. [20] The President's Committee on Urban Housing found this factor to be part of the social and environmental disadvantages of the ghetto that could invalidate any improved housing in it. [21]

As Myrdal stated: "Residential segregation is basic in a mechanical sense. It exerts an influence in an indirect and impersonal way: because Negro people do not live near white people, they cannot—even if they otherwise would—associate with each other in the many activities founded on common neighborhood." [22] At present the South's substantial school integration may give it some head start in race relations. But

TABLE 6.3. *Percentage of South's Metropolitan Population, White and Nonwhite, in Central Cities and Suburban Rings of Ten Southern States, 1960-70*

	Total Area	1960 Central City	1960 Suburban Ring	1960 Total Area	1970 Central City	1970 Suburban Ring
White	77.7	72.6	83.3	79.1	70.8	86.3
Nonwhite	22.2	27.4	16.7	20.9	29.2	13.7

Source: U.S. Department of Commerce, Bureau of the Census, *Census of Population and Housing, 1970*, Final Reports, Series PHC (2), table A.
Note: The ten states are Alabama, Arkansas, Florida, Georgia, Kentucky, Louisiana, Mississippi, North Carolina, Oklahoma, and South Carolina.

repercussions from the Supreme Court's busing decision in *Swann* v. *Charlotte-Mecklenburg Board of Education* suggest that once a school district has been totally segregated, then the de facto forces that have segregated the rest of the nation's schools will go to work. [23] The South's schools could then become resegregated.

Throughout the country the costs of city government services are beginning to rise more quickly than revenue because of the influx of the poor and the outward flow of wealthier whites, some of the latter motivated by racial considerations. Without annexations, Southern central cities would have lost population during the 1960s.

The other aspect of the urban dilemma is the suburbanization of employment. Without this complication there might be hope that increases in the income of blacks would break down some socioeconomic barriers, but with it the situation becomes more difficult. A study encompassing forty large SMSAs (eleven in the South) from 1948 to 1963, with rough corrections for annexation, showed wide disparities in the mean annual percentage growth of employment for central cities and metropolitan rings (see table 6.4). In all areas of employment—

TABLE 6.4. *Estimated Mean Annual Percentage Changes in Employment for the Central Cities and Suburban Rings of Forty Large SMSAs*

Type of Employment	Central City			Suburban Ring		
	1948-54	1954-58	1958-63	1948-54	1954-58	1958-63
Manufacturing	1.9	-1.7	-0.4	13.2	6.9	6.0
Wholesaling	0.8	0.2	-0.2	24.9	16.6	15.1
Retailing	-0.6	0.1	-2.0	11.3	13.5	13.4
Services	1.6	3.9	0.9	18.0	16.6	13.5

Source: John F. Kain, "The Distribution and Movement of Jobs and Industry," in *The Metropolitan Enigma: Inquiries into the Nature and Dimensions of America's "Urban Crisis,"* ed. James Q. Wilson (Cambridge, Mass.: Harvard University Press, 1968), p. 13, (IB) table 4, and p. 17, (IC) table 5.

Note: Central city boundaries are from 1950 figures.

wholesaling, retailing, and services—the gains in the metropolitan rings were greater than in the central cities, and only in service employment was the absolute number of employment opportunities even close. [24] By 1970 the suburbs of the nation's fifteen largest metropolitan areas provided as many jobs as the central cities. [25] When jobs develop outside the central city, John M. Kain suggests that three factors operate to limit blacks' chances to share in them: (1) the distance, difficulty, time, and expense of traveling to these jobs on transportation designed to move in the opposite direction; (2) the economic and social isolation of central-city black residential centers, which inhibits access to information concerning job opportunities developing outside the city; (3) discrimination by outer-ring employers motivated by the real or imagined animosity white residents will feel if black workers are brought into the neighborhood, where they will have reason to seek housing. [26]

Data on the location of new construction of nonresidential buildings is available by census regions, uncorrected for annexation. From 1954 to 1965 more than half of new industrial buildings (63 percent) and stores and other mercantile structures (53 percent) were located outside central cities while only 27 percent of office buildings were so placed. For the South, figures for all three categories were lower (47 percent, 33 percent, and 20 percent, respectively). [27] These figures give no indication of the relative importance of annexation (noted earlier as an important factor in Southern central city growth) and of the availability of larger amounts of vacant land in Southern cities to be expected from their lower density.

Annexation is not likely to remain for long the effective tool that it has been in the South, unless state laws are changed to prohibit or make more difficult incorporations around major cities. Annexation, difficult at best, becomes virtually impossible to accomplish once an outlying area is incorporated. [28] Even when annexation is not responsible for regional differences, the South's advantage is only temporary. Vacant land, under increased demand, cannot remain economically "available" for long. The developing price differentiation between the inner city and the outer ring, together with changes in transportation and production methods that originally allowed and are now beginning to demand suburban locations for industry, are unlikely to be reversed— except possibly by long-term and pronounced energy shortages. The preference for single-level stores and factories probably is here to stay, [29] as are the higher tax rates of the central city. [30]

Blacks, like other minority groups before them, moved into large central cities to be near blue-collar employment centers and to take advantage of the lower housing costs. However, unlike previous minorities, they encountered a resilient racism that denied them equal access to employment. Even if this barrier had been overcome, they then lacked the opportunity to move from the ghetto to the suburbs. Black migration to the cities also occurred during the rise of the automobile, with its decentralizing impetus; the city is ceasing to be the working-class employment center that it has been throughout American history. Finally, the movement of employment centers and other forms of wealth from the central cities now threatens to deny blacks the services and financial assistance required for a better life, just when black numerical concentration and political activism have provided an opportunity for commanding these resources. For the first time, the central city is without the means to solve its minority-residents' problems. [31] The answer lies within the new city that the automobile has created, the metropolitan area.

The chance to exert political influence, for so long denied to blacks, could easily produce an empty victory. As the Kerner Commission stated: "In a country where the economy, and particularly the resources of employment, are predominantly white, a policy of separation can only relegate Negroes to a permanently inferior economic status." [32] One can also imagine a white majority, under certain circumstances, being willing to abandon to blacks the central cities, emptied of most of their wealth. [33] For these reasons, policies to bring about residential integration rather than heightened separation would be of the greatest benefit to urban development and to blacks and whites in the long run.

Blacks are understandably unwilling to bear the entire price of integration. City officials must realize that when they offer their black constituents the choice of having predominantly black and financially troubled cities or of being thrown to the political mercy of white suburbanites, they are offering no viable option at all.

Substandard Housing

The South has by far the highest concentration of substandard housing stock of any region. In 1968, 16 percent of its housing was rated substandard in that it lacked some plumbing facilities or was rated "dilapidated" by census standards, as compared with 6.4 percent for the rest of the nation. [34] Both whites and nonwhites are victims, but the burden is far from equally shared. Nonwhites in the rest of the nation are slightly more than twice as likely to live in such substandard dwellings as whites, while in the South nonwhites are four times more likely to be in this situation. Thirty-six percent of all nonwhite housing units in the South were classed as substandard (see table 6.5).

TABLE 6.5. *Percentage of Occupied Housing Lacking Complete Plumbing Facilities or Rated Dilapidated, 1968*

Location	North and West		South[a]	
	Nonwhite	White	Nonwhite	White
Central cities of metropolitan areas	9	4	9	3
Suburban ring	12	3	22	3
Nonmetropolitan areas	22	7	61	16
Total	11	5	36	9

Source: U.S. Department of Commerce, Bureau of the Census, and U.S. Department of Labor, Bureau of Labor Statistics, *The Social and Economic Status of Negroes in the United States, 1969,* Current Population Reports, Series P-23, no. 29, Bureau of Labor Statistics, Report no. 375, p. 58.
[a]Census South.

In the South, substandard housing is primarily, but not entirely (see table 6.6), a nonmetropolitan problem. Within metropolitan areas nonwhites are 4.6 times as likely as whites to live in units lacking plumbing facilities and are 3.2 times as likely to live in overcrowded conditions. Nonwhites living in the outer metropolitan ring lack complete plumbing facilities 7.3 times more frequently than their white counterparts, and are overcrowded 2.7 times as often. That whites share proportionally more in the problem of overcrowding runs counter to conventional white wisdom that larger families among blacks is the major cause of their inadequate housing.

Since a high correlation exists between income and housing quality, and since blacks in 1970 had a median income of only 57 percent of that of whites, [35] one could expect that programs that raised the income of blacks would ease their housing problems. But not all of the explanation is economic; discrimination in the rental housing market is important. "Across the metropolitan United States . . . in every rent class the median rent-income ratios of Negro renters is higher than that of whites, and regardless of income Negroes show a higher proportion of substandard units that do whites."[36] Thus blacks spend more of their income on housing and get less for each dollar spent.

TABLE 6.6. *Metropolitan Housing Lacking Complete Plumbing Facilities or Rated Overcrowded, 1970*

Location and Status of Plumbing and Housing	Nonwhite	White
Total metropolitan area		
Housing lacking complete plumbing	154,777	175,209
Total housing	927,608	4,825,196
% housing lacking complete plumbing	16.7	3.6
Central cities of metropolitan areas		
Housing lacking complete plumbing	57,503	52,879
Total housing	640,083	2,189,205
% housing lacking complete plumbing	9.0	2.4
Suburban ring		
Housing lacking complete plumbing	97,274	122,330
Total housing	287,525	2,635,991
% housing lacking complete plumbing	33.8	4.6
Total metropolitan area		
Housing rated overcrowded	177,964	262,927
Total housing	927,608	4,447,085
% housing rated overcrowded	19.2	5.9
Central cities of metropolitan areas		
Housing rated overcrowded	127,973	107,198
Total housing	640,083	2,000,058
% housing rated overcrowded	20.0	5.4
Suburban ring		
Housing rated overcrowded	49,991	155,729
Total housing	287,525	2,447,027
% housing rated overcrowded	17.4	6.4

Source: U.S. Department of Commerce, Bureau of the Census, *Census of Population and Housing, 1970*, Final Reports, Series PHC (2), table 5.
Note: Because of peculiarities in the census classifications the percentage lacking complete plumbing facilities is computed by subtracting those units without complete plumbing occupied by nonwhites from all units lacking such facilities (including vacant year-round units) and dividing that by the total year-round units minus nonwhite occupied units. For nonwhites the figures are only for occupied units.
Overcrowded units have at least 1.01 persons on the average per room. For both whites and nonwhites these figures are for occupied units with complete plumbing facilities. Therefore, figures are not given for housing both overcrowded and lacking complete plumbing facilities.

Urban Sprawl and Governmental Clutter and Misfit

Anyone who has recently driven through the rapidly growing sections of Houston, Dallas, Austin, Atlanta, Miami, Fort Lauderdale, Gainesville, West Palm Beach, Raleigh, Fayetteville, and Huntsville has come face to face with urban sprawl. The downtown sections of some of these cities are indeed becoming more attractive, but they are not the rapidly growing sections. In many cases the incorporated areas lost population within their 1960 boundaries during the subsequent decade, and in no case did growth within that area match the population added through annexation. [37] The areas of rapid growth were outside the cities, and these suburbs are now the sites of sprawl, clutter, and waste.

To bemoan sprawl is not to say that these areas should be of the high density of inner cities. In fact, by national standards, high density has not characterized many Southern cities since dependence on water transportation ended. Southern cities have experienced three-fourths of their growth since the automobile gained importance circa 1925. [38] As a result of this and other factors, Southern cities have failed to develop the extremely dense inner cities common to the Northeast and North Central regions. In 1960 the region's central cities had a density of only 3,600 persons per square mile as compared with 6,200 persons per square mile for the rest of the nation, that is, they were only 58 percent as dense.

The opportunity was lost to do a better job than was done with Southern urban growth. Areas surrounding major transportation intersections, which could have supported some types of outer-ring, relatively high-density development with their attendant varieties of employment, housing, entertainment, and environmental possibilities, [39] were instead cluttered with service stations, shopping centers, and hamburger stands. Open land that should have remained untouched for years to come was developed, with the added expense of extending public services to a needlessly distant point, while land closer to the inner city was skipped over. [40] In many cases land was used with no regard for, and frequently with detriment to, the environment of the area and the growth needs of the metropolitan area. Finally, much growth took place outside of the inner city without provisions for including all racial, economic, and social groups.

The eleven metropolitan areas mentioned above each grew at least 35 percent from 1960 to 1970. [41] If metropolitan, state, or regional authorities with the responsibility to help direct growth had been operating during the decade, they might have predicted these to be high growth centers and made plans for their most efficient utilization. Properly manned and given the resources and the power necessary, such authori-

ties might have given the region more for its public and private developmental expenditures. The South continued to pace the nation in
population growth in the early 1970s. If the growth that the South will
experience during the next decade is uncontrolled, continued sprawl
and clutter will be the legacies.

According to the 1967 Census of Governments, 76 designated Southern SMSAs contained an average of 37.6 governmental units, including
county and municipal governments and school and single-function
special districts, with and without taxing power. Since the average
number of units per SMSA for the remainder of the nation is 118.2, the
South presently has a substantial advantage in regard to the problem of
"governmental clutter"; but here again time is already operating to
debilitate that advantage. [42]

Only five years earlier the 71 then-recognized Southern SMSAs had an
average of only 30 governments within their boundaries as compared
with 115 for the remainder of the nation. As a percentage of the number
in existence, the increase is much larger for the South's metropolitan
areas (see table 6.7).

TABLE 6.7. *Governments of All Types within SMSAs*

	1962	1967	% Increase
Number in South (average)	30.0	37.6	25.3
Number in non-South (average)	115.0	118.2	2.8
Number in United States (average)	87.1	91.2	4.7
Percentage of Southern SMSAs in terms of number of governments			
Lowest third	62.0	52.6	
Bottom half	84.5	78.9	
Bottom two-thirds	91.5	92.1	

Source: U.S. Department of Commerce, Bureau of the Census, *Census of Governments, 1967,*
vol. 1, *Governmental Organization,* table 19, and U.S. Department of Commerce, Bureau of the
Census, *Census of Governments, 1962,* table 15.

Of the four census regions, the South also was the only one to show an
increase in total number of governments. [43] For the thirty Southern
metropolitan areas with populations over 300,000, the average number
of governmental units increased from 47.2 in 1962 to 59.8 in 1967.

Increases in single-function special districts amounted to 57 percent of the total increase (see table 6.8).

TABLE 6.8. *Number and Types of Governments within Southern SMSAs over 300,000 in Population*

	1962	1967	% Increase
All governments (average)	47.2	59.8	26.7
School districts (average)	11.4	13.2	7.0
Special districts (average)	13.2	20.2	53.0
Others (average)	22.6	27.5	21.7

Source: U.S. Department of Commerce, Bureau of the Census, *Census of Governments, 1967,* vol. 1, *Governmental Organization,* table 19, and U.S. Department of Commerce, Bureau of the Census, *Census of Governments, 1962,* table 15.

This rapid expansion probably was caused by (1) rapid growth (during this period Southern SMSA growth was well above the national average); (2) large size (the thirty largest metropolitan areas in the region gained on the average more governments than the average for the entire 76); (3) greater demand for services by the South's larger and more affluent metropolitan population—witness the use of special districts, which more frequently are being used to provide such expanded service. There is little reason to expect the growth rate of governmental units to slow on its own.

In understanding the danger of such growth, one must begin with the proposition that the SMSA is a rough approximation of the modern urban community. This community is highly interdependent and relies on its parts for its existence, its day-to-day needs, and its continued growth. In order to survive and prosper, the community must have various types and price ranges of housing, various types of laborers possessing a range of skills, facilities for the sick, the poor, and for cultural and educational activities, and other resources. Without all these component parts, some of the community's needs would go unfulfilled; the vital process out of which city growth historically has emerged would be inhibited.

Within this community today the suburban ring bears few burdens. Because of market factors and because of the discrimination and exclusion practiced by the suburbs, they have less of the ugliness, filth, and old buildings of the inner city, and still fewer nonwhites, rich or poor. As a result, the suburbs receive an array of subsidies from the inner city. A subsidy is involved when suburban residents shop or work downtown and use the city's facilities but pay the city no taxes. They receive the general benefits (e.g., entertainment) of a thriving city, which also help to attract people with lower skills and higher service needs, without sharing the financial burden of this component of the community.

This subsidy argument may be challenged, since it is based on the proposition that the SMSA approximates an interdependent urban community; no doubt the argument may be losing some of its validity as suburban rings become more self-sufficient.[44] However, Southern metropolises still are "strikingly different from the Northeast where more often than not metropolitan communities are continuous. This means that the fringe of a southern metropolis, with few exceptions, does not have much importance independent of the central city."[45]

Layering of government involves (1) the problem of clutter itself, yielding inefficiency and reduced accountability, and (2) the problem of poor fit between the expenses of the functions that government is called upon to perform and its tax base. Associated with the first are inability to take advantage of economies of scale; waste and duplication of effort through overlap and fractionalization of governments; inability of voters and patrons to locate and fix responsibility; the probability that the decision-making body will not include all interested and concerned parties; and the difficulty of balancing total needs and resources involved in what are often area-wide functions without an area-wide government.[46] Associated with the second are the economic subsidy problem, and the problem of social goods, whereby if the good is provided for a single person it may be enjoyed by others who cannot be required to pay for the benefit.[47]

SPECIFICATION OF OUTPUTS

As defined here, the city is a concentration of institutions: outputs are shaped by the interaction of one institution with another. These institutions will affect the availability and character of jobs, the level of support for the schools, the production and placement of housing, the uses to which land will be put, and the race of the inhabitants of a neighborhood. The city government can alter the outputs of other institutions. In determining the ground rules of development, the city can affect whether future growth will be used to break down segregation in housing, to integrate the suburbs, to spread the costs of handling problems throughout the urban community, and to create attractive environments. Since it is far more difficult to correct a situation already laid in concrete than it is to avoid the problem initially, the hope of

Southern cities lies with the proper channeling of anticipated growth.

Historical Summary

The relatively small size of Southern cities at present and their recent rapid growth, as the most distinctive aspects of the region's metropolitan areas, will be examined historically.

1565-1920

Beginning with St. Augustine in 1565 cities were founded along the Southern seacoast to serve as naval, military, and administrative centers for the European powers then colonizing the New World. Political as well as economic motives were important in the founding and development of cities. [48] With few exceptions, Southern cities did not develop as centers of industrial activity. Instead they had their origins as "ports, railway and commercial centers, as local trading and marketing towns, or as temporary residences of wealthy planters' families." [49] The region and its industrial activity, such as it was, remained primarily rural. The extractive processes, which made up the bulk of the Southern industrial operations, were carried out in small towns or rural areas; as a result, Southern cities remained primarily transportation centers almost totally dependent on commerce for their existence. Unlike many commercial cities in Europe, there was no accompanying development of skilled handicraft trades.

Of the four factors mainly responsible for retarding industrialization (see chapter 2), insufficient effective demand was the greatest inhibitor of city growth during this period. Had such demand been present, the region's cities might have been able to expand through their own efforts as capital became concentrated there, but without it, they continued to remain small, slow-growing, and heavily dependent on the surrounding region.

The first census in 1790 found the South with only 1.8 percent of its population in urban places as compared with over 7 percent for the non-South. (It was not until seventy years later that the South reached the 7 percent level.) With the exception of only the decade from 1810 to 1820, the rest of the nation continued to urbanize at a faster rate than did the South. [50]

Greater industrialization did follow the Civil War, since lucrative agricultural investment opportunities had diminished. But in most cases it was of limited value to city growth because the region maintained its colonial status as the producer of raw materials for Northern industry and as the performer of low-wage, low-value-added extractive processes. Occasionally, another user of the same raw material, such as a furniture manufacturer in a sawmill town, contributed to city development, but in general the industrialization that developed in the South was not the type to produce city growth.

1920-1950

In 1920 the South was only 41 percent as urbanized as the rest of the nation, which was by that time predominantly urban. But in the 1920s the South began to close the urbanization gap. World War I helped to bring the South at least temporarily into the national economy and to speed up industrialization. The collapse of agricultural prices after the war helped to push the region away from its dependence on agriculture, which had inhibited urbanization. The dependence on agriculture was reduced even further during World War II.

Southern industries have not been the type on which large city development is built. Textiles, tobacco and cigarettes, and furniture all had periods of great growth after electrification and were able to draw upon an ample rural labor supply. But they have neither required nor produced sizable urban centers. The growth of automobile transportation also has militated against the growth of metropolitan centers because workers, who in an earlier age would have moved to locations near their employment, now commuted. The petro-chemical industry, also important to the South, had little direct effect on urban development since it created few jobs, but unlike the three industries mentioned above, it was a high wage-producing activity; it did much to build related and auxiliary industries and to stimulate services and trade. Furthermore, it has been a considerable source of capital important in the development of large Southwestern cities. World War II brought the South into the nation's economy to an unprecedented degree.

1950- PRESENT

Cities in the South perform economic functions different from those of cities in the rest of the nation. Otis Duncan et al. categorized metropolitan areas with populations of 300,000 or more (1950 census data). In the categories defined on the basis of manufacturing, not one Southern metropolitan area is to be found. But of the twenty-one metropolitan areas in the Regional Metropolis and Regional Capital classifications, twelve are Southern. These classifications are both defined in terms of their "reciprocal regional relationship . . . with an adjacent hinterland." Atlanta and Dallas are the two Regional Metropolises that have clear dominance over their hinterlands primarily because of size. These metropolitan areas act as industrial processors of regionally extracted raw materials, regional commercial and wholesale centers, personal and business service centers, and transportation hubs.[51]

Economic classification performed with 1960-63 data shows that Southern SMSAs have maintained much of their distinctiveness, though manufacturing is becoming more important.[52] In over 31 percent of the region's metropolitan areas, retailing employment was greater than manufacturing employment. This was true of only 17 percent of SMSAs in the rest of the nation. Manufacturing provided more than half of the employment in 18.4 percent of Southern metropolitan areas and in 60.6 percent of non-Southern areas. Thus the metropolitan areas of the South remain to a large degree dependent on retailing employment, the mark of an interdependent relationship with the adjacent hinterland. And because of the importance of retail employment, Southern cities remain far more dependent on fluctuations in the general economy than are cities elsewhere (see table 6.9). Larger Southern cities have grown rapidly, then, because of the increased industrialization stimulated by

TABLE 6.9. *Functional Classification of Cities over 10,000 Population, and SMSAs, 1963 (in Percentages)*

Classification	Southern SMSA	Non-Southern SMSA	Total SMSA	Southern Cities	Non-Southern Cities	Total Cities
Manufacturing[a]	15.8	57.3	43.4	19.8	34.3	30.8
Industrial[b]	2.6	3.3	3.1	2.2	4.6	4.0
Diversified manufacturing[c]	43.4	19.3	27.4	18.8	10.7	12.7
Diversified retailing[d]	23.7	16.7	19.0	22.7	10.5	13.5
Retailing[e]	7.9	.7	3.1	16.3	8.8	10.7
Dormitory[f]	0	0	0	12.2	25.1	21.8
Specialized[g]	6.6	2.7	4.0	8.4	6.0	6.6

Source: Richard L. Forstall, "Economic Classification of Places Over 10,000, 1960-1963," in *The Municipal Year Book, 1967* (Chicago: International City Management Association, 1967), p. 40, table 1, and pp. 45-48.

[a]50 percent or more of total employment in manufacturing, and less than 30 percent in retail trade.

[b]50 percent or more of total employment in manufacturing, and over 30 percent in retail trade.

[c]Employment in manufacturing greater than retail employment, but less than 50 percent.

[d]Greater employment in retailing than in manufacturing, but manufacturing at least 20 percent of total.

[e]Retail employment is greater than any other component of total employment and manufacturing is less than 20 percent.

[f]Primarily residential.

[g]Some type of unusual economic activity forms the principal source of employment for the community.

World War II and subsequent events, and because of the increased prosperity of outlying areas. There are special factors that have spurred growth: for Florida, the tourist and retirement business attracted by its pleasant climate; for the South in general, armed forces installations and space expenditures. Southern cities have received federal largesse in slightly greater amounts relative to population than have cities in other regions. [53]

The classification of cities for 1960-63 cited above shows armed forces installations as the primary employment source for only two SMSAs, both in the South. Of the 23 SMSAs that had such employment as a secondary and important source, 14 were located in the South. These were 21 percent of the Southern SMSAs recognized at that time. [54] The importance of military-base spending in the South has not declined since then. Huntsville and Houston, two of the eleven metropolitan areas in the region with a growth of more than 35 percent in the 1960s, are also

TABLE 6.10. *SMSAs: Their Growth by Population Size, 1960-70*

Size of SMSA, 1970	Number in the South	% in the South	Population in the South	% of Pop. in the South	% of South's Growth, '60-'70[a]	% of U.S. Growth, '60-'70[a]
2,000,000 and above	0	0	0	0	0	12.0
1,000,000- 1,999,999	6	28.6	8,258,001	29.0	33.9	26.6
750,000- 999,999	4	40.0	3,222,773	37.7	19.8	22.0
500,000- 749,999	8	36.4	4,872,924	36.4	21.2	15.6
400,000- 499,999	4	44.4	1,713,701	43.4	20.5	19.1
300,000- 399,999	8	30.8	2,655,629	29.8	16.4	15.0
200,000- 299,999	15	31.2	3,821,489	31.8	20.1	17.8
150,000- 199,999	8	29.6	1,424,977	30.8	14.3	13.3
100,000- 149,999	18	42.9	2,218,766	42.3	9.2	10.8
50,000- 99,999	11	35.5	29,076,301	21.7	22.5	16.5

Source: U.S. Department of Commerce, Bureau of the Census, "Rank by Population Size of Many U.S. Metro Areas Changed as a Result of 1970 Census," 23 March 1971 news release.
[a]These percentages total more than 100 percent because areas with smaller populations showed declines in population between 1960 and 1970.

the beneficiaries of large government expenditures for missile development and space exploration.[55] Although figures in chapter 2 indicate that the South's share of total federal expenditures was not far out of line with its share of the population, in an under-urbanized region the receipts had a profound effect and helped to designate which localities were to grow.

Today the South has more than its share of growth centers. Although only 28 percent of the nation's population and 22 percent of its metropolitan population is Southern, 34 percent of SMSAs are Southern. On the basis of its percentage of the nation's population, the region could be predicted to have only 67 percent, or 53 SMSAs, rather than the 82 it actually has. The explanation for these extra metropolitan areas is that Southern SMSAs are generally smaller than those in the rest of the nation. The South in 1970 had no SMSA with a population of more than two million, but there are 12 outside the South, accounting for 47 percent of the non-South's metropolitan population.[56] The South is overrepresented in all other SMSA size categories (see table 6.10).

BLACKS AND URBAN GROWTH

Not since 1890 have blacks been more urbanized than whites in the South; furthermore, in only three decades since 1900 have blacks in the South urbanized more quickly than whites. After 1910 blacks formed a far higher percentage of those migrating from the South than their percentage of the region's population.[57] "The net migration to an area corresponds very closely to its income level and its production of new jobs as compared with other potential destinations for migrants."[58] Assuming that this proposition has been valid throughout the country, it appears that while the Southern city became the center of opportunity for the rural white population, racial discrimination until recently denied it that function for blacks.

Blacks have been declining as a percentage of the South's total, rural, and metropolitan population (see table 6.11). In only one part of the Southern city have they been increasing—the inner city. The South was once the least segregated region residentially, a condition that lingered for some time in the older cities. As the cities of the "New South" developed in this century, blacks were housed in areas set aside for them.[59] A study done with 1960 data showed that the age of a city (among smaller cities) was a significant determinant of the degree of residential segregation present.[60] As noted earlier, the South by 1960 was the most segregated region.

TABLE 6.11. *Blacks and Urban Growth in the South*

	1890	1900	1910	1920	1930	1940	1950[a]	1960[a]	1970
% of black population in urban areas	13.6	15.5	19.6	23.5	29.8	34.4	45.3	55.9	
Black urbanization change (by decade, in percentages)		1.9	4.1	3.9	6.3	4.6	10.9	10.6	
% of nonblack population in urban areas	13.3	15.1	20.4	26.2	32.8	34.9	47.6	58.1	
Nonblack urbanization change (by decade, in percentages)		1.8	5.3	5.8	6.6	2.1	12.7	10.5	
Black % of South's urban population	36.1	34.9	30.8	26.4	24.3	24.8	21.6	20.3	
Black % of South's rural population	35.5	34.3	30.7	29.3	26.9	25.2	23.3	21.8	
Black % of South's total population	35.6	34.3	30.7	28.6	26.1	25.0	22.5	21.0	19.1

Sources: U.S. Department of Commerce, Bureau of the Census, *Changing Characteristics of the Negro Population,* by Daniel O. Price (Washington, D.C.: Government Printing Office, 1969), table B-1; U.S. Department of Commerce, Bureau of the Census, *Thirteenth Census of the United States, 1910,* vol. 1, *Population,* table 42; U.S. Department of Commerce, Bureau of the Census, *Fourteenth Census of the United States, 1920,* vol. 2, *Population,* table 24; U.S. Department of Commerce, Bureau of the Census, *Fifteenth Census of the United States, 1930,* vol. 2, *Characteristics of the Population,* table 21; U.S. Department of Commerce, Bureau of the Census, *Sixteenth Census of the United States, 1940,* vol. 2, *Characteristics of the Population,* part 2, Kansas-Michigan, Kentucky, table 5, and part 5, New York, Oregon, Oklahoma, table 5; U.S. Department of Commerce, Bureau of the Census, *Census of Population, 1950,* vol. 2, *Characteristics of the Population,* part 17, Kentucky, table 14, and part 36, Oklahoma, table 14; U.S. Department of Commerce, Bureau of the Census, *Census of Population, 1960,* vol. 1, *Characteristics of the Population,* part 19, Kentucky, table 15, part 38, Oklahoma, table 15, and part 1, U.S. Summary, tables 9 and 20.
[a]"New definition" figures are used for 1950 and 1960. For definition, see table 6.1.

Inputs to the Southern City

ENDOWMENTS

Smaller Metropolitan Areas

Southern metropolitan areas, as mentioned earlier, are generally smaller than those elsewhere; on the average they are only 53 percent as big as those in the rest of the nation. Of the nation's metropolitan population, 75.7 percent resides in SMSAs of less than one million in size while the comparable figure in the rest of the nation is 32.9 percent. Something about extremely large size increases most urban problems in a qualitative respect. The South's cities, then, should be manageable if the region acts before growth removes this advantage.

Younger Cities

> While 64 percent of Northeastern cities and 10 percent of North Central cities had attained one half of their 1960 population prior to 1900, only 8 percent of Southern cities had done so. Furthermore, while 32 percent of Northeastern cities and 71 percent of North Central cities attained one half of their 1960 population between 1905 and 1920, only 18 percent of Southern cities did. Thirty-eight percent of Southern Central cities attained one half of their 1960 population between 1925 and 1945, and another 36 percent attained it between 1945 and 1960. Between 1925 and 1960, therefore, 74 percent of Southern cities reached this level, in contrast to only 19 percent of North Central cities and only 4 percent of Northeastern cities. [61]

Since the South's cities are younger, less of the social capital of its central cities is deteriorating, and repair and replacement is less of a drain on resources.

Less Dense Metropolitan Areas

The fact that much of the growth of Southern cities came during the age of the automobile made them less dense. SMSAs in the South were only 79 percent as dense in 1960 as those in the rest of the nation.

Healthier Central Cities

Because of expansion through annexation, Southern central cities have continued to grow. However, like those in the rest of the country, they are losing population within their old boundaries. In terms of the location of building activity, Southern central cities have shown themselves to be more constructive than those in the non-South.

Strong County Governments

The county in the South traditionally has been a stronger unit of government than in other regions. This factor is especially important to those metropolitan areas contained entirely by a single county, of which there were 32 out of the South's 77 in 1967. [62] For these SMSAs, metropolitan functions can be undertaken by an already-established unit of government, which is a great practical advantage.

Prospects for Healthy Future Growth

Population projections for large metropolitan areas reaching 100,000 population by the year 2000 show the South continuing to experience

TABLE 6.12. *Mean Annual Population Growth Rate for Urbanized Areas Attaining Population Size of 100,000 by 2000 (in Percentages)*

Area	1960-70	1970-80	1960-2000	1980-2000
Florida	3.96	3.88	2.45	2.98
Southeast[a]	2.56	2.29	2.15	1.88
Mid-Southwest[b]	2.86	2.76	2.47	2.13
United States	2.14	2.24	2.03	1.87

Source: Jerome P. Pickard, *Dimensions of Metropolitanism* (Washington, D.C.: Urban Land Institute, 1967), p. 66.
[a]Includes Alabama, Arkansas, Georgia, Mississippi, North Carolina, South Carolina, Tennessee, Kentucky (excluding Louisville), Virginia (excluding Washington, D.C. suburbs), and east Louisiana.
[b]Includes Texas, Oklahoma, and west Louisiana.

growth in excess of the national average (see table 6.12). The South may be fortunate that so much of its growth will be coming during an age in which environmental and energy matters are of major concern and industrial development and growth in general are viewed as mixed blessings to be carefully controlled. [63] Governor Reubin Askew of Florida and other governors in the early 1970s suggested that the region had reached a point in its economic development that it could afford to curtail "undesirable" industrial and urban expansion. The Southern Growth Policies Board, an interstate compact organization established in 1971, had as its mandate planning for controlled growth.

EXTERNAL FACTORS

Expansion of the National Economy and Federal Largesse

The expansion of the national economy to include the South, especially after 1940, and the impact of federal expenditures on an under-urbanized region have been significant, as previously discussed.

The Federal Judiciary

Federal judicial actions in two areas have had profound impact on Southern cities. The first is school desegregation. *Brown* v. *Board of Education*[64] not only began the process of integrating the nation's schools but also gave impetus to the growing political activism of urban blacks, which was to help produce legislation on equal employment opportunity, fair housing, and equal access to public accommodations. Decisions on busing to achieve integration[65] have potential for integrating schools in large urban centers where housing segregation makes techniques other than busing ineffective. Unfortunately, this same development has the potential for aggravating destructive political forces. The Charlotte experience can serve as the model for a Southern nightmare. There the Concerned Parents Association formed to oppose busing and quickly grew into what the *Charlotte Observer* characterized as the "strongest and most single-minded bloc of voters this county has ever known."[66] But they were not so single-issue-oriented that they could not oppose the city-county consolidation plan, which contained some school-related proposals,[67] and the merger went down in defeat.

Baker v. *Carr* and subsequent one-man, one-vote decisions, in state legislative and congressional apportionment, have given the region's urban population a greater voice in determining state and national policies. In some areas increased governmental activity in urban affairs has ensued.

A new field in which the federal judiciary may produce important results was opened by *Hawkins* v. *Town of Shaw, Mississippi*.[68] In this case city action, which resulted in Shaw's black population's receiving municipal facilities of a quality inferior to those of the white population, was held to be a denial of equal protection of the laws. This and similar decisions have a long road ahead before becoming the "law of the land," but promise to have great impact on the South.

The U.S. Supreme Court was moving toward a more cautious approach to school desegregation and related matters in 1972-74. A 1971 decision on the west coast also went against the earlier antidiscriminatory trend: *James* v. *Valtierra*[69] found constitutionally acceptable a California constitutional provision that allowed a suburb to vote on whether to allow low-income housing within its boundaries. Finding the alleged discrimination to be based on poverty rather than race, the court held the voting provision did not violate the "equal protection" provision of the Fourteenth Amendment. Race and poverty, of course, are in many cases indistinguishably entangled.

POLICY DECISIONS

Federal

Congress sought to guarantee equal access and opportunity in public accommodations and employment in the 1964 Civil Rights Act and in housing in the 1968 Civil Rights Act. The potential impact of this legislation is considerable for Southern cities. Among other things, by discouraging segregation it might also lessen the region's loss through out-migration of so many blacks. However, unlike school desegregation, the impact of this legislation is difficult to assess. One reason is the lack of clear commitment to enforcement by Congress and the administration.[70] The record of the federal executive in the creation of segregated housing has been nothing short of tragic.

> From 1935 to 1950—a period in which about 15 million new dwellings were constructed—the power of the national government was explicitly used to prevent integrated housing. Federal policies were based upon the premise that economic and social stability could best be achieved through keeping neighborhood populations as homogenous as possible. Thus the *Underwriting Manual* of the Federal Housing Administration . . . warned that "if a neighborhood is to retain stability, it is necessary that properties shall continue to be occupied by the same social and racial group." It advised appraisers to lower their valuation of properties in mixed neighborhoods, "often to the point of rejection." FHA actually drove out of business some developers who insisted upon open policies.[71]

Since that time its record has been only modestly improved. According to the U.S. Commission on Civil Rights it was not until the 1962 Executive Order on Equal Opportunity in Housing that "it could be said that FHA and VA policy was one of nondiscrimination," and even that policy change applied mainly to new housing.[72] The tacit support of segregation is seen in programs that reinforce inequality and in the choices of location of low-income federally assisted housing. There has been extensive subsidization of privately constructed and owned middle-income housing in comparison with the investment made in low-income housing.

> In 1962, the U.S. Government expended an estimated $820 million to subsidize housing for poor people. (The sum includes public housing, public assistance, and savings because of income tax de-

ductions.) In the same year, the Federal Government spent an estimated $2.9 billion to subsidize housing for those with middle incomes or more. This sum includes only savings from income tax deductions. . . . The two programs that express the national conscience in housing—public assistance and public housing—together manage to raise poor families to per capita equality with the income tax subsidy that goes to all the rest. [73]

Finally, "the few Federal programs that do seek to provide . . . [low income] housing do not provide it on a metropolitan basis. Indeed, they are having the effect of intensifying concentrations of the poor and nonwhite within central cities." [74] Of the quarter of a million public housing units built in the nation's twenty-four largest cities by 1966, only 76 units were located outside of the central city. And the other federal programs that provide units for low- and moderate-income people are largely ineffective in locating outside of the central city because of placement requirements that have the effect of allowing suburban locations to choose whether such housing will be constructed within their boundaries. [75] The Nixon administration made it clear that it would not force "economic integration" of the suburbs. Former HUD Secretary George Romney attempted to tie federal sewer, water, and urban renewal funds to the acceptance of low- and moderate-income housing within a suburb, but since these funds are of relatively small importance to most suburbs, little could be expected from his gesture. [76]

Through federal financial-aid requirements, a promising movement toward metropolitan planning and control of matters of regional concern has begun. The metropolitan councils of government and planning agencies have not been very effective so far, because they are powerless to do more than threaten restraining action as a sanction. [77] Nevertheless, guidelines tied to the massive federal expenditures in metropolitan areas, coupled with political astuteness in their administration, might alter the picture.

State

Rather than developing on a statewide basis to deal with general and continuing urban problems, political-support groups usually arise in response to particular crises in particular urban areas. With this in mind, the tendency of the region's legislatures to pass special local legislation, detrimental in most ways, may have benefited urban areas. As the National Commission on Urban Problems put it, "it has generally been more feasible in the South than elsewhere to obtain needed State action focused directly upon the unique problems of particular areas where there was strong local backing for change."[78] These are not situations out of which general solutions to urban difficulties can come.

Southern states rely far less than other states on the property tax as a source of local and state revenues, with only Texas of the thirteen states approaching the national average. The states of the region rank almost as low when the tax is related to each $1,000 of personal income as when it is presented on a straight per capita basis (see table 6.13). Southern states rely more on state-imposed sales taxes and provide fewer public services.[79] Southern state governments also generally bear a larger share of the financial burden of public education than do other states. Of the twelve Southern states for which figures are available, ten rank within the top seventeen states in the nation in the percentage of the cost of public education borne by the state government (see table 6.14). These two facets of Southern governmental finance are important because school expenditures are the most significant expenditure item of local governments and are one of the primary motivations to zone out low- and moderate-income housing as net financial burdens upon the community. Of ten Southern states, seven are in the lower half of states both in terms of locally raised property tax dollars expended on public education and the percentage this source forms of the total expended.[80]

Local

Annexation / From 1950 to 1960, of the 103 cities in the United States with populations over 25,000 that annexed areas containing 10,000 or more inhabitants, 47 (or 46 percent) were in the South,[81] a percentage far in excess of what might be expected on any population or growth basis. Of the 28 cities that annexed 2,000 or more residents from 1960 to 1965, 10 were in the South, and the region maintained this approximate share during 1966-67 among cities annexing 1,000 or more inhabitants.[82] The importance of this annexation activity was shown in the 1970 census figures. During the 1960s the central cities of Southern SMSAs sustained better than 10 percent growth, of which over 100 percent was due to annexation.[83] Without annexation the central cities of the region, like those of the nation,[84] would have lost population. The widespread use of annexation also may have helped to curtail the expansion in layers of government in the region's metropolitan areas.[85]

It is not clear to what degree widespread annexation is the result of the fact that younger cities are less likely to be surrounded by incorporated suburbs that make annexation all but impossible, and to what degree it results from decisions by Southern states to set up annexation procedures that are easily operated. The latter factor is important in determining

TABLE 6.13. *Property Tax, 1968-69*

	Property Tax as % of All State and Local Tax Revenue	Per Capita Property Tax		Property Tax per $1,000 of Personal Income	
		Amount	State Rank	Amount	State Rank
South	30.0	....	...	....	...
United States (average)	40.0	151.92	...	44.86	...
Alabama	16.1	36.20	50	15.37	50
Arkansas	26.4	58.37	48	25.25	45
Florida	34.5	113.74	34	36.82	34
Georgia	30.4	81.85	40	29.89	37
Kentucky	23.1	64.23	44	24.37	46
Louisiana	20.2	60.32	46	23.01	47
Mississippi	24.7	59.84	47	28.95	38
North Carolina	26.1	67.66	43	25.81	42
Oklahoma	31.0	89.00	37	31.48	35
South Carolina	21.9	49.32	49	20.93	48
Tennessee	27.1	68.38	42	26.58	41
Texas	42.9	118.37	32	39.82	29
Virginia	26.3	82.53	39	27.33	40

Source: U.S. Department of Commerce, Bureau of the Census, *Governmental Finances in 1968-69,* Series G.F. 69, no. 5, tables 17, 22, and 24.

TABLE 6.14. *State Support of Public Education, 1968-69*

	% State Support of Public Education	State Rank
Alabama	75	6
Arkansas	53	16
Florida	...	...
Georgia	67	9
Kentucky	58	15
Louisiana	68	8
Mississippi	40	24
North Carolina	76	5
Oklahoma	28	41
South Carolina	66	10
Tennessee	59	13
Texas	52	17
Virginia	38	29

Source: U.S. Department of Health, Education, and Welfare, *Pulbic School Finance Programs, 1968-69,* by Thomas L. Johns (Washington, D.C.: Government Printing Office, 1969).

whether annexation will even be attempted.[86] Cities from three states with easily operated procedures appeared most frequently in lists of annexers.[87]

Six of the thirteen Southern states have easily operated annexation procedures that avoid referendums: Kentucky, Mississippi, North Carolina, Tennessee, Texas, and Virginia. The differences between the Texas and North Carolina procedures are perhaps the greatest. Texas empowers certain of its home rule cities to annex unilaterally and almost without restrictions. While North Carolina allows municipal councils to annex unilaterally, rather extensive requirements concerning the urban character, development, and location of the area to be annexed, together with services to be provided to the new area by the annexing municipality, must be met before annexation takes place. North Carolina's statute provides for the more orderly method of annexing land and is less likely to produce massive preemptive "land-grabs" of rural areas not ready to be urbanized. An important advantage of Texas's annexation mechanism is that it allows more of a metropolitan area to be included within a central city, reducing the problems of governmental clutter and misfit. Both states, however, fail to deal with the problem of new incorporations within or near the metropolitan area. Once the suburbs have developed and incorporated, the city has reached its final size.

Exclusionary and Fiscal Zoning / Zoning began in the United States as an extension of the common-law nuisance doctrine, which allowed limitations to be placed on certain objectionable uses of land, and under this extension (based on the state's power to protect the "general welfare"), it was broadened into a land-use regulatory technique. However, primarily as the result of the misfit of governments within metropolitan areas, the meaning of "general welfare" employed by local decision-makers has become narrow and warped. The "legitimate interests of all . . . parties—landowner, neighbor, municipality, and region" are not adequately represented because municipal boundaries do not include all those who need to be involved.[88] "The problems of air and water pollution, transportation, open space, solid waste disposal, housing, and employment do not end" locally.

> The problem takes on momentous proportions when compounded by the reliance of local governments on the property tax as their major source of revenue. How land within their borders is used becomes not merely a question of esthetic and social sensitivity, it is a matter of governmental solvency. Land-use controls have become a major weapon in the battle for ratables.

The game of "fiscal zoning" requires the players—i.e., zoning jurisdictions—to attract uses which add more in property taxes or local sales taxes than they require in expensive public services and to exclude uses which do not pay their own way. In essence, this means that jurisdictions are influenced to seek industrial and commercial uses and luxury housing and discourage or prohibit such uses as housing for low- and moderate-income persons. A further refinement is the desire to exclude housing which attracts families with many children in favor of housing with no children or as few as possible—all this because children require schools, the most significant expenditure item of local governments. Low-income housing is bad from a purely fiscal perspective because it does not add to the tax rolls the same amount of assessed value as luxury housing and because it often brings large families into a community. In addition, the families occupying such housing may require welfare and, it is widely believed, more of other services from local government than higher income families require. [89]

Some of the techniques employed in exclusionary and fiscal zoning include:

1. Zoning vacant residential land for large minimum-lot size, thereby reducing the supply of developable land and increasing its cost.
2. Zoning for excessively large minimum-house size, without regard to the size of families occupying the house or a generally accepted minimum standard of floor area.
3. Prohibiting all forms of multifamily housing from an entire municipality, thereby zoning out the people who cannot afford their own homes.
4. Spot-zoning of land for multifamily housing through the use of special or conditional permits, thereby allowing only expensive apartments in the suburbs.
5. Imposing unduly expensive subdivision requirements which increase the cost of land development by shifting the burden of public improvements from the public at large to new homeowners. [90]

There is no indication that Southern governments are any less willing or able to utilize these tools to exclude the poor and minority groups.

POLITICAL

As long as the region remained predominantly rural, and rural interests exerted control in state legislatures and congressional delegations far in excess of the numbers that they represented, there was little reason to expect state and federal action to meet the needs of the city. External economic inputs after 1940 largely produced the region's rapid urban growth, and *Baker* v. *Carr*[91] brought reapportionment to produce political changes from these demographic trends. In 1970, for the first time, more than half of the South's population lived in metropolitan areas, and—unlike smaller urban areas—these metropolises often produce citizenries with more progressive political values than those of the rural South.

Two new, politically active groups have risen to regional importance with increased urbanization: an urban middle class and an urban black population. Traditionally, the first group has been a prime mover for social and political changes, generally of a progressive nature, in its own behalf.[92] However, this predominantly white middle class has, like its national counterpart, become suburban, and often its interests are viewed narrowly as in opposition to the needs of the residents of the inner city. The loss of power by conservative rural elements may have been only temporary; the development of a new rural-suburban coalition is possible. Therefore, it is with the second emerging group, the urban blacks, that much of the Southern hope to solve its urban problems rests, perhaps in a white labor-black coalition.[93]

Governments, through their persuasive and coercive powers, are the institutions that ultimately may shape the development of metropolitan areas into desired forms. The city itself, as the primary victim of segregation and metropolitan governmental clutter and misfit, is the level of government most ready to act upon urban problems. To be effective, many problem-solving mechanisms will have to extend beyond the city's boundaries and must therefore wait upon state action; it is impossible to fashion from the city's own powers and resources a comprehensive solution to urban problems. The federal government, though furthest from the problem, is the other level of government that has shown signs of recognizing the magnitude of urban problems.

The county government's strengths are also its weaknesses. As a strong, existing unit it could be utilized without developing a new structure; its officials could offer important political assistance in winning acceptance of changes. These qualities mean, however, that the county may have neither the proper orientation to the solution of the problems nor the flexibility necessary to operate in a new area. It is conservative and rural-dominated; it is where suburbanites now exercise their political power.

State governments have the authority and resources to deal effectively with a wide range of problems, while operating at some distance from the difficulties. But since the South has only recently become predominantly urban, since it still has few large cities, and since its urban problems are not yet at the crisis point, state governments may remain inactive until the problems get out of hand.

SOCIAL

Until recently, indigenous social institutions have tended to inhibit urban growth. That growth was discouraged by the attitudes of a rural age, and the political and social dominance of an elite opposed to the development of a change-oriented urban community. The forces that broke the fetters of tradition were primarily post-1940 and exogenous. World War II exposed Southerners to the rest of the nation and the world and exposed non-Southerners to the South, introduced more industry and technological development to the region, brought the South into the national economy, and opened lines of national communication. In the 1950s and the 1960s black political activism, which fed and was fed by federal actions, further accelerated the rate of change. "Taken together these events comprised a force for social change too large and too insistent for the South to withstand as it had done more or less successfully in the past. It could no longer choose the kinds of social changes it would allow. . . ."[94]

EDUCATIONAL

The need to contribute to the financing of local public schools has been met by communities in the South, as elsewhere, by levying property taxes. The quality of education a child receives thus becomes partly dependent upon the wealth of his community and the priority placed upon education by its residents when they vote upon tax rates to support education.

An oft-repeated reason given by people for moving from cities to suburbs is the alleged inferiority of city school systems. Once ensconced in their suburban enclaves, residents are loath to admit low-income families with children because the newcomers will make demands on the schools without adding much to the property-tax base. Through zoning restrictions and refusal to build public housing, many suburbs have prevented intrusions from inner-city residents. Two federal court decisions—one requiring a merger of the school systems of Richmond and its surrounding suburban counties, the other (not upheld by the Supreme Court) challenging the constitutionality of school financing based upon the local property tax—raised a host of questions.

Policy Recommendations

Reforming city governments has been, at least since the muckraker movement, a major goal of American reform. Some of the reforms—for example, nonpartisan elections—have moved city government in the wrong direction, and others have had little impact on the substance of policy decisions. "Reformed" governments have been found to be less responsive to the characteristics of their populations than have other urban governments.[95] Environmental factors such as income levels appear to have more effect on urban expenditure levels than do structural characteristics of city governments. The policy recommendations below deal primarily with substantive policy choices and to a lesser extent with institutional reforms. (Structural characteristics *do* have some independent effect on policy. Also, these characteristics are in some cases more directly amenable to citizen control, and are thus more likely to be changed in a short span of time, than are environmental characteristics.)

No one level of government can solve the problems of urban areas, so the recommendations below are directed at federal, state, and local levels.

FEDERAL

Continue Federal Aid to Cities

The only level of government located in the South that has recognized the urgency of urban problems is the city, and without state cooperation the city lacks the resources to fashion effective solutions. The South's position as the least urbanized area with the fewest severe urban problems, and the continued importance of racial divisions suggest that the states may not act until it is too late.

The most likely source of funds for various purposes remains the federal government; its incentives to metropolitan cooperation, planning, and racial and economic integration of the suburbs could operate through guidelines and restrictions placed on all federal expenditures in urban areas, and through monies for urban development. Some have feared that general revenue-sharing—in which federal tax revenues are returned to localities and states with few strings attached to their use—would turn the clock back. The problems of the cities in the South, it is feared, would be unlikely to receive as much attention as they would if the federal government continued to be the source of direct aid. [96] However, the problems have not been with revenue-sharing as such, but with the proposed federal program cuts that accompanied it, and with the incapability of many state and local governments at present to spend additional money wisely. A small-scale revenue-sharing program, on its own merits, would be acceptable.

A separate problem with revenue-sharing is the possibility that the program will discourage consolidation of governments and annexation efforts by providing funds for small and financially insecure governments.

Attempt to Influence Corporate Location

When corporations move from the central city to suburban locations, the problems of blue-collar employees are often ignored. Corporations should be encouraged to act voluntarily to insure that the housing and transportation needs of their nonexecutive employees are met as adequately as the needs of their executives. The federal government may have to use civil rights laws to influence corporations to act in this manner; some argue that a corporate move from the city to the suburbs, with its detrimental effect on previous minority employment, constitutes a violation of the equal employment provisions of the 1964 Civil Rights Act. Legislation similar to the facilities location bill of 1970, introduced by Senator Abraham Ribicoff, might become necessary. The proposed legislation

> would require Federal agencies, Federal contractors and State and local governments to insure that adequate housing is available wherever they locate or expand their facilities. It would require [that] moderate income housing in the vicinity of the facility be provided for by the community in which such facilities are located with Federal subsidization of the communities concerned. The bill forbids the location of new facilities in communities which have failed to develop an acceptable plan to provide the requisite housing. A corporation which violates this requirement can lose its Federal contracts; a State or local government can lose Federal assistance. [97]

Develop a National Housing Policy

The federal government acknowledged the magnitude of housing problems when it established the Department of Housing and Urban Development. Unfortunately, statements about a national commitment to meet housing needs have consisted chiefly of rhetoric. The situation deteriorated further in 1973 when the Nixon administration sought to halt a number of the HUD programs that did exist. As well as facilitating the building of housing in sufficient quantity to meet the need, the federal government should promote the type of housing construction normally avoided by private builders. Two proposals that would benefit the urban South follow.

Increase Federal Subsidies for Low-Cost Housing / The federal effort to provide housing for low-income people looks impressive until it is compared with the greater housing subsidy to middle-income groups. Not only does FHA insure mortgages for those able to buy their own homes, but the tax deduction allowed for interest payments on a mortgage amounts to a subsidy of millions of dollars every year to home-owners. It is time to correct this inequity by increasing low-cost housing programs for the growing number of people being priced out of the housing market. Direct income supplements that could be used to buy private or public housing also might be provided.

Use Financial Power of Federal Government to Affect Housing Patterns / The Southern Regional Council has pointed out that "only the federal government has the power and resources to make dramatic changes in the nation's residential patterns."[98] Through vigorous enforcement of existing civil rights legislation and through use of federally assisted housing programs, the government could attempt to bring about a greater mix of housing types in the suburbs, promoting the building and dispersal of multifamily, low- and moderate-income, and public housing, as well as private single-family, middle-class dwellings. Changes here would have to be achieved painfully, over a long period. If more traditional measures fail, the federal government may have to begin insuring property values in neighborhoods with a certain racial balance.

Assist Development of Public Mass Transportation

Mass transit is need to facilitate movement within cities and between cities and outlying areas. Instead of continuing to pour money into the building of highways, which perpetuates dependence on the private automobile with its attendant energy, pollution, and traffic and parking problems, the federal government should assist cities in developing modern public mass transportation. Access to such transportation would help to expand employment opportunities, making it possible for city dwellers to travel to various job locations. The quality of life of such transit-dependent groups as the aged also would be improved. Most Southern cities have poorly developed mass transportation systems and could especially benefit from federal aid in this area.

Enforce National Standards for Purity of Air and Water

The fouling of the water and the air is a particular problem in congested urban areas. Pollution cannot be handled realistically by cities or states because it transcends their boundaries. Therefore, national standards for the purity of air and water resources should be vigorously enforced, even in the face of energy shortage. Each governmental unit should see that these standards are met within its jurisdiction; for instance, cities would be responsible for seeing that their sewerage treatment is adequate to avoid water pollution, with the federal government stepping in to fill jurisdictional gaps.

STATE

Prohibit New Incorporations Anywhere Within SMSAs

None of the Southern states, regardless of annexation procedures, has solved the related problem of new incorporations within or near metropolitan areas. Once the suburbs have incorporated, the city has reached its final geographical size. What is needed is a statutory prohibition on new incorporations anywhere within a SMSA. Coupled with this restriction, the annexation model referred to below would be appropriate. Without a limitation on incorporations, however, annexation powers should be as broad as possible.

Encourage Annexation

Of the Southern state requirements that relate to the power of cities to annex, outlined previously, North Carolina's annexation procedure is the one endorsed by the Advisory Commission on Intergovernmental Relations. [99] Difficult issues often accompany annexation; for example, the city government's desire to strengthen the economy by annexing more territory may conflict with the political ambitions of inner-city blacks, who often lose their numerical predominance after annexation. Thus a two-tiered form of government (as recommended below) might be established in circumstances where there has been large-scale annexation.

The power to exercise extraterritorial planning and zoning control, discussed below, also should be granted to cities by the states.

Aid City-County Consolidation Through Permissive Legislation

City-county consolidation, some believe, has the potential to ameliorate metropolitan problems. [100] In most Southern SMSAs one county contains the central city and a substantial part of its suburban ring. In these cases consolidation of the city and county governments reduces the problem of governmental misfit, and gives a single unit additional resources to deal with other problems.

Since 1947 three of the four or five major city-county consolidations have taken place in the South—Baton Rouge and East Baton Rouge Parish in 1947, Nashville and Davidson County in 1962, and Jacksonville and Duval County in 1967. In addition, in 1957 Miami and Dade County adopted a two-tiered, federation form of government in which Miami and twenty-seven suburban cities continued to perform local functions while the county took over functions that were metropolitan in nature. [101] In general, however, the record of consolidation attempts has been filled with failure. Various political considerations often make it impossible. However, consolidated governments show enough potential for solving urban problems that they should be encouraged. States should pass general enabling legislation that allows their large cities to establish charter study commissions and to conduct referendums on consolidation. Blacks and other segments of the population are likely to fear that they will be sacrificed in the interest of "saving the city"; therefore, the recommendations often given for making consolidation easier by reducing voting requirements [102] should not be followed. States should remove the restrictions that keep metropolitan areas from considering consolidation, but they should not force the union. The best compromise might be a two-tiered form of government; [103] this would combine the advantages of "community control," with power over certain functions at the local level, and area-wide control over other functions. This plan might be particularly appropriate for larger cities.

Create State Urban Development Authorities

Future growth should contribute to the solution rather than the worsening of the region's urban problems. A state urban development authority would need to be able to do the following things.

Develop a Statewide Population Growth Location Plan / The first responsibility of the authority would be to develop a statewide population growth plan designed to encourage the location of the poor and black throughout urban areas. Other developmental issues of statewide concern include environmental quality and economic growth. The authority would devise detailed plans for every urban area, indicating the responsibilities of each division of government.

Approve Expenditure of Urban Development Funds and Placement of State Facilities / To win acceptance of its plans, the authority would need powers to approve the expenditures of all urban development funds and to approve the placement of all state facilities. The state probably could expect support from the federal government in its attempts to have federal aid and contracts used and facilities located so as to conform to state guidelines for urban development.

Require Local Governments to Use Zoning Powers to Accomplish Specific Purposes / The enabling legislation that makes zoning by local governments possible should be altered to enumerate specific purposes for which this power is to be used—e.g., insuring the maintenance of a healthful environment and beneficial economic growth, and the provision of adequate sites for housing persons of all income levels and races. The local governmental unit would be required to justify its zoning decisions in terms of these stated purposes. [104]

Override Zoning Decisions That Hamper Authority's Growth Plan / In extreme cases in which municipalities refuse to use their zoning powers as intended by the state to facilitate its population growth location plans, the state authority should have the power to override zoning decisions.

Exercise Power of Eminent Domain / Centers of relatively high population density have the ability to attract wide varieties of employment, housing, entertainment, and economic growth opportunities. One of the most difficult problems in developing these high-density centers is the assembly of land. The state urban development authority must be able to assist in land assembly through the exercise of eminent domain powers, as well as by offering financial support for government purchase of land. [105]

Use Government Land Purchases, Loan Guarantees, and Land Banking / Since the returns from massive investment in urban development often lag so far behind the initial outlay, private sources may not be able to undertake the endeavor. Therefore, government land purchases, loan guarantees, and land banking should be used. These measures would provide additional incentives for compliance with state plans.

Locate and Build Transportation Systems to Support High-Density Development / The location of transportation systems is important in determining where other development will occur. States should plan transportation systems to support the growth of higher-density suburban areas.

Support Regional Planning / Although the South is not a single region, its subregions have characteristics in common. The Southern Growth Policies Board has the potential to assist the South. By planning across state borders, it can reduce the natural competition between states, and should be helpful in dealing with the growth of urban areas across state boundaries. [106]

Promote Development Around Existing Small Cities Instead of Building New Cities / To what extent the problems of urban areas are caused by size alone and to what degree by inability or unwillingness to fashion and operate effective controls is uncertain. Thus, caution is needed in considering "new cities" of the free-standing, self-supportive type, outside commuting distance to other urban centers, as a solution to the problems brought on by size. By suggesting that new cities are possible, one assumes that the tools and powers necessary to develop them will be given to state and local governments. But if these tools were available, perhaps new cities would be unnecessary; states could then locate growth on the periphery of smaller cities. New cities involve extra expenses in construction and development. [107] Smaller cities have slower growth rates (see table 6.10) and lower hourly wages. [108] With an unusually large number of small metropolitan areas, the region would do well to promote development around them.

One advantage to smaller cities is that if growth centers are located in rural areas or small towns, the residents of those areas can continue to enjoy the advantages of living away from crowded, large cities without having to pay the price of economic deprivation. However, the idea of development of this type should be separated from the exotic concept of new cities; the region's growing population can be located more efficiently around small, growing SMSAs.

LOCAL

Pass Local Open-Housing Ordinances

To a large degree the problem of segregated housing lies outside the control of Southern cities, in their white suburban rings. Nevertheless, for many of their residents integrated central-city housing would improve housing quality, living environment, and, perhaps, employment opportunities. Unless the central city acts, it can hardly expect the suburban ring to help integrate the metropolitan area. Local and open-housing ordinances are needed because of the ineffectiveness and lack of commitment demonstrated by federal authorities in enforcing the open-housing provisions of the 1968 Civil Rights Act. However, of the 373 municipalities in the nation with local open-housing ordinances in 1971, only 12 were in the South. Among these 12 are several good models— Dade County, Florida, and Alexandria, Arlington, and Fairfax counties, Virginia. "These laws appear to be 'substantially equivalent' to the federal law in terms of coverage and prohibitions and to provide for more effective enforcement mechanisms, granting the local enforcement agency not only power to conciliate cases of discrimination, but power to impose fines, secure injunctions, and require affirmative action by parties found guilty of discriminating." [109] Open-housing laws cannot achieve large-scale desegregation by themselves. They need wide publicity and a strong commitment to enforcement to achieve even limited success.

Although some liberals argue that all that is required is tougher federal open-housing laws or state laws that ban discrimination in housing, it is our opinion that neither of these alternatives is politically feasible at the present time. The elimination of racial discrimination in housing is second only to busing as an issue to arouse widespread resistance in both the South and the North. It seems unlikely that Congress will pass a significant new open-housing law during the next few years, and it is even less likely that significant legislation will pass in any Southern legislature soon.

While it may be impossible to pass strong open-housing laws, it may be possible on the national level to pass legislation offering financial incentives to those who choose to remain in the central cities of the South and the nation in integrated neighborhoods. Perhaps city councils in places such as Atlanta and New Orleans could pass local legislation to provide such incentives. At any rate, we need to ask ourselves how to motivate people to live in integrated neighborhoods.

Assist in Searches for Jobs and Housing

Job opportunities opening outside the urban ghetto are often never communicated to those living within it because of the ghetto's isolation.

Southern cities should encourage corporations locating outside their boundaries to publicize their job openings throughout the metropolitan area. Perhaps in cooperation with the state employment service, the city itself should keep an up-to-date listing of such jobs to provide information for those seeking employment.

If suburban jobs are obtained, there probably will be a strong motivation to find housing nearby. [110] The lack of lower-priced housing is primarily responsible for the fact that when corporations move to suburban locations, the majority of nonexecutive-level employees do not remain with the corporation, while the vast majority of executives do. Housing is thus integrally tied to job opportunities.

Corporations should be encouraged to secure housing for their employees near the new plant location. They can assist minorities, who are especially victimized by plant relocations, by "(a) informing all employees of the existence and operation of fair housing laws; (b) cooperating with the city, county, State and Federal agencies in handling complaints of housing discrimination; (c) assisting employees to find fair housing through multiple listing systems in which the [corporation] participates; and (d) providing legal assistance where any form of discrimination is encountered." [111] If a corporation makes certain to locate where housing in a variety of price ranges is available and then insures fair treatment for its employees as they seek housing, it risks creating animosity among its suburban neighbors. The city and interested citizens' groups should exert whatever influence and coercive powers they possess to convince corporations not to back away from this task.

Exercise Control Over Development in Suburban Fringes

The problems of the central city cannot be dealt with in isolation from the rest of the metropolitan area. For this reason the authority of the city often must be extended over much of the surrounding community; the most common method used in the South has been annexation.

Some of the problems that suburbs create for their parent cities can be dealt with short of annexation. If city governments, with their greater concern about segregation, are given zoning powers within the suburban fringe, then the problems of exclusionary zoning may be reduced. The self-interest of the city government should be closer to the interests of the entire urban community than is that of the suburban governments representing less populous areas. Unless such extraterritorial powers are granted to the central city, step-by-step annexation loses much of its attractiveness. North Carolina's statute provides for representation of the fringe area on city planning and zoning boards but leaves formal adoption power to the city. [112] Insofar as possible the geographic scope of this regulatory power should be the boundary of the SMSA.

Reduce Property Taxes and Shift Their Collection Upward

The South has an advantage over the rest of the nation in that it relies less on the local property tax because state support for education is greater. The region should move to increase the advantage. Since the local property tax is especially regressive in relation to central-city housing[113] and causes fiscal zoning, strategies to remedy the problems should aim at reducing property taxes in general and shifting their collection and disbursement upward to the metropolitan, state, or federal level.

Before the California Supreme Court decision in *Serrano* v. *Priest* (which found local property taxes as the basis of support for public education to be unequal protection of the laws) was overturned, many states considered replacing such taxes with a statewide property levy. We prefer state income taxes, with substantial progressivity, but if property taxes are to be collected, they should cover a broad area. A tax that is collected and disbursed equally statewide would help to guarantee a child from an impoverished area an opportunity for schooling more equal to that of a child from an affluent suburb. Any shift away from property taxation as a major source of school funds will help the cities.

To the extent that property taxes are relied upon by local governments, the taxes should apply equally. Equalized tax rates in cities such as Atlanta and Nashville would increase the market value of many blighted properties in the central city by making owners of higher-income properties bear more of the tax burden. Many local governments' assessment practices need to be reformed.

Give County Governments or Metropolitan Authorities
Responsibility for Water, Sewerage, and Transportation

The financing and administering of transportation, water, and sewerage systems should be shifted upward either to the county or to a metropolitan governmental structure. [114] The metropolitan structure does carry with it the problems of governmental fragmentation and possible loss of accountability inherent in special districts; these are counterbalanced by the regional character of the above functions and the need for their operation on a regional scale. In addition, the metropolitan structure has a better chance of acceptance than does consolidation because it does not threaten the existence of any level of general government; the Miami federation form of government serves as a model. The fledgling metropolitan councils of government and planning agencies, perhaps with additional federal financial incentives, could be built upon.

Adopt Modern Approaches to Urban Planning and Budgeting

We recommend the adoption of Planning, Programming, Budgeting Systems for all Southern cities with a population over 50,000. We also recommend that the four-step methodology proposed for state planners be implemented by Southern cities: (1) formulation of a conceptual framework for urban planning, (2) determination of goals and priorities for urban planning, (3) development of an urban management information system and data base, and (4) formulation of an urban planning model to evaluate the effects of alternative plans.

7. Agrarianism:
Through a Different Looking Glass

The Setting

DEFINITION OF THE PROBLEM

Rural problems have been largely ignored in recent years, and as a result they have festered. The rush for progress and the modernization of

TABLE 7.1. *Rural and Urban Population, 1970*

	Urban		Rural		
	Total (x1,000)	*Percent*	*Total (x1,000)*	*Percent*	*% Change from 1960 Absolute Number of Rural People*
United States	149,235	73.5	53,886	26.5	-0.3
South	35,684	63.9	20,120	36.1	
Alabama	2,012	58.4	1,432	41.6	-2.9
Arkansas	961	50.0	962	50.0	-5.7
Florida	5,468	80.5	1,321	19.5	2.4
Georgia	2,768	60.3	1,822	39.7	3.3
Kentucky	1,684	52.3	1,535	47.7	-8.9
Louisiana	2,406	66.1	1,235	33.9	3.2
Mississippi	987	44.5	1,230	55.5	-9.4
North Carolina	2,285	45.0	2,797	55.0	1.5
Oklahoma	1,740	68.0	819	32.0	-5.1
South Carolina	1,232	47.6	1,358	52.4	-3.1
Tennessee	2,305	58.8	1,618	41.2	-4.9
Texas	8,921	79.7	2,276	20.3	-4.9
Virginia	2,935	63.1	1,714	36.9	-7.4

Source: U.S. Department of Commerce, Bureau of the Census, *Statistical Abstract of the United States, 1971,* p. 18.

American life have left behind the anachronisms and nostalgia that perpetuate the agrarian myth. In some places, cities still are viewed as centers of dissoluteness. But rural Southerners, confronted with the real prospect of continuing poverty, substandard education, and communities going nowhere, have fled to the cities in large numbers since 1946. Despite this mass migration, predominantly of black workers, in 1970 over 36 percent of the South's population still lived in rural localities, in contrast to a national average of 26.5 percent (see table 7.1).

Difficulties facing both farm and non-farm rural Americans have thus had their greatest impact in the South. A 1970 study by the Department of Agriculture listed four features that differentiate rural problems from those of urban America: "(1) rural family incomes are generally lower and a greater proportion of rural people live below the poverty line; (2) the rural population has more older persons and youths and fewer adults of working age; (3) the average level of education of rural people is lower; and (4) rural people must travel longer distances to health centers."[1] And racial hostilities loom larger in the South, both historically and because 53 percent of the nation's blacks still live in Southern

TABLE 7.2. *White and Black Population, 1960 and 1970*

	1960		1970		
	White (x1,000)	Black (x1,000)	White (x1,000)	Black (x1,000)	Blacks as % of Total
United States	158,832	18,872	177,612	22,673	11.2
Alabama	2,284	980	2,529	908	26.4
Arkansas	1,396	389	1,561	357	18.6
Florida	4,064	880	5,711	1,050	15.5
Georgia	2,817	1,123	3,388	1,191	25.9
Kentucky	2,820	215	2,971	241	7.5
Louisiana	2,212	1,039	2,540	1,089	29.9
Mississippi	1,258	915	1,393	815	36.8
North Carolina	3,339	1,116	3,892	1,138	22.4
Oklahoma	2,108	153	2,275	178	7.0
South Carolina	1,551	829	1,794	789	30.5
Tennessee	2,978	587	3,283	631	16.1
Texas	8,375	1,187	9,697	1,420	12.7
Virginia	3,142	816	3,757	865	18.6

Source: U.S. Department of Commerce, Bureau of the Census, *Statistical Abstract of the United States, 1971*, p. 27.

states (not including Kentucky) and 25 percent in rural parts of the South (see table 7.2).

These factors have reinforced one another to produce poor housing, malnutrition, underemployment and lack of opportunity. This chapter analyzes key problems in the rural South, and recommends policies to help check the outflow of human resources and to revitalize this long-neglected area.

SPECIFICATION OF OUTPUTS

Low Incomes

Low per capita income has always plagued the South, especially in rural areas, where illiteracy, cyclical poverty, and powerlessness have tied men to the land. With its backward system of political, social and economic institutions, agrarian society remained relatively static while the rest of the United States was making rapid progress. Growing industrialization in the South should cause Southern per capita incomes to converge gradually with those of the rest of the nation; rural areas, however, continue to lag behind, particularly as the substitution of capital for labor on farms displaces farm workers and compounds the unemployment problem.

Rural America accounts for only 27 percent of the nation's population, and yet 70 percent of the nation's poor. In 1971 George Wallace stated that per capita incomes in Alabama counties vary directly with the size of their populations: "The average income in the six counties with populations over 100,000 was $3,095 whereas the average was $1,608 in the 30 rural counties having populations between 10,000 and 24,999." [2]

Practically all rural Southern poor are employed; yet in 1966 one-third of the nonwhite males and one-seventh of the white males who worked full-time were still below the poverty level. A study of the northeastern coastal plain of South Carolina revealed that the heads of rural households there are usually the working poor. All "able-bodied male heads" were in the labor force at the time of the study, with only 1 percent unemployment. No household headed by an "able-bodied man" under forty-five received welfare assistance—despite per capita incomes averaging under $3,000 a year. Two effects of low per capita income in the rural South are poor diet and lack of adequate housing. The Coleman Report indicates that nearly 40 percent of low-income families in the South are malnourished. Nationally, 28 percent of all rural housing is substandard, but in the Southeast the figure reaches 66 percent; in the Alabama Black Belt it rises to 76 percent.

Discrimination

After Reconstruction, Southern legislatures devised legal structures to keep the Negro in a position of economic and social inferiority; consequently the average black man remained poor, uneducated, and hidden in rural localities.

Many black veterans returned home to the South after World War II and found their old life-style unacceptable after the relative sufficiency of military standards of living. In 1940, 77 percent of all blacks in the United States lived in the South, but by 1970 only 53 percent lived there. For the past thirty years, the average annual net out-migration of blacks from the South has been over 147,000. Black Americans still form over 25 percent of the population in five Southern states and 19 percent in the South as a whole. Their difficulties are still at the very core of the Southern problem of how to "catch up" with national prosperity.

Black-operated farms numbered 560,000 in 1959, although in 1970 only 98,000 remained; the black farm population has been correspondingly decreasing at an annual rate of 10.5 percent as compared to a 3.9 percent decrease among white farmers. The widening racial income gap among farm operators adds impetus to this wholesale exodus of blacks. Farm incomes for whites have risen at six times the rate of those earned by black farm operators since 1960. Economist Ray Marshall notes that, "because of their limited incomes, education, farm sizes, and access to credit, the Negro farmers' ability to adjust to technological and market changes has been markedly different from that of whites, as is evident from the following: the average size of farms operated by Negroes is one-fourth the average size of farms operated by whites; Negroes have less livestock, crop yields per acre, and machinery per farm; and are much more dependent upon cotton and tobacco, which are hardest hit by technological changes and Federal agricultural policies." [3]

Against the background of the rural South as the poorest section of the country, living conditions for poor rural blacks take on a Gothic character. In the United States, 10 percent of all whites and 31 percent of all blacks are poor. Although 22.5 percent of white families in the rural South were poor in 1970, 53.6 percent of all minority families were classified as poverty-stricken—not a great improvement since Reconstruction.

Inputs to the Rural South

ENDOWMENTS

Natural Resources

Land in the South was the "black gold" of the Colonial period and the early days of the Confederacy. The heavy black or brown loam soils of the Alabama-Mississippi Black Belt made this region famous for tobacco and later it became the richest cotton-producing area in the world. Fertile land along the rivers and bayous of southeastern Louisiana combined with a long growing season to produce fortunes in sugar cane during the 1800s. Coastal lands in South Carolina and Georgia proved ideal for rice cultivation. Over the years, however, alarming soil depletion and erosion have taken permanent toll of once vast croplands. Methods of cultivation were inefficient and wasteful, not because of the slavery system, but because land was readily available in large quantities. Today, with a fair amount of coddling, cotton and tobacco can still be coaxed from formerly rich soils and from the more predominantly clay soils of the Southeast.

Timber is still a major resource in Georgia and neighboring states. Exploitation in the 1930s laid waste pine forests in the South as well as in other regions, but conscientious reforestation and natural seeding are bringing back this valuable asset. Aside from lumber production, timber has attracted other badly needed industries to Southern states, although industrial effluents from chemical derivative and paper-producing plants have been responsible for a growing pollution menace. Threats to the air and water occur more particularly in hill and mountain areas where dense air pollution can be trapped in valleys and the water resources for lower municipalities contaminated for hundreds of miles. Prospects for maintaining this industry are still very favorable, with 39 percent of the nation's commercial forest land in the South. This figure includes 36 percent of the hardwoods used mainly for manufacturing and pulpwood and 19 percent of the national inventory of sawtimber, i.e., trees of sufficient size and quality to contain at least one log suitable for lumber or veneer.

In some respects the greatest physical asset of the South is its climate. Long, warm summers and relatively short and mild winters produce long growing seasons that vary from six to nine months. Although ideal for many varieties of food and fiber, these factors are still put to greatest use in cotton and tobacco production. A number of economic elements have contributed to the underutilization of the inputs of land and climate.

An extensive network of rivers, lakes, and streams have given many rural Southerners easy access to markets for farm products; the inland waterway supplements those formed naturally. Inland lakes provide natural reservoirs for farm use. Water resources are extensive except in the Southwest.

Human Resources

The living conditions of the average rural Southerner are remarkable for the absence of such essentials as adequate housing, good diet, quality education, and sufficient income. The lack of these basic necessities inevitably affects the quality of human resources as an input into the economy.

Because of inadequate opportunities for development, managerial skill and entrepreneurship have been almost nonexistent in rural areas, the small merchant being a small exception. The industries that have settled in the rural South import managers and high-wage, skilled workers. Most jobs available to local citizens are menial or low-paid.

Capital

Capital has always been in short supply in the South; even the wealthiest antebellum Southerner was often short of ready cash with his assets tied up in land and slaves. When crops and homes were destroyed in the Civil War and the slaves freed, physical capital vanished also. The population of the South doubled in the thirty years after 1865, but the amount of currency in circulation actually declined. Tenant farmers rarely saw any money from one season to the next. As recently as 1940, more than one-third of Southern farm income took the form of products consumed at home. Only by 1961 had this noncash farm income been reduced to less than 25 percent.

The shortage of capital for Southern economic development has induced many Southern industries to exploit the cheap labor supply. The South has had the lowest capital-labor ratio of any region in the United States. For even its limited capital the South has depended to a considerable degree on Northern capital markets. When credit was tight in financial markets, Southern loan applications were frequently the first to be rejected. Dependence upon imported capital inevitably resulted in the exporting of profits.

EXTERNAL FACTORS

External factors determine the future of a system in ways beyond the control of the system itself. Important external considerations for the rural South include federal government policies, the influence of the national economy, agricultural prices, and Supreme Court decisions.

Federal Agricultural Policies

In a recent analysis of the U.S. Department of Agriculture's farm subsidy program, Charles L. Schultze questioned whether subsidies to agriculture transfer income from a relatively prosperous urban population to a relatively depressed, low-income farm community, or whether they benefit primarily the efficient, well-to-do farmer. He found that the latter was true and that most of the small farmers were helped relatively little by these programs.

Schultze argues that two factors explain why the present agricultural program is a poor device for helping low-income farmers. First, in the United States most of the agricultural goods sold are produced by a relatively small number of farmers. Three-fourths of the sales of farm products come from only 19 percent of the farms, while at the other tail of the distribution 1.5 million small farms account for only 5 percent of sales. Since farm subsidies are directly related to farm size and production, the largest farms receive the largest share of subsidies.

Second, most farm programs are vested in the land rather than in the farmers. The benefits from farm subsidies are gradually reflected in farmland prices. The current generation of farmers must pay the higher carrying costs of inflated land prices as land changes hands over time. Since a significant portion of the subsidy benefits has been realized in the form of capital gains, or in higher rents paid to nonfarm landlords, the current generation of active farmers receives relatively few benefits.

Ray Marshall has observed that three federal programs whose alleged objective was to provide assistance to small farmers have been guilty of blatant racial discrimination in the distribution of benefits to black farmers in the South. As recently as the end of 1968 the Agricultural Stabilization and Conservation Service (which administers the farm subsidy program) had no black members serving on any of its county committees. Since 1969 blacks have had only token representation on state ASCS committees. With the exception of a few nondescript positions, very few blacks were employed by the ASCS in the South. The story was virtually the same for the administration and employment practices of the Cooperative Extension Service (CES) and the Farmers Home Administration (FHA). The former, segregated until 1964, was established to help farmers improve their productivity by providing advice on management and technical aspects of farming. The FHA makes loans to small farmers to improve their homes, to buy or expand farms, to raise and market crops, to buy machinery, and to finance business firms.

Agricultural Prices

A region dependent upon agriculture for its major source of income is plagued with cyclical fluctuations in economic conditions. The forces of supply and demand determine the price of any good, and the demand for products is a function of particular taste and general economic conditions. Because the manufacturer has limited control over the supply of his product, agricultural workers are unable to determine how much of any good they are going to produce. After successful planting, weather changes or pests may destroy a bumper crop. Hence agricultural incomes are inherently unstable. However, a growing worldwide demand for American agricultrual products in the 1970s offered the promise of good prices in the future.

Analysis of Specific Rural Institutions

ECONOMY

Farming has always been the most important economic institution in the rural South. In recent years, however, a migration from farm employment to rural nonfarm employment has paralleled the rural-to-urban migration. Both migrations have been in response to farm consolidation and mechanization. Between 1947 and 1969 total Southern farm output increased by 50 percent even though the number of farms declined by almost half with the absorption of small farms by the larger and more efficient. Former owners of farms had to seek other employment. As larger farms became increasingly mechanized, they displaced more and more farm workers, an annual average of 115,000 over the past twenty years. Although the farm population has declined, the rural population has remained almost constant over the past decade.

The next major displacement of farm workers may come in the Carolina-Virginia tobacco belt where an automatic harvester is being introduced. It is expected ultimately to drive thousands of small farmers from their land—perhaps as many as 50,000 in North Carolina alone—and to displace thousands of farm workers. (In order for displaced farm workers to remain in rural areas, new economic institutions must be developed to provide adequate jobs. The policy recommendations for this chapter explore proposals to meet this need.)

The economies of rural municipalities in the South have been dependent for survival on what is usually a single local industry. [4] The location of military bases in small towns in the South also has had a major impact. These potentially unstable economies may feel the brunt of cutbacks in military spending in coming years and need only look at past experiences to realize that planning is necessary now to put these vast facilities to new uses through vocational training or by the development of new small industries. Every Southern state except Tennessee and Arkansas is dependent in major ways on military base spending.

EDUCATION

Public education at the primary level has suffered from dual school systems and inadequate state support. Most Southern states provide a minimum expenditure floor that is supplemented by local funds. Rural districts lack the population and income base to raise the funds needed to bring their schools up to urban levels. Rural schools are generally less well equipped and less likely to have the opportunity to experiment with modern facilities in the fields of science and language. Consequently they have had difficulty attracting qualified teachers because of low salaries and the inadequacy of other services and opportunities. Students in rural schools are twice as likely to have uncertified teachers as their urban counterparts.

Students from the South have historically ranked lower on standardized tests than students from other regions, and rural Southerners, especially blacks, have been among the lowest-scoring students. The Coleman Report finds that verbal ability scores of blacks from the nonmetropolitan South averaged 5.2 grades behind those of white students in the Northeast. White students from the rural South scored 1.5 grades behind the same age groups from the Northeast.[5] Many rural Southern students are handicapped further by being forced to drop out of school to work full-time to help supplement the family income. Still others simply drop out and migrate to the cities. Ray Marshall has observed that 80 percent of the black males who leave Southern agriculture have, in effect, less than a seventh-grade education, and more than half have attended fewer than four years of school.

POLITICS

Until legislative reapportionment in the 1960s, rural political influences in the South dominated both state and federal legislatures. This domination did not, however, represent all rural residents equally but was instead a guise for planter and large-farmer control of legislatures at the expense of poor blacks and whites who comprised most of the population in the rural South. Thus Southern representatives have historically opposed legislation that would better the life of the farm worker. The possible mutuality of interest between poor whites and blacks that might have reversed the priorities of state and local governments has so far remained unexplored because of the manipulation of racial tensions by entrenched interests. Owners of large farms desire a readily available supply of cheap labor in rural areas. That such programs as a minimum wage, workman's compensation, unemployment insurance, and collective bargaining have not been extended to farm workers is a manifestation of "planter power." Federal agricultural policies and low welfare payments were not designed to create the good life for farm employees.

Political dominance is now gravitating to an increasing number of black voters and the rapidly developing urban areas of the South. The irony of this trend is that urban-dominated assemblies may continue the neglect of the rural poor.

SOCIAL FACTORS

Farm organizations have a long history in the South. Agrarian attitudes have placed owners of large farms at the top of the social structure, where they have wielded influence through organizations such as the Farm Bureau. The largest farm organization in the country, the Farm Bureau was founded in Chicago in 1920. Farm workers, in contrast to farm owners, can obtain only a nonvoting associate membership in this organization. Prosperous farmers have used the bureau to elect roadblocks to decisive government action to help the country's farm workers. The Farm Bureau has given large planters legal help in maintaining cheap labor in rural areas.

The Ku Klux Klan was organized in 1865 by Confederate veterans to defend the interests of the debilitated planter class against the forces of Reconstruction and the increasing economic and political influence of blacks. It has been revived twice as an instrument of racial intimidation and into the fifties was a force in the region's politics. Its members paraded down the streets of Southern towns and bragged of their latest deeds. After the 1954 school decision the Klan "became a refuge for the small group of violent anti-Semitic and anti-Negro crackpots. Among these were the terrorists who did the dynamiting of schools, homes, and churches."[6]

The White Citizens' Councils were organized in Indianola, Mississippi, in 1954; the "white collar Klan" became a means for some respectable whites to gather and make decisions regarding blacks. One of the functions of the Citizens' Councils and parallel organizations has been the building of private, all-white schools.

Policy Recommendations

To accomplish the goal of rural redevelopment, the out-migration pattern in the rural South must be halted. Many people would prefer to live in small towns but must move to large cities to find jobs. The recommendations of this chapter will be concerned with establishing "the right of all people to have a realistic choice about where they will live and work." [7]

One reason for rural-to-urban migration has been the lack of adequate services in rural areas—medical and educational facilities, transportation systems, day care centers for working mothers, cultural centers, police and fire protection. But the paramount consideration that has caused Southerners to leave rural areas has been the lack of ways and means of earning an adequate income. The following programs would hasten the redevelopment of these potentially self-sustaining areas.

HUMAN RESOURCES

Subsidize Human Redevelopment

Federal and state governments should undertake an immediate program directed toward the goal of making all citizens in the rural South productive and insuring that they can provide basic necessities for themselves. This program should include (1) a guaranteed annual income based on the poverty level, (2) guaranteed jobs for all citizens, and (3) a massive job training program.

The present welfare system in the United States has proved inadequate both in terms of costs and in its attempts to get people off the welfare rolls and back on the job. The flaws of this system are especially felt in the rural South. Welfare benefits are lowest in states where rural deprivation is most serious. In Mississippi families receiving Aid to Families with Dependent Children subsidies have been expected to survive on $564 a year and in Louisiana on $1,000 a year, although the national average for aid to AFDC recipients has been $2,160. In these states many eligible welfare recipients are arbitrarily excluded from coverage by local welfare boards. A USDA survey of poverty in the rural Mississippi Delta found only 11 percent of poor families on public assistance. [8]

A guaranteed annual income financed through the federal government would give funds directly to poor people. Since the South has a larger percentage of population below the poverty level, a substantial share of these funds would go to the South. Under the Family Assistance Program proposed by President Nixon, 61.8 percent of the increase in welfare benefits would be allotted to the South and 32.2 percent to the rural South.[9]

We favor requiring each state to provide jobs for recipients of welfare payments; the subsidy would then be a salary. A minimum subsistence would be paid to those who did not work, and payments would rise according to how much work was performed by the individual; of course, setting precise levels would require painstaking analysis.

Each state would have control over the jobs it provided to welfare recipients. Rural areas could benefit especially from such a work force. Needed services could be provided in this manner: roads and sewers could be repaired and maintained; parks, sanitation services, and additional fire protection could be provided; and public service projects such as levies, land restoration and irrigation, and lakes could be undertaken. Rural areas could be made better places to live in as a result of these programs.

The third part of our proposal concerns an expanded job training program. Such programs should be coordinated with community colleges and technical schools in the area and with local industrial plants. People would be trained for available jobs, and new industry could be attracted with the promise of a trained (not a "cheap") labor supply waiting when a plant opened. Incoming industry would then be subsidized by developing human resources in the area instead of being granted long-term tax incentives.

Reorganize Housing Programs

The housing policy of the federal government has primarily aided middle- and upper-income groups, most of which have been in urban areas. Nonmetropolitan localities have more than half the low-income families and two-thirds of the worst housing, yet these areas receive only one-fifth of the budget of low-income housing programs. Areas defined as rural receive only about 10 percent of all federal housing funds, and little of this money reaches the poor.[10] Eighty-seven percent of the nation's housing subsidy remains in the form of tax provisions such as homestead exemptions. Each year over $6 billion in taxes is foregone because of tax subsidies to middle- and upper-income families, while programs to help finance low-income housing have been budgeted at less than $1 billion.

We prefer a reorganized housing program that rejects the present philosophy. Tax provisions that discriminate against those people unable to own a home should be eliminated. Low-income public-housing and loan programs should be expanded. Special programs should be adopted to reach the rural poor who occupy substandard housing and should include public housing in small rural towns.

Develop Updated Health Care Services

Among services, personal health care is vital. Rural areas seldom provide adequate health care because small communities cannot usually support medical centers. [11] Often it is impossible to keep even one doctor in town. Federal or state funds are needed to help rural areas maintain health centers; they need not have a full staff of doctors—a "physician's associate" may be enough—but they must be able to meet routine, daily health needs of rural residents. In case a need arises for prolonged hospitalization, these centers could provide transportation to the nearest hospital.

Historically, the South has remained a region of high natural birth rates and low economic opportunity. Thus birth control information and family planning programs are basic needs in rural localities.

DEVELOPMENT

Reorient Land-Grant Colleges and Universities

Rural-oriented programs of some land-grant colleges and universities in the South and the rest of the nation have served segments of agriculture well, but too few of their graduates know much about broader rural development. Schools of planning, for the most part, have specialized in urban planning with little or no emphasis placed on rural planning or development, and schools of agriculture and state extension services have had too narrow a conception of their role.

Develop a Federal Program for Rural, Nonfarm Development

A first priority item should be to create a new federal program of rural, nonfarm development. Although substantial sums of federal money have been available since the 1930s for the agricultural South, the nonfarm rural South has been greatly ignored. Price supports, agricultural extension services, and land-grant colleges were all available to support the agricultural South. Urban renewal, model cities, and many other programs have benefited Southern cities, while residents of the nonfarm rural South, including the small towns, have been left behind. In order for these areas to receive the benefits of the limited federal programs available to them, the services of an astute administrator are usually necessary.

In part with resources freed by the elimination of the farm price-support system, we propose a program of rural development that would do for the nonfarm rural South what the New Deal did for the agricultural South. Such a program (including existing efforts) would include loans to rural areas for community improvements, moderate tax incentives for industrial development, liberal financial terms for housing, and direct grants for improved government services, including fire protection, police protection, and water and sewer facilities. Special grants should also be made to encourage the consolidation of county and municipal governments in rural areas, and the creation of multicounty governmental units.

With the creation of the rural development program it would be possible to discontinue or combine the Commodity Credit Corporation, the Economic Development Administration, the Resource, Conservation and Development Program, and the regional commissions, including the Appalachian, Ozark, and Coastal Plains Commissions, which provide assistance to rural areas.

Subsidize Marginal Enterprises in the Rural South

Many economists have argued that to raise per capita income in the South the region should attempt to attract industry that is capital-intensive and thus increase the mobility of the labor force from low to higher productivity fields. Few would question the efficacy of this approach as a long-run strategy. However, economist Marshall argues that any human resource development program should also include a strategy for the development of labor-intensive activities, at least in the short run. Marshall contends that many of the displaced farm workers in the rural South are simply not qualified to hold high-wage positions in capital-intensive industries. Yet many of these individuals are capable of holding positions in labor-intensive operations such as vegetable farming and livestock production. Given the immobility of many of these displaced farm workers, a sensible short-run strategy would be for the Department of Agriculture to subsidize labor-intensive marginal enterprise in the rural South through technical assistance and loan programs. This, of course, would be a striking departure from the present policies of the department, which has for nearly forty years subsidized large-scale, capital-intensive farm operations in the South. Marginal enterprises run by blacks should receive particular attention. If such a program is established, it should be set up for a period not to exceed ten years, with explicit plans to retire the program at the end of that period. This is a short-run, stop-gap program to provide relief to those Southern farm workers who have a desire to work but simply do not possess the skills to survive in a technological age.

Utilize Land-Use Planning

Great promise lies in land-use planning because to date land in this region had been exploited as a speculative commodity rather than husbanded as a public utility. When the Southeast was first settled, men were allowed to appropriate their allotted acreage from any untaken land, usually in fifty-acre sections. Property lines ran different ways, and pieces of land lay unclaimed between larger plots, inviting disputed claims. By contrast, land in the Northeast was granted only to groups of people intending to form a community, and surveying combined with strict allotments for roads and commons areas to produce clearly designated boundaries and maximum productivity. The South has remained attached to the "prairie psychology" that manifests a "general unconcern for the rate at which land is consumed by new development, born of the confidence that the supply is virtually unlimited. . . . And it is not altogether fanciful to see the persistence of the log-cabin tradition in the overwhelming American preference for the detached one-story house on a large plot."[12]

A solution to the waste of land resources in the South lies in rural zoning to designate land as forest, crop land, or "holding zones" for future development. The reform of tax laws regarding rural lands is also an integral part of land reform in the South. John Delafons notes that "the fact that even if land is zoned for agricultural use it may still be taxed for its speculation value is the biggest anomaly in American land-use planning."[13] Superintendence of zoning at the state level, in cooperation with county officials, would seem to produce the most coordinated effort and optimal perspective for Southern land-use planning. The Maryland legislature has enacted laws "to prevent the forced conversion of open space to more intensive uses as a result of economic pressures caused by the assessment of land at a rate or level incompatible with the practical use of such land for farming,"[14] a philosophy much needed to forestall the uncontrolled urban sprawl already eating up the countryside in many parts of the South.

One irony of present neglect of rural lands is that planning ideas existed thirty years ago, which, if enacted, would have done what we are now struggling against the accumulations of time to accomplish. "The intermingling of poor and good lands, such as is to be found in many parts of the Southern uplands, enormously complicates the task of zoning. . . . In the South, zoning must be used the way cities have long used it, to impose different types of utilization upon contiguous lands, frequently lands within a single farm enterprise. In brief, rural zoning in the South is needed to prevent population backwashes, and in addition to reinforce sound agricultural practices on individual farms."[15] Con-

scientious land-use planning in the South can make a vast neglected resource productive to an extent hardly visualized today; at a time when
land is already becoming a scarce commodity, the South may "clean its
closet" to find the greatest investment just waiting to be uncovered.

An additional consideration in careful land use is proper regard for
timber resources, presently still a lucrative enterprise in the South. Timber can continue to produce important revenue if planning officials inhibit the unlimited encroachment on forest lands by the industry. With
proper reforestation and selective cutting, the South should be able to
prosper indefinitely from its yearly timber harvest, which should increase in value substantially in coming years.

AGRICULTURE

Eliminate Farm Price-Support Program

Before the sharp increase in food prices in 1973 the federal farm price-
support program cost the American taxpayer $5 billion a year in direct
budgetary outlays and an additional $4.5 billion in higher food prices. If
this program were being used to transfer income to low-income farm
families, some justification might exist for continuing this form of subsidy to agriculture. But, as a study by Charles L. Schultze has demonstrated, benefits of the farm price-support program are distributed in
proportion to the volume of production on each farm rather than in ac-
cordance with income levels—wealthy families receiving the most assistance and poor families the least. Given that the tight world market
for agricultural products probably will continue, large-scale farmers
should be able to compete without subsidies. The Nixon administration
discussed removing supports for wheat, feed grains, and cotton. We
recommend a phasing out of the price-support program with the objective of completely terminating it within five years.

Reorganize the Department of Agriculture

The U.S. Department of Agriculture is a classic case of institutional ob-
solescence. It is an institution whose present policies were designed to
solve problems that existed in the 1930s. Consider the situation in the
South. Our present national farm policy does virtually nothing to alleviate the problems of the rural South. It is time that the Department of
Agriculture broadened its mission to encompass all rural problems including poverty, health and sanitation, discrimination, unemployment,
education, and inadequate government services, rather than continuing
to funnel the majority of its resources into direct subsidies for wealthy

farmers. The department's unwillingness in 1973-74 to draw up a rural development plan with specific goals is indicative of its recent attitude.

We recommend that the Department of Agriculture be reorganized as the Department of Rural Development with a substantial reduction in its direct outlays for agriculture and a major increase in expenditures for other purposes such as the development of small towns in rural areas.

Review Rural Credit Needs

Provisions for rural credit have historically been handled poorly, in many instances intentionally for the advantage of lending parties. The original form of rural credit was the crop lien system, which was at best a makeshift. Not only the rate of interest, but even the amount of the loan was left unspecified. Interest rates of 30 to 70 percent trapped the small farmer in a cycle of indebtedness. At one time farm mortgage payments fell due in the full amount on a given date. But the Federal Farm Loan Act of 1916, which stipulated that annual payments be spread out over the years, is still far from serving the needs of an uncertain occupation. Installment payments might be allowed to flucuate with income. Deferred-payment loans are sometimes essential to getting a farming enterprise going. The fixed payment is the Juggernaut that in the end forces many farmers off the land and into the unemployment statistics.

Insure Small Farmers and Farm Workers a Voice in Policies

Small farmers would be more likely to remain on the land with an increased influence over their own destinies. Large-scale farmers, whose more efficient operations allow them to underbid other farmers in the marketplace, are always going to have an advantage in the free-enterprise system. But in many local cooperatives there are strict limitations on who may vote in determining local policies; ownership of land or of a certain amount of land is a primary criterion. Federal or state regulation of cooperatives would assure all farmers protection from this misuse of economic power by more prosperous members. The further development of the cooperative as an institution also could have far-reaching benefits for the South.

In chapter 2 we referred to job democracy. This concept also applies to workers on farms owned by corporations. Employees of these farms should be allowed participation on corporate boards of directors. In the case of farms owned by partnerships or single proprietorships, we recommend establishment of a managerial policy committee in which workers are represented.

8. Summary and Conclusions

A number of themes have recurred throughout this book, among them an emphasis on the need for serious planning by public agencies of all types, and on the necessity to develop new forms by which institutions can be held accountable to the people. The intent of this book is not to foster a doctrine of newness so much as a doctrine of awareness—awareness of the possibilities and pitfalls of change.

Major Policy Recommendations

A number of the policy recommendations in chapters 2 through 7 dealt with proposals to increase per capita income, improve the educational system, and contain racial discrimination. Many, but not all, of the recommendations relate specifically to the South. The following are central recommendations from each chapter.

THE ECONOMY

1. Expand business ownership.
2. Seek to expand international trade and abandon support for protectionist policies.
3. Adopt state antidiscrimination laws for employment.
4. Require provision for employee participation in corporate policy-making.
5. Eliminate federal and state minimum-wage laws.
6. Use the corporate income tax as a growth policy instrument, and rely more heavily on state personal income taxes.

PUBLIC EDUCATION

1. Clearly establish the principle of educational accountability.
2. Devote a larger share of resources to early childhood development and to vocational education.

3. Merge city and county school systems.
4. Discontinue reliance on local property taxes to finance public schools.
5. Explore the feasibility of education voucher plans.

HIGHER EDUCATION

1. Establish a single board of higher education at the state level, and develop long-range planning and budgeting procedures.
2. Adopt an "academic common market" plan for the region.
3. Adopt as fundamental policy that ability to pay shall not be a criterion for admission to public institutions.
4. Direct the energies of universities toward societal problem-solving.

POLITICS

1. Hold constitutional conventions to rewrite state constitutions that have not been rewritten in the last three decades.
2. Restructure state agencies to give the governor more authority, and make the governor the chief budget officer and planner for the state.
3. Operate state government "in the sunshine."
4. Adopt unified court systems.
5. Avoid creating special districts, and aid city-county and county-county consolidation.

URBAN DEVELOPMENT

1. Prohibit new incorporations anywhere within SMSAs.
2. Develop statewide population growth and location plans.
3. Require local government to use zoning powers to accomplish specified purposes.
4. Promote development around existing small cities rather than the development of "new cities."
5. Adopt modern approaches to state and urban planning, including Planning, Programming, Budgeting Systems (PPBS).

RURAL DEVELOPMENT

1. Eliminate farm price-support programs.
2. Reorganize the U.S. Deparment of Agriculture as the Department of Rural Development.
3. Make improved health care delivery, especially for rural areas, a priority concern.

Implementation

What are the chances that recommendations such as these actually will be put into practice? The answer depends on Congress, thirteen state legislatures, city councilmen, county commissioners and school officials throughout the South, and the political parties. Among the less controversial proposals are those dealing with expanded business ownership and the adoption of modern planning and budgeting techniques. Some of our recommendations are likely to receive a positive response from Democrats and Republicans as well as from people at all levels of government. Liberal Democrats are likely to be unhappy with our proposal to abolish minimum-wage laws. On the other hand, conservative Republicans are likely to rebel at the idea of blue-collar workers' participation in corporate decision-making. The policy proposals vary in political feasibility at different levels of government. But no party or governmental unit as now constituted is likely to embrace more than a bare majority of the recommendations in this book. New political coalitions and leaders may need to emerge in the near future.

A so-called new breed of Southern governors emerged in the early 1970s—Reubin Askew of Florida, Dale Bumpers of Arkansas, Jimmy Carter of Georgia, James Holshouser of North Carolina, Linwood Holton of Virginia, and John West of South Carolina. They were elected in several cases by a "new populism" coalition of blue-collar workers, farmers, blacks, and George Wallace supporters suspicious of the "establishment." They represented "change"; they were new faces, relatively unscarred by previous political battles. They entered the statehouses with inaugural addresses proclaiming the end of racism and the beginning of a progressive era in state government. Governors Holton and West took positive steps to eliminate racial discrimination in state government and Governor Askew defended busing and spearheaded a successful campaign to enact a corporate income tax in Florida. There were signs of new caution about the virtues of unrestricted growth. But in many fields state governments in the South remain lethargic, incompetent, or oblivious to progressive attitudes and techniques. Although many of the new Southern governors are orders of magnitude more progressive than their predecessors, they and others like them cannot promote and implement the kind of policy recommendations set forth in this book without new supporting coalitions.

What about the Democratic and Republican parties, in the South and nationally? Neither is likely soon to provide the type of leadership required to implement this program. In spite of the life that Watergate gave the Democratic party, the McGovern debacle left the party weakened in the South. In Washington the party appears unlikely to identify with policies that represent significant departures from its programs of the past; it still is unwilling to admit the failure of many past programs to help the people they were intended to help. As for the Republican party, there is little evidence that the national leadership, especially those who supported the so-called Southern strategy of President Nixon, would provide much support for this program.

At present in most states and on most issues neither the Democratic nor the Republican party is an effective vehicle for change in the South. The success of Governor Wallace has been due in part to his recognition that many people in the South are alienated from both parties and from all levels of government. Party labels often have become a liability rather than an asset.

If the program proposed in this book is to be implemented, it needs the support of a new coalition of Southerners: small farmers, farm workers, and blue-collar workers (many of whom have supported George Wallace in the past); blacks and other minorities; concerned women and young people; the neglected "senior citizens"; and white progressives among the professional and business classes. Now that integration is a fact of life in the South, it may be possible to form stable coalitions of working-class whites and blacks. Since the 1890s there have been repeated attempts to form coalitions of black and white working-class people in the South. In the past such coalitions were precarious, in part because blue-collar workers viewed integration as a threat to their economic security. But these threats have not materialized. Industrialization has brought more jobs to most parts of the South than there are whites who are seeking jobs. A new Southern coalition is needed to light a fire under present leaders and to put forward new leaders. In part, we have tried to provide a program around which such a group could be organized—not to repeat the mistakes of the past, but to produce a set of strategies that will benefit all of the people in the South. For those who disagree with our proposals, in part or in whole, as well as for those who agree with them, we hope that this analysis has helped promote a clearer understanding of the region, its problems, and its opportunities.

Notes

Chapter 1

1. "The New Rich South: Frontier for Growth," *Business Week*, 2 September 1972, pp. 30-37.

2. John Shelton Reed, *The Enduring South* (Lexington, Mass.: D. C. Heath & Co., 1972).

3. Robert Harris, "The South: Research for What?," in *Perspectives on the South: Agenda for Research*, ed. Edgar T. Thompson (Durham, N.C.: Duke University Press, 1967), pp. 37-58.

4. From public opinion surveys conducted between 1968 and 1973 by William R. Hamilton and Staff, a division of the Washington, D.C., firm of Independent Research Associates, Inc. The data were obtained by the authors from the firm.

5. From public opinion surveys conducted by Louis Harris and Associates, Inc., and stored in the Louis Harris Data Center, University of North Carolina, Chapel Hill, N.C.

Chapter 2

1. The U.S. Bureau of the Census definition of the South includes Delaware, the District of Columbia, Maryland, and West Virginia in addition to our thirteen states—Alabama, Arkansas, Florida, Georgia, Kentucky, Louisiana, Mississippi, North Carolina, Oklahoma, South Carolina, Tennessee, Texas, and Virginia.

2. U.S. Department of Commerce, Bureau of the Census, and U.S. Department of Labor, Bureau of Labor Statistics, *The Social and Economic Status of Negroes in the United States, 1970*, Current Population Reports, Series P-23, no. 38, Bureau of Labor Statistics Report no. 394, p. 90.

3. Ibid., p. 27.

4. U.S. Department of Commerce, Bureau of the Census, *Statistical Abstract of the United States, 1971*, p. 67.

5. Ibid., p. 69.

6. U.S. Department of Commerce, Bureau of the Census, and U.S. Department of Labor, Bureau of Labor Statistics, *Social and Economic Status of Negroes in the United States, 1970*, p. 90.

7. Ibid.

8. See, for example, James G. Maddox, E. E. Liebhafsky, Vivian Henderson, and H. M. Hamlin, *The Advancing South: Manpower Prospects and Problems* (New York: Twentieth Century Fund, 1967); Clarence H. Danhof, "Four Decades of Thought on the South's Economic Problems," in *Essays in Southern Economic Development*, ed. Melvin L. Greenhut and W. Tate Whitman (Chapel Hill: University of North Carolina Press, 1964), pp. 7-68; William H. Nicholls, *Southern Tradition and Regional Progress* (Chapel Hill: University of North Carolina Press, 1960); Joseph J. Spengler, "Southern Economic

Trends and Prospects," in *The South in Continuity and Change*, ed. John C. McKinney and Edgar T. Thompson (Durham, N.C.: Duke University Press, 1965), pp. 101-31; and Calvin B. Hoover and B. U. Ratchford, *Economic Resources and Policies of the South* (New York: Macmillan Co., 1951).

9. Nicholls, *Southern Tradition and Regional Progress*, pp. 14-15.

10. Ibid., p. 19.

11. Francis Butler Simkins, *A History of the South* (New York: Alfred A. Knopf, 1958), p. 133.

12. A. H. Conrad and John R. Meyers, "The Economics of Slavery in the Ante-Bellum South," *Journal of Political Economy* 66 (1958): 95-130.

13. William E. Dodd, *The Cotton Kingdom* (New Haven: Yale University Press, 1919), p. 24.

14. Conrad and Meyers, "Economics of Slavery in the Ante-Bellum South."

15. W. J. Cash, *The Mind of the South* (New York: Alfred A. Knopf, 1941), p. 45.

16. Danhof, "Four Decades of Thought on the South's Economic Problems," p. 8.

17. Richard A. Easterlin, "Interregional Differences in Per Capita Income, Population, and Total Income, 1840-1950," in *Trends in the American Economy in the Nineteenth Century*, National Bureau of Economic Research Publications (Princeton: Princeton University Press, 1960), pp. 97-98.

18. Nathaniel A. Ware, *Notes on Political Economy* (New York: Leavitt, Trow, and Co., 1844).

19. Clarence H. Danhof, *Three Decades of Thought on the South's Economic Problems* (Washington, D.C.: Brookings Institution, 1962), p. 1.

20. Easterlin, "Interregional Differences," pp. 97-98.

21. Douglass C. North, *The Economic Growth of the United States, 1790-1860* (Englewood Cliffs, N.J.: Prentice-Hall, 1961), pp. 131-32.

22. William H. Nicholls, "Some Foundations of Economic Development in the Upper Tennessee Valley, 1850-1900," *Journal of Political Economy* 64 (1956): 50.

23. Cash, *Mind of the South*, p. 46.

24. Ware, *Notes on Political Economy*, p. 201.

25. Cash, *Mind of the South*, p. 25.

26. Easterlin, "Interregional Differences," pp. 97-98, 128.

27. Ware, *Notes on Political Economy*, pp. 30-31.

28. Ernest M. Lander, "Manufacturing in South Carolina, 1815-1860," *Business History Review* 28 (1954): 66.

29. Nicholls, *Southern Tradition and Regional Progress*, pp. 45-46.

30. Louis R. Harlan, *Separate and Unequal: Public School Campaigns and Racism in the Southern Seaboard States, 1901-1915* (Chapel Hill: University of North Carolina Press, 1958), pp. 4-5.

31. North, *Economic Growth of the United States, 1790-1860*, p. 9.

32. Nicholls, *Southern Tradition and Regional Progress*, p. 21.

33. Eugene M. Lerner, "Southern Output and Agricultural Income, 1860-1880," in *Economic Impact of the American Civil War*, ed. Ralph Andreano (Cambridge, Mass.: Schenkman Publishing Co., 1962), pp. 97-98.

34. Easterlin, "Interregional Differences," pp. 99-100.

35. Ibid., pp. 102-3.

36. C. Vann Woodward, *Origins of the New South, 1877-1913* (Baton Rouge: Louisiana State University Press, 1951), pp. 291-92.

37. Ibid., pp. 309-10.

38. Danhof, "Four Decades of Thought on the South's Economic Problems," p. 11.

39. George B. Tindall, *The Emergence of the New South, 1913-1945* (Baton Rouge: Louisiana State University Press, 1967), p. 111.

40. Ibid., pp. 111, 354.

41. Ibid., p. 112.

42. Danhof, "Four Decades of Thought on the South's Economic Problems," pp. 11, 12.

43. Hoover and Ratchford, *Economic Resources and Policies of the South.*

44. Maddox et al., *Advancing South*, pp. 41-43.

45. Ibid., p. 43.

46. Ibid., p. 45.

47. U.S. Department of Commerce, Bureau of the Census, and U.S. Department of Labor, Bureau of Labor Statistics, *The Social and Economic Status of Negroes in the United States, 1969*, Current Population Reports, Series P-23, no. 29, Bureau of Labor Statistics Report no. 375, p. 4.

48. U.S. Department of Commerce, Bureau of the Census, *Statistical Abstract of the United States, 1970*, p. 219.

49. Ibid., p. 699.

50. *Survey of Current Business* 50 (August 1970): 41.

51. U.S. Department of Commerce, Bureau of the Census, *Statistical Abstract of the United States, 1970*, p. 232.

52. U.S. Federal Home Loan Bank Board, *Trends in the Savings and Loan Field* (Washington, D.C.: U.S. Federal Home Loan Bank Board, 1970).

53. *Survey of Current Business* 50 (April 1970): 7-10.

54. Joe Floyd, "Trends in Southern Money, Income, Savings, and Investment," in *South in Continuity and Change*, ed. McKinney and Thompson, p. 132.

55. This material is based on George H. Brown's "The Changing South" (Paper delivered at the International Conference on Population Priorities and Options for Commerce and Industry, University of North Carolina, Chapel Hill, N.C., 23 October 1970).

56. Ibid.

57. Werner Hochwald, "Interregional Income Flows in the South," in *Essays in Southern Economic Development*, ed. Greenhut and Whitman, pp. 336-37.

58. Maddox et al. *Advancing South*, p. 54.

59. F. Ray Marshall and Virgil L. Christian, "Human Resource Development in the South," in *You Can't Eat Magnolias*, ed. H. Brandt Ayers and Thomas H. Naylor (New York: McGraw-Hill Book Co., 1972), pp. 231-72.

60. See Thomas H. Naylor, *Computer Simulation Experiments with Models of Economic Systems* (New York: John Wiley & Sons, 1971).

61. Nicholls, *Southern Tradition and Regional Progress*, p. 159.

62. Ibid., p. 161.

63. Thomas H. Naylor, John W. Wall, and Horst Schauland, SIMPLAN: *A Planning and Budgeting Language* (Durham, N.C.: Duke University Press, 1975).

64. President's Advisory Council on Minority Business Enterprise, *Minority Enterprise and Expanded Ownership: Blueprint for the 1970's* (Washington, D.C.: U.S. Government Printing Office, 1971), p. 5.

65. U.S. Department of Commerce, Bureau of the Census, and U.S. Department of Labor, Bureau of Labor Statistics, *Social and Economic Status of Negroes in the United States, 1970*, p. 90.

66. In chapter 7 we propose the establishment of a Department of Rural Development with cabinet level status in the federal government.

67. For a detailed description of the methodology outlined in this section, see Naylor, Wall, and Schauland, SIMPLAN.

68. Some states such as Michigan are turning to survey data to determine priorities for state government. The division of state planning in Michigan recently conducted a survey of legislators, state government officials, and opinion leaders in the state to determine goals and priorities.

Chapter 3

1. Charles Silberman, *Crisis in the Classroom* (New York: Random House, 1970), p. 6.

2. Gunnar Myrdal, *An American Dilemma: The Negro Problem and Modern Democracy* (New York: Harper & Brothers, 1944), p. 882.

3. W. Lee Hansen and Burton A. Weisbrod, *Benefits, Costs and Finance of Public Higher Education* (Chicago: Markham Publishing Co., 1969), pp. 18 ff.; and Mark Blaug, ed., *Economics of Education*, Modern Economic Series, vol. 2 (Middlesex, Eng.: Penguin, 1969).

4. Moses Abramovitz, "Economic Growth in the United States: A Review Article," *American Economic Review* 52 (1962): 401.

5. Alexis de Tocqueville, *Democracy in America* (New York: Oxford University Press, 1947), pp. 335-36.

6. Alexander Heard, "Southern Education: The Continuing Frontier" (Paper delivered at the L. Q. C. Lamar Society symposium, "The Emerging South," Memphis, Tenn., April 1970).

7. U.S. Department of Health, Education, and Welfare, Office of Education, *Equality of Educational Opportunity*, by James S. Coleman, Carol J. Hobson, James McPartland, Frederick D. Weinfield, Ernest Q. Campbell, Alexander Mood, and Robert L. Yonk, 2 vols. (Washington, D.C.: Government Printing Office, 1966), 1:29 (hereafter cited as Coleman, *Educational Opportunity*).

8. See ibid., 1:218. Describing the tests used in his survey of 600,000 elementary and secondary students, Coleman stated that "such tests are not in any sense 'culturally fair'; in fact, their very design is to determine the degree to which the child has assimilated a culture appropriate to modern life in the United States."

9. The Selective Service mental examination does not sample a representative portion of the population—i.e., very few college students and virtually no women are tested. The skills that it tests are basic but limited.

10. Coleman, *Educational Opportunity*, 1:219.

11. Ibid., pp. 274-75.

12. U.S. Commission on Civil Rights, *Racial Isolation in the Public Schools* (Washington, D.C.: Government Printing Office, 1967), p. 110. Other studies favorable toward school busing for desegregation purposes have been undertaken by the Metropolitan Applied Research Center of New York, the National Education Association, the Washington Research Project, the Center for National Policy Review, the Resource Management Corporation (for the U.S. Office of Education), and the Southern Regional Council. A study by David J. Armor suggested that integration through busing in six Northern cities neither raised the academic achievements, aspirations, and self-esteem of black children nor improved race relations ("The Evidence on Busing," *Public Interest* 28 [1972]: 90-126).

13. Southern Regional Council, *The South and Her Children: School Desegregation 1970-1971* (Atlanta: Southern Regional Council, 1971), p. 6. Nationally, the percentage of Negroes in majority-white schools increased from 23.4 percent to 33.1 percent between 1968 and 1970 (*Race Relations Reporter*, 6 July 1971, p. 1).

14. W. J. Cash, *The Mind of the South* (New York: Alfred A. Knopf, 1941), pp. 14-17; and Myrdal, *American Dilemma*, p. 459.

15. Walter Hines Page, *The Rebuilding of Old Commonwealths: Being Essays Toward the Training of the Forgotten Man in the Southern States* (New York: Doubleday & Co., 1902), p. 6. Also see Edgar Knight, *Public Education in the South* (Boston: Ginn & Co., 1922); and William Dabney, *Universal Education in the South*, vol. 1, *From the Beginning to 1900* (Chapel Hill: University of North Carolina Press, 1936).

16. Knight, *Public Education in the South*, pp. 156-57.

17. William Taylor, "Toward a Definition of Orthodoxy: The Patrician South and the Common Schools," *Harvard Educational Review* 36 (1966): 412-26.

18. Wariness of the potentially disruptive influence of education provided the rationale, for example, for making it a crime to teach a slave how to read (see Winthrop Jordan, *White Over Black: American Attitudes Toward the Negro, 1550-1812* [Chapel Hill: University of North Carolina Press, 1968]).

19. Knight, *Public Education in the South*, p. 463. Also see Henry A. Bullock,

History of Negro Education in the South: From 1619 to the Present (Cambridge, Mass.: Harvard University Press, 1967).

20. Harry Ashmore, *Epitaph for Dixie* (New York: W. W. Norton & Co., 1958), p. 155.

21. Southern Regional Council, *South and Her Children*, p. 17.

22. *Race Relations Reporter*, 6 July 1971, p. 1.

23. Calculated from National Education Association, Research Division, *Estimates of School Statistics, 1970-71* (Washington, D.C.: National Education Association, 1971), p. 31.

24. U.S. Department of Health, Education, and Welfare, Office of Education, National Center for Educational Statistics, *Digest of Educational Statistics, 1970*.

25. Coleman, *Educational Opportunity*, vol. 1, tables 2.32.1, 2.32.2, 2.32.3, 2.32.4, 2.32.5, 2.33.6, 2.33.7, 2.33.8.

26. James G. Maddox, E. E. Liebhafsky, Vivian Henderson, and H. M. Hamlin, *The Advancing South: Manpower Prospects and Problems* (New York: Twentieth Century Fund, 1967), p. 91.

27. Silberman sees this result from that type of structure: children do not develop self-discipline, self-motivation, or responsibility for their own learning because everything is imposed from the outside. He claims that "the schools are not organized to facilitate learning. They are organized to facilitate order and the result is a whole set of rules and an insistence on silence and lack of motion that we adults find impossible to observe" (U.S. Congress, Senate, Select Committee on Equal Educational Opportunity, *Hearings before the Select Committee of the Senate on Equal Educational Opportunity*, 91st Cong., 2d sess., 1970, pt. 1A, p. 231).

28. Ibid., p. 233.

29. U.S. Department of Health, Education, and Welfare, *Statistics of Public Schools, Fall 1970*, pp. 28-29.

30. Ibid., p. 32.

31. Ibid., pp. 32, 34.

32. *Race Relations Reporter*, 3 January 1972, p. 16. Although most busing opponents claim to oppose only the transporting of children beyond their neighborhood schools, some see "no forced busing" as a code phrase whose true meaning is "no further integration." William Steif says, "The anti-busing sentiment is only symbolism: It focuses the feelings of middle-class whites who are fed up with the complaints of blacks and other minorities. It points to the whites' refusal to sacrifice status or comfort to try to achieve a more integrated society. It hints of a national rigidity that has created a permanent under-class" (ibid., p. 17).

33. Robert W. Hooker, *Displacement of Black Teachers in the Eleven Southern States* (Nashville: Race Relations Information Center, 1970), p. 1.

34. Ibid., p. 4.

35. Ibid.

36. Ibid., p. 5.

37. National Education Association, Research Division, *Estimates of School Statistics, 1970-71*, p. 7.

38. Ibid., p. 6.

39. U.S. Department of Health, Education, and Welfare, Office of Education, National Center for Educational Statistics, *Digest of Educational Statistics, 1970*, p. 33.

40. *New York Times*, 7 March 1972, p. 1.

41. Coleman, *Educational Opportunity*, 1:318, 313, 316.

42. Ibid., pp. 21-22.

43. See, for example, Henry S. Dyer, "School Factors and Equal Educational Opportunity," *Harvard Educational Review* 38 (1968): 46.

44. Coleman, *Educational Opportunity*, 1:318, 302.

45. *New York Times*, 18 May 1954, p. 15.

46. Ibid., 21 April 1971, p. 15.

47. For data concerning the fate of bond issues in the country as a whole, see U.S.

Department of Health, Education, and Welfare, Office of Education, National Center for Educational Statistics, *Digest of Educational Statistics, 1970*, pp. 95-96.

48. See U.S. Commission on Civil Rights, *Racial Isolation in the Public Schools*, p. 31 ff., for case studies of successful integration programs in other parts of the country.

49. Ibid., pp. 158 and 166, and Coleman, *Educational Opportunity*, 1:29. Research on this crucial subject, however, remains inconclusive.

50. Ashmore, *Epitaph for Dixie*, p. 148.

51. Willie Morris, *Yazoo* (New York: Harper's Magazine Press, 1971), pp. 33-36.

52. See Myrdal, *American Dilemma*, p. 879, for an early discussion of Negro class structure. Also see James S. Coleman, *Resources for Social Change: Race in the United States* (New York: John Wiley & Sons, 1971).

53. Robert Highsaw, ed., *The Deep South in Transformation: A Symposium* (University, Ala.: University of Alabama Press, 1964), p. 103.

54. Governor's Committee on Public School Education, *Report of the Governor's Committee on Public School Education* (Austin: Governor's Committee on Public School Education, 1968), p. 8.

55. U.S. Department of Commerce, Bureau of the Census, *Statistical Abstract of the United States, 1970*, p. 25, table 25.

56. Samuel S. Hill, Jr., *Southern Churches in Crisis* (New York: Holt, Rinehart & Winston, 1966), p. 31.

57. Wallace M. Alston, Jr., and Wayne Flynt, "Religion in the Land of Cotton," in *You Can't Eat Magnolias*, ed. H. Brandt Ayers and Thomas H. Naylor (New York: McGraw-Hill Book Co., 1972), p. 115.

58. Ibid.

59. Also see Willis D. Hawley, *Nonpartisan Elections and the Case for Party Politics* (New York: John Wiley & Sons, 1973).

60. *VEP News* 6, no. 1 (October 1971): 1.

61. Susan S. Stodolsky and Gerald Lesser, "Learning Patterns of the Disadvantaged," *Harvard Educational Review* 37 (1967): 582.

62. National Education Association, Committee on Educational Finance, *Financial Status of the Public Schools, 1970* (Washington, D.C.: National Education Association, 1970), pp. 52-53.

63. Eva Galambos, *The Tax Structure of the Southern States* (Atlanta: Southern Regional Council, 1969), pp. 4-5.

64. See the *Saturday Review*, 20 November 1971, p. 82, for a discussion of the California Supreme Court decision in *Serrano* v. *Priest*.

65. Education Commission of the States, *Early Childhood Development: Alternatives for Program Implementation in the States* (Denver: Education Commission of the States, 1971), p. 20.

66. Ibid., p. 14.

67. *Charlotte Observer*, 19 January 1972, p. 3A.

68. Ibid., 15 March 1972, p. 8A.

69. Virginia Department of Education, *Vocational Education in Virginia* (Richmond: Virginia Department of Education, 1971), p. 21.

70. Georgia Department of Education, *Georgia Needs Comprehensive High Schools* (Atlanta: Georgia Department of Education, 1970).

71. Oklahoma Department of Education, *Adult Basic and Continuing Education Through Oklahoma Learning Centers* (Oklahoma City: Oklahoma Department of Education, 1970), pp. 1-3.

72. Virginia Department of Education, *Annual Report of the Superintendent of Public Instruction* (Richmond: Virginia Department of Education, 1971), p. 48. Also see the studies of the Carnegie Commission on Non-Traditional Study.

73. Replies to authors' questionnaire by state departments of education.

74. *Greensboro Daily News*, 12 July 1971, p. 1. The Mississippi private school movement is examined in James M. Palmer, Sr., "Mississippi School Districts: Factors in the Disestablishment of Dual Systems" (Ph.D. diss., Mississippi State University, n.d.).

Some sources reported that white applications to private schools were decreasing (see "Schools' White Flight Slowing," *Charlotte Observer*, 20 November 1972, pp. 1-7).

75. *Charlotte Observer*, 15 December 1971, p. 17A.

76. *Greensboro Daily News*, 12 July 1971, p. 1.

77. *Charlotte Observer*, 15 December 1971, p. 17A.

78. "School Role in Poverty Contested," *New York Times*, 8 January 1973, pp. 55-56.

79. Education Commission of the States, *National Assessment of Educational Progress: A Project of the Education Commission of the States, Report 1* (Washington, D.C.: Government Printing Office, 1970). The study cautions, however, that "National Assessment supplies only 'facts' in the hope that they will assist others to find 'answers.'"

80. Florida Department of Education, *Florida's Public Education Program* (Tallahassee: Florida Department of Education, p. 31.

81. "Atlanta, U.S. NAACP's at Odds on Busing," *Durham* (N.C.) *Morning Herald*, 16 July 1973.

82. Charles Clotfelter, "School Desegregation and 'White Flight': The Effects of Desegregation Policies on Urban Markets for Housing and Schooling" (Ph.D. diss., Harvard University, 1973). Also see Frederic B. Glantz and Nancy J. Delaney, "Changes in Nonwhite Residential Patterns in Large Metropolitan Areas, 1960 and 1970," *New England Economic Review* (March/April 1973): 2-13.

83. *New York Times*, 25 October 1971.

Chapter 4

1. Mary Louise Naylor, "The Political Effects of Alternative Schemes of Financing Higher Education," mimeographed (Chapel Hill: University of North Carolina, 1971), pp. 6-7.

2. Russell Middleton, "Racial Problems and the Recruitment of Academic Staff at Southern Colleges and Universities," *American Sociological Review* 26 (1961): 960-70.

3. Otis A. Singletary, "Higher Education in the South: A Contemporary View," *South Atlantic Quarterly* 68 (1969): 86.

4. Ibid.

5. Kenneth D. Roose and Charles J. Andersen, *A Rating of Graduate Programs* (Washington, D.C.: American Council on Education, 1970).

6. Singletary, "Higher Education in the South, " pp. 93-95.

7. Southern Regional Education Board, *Fact Book on Higher Education in the South, 1970* (Atlanta: Southern Regional Education Board, 1970), pp. 30-31.

8. Southern Regional Education Board, *A Profile of Degrees Awarded* (Atlanta: Southern Regional Education Board, 1965), p. 4.

9. Singletary, "Higher Education in the South," p. 92.

10. Carnegie Commission on the Future of Higher Education, *A Chance to Learn* (New York: Carnegie Commission on the Future of Higher Education, 1970), p. 2.

11. Ibid.

12. Robert Scott, "Higher Education in North Carolina" (Address delivered to the North Carolina Association of Colleges and Universities, Raleigh, N.C., November 1970).

13. Southern Regional Education Board, *Fact Book on Higher Education in the South, 1970*, p. 44.

14. Southern Regional Education Board, *Within Our Reach* (Atlanta: Southern Regional Education Board, 1961), p. 9.

15. William H. Nicholls, *Southern Tradition and Regional Progress* (Chapel Hill: University of North Carolina Press, 1960), pp. 132-33, 143-44. Nicholls says that settlers on the Southern frontier "were soon outside the mainstreams of American migration and, with their increasing cultural isolation and heavy inbreeding, tended to lose whatever appreciation of book learning they may have started with. When they responded almost

en masse to the emotionalism of the great religious revivals of the early nineteenth century led by an uneducated lay ministry, their newly acquired religiosity reinforced their intolerance of dissent and encouraged the view that formal education was inconsistent with either spiritual salvation or physical virility."

He also wrote: "After founding its society on the 'violent abstraction' of slavery, the South desisted from further abstraction while the North never ceased to abstract—that is, it continued to employ intellectual processes as a means of attaining both technological and social progress. . . . Not only had the South become basically anti-intellectual, but this hostility had permeated even into the ivory towers of the better Southern universities. It is little wonder that the savage ideal and its inherent intolerance succeeded . . . in draining most Southern campuses of their best intellectual talent."

16. E. Merton Coulter, *The South During Reconstruction, 1865-1877* (Baton Rouge: Louisiana State University Press, 1957), p. 321. In 1884 six Southern states were attempting to support 67 colleges for men, while six equivalent states in the North supported only 17.

17. C. Vann Woodward, *Origins of the New South, 1877-1913* (Baton Rouge: Louisiana State University Press, 1951), p. 437.

18. For discussion of the history of Southern higher education see: Howard Odum, *Southern Regions of the United States* (Chapel Hill: University of North Carolina Press, 1936); Robert H. Salisbury, "State Politics and Education," in *Politics in the American States*, ed. Herbert Jacob and Kenneth Vines (Boston: Little, Brown & Co., 1965); Allan M. Cartter, "The Role of Higher Education in the Changing South," in *The South in Continuity and Change*, ed. John C. McKinney and Edgar T. Thompson (Durham, N.C.: Duke University Press, 1965); Ronald F. Howell, "Education for the Uncommon Man," in *The Lasting South*, ed. Louis D. Rubin, Jr., and James Jackson Kilpatrick (Chicago: Henry Regnery Co., 1957); Clement Eaton, *The Freedom-of-Thought Struggle in the Old South* (New York: Harper & Row, 1964); W. J. Cash, *The Mind of the South* (New York: Alfred A. Knopf, 1941); Howard Odum, *An American Epoch* (New York: Henry Holt & Co., 1930); Virginius Dabney, *Below the Potomac* (New York: Appleton-Century, 1942).

19. See Horace Mann Bond, *The Education of the Negro in the American Social Order* (Englewood Cliffs, N.J.: Prentice-Hall, 1934); Dwight Oliver Wendell Holmes, *The Evolution of the Negro College* (New York: Arno Press, 1934).

20. An example was the cooperative educational program planned for the Atlanta-Athens region of Georgia. Aided by the General Education Board, the program was designed to combine the library and laboratory facilities of a number of colleges and universities in the area and to improve graduate research facilities. Once again, however, political interference blocked development of the program: it was halted in 1941 when Governor Eugene Talmadge objected to its biracial nature.

21. Cartter, "Role of Higher Education in the Changing South," p. 92.

22. "Trustee Raps USC Use of Bequest," *Charlotte Observer*, 25 December 1970, p. 4A.

23. Sam Wiggins, *Higher Education in the South* (Berkeley: McCutchan Publishing Corp., 1966), p. 67.

24. Singletary, "Higher Education in the South," p. 92.

25. Southern Regional Education Board, *Fact Book on Higher Education in the South, 1970*, pp. 64, 57, 28.

26. Cartter, "Role of Higher Education in the Changing South," pp. 296-97.

27. American Council on Education, *A Fact Book on Higher Education: Third Issue, 1969* (Washington, D.C.: American Council on Education, 1969), p. 9137.

28. Southern Regional Education Board, *Fact Book on Higher Education in the South, 1970*, p. 63.

29. Ibid., p. 62.

30. Ibid., pp. 30, 33-34; American Council on Education, *A Fact Book on Higher Education: First Issue, 1973* (Washington, D.C.: American Council on Education, 1973), p. 7310.

31. American Council on Education, *Fact Book on Higher Education: First Issue, 1973*, pp. 2-15.

32. Southern Regional Education Board, *The Future South and Higher Education* (Atlanta: Southern Regional Education Board, 1968), p. 89.

33. U.S. Department of Commerce, Bureau of the Census, *Statistical Abstract of the United States, 1970*, p. 107.

34. Southern Regional Education Board, *Fact Book on Higher Education in the South, 1970*, pp. 54, 51.

35. C. Arnold Anderson, "Southern Education: A New Research Frontier," in *Perspectives on the South: Agenda for Research*, ed. Edgar T. Thompson (Durham, N.C.: Duke University Press, 1967).

36. Joseph J. Spengler, "Demographic and Economic Change in the South, 1940-1960," *Change in the Contemporary South*, ed. Allan P. Sindler (Durham, N.C.: Duke University Press, 1963), p. 54.

37. Salisbury, "State Politics and Education," p. 363.

38. James G. Maddox, E. E. Liebhafsky, Vivian Henderson, and H. M. Hamlin, *The Advancing South: Manpower Prospects and Problems* (New York: Twentieth Century Fund, 1967), pp. 111-12.

39. Southern Regional Education Board, *College Students on the Move* (Atlanta: Southern Regional Education Board, 1968), p. 6.

40. Middleton, "Racial Problems and the Recruitment of Academic Staff," pp. 960-70.

41. Southern Association of Colleges and Schools, "Report of the Commission of the Study of the Statutes Related to Visiting Speakers at State Supported Educational Institutions," in *Proceedings of the Seventieth Annual Meeting* (Atlanta: Southern Association of Colleges and Schools, 1965), p. 67.

42. Southern Association of Colleges and Schools, "The 1963 Legislation—General Statutes of North Carolina—Article 22," in ibid., pp. 72-73.

43. Lanier Cox and Lester Harrell, *The Impact of Federal Programs on State Planning and Coordination of Higher Education* (Atlanta: Southern Regional Education Board, 1969), p. 2.

44. John C. McKinney and Linda B. Bourque, "The Changing South: National Incorporation of a Region," *American Sociological Review* 36 (1971): 407.

45. Maddox et al., *Advancing South*, p. 85.

46. Anderson, "Southern Education," p. 178.

47. *New York Times*, 24 June 1972, pp. 1, 15.

48. Paul Delaney, "Negro Colleges Not Using U.S. Aid," *New York Times*, 3 January 1971.

49. James L. Miller, Jr., "Conference Summary: Review of the Issues and Emerging Directions," in *New Directions in Statewide Higher Educational Planning and Coordination* (Atlanta: Southern Regional Education Board, 1970), p. 48.

50. Commission on Research and Service, *Changes in Admission Policies of Colleges and Universities in the South* (Atlanta: Commission on Research and Service, 1962), p. 25.

51. "Race and I.Q.," *Time*, 7 September 1970, p. 27. The Southern Regional Council sponsored the Symposium on Human Intelligence, Social Science, and Public Policy in spring 1973.

52. Charles A. Nelson, "Quantity and Quality in Higher Education," in *Higher Education and Modern Democracy*, ed. Robert A. Goldwin (Chicago: Rand McNally & Co., 1965), p. 159.

53. Southern Regional Education Board, *A Profile of Degrees Awarded*, p. 2.

54. Southern Regional Education Board, *Fact Book on Higher Education in the South, 1970*, pp. 2-15, 30.

55. Southern Regional Education Board, *Statistics for the Sixties: Higher Education in the South* (Atlanta: Southern Regional Education Board, 1963), pp. 72-73.

56. Southern Regional Education Board, *Fact Book on Higher Education in the*

South, 1970, p. 48.

57. Robert Scott, "Higher Education in North Carolina."

58. William F. McFarlane, *State Support for Private Higher Education?* (Atlanta: Southern Regional Education Board, 1969), p. 3.

59. North Carolina General Assembly, House Bill 780 (1971).

60. U.S. Department of Health, Education, and Welfare, Office of Education, and National Center for Educational Statistics, *Education Directory, 1970-71: Higher Education*, passim.

61. Wiggins, *Higher Education in the South*, p. 271.

62. McFarlane, *State Support for Private Higher Education?*, pp. 3-4. "The major objective would be to stimulate larger enrollments in the private sector by equalizing the costs of attending public and private institutions; to use facilities and programs of private institutions in the public interest when, by virtue of location or special resources, there would be a net gain in the educational and/or financial advantages; and, in general, to provide for a more equitable distribution of effort among public and private institutions in meeting overall state needs."

63. Southern Regional Education Board, *Fact Book on Higher Education in the South, 1970*, p. 30.

64. Donald Phillips, "14 Universities in the Red, Many Cut Back, Study Finds," *Atlanta Constitution*, 7 July 1971.

65. McFarlane, *State Support for Private Higher Education?*, p. 3.

66. Adam Smith, *The Wealth of Nations* (New York: Random House, Modern Library, 1937), p. 248.

67. *Vlandis* v. *Kline*, 37 U.S. 63 (1973).

68. Southern Regional Education Board, *Sources of Financing* (Atlanta: Southern Regional Education Board, 1966), p. 8.

69. Southern Association of Colleges and Schools, *Education: The Southern Hope* (Atlanta: Southern Association of Colleges and Schools, 1965), p. 45.

70. Southern Regional Education Board, *Within Our Reach*, p. 32. In 1961 the Southern Regional Education Board recommended the year-round operation of colleges and universities: "Year-round operation is not the same as a summer school program. It means the addition of a full fourth quarter or third semester to the school year. It means that courses are offered during the summer months on the same basis as the rest of the year. It means that faculty are expected to teach and students to study a minimum of 45 weeks out of the year.

In addition to increasing the number of students who can be accommodated in existing facilities, year-round operation will reduce the time required to complete graduate, undergraduate or professional studies. By making fuller use of faculty time, it will reduce the need for new teaching staff and make possible higher total salaries for faculty."

71. "Will Everyman Destroy the University?," *Saturday Review*, 20 December 1969, p. 55.

72. Ben E. Fountain, "What Will the Future Bring?" *Open Door* 17 (1969): 20.

73. Edmund J. Gleazer, Jr., *American Junior Colleges*, 6th ed. (Washington, D.C.: American Council on Education, 1963), p. 3.

74. John E. Roueché, "Accountability in the Two-Year College," mimeographed (Durham, N.C.: Regional Education Laboratory for the Carolinas and Virginia, 1971), p. 4.

75. Southern Regional Education Board, *The Community College* (Atlanta: Southern Regional Education Board, 1964), p. 4.

76. Southern Regional Education Board, *Fact Book on Higher Education in the South, 1970*, pp. 2-15, 36.

77. Carnegie Commission on the Future of Higher Education, *The Open-Door Colleges* (New York: Carnegie Commission on the Future of Higher Education, 1970), p. 29; Miami-Dade Junior College claimed an enrollment of over 24,000 in 1968 (Southern Regional Education Board, *Fact Book on Higher Education in the South, 1970*, p. 45).

78. James L. Wattenbarger, "Community Colleges: A Friendly Critique," in *Effective Use of Resources in State Higher Education* (Atlanta: Southern Regional Education Board, 1970), p. 22.

79. National Laboratory for Higher Education, *The EDO: New Man on the Junior College Campus* (Durham, N.C.: National Laboratory for Higher Education, 1971), p. 1.

80. Arthur M. Cohen, *Dateline '79: Heretical Concepts for the Community College* (Beverly Hills: Glencoe Press, 1969), p. xvii.

81. Leland L. Medsker, *The Junior College: Progress and Prospect* (New York: McGraw-Hill Book Co., 1960), p. 185. More attention should be given to the preservice training of community-college instructors, especially with increasing numbers of research-oriented Ph.D.s taking such positions.

82. Carnegie Commission on the Future of Higher Education, *Open-Door Colleges*, pp. 30-31.

83. Patricia K. Cross, *The Junior College's Role in Providing Postsecondary Education for All* (Berkeley: Center for Research and Development in Higher Education, 1969), p. 5.

84. Southern Regional Education Board, *The Negro and Higher Education in the South* (Atlanta: Southern Regional Education Board, 1967), p. 29.

85. Southern Regional Education Board, *New Challenges to the Junior Colleges* (Atlanta: Southern Regional Education Board, 1970), pp. 5-7.

86. Wattenbarger, "Community Colleges," p. 22.

87. Southern Regional Education Board, *Negro and Higher Education in the South*, p. 1.

88. Freda H. Goldman, *Educational Imperative: The Negro in the Changing South* (Chicago: Center of Liberal Education for Adults, 1963), pp. 2-3.

89. Southern Regional Education Board, *Negro and Higher Education in the South*, p. 3; David Riesman and Christopher Jencks, "The American Negro College," *Harvard Educational Review* 37 (1967): 26.

90. Southern Regional Education Board, *Negro and Higher Education in the South*, pp. 23, 30.

91. Riesman and Jencks, "American Negro College, " p. 25. Nathan Hare wrote of his interview with a black college registrar who, "before fleeing mid-year to a white university . . . showed me figures indicating that his college, despite a high flunk-out rate, lost more students each year who earned a 'C' or better average than students who earned less than a 'C' average" ("The Legacy of Paternalism," *Saturday Review*, 20 July 1968, p. 58).

92. Southern Regional Education Board, *Negro and Higher Education in the South*, pp. 3-5.

93. Ibid., pp. 21-22.

94. Riesman and Jencks, "American Negro College," p. 48.

95. Southern Regional Education Board, *Negro and Higher Education in the South*, p. 15.

96. Riesman and Jencks, "American Negro College," p. 25.

97. Ibid.

98. Earl J. McGrath, *The Predominantly Negro Colleges and Universities in Transition* (New York: Teachers College, Columbia University, 1965), p. 25.

99. Ibid, p. 39.

100. Riesman and Jencks, "American Negro College," p. 25.

101. "Up from Isolation," *Newsweek*, 1 March 1971, p. 68.

102. Southern Regional Education Board, *Negro and Higher Education in the South*, p. 7.

103. James M. Godard, "Introduction," in *Expanding Opportunities: Case Studies of Interinstitutional Cooperation, 1969* (Atlanta: Southern Regional Education Board, 1969), pp. 1-2, 23. A number of programs involving interinstitutional cooperation are already in operation in the South. Florida's Stetson University and Bethune-Cookman

College, one predominantly white and the other predominantly black, offer a joint seminar in social problems and are developing plans for the establishment of several joint professorships. Livingstone and Catawba colleges, both in North Carolina, share a single sociology department. The Texas Association of Developing Colleges is a consortium of six private, traditionally Negro colleges, but plans are being developed for cooperative programs with predominantly white colleges and universities in the area.

104. McGrath, *Predominantly Negro Colleges*, pp. 9-11.

105. Southern Regional Education Board, *Negro and Higher Education in the South*, p. 21.

106. "Up from Isolation," p. 69.

107. Riesman and Jencks, "American Negro College," p. 57.

108. Lyman A. Glenny, "Doctoral Planning for the Seventies: A Challenge for the States," in *Effective Use of Resources in State Higher Education* (Atlanta: Southern Regional Education Board, 1970), p. 3.

109. Southern Regional Education Board, *Statistics for the Sixties*, pp. 77-79.

110. Southern Regional Education Board, *Profile of Degrees Awarded*, p. 5.

111. Cartter, "Role of Higher Education in the Changing South," p. 291.

112. Roose and Andersen, *Rating of Graduate Programs*, pp. 2-3, 11, 18.

113. Miller, "Conference Summary," p. 48.

114. Glenny, "Doctoral Planning for the Seventies," p. 4.

115. Scott, "Higher Education in North Carolina."

116. Allan M. Cartter, "Reflections on the Cost of Graduate Education" (Memo to participants at the Conference on the Future of Graduate Education, Woods Hole, Mass., August 1969), p. 9.

117. Roose and Andersen, *Rating of Graduate Programs*, p. 25; "In the Southern states and in the Western Plains states interstate arrangements could be made to establish a few, first-rate, graduate-research-teaching centers. . . . Both regions have too many poor-quality programs . . . both have a number of institutions which ought never to have been authorized to offer advanced degrees. . . . Both regions have the mechanism for planning and for facilitating [this kind of] development" (Glenny, "Doctoral Planning for the Seventies," p. 80).

118. "OK Given 'Academic Common Market' Plan," *Durham* (N.C.) *Morning Herald*, 15 June 1973, p. 7.

119. Howard Y. McClusky, *Background Paper on Education* (Washington, D.C.: White House Conference on Aging, 1971).

120. Horst Schauland, Thomas H. Naylor, and Allan Kornberg, "ELECTION: A Campaign Simulator" (Paper delivered at the annual meeting of the American Political Science Association, Chicago, September 1971). Within the classroom students can learn the probable consequences of decisions through gaming or physical or social system model-building.

121. Carnegie Commission on the Future of Higher Education, *Chance to Learn*, p. 13.

Chapter 5

1. Lewis A. Froman, Jr., *Congressmen and Their Constituencies* (Chicago: Rand McNally & Co., 1965), pp. 37-38.

2. Thomas R. Dye, *Politics, Economics and the Public* (Chicago: Rand McNally & Co., 1966), p. 71.

3. Angus Campbell, Philip E. Converse, Warren E. Miller, and Donald E. Stokes, *The American Voter* (New York: John Wiley & Sons, 1964), pp. 86-87; and Frank J. Sorauf, *Party Politics in America* (Boston: Little, Brown & Co., 1968), p. 138. It is hypothesized by Campbell et al that family relationships are a primary influence on registration and voting behavior.

4. George B. Tindall, "Southern Strategy: A Historical Perspective," mimeographed

(Chapel Hill: University of North Carolina, 1971), p. 23.

5. Thad Beyle and Angel Beza, "The Politics of North Carolina," mimeographed (Chapel Hill: University of North Carolina, 1970), p. 6, quotes Douglas S. Gatlin, "Socioeconomic Basis of Party Competition: A Case Study of North Carolina" (Ph.D. diss., University of North Carolina, 1970).

6. F. Glenn Abney, "Partisan Realignment in a One-Party System—The Case of Mississippi," *Journal of Politics* 31 (1969): 1104. The conclusion reached was that "as long as Mississippi Democratic leaders distinguish themselves from the nation's Democratic party and as long as the courts allow the 'regulars' to use the Democratic label, Mississippians will probably continue to decide their elections in Democratic primaries." Also see Earl Black and Merle Black, "Party Institutionalization in the American South: The Growth of Contested Republican Primaries" (Paper delivered at the annual meeting of the Southern Political Science Association, Atlanta, 1973).

7. James Clotfelter and William R. Hamilton, "Wallace Supporters and Southern Political Attitudes: . . . in Which Certain Questions Are Raised Regarding Wallace Supporters" (Paper delivered at the annual meeting of the Southern Political Science Association, Atlanta, 1973); James Clotfelter and William R. Hamilton, "The Wallace Electorate and the Future of Southern Politics" (Paper delivered at the annual meeting of the Southern Humanities Conference, Houston, 1973). The surveys used in these papers were conducted by William R. Hamilton and Staff, a division of the Washington, D.C., firm of Independent Research Associates, Inc.

8. Donald S. Strong, *Negroes, Ballots and Judges* (University, Ala.: University of Alabama Press, 1968), p. 56.

9. U.S. Department of Commerce, Bureau of the Census, *The Social and Economic Status of the Black Population in the United States, 1972*, Special Studies, Series P-23, no. 46 (1973), p. 99, table 77.

10. V. O. Key, *Southern Politics in State and Nation* (New York: Alfred A. Knopf, 1949), p. 20.

11. Senator Long was elected to the Senate in 1948. He has been opposed since then only once, in 1962, when he won with 76 percent of the vote. He was reelected unopposed in 1968.

12. Alexander Heard, *A Two-Party South?* (Chapel Hill: University of North Carolina Press, 1959), p. 247.

13. Bernard Cosman, *Five States for Goldwater* (University, Ala.: University of Alabama Press, 1966), p. 90.

14. Donald R. Matthews and James W. Prothro, *Negroes and the New Southern Politics* (New York: Harcourt, Brace & World, 1966), p. 398.

15. James Clotfelter and William R. Hamilton, "Beyond Race Politics," in *You Can't Eat Magnolias*, ed. H. Brandt Ayers and Thomas H. Naylor (New York: McGraw-Hill Book Co., 1972), pp. 136-59.

16. *Baker* v. *Carr*, 369 U.S. 186 (1962); and *Reynolds* v. *Simms*, 377 U.S. 533 (1964).

17. Frank Trippitt, *The States—United They Fell* (New York: World Publishing Co., 1967), passim.

18. Institute of Government, *North Carolina Governor's Committee on State Government Reorganization: Final Report to 1971 General Assembly* (Chapel Hill: Institute of Government, University of North Carolina, 1971), p. 1.

19. Coleman B. Ransome, "Political Leadership in the Governor's Office," *Journal of Politics* 26 (1964): 201.

20. Malcolm E. Jewell, "State Legislatures in Southern Politics," *Journal of Politics* 26 (1964): 188.

21. Southern Regional Council, *Southern Justice: An Indictment* (Atlanta: Southern Regional Council, 1965), p. 2.

22. Louis H. Pollok, ed., *The Constitution and the Supreme Court* (New York: World Publishing Co., 1966), vol. 2, chap. 4.

23. Daniel J. Elazar, ed., *Cooperation and Conflict: Readings in American Federal-*

ism (Itasca, Ill.: F. E. Peacock, 1969), p. 162.

24. Dana B. Brammer, *A Study of the Office of Sheriff in the Southern Region, 1967* (University, Miss.: Bureau of Governmental Research, University of Mississippi, 1968), p. 20.

25. National Advisory Commission on Rural Poverty, *The People Left Behind* (Washington, D.C.: National Advisory Commission on Rural Poverty, 1967).

26. Clyde F. Snider, *Local Government in Rural America* (New York: Appleton-Century-Crofts, 1952), p. 39.

27. Herbert Jacob and Kenneth N. Vines, *Studies in Judicial Politics*, Tulane Studies in Political Science, vol. 8 (New Orleans: Department of Political Science, Tulane University, 1963), p. 118.

28. Paul W. Wager, ed., *County Government Across the Nation* (Chapel Hill: University of North Carolina Press, 1960).

29. William H. Nicholls, *Southern Tradition and Regional Progress* (Chapel Hill: University of North Carolina Press, 1960); Monroe L. Billington, *The American South: A Brief History* (New York: Charles Scribner's Sons, 1971); Dewey W. Grantham, *The Democratic South* (Athens: University of Georgia Press, 1963); Allan P. Sindler, "The South in Political Transition," in *The South in Continuity and Change*, ed. John C. McKinney and Edgar T. Thompson (Durham, N.C.: Duke University Press, 1965); Pat Watters and Reese Cleghorn, *Climbing Jacob's Ladder: The Arrival of Negroes in Southern Politics* (New York: Harcourt, Brace & World, 1967).

30. See National Municipal League, Committee on State Government, *Model State Constitution*, 6th ed. (New York: National Municipal League, 1963).

31. Richard H. Leach, ed., *Compacts of Antiquity: State Constitutions* (Atlanta: SNPA Foundation, 1970), pp. 97, 93, 91.

32. "The Black Officeholder," *Birmingham News*, 22 February 1973. Also see Charles Bullock III, "Southern Black Elected Officials" (Paper delivered at the annual meeting of the Southern Political Science Association, Atlanta, 1973).

33. *VEP News* 6, no. 1 (October 1971): 1.

34. Samuel D. Cook, "Political Movements and Organizations," in *The American South in the 1960's*, ed. Avery Leiserson (New York: Frederick A. Praeger, 1964), p. 132.

35. *Plessy* v. *Ferguson*, 163 U.S. 532 (1896).

36. Pollok, *Constitution and the Supreme Court*, p. 360.

37. Matthews and Prothro, *Negroes and the New Southern Politics*, p. 75.

38. *Baker* v. *Carr*, 369 U.S. 186 (1962); *Reynolds* v. *Simms*, 377 U.S. 533 (1964).

39. Frank Smothers, ed., *The Book of the States, 1966-1967* (Chicago: Council of State Governments, 1966), p. 38.

40. William J. Keefe and Morris S. Ogul, *The American Legislative Process, Congress and the States* (Englewood Cliffs, N.J.: Prentice-Hall, 1964), p. 25.

41. James Nathan Miller, "Florida Fires the Pork Chop Gang," *Reader's Digest*, August 1971, p. 109.

42. Howard F. Mahan, "Alabama," in *Apportionment in the 1960's* (1967; rev. ed., New York: National Municipal League, 1970), p. 1.

43. *Fatson* v. *Dorsey*, 379 U.S. 433 (1965).

44. Thomas R. Dye, *Politics in States and Communities* (Englewood Cliffs, N.J.: Prentice-Hall, 1969), p. 101.

45. Richard H. Leach, *American Federalism* (New York: W. W. Norton & Co., 1970), p. 34.

46. John M. DeGrove, "Help or Hindrance to State Action?: The National Government," in *The States and the Urban Crisis*, ed. Alan K. Campbell (Englewood Cliffs, N.J.: Prentice-Hall, 1970), p. 148.

47. Deil S. Wright, *Federal Grants-in-Aid: Perspectives and Alternatives* (Washington, D.C.: American Enterprise Institute for Public Policy Research, 1968), p. 7.

48. Leach, *American Federalism*, pp. 201-2. The proliferation of narrowly categorical federal grants, entailing much duplication, has had other negative consequences for state policy and administration. Their conditional and functional character engen-

dered a sense of independence and single-program focus among administrators; aided by fragmented state administrative structures, administrators have often achieved "substantial immunity from control by their governors, legislators, and other politically responsible officials" (Wright, *Federal Grants-in-Aid*, p. 48). In setting conditions and offering financial inducements, federal administrators intervene in the state policy-making process and restrict the discretion of elected state or local officials. While this is designed to assure conformity with policies of national importance, the review of state plans and proposals by federal officials with little knowledge of local problems often leads to unrealistic appraisals that can undermine a program (Terry Sanford, *Storm Over the States* [New York: McGraw-Hill Book Co., 1967], pp. 89-90). The federal government itself has not set meaningful priorities among its plethora of grants programs so that the insufficient funds allocated to domestic needs chase too many goals, sometimes in conflicting ways (Dye, *Politics in States and Communities*, p. 469). Furthermore, while grants programs have encouraged state planning efforts, they have usually been confined to the narrow functional area covered by a single program and have been divorced from any comprehensive plan that could help to eliminate duplication and waste of scarce resources.

49. Sorauf, *Party Politics in America*, p. 187.

50. Ibid., pp. 143-45.

51. William L. Chase, "Southern Hospitality Reaches Unions Slowly," *Durham* (N.C.) *Morning Herald*, 20 June 1971.

52. "A New Life for the County," *American County*, October 1970, p. 43.

53. A. Wade Martin, "Technical Training: The South Carolina Approach," in *American Cooperation 1970* (Raleigh: Agricultural Policy Institute, North Carolina State University, 1970), p. 85.

54. Deil S. Wright, "Political Economy, Fiscal Outcomes and Intergovernmental Relations," mimeographed (Chapel Hill: University of North Carolina, 1970); and Eva Galambos, *The Tax Structure of the Southern States* (Atlanta: Southern Regional Council, 1969), p. 8; Galambos's study covers the eleven states of the Confederacy.

55. Galambos, *Tax Structure of the Southern States*, p. 14.

56. See Pollok, *Constitution and the Supreme court*, p. 266.

57. Matthews and Prothro, *Negroes and the New Southern Politics*, pp. 85, 127, 343, 128. Also see Chandler Davidson, *Biracial Politics* (Baton Rouge: Louisiana State University Press, 1972).

58. Felton J. Capel, "A Rural Politician Looks at the South," *Black Politician*, January 1971, p. 18.

59. Nicholls, *Southern Tradition and Regional Progress*, p. 84.

60. Ibid., p. 86.

61. Numan V. Bartley, *The Rise of Massive Resistance: Race-Politics in the South during the 1950's* (Baton Rouge: Louisiana State University Press, 1969), p. 19.

62. Beyle and Beza, "Politics of North Carolina," p. 5.

63. John M. Winters, *State Constitutional Limitations on Solutions of Metropolitan Area Problems* (Ann Arbor: Michigan Legal Publications, 1961), p. 47.

64. John L. Sanders, "Modern Forms of County Administration," *County Government Review* 19 (1966): 22.

65. Cosman, *Five States for Goldwater*, p. 25; and H. D. Price, *The Negro and Southern Politics* (New York: New York University Press, 1957).

66. North Carolina General Statute 163-15 has been so interpreted by some local officials.

67. Sorauf, *Party Politics in America*, p. 331.

68. C. Vann Woodward, *Reunion and Reaction: The Compromise of 1877 and the End of Reconstruction* (Boston: Little, Brown & Co., 1951).

69. Cosman, *Five States for Goldwater*, p. 112.

70. Malcolm E. Jewell, *The State Legislatures, Politics and Practice* (New York: Random House, 1963), pp. 48, 77.

71. Coleman B. Ransome, *The Role of the Governor in the South* (University, Ala.:

Bureau of Public Administration, University of Alabama, 1951), p. 69.

72. Joseph J. Ferrell, "The Local Government Study Commission Recommends," *Popular Government*, March 1969.

73. Trippitt, *The States—United They Fell*, p. 151.

74. Malcolm E. Jewell, *Legislative Representation in the Contemporary South* (Durham, N.C.: Duke University Press, 1967), p. 23.

75. *Folson* v. *Dorsey*, 85 Sup. Ct. 489 (1965).

76. Jewell, *Legislative Representation in the Contemporary South*, p. 130.

77. Malcolm E. Jewell, "The Political Setting," in *State Legislatures in American Politics*, ed. Alexander Heard (Englewood Cliffs, N.J.: Prentice-Hall, 1966), pp. 70-97.

78. Dye, *Politics, Economics and the Public*, p. 273.

79. Trippitt, *The States—United They Fell*, p. 33; and Miller, "Florida Fires the Pork Chop Gang," p. 109.

80. National Conference of State Legislative Leaders, *Yearbook, 1969* (Milwaukee: Office of the Secretariat, National Conference of State Legislative Leaders, 1969), p. 8.

81. Coleman B. Ransome, "Political Leadership in the Governor's Office," in *American South in the 1960's*, ed. Leiserson, p. 200.

82. Joseph A. Schlesinger, "The Politics of the Executive," in *Politics in the American States*, ed. Herbert Jacob and Kenneth N. Vines (Boston: Little, Brown & Co., 1965), pp. 222-23.

83. Ibid., pp. 225-27; and Ransome, "Political Leadership," p. 203.

84. Grant McConnell, *Private Power and American Democracy* (New York: Alfred A. Knopf, 1966), p. 193.

85. Schlesinger, "Politics of the Executive," pp. 227-28.

86. Thomas R. Dye, *Politics in States and Communities* (Englewood Cliffs, N.J.: Prentice-Hall, 1969), p. 142.

87. Malcolm E. Jewell, "State Legislatures in Southern Politics," in *American South in the 1960's*, ed. Leiserson, p. 188.

88. Austin Ranney, "Parties in State Politics," in *Politics in the American States*, ed. Jacob and Vines, p. 89.

89. McConnell, *Private Power*, p. 192.

90. Jewell, "State Legislatures in Southern Politics," pp. 189, 191.

91. Clyde L. Ball, *Report on Court Structure and Jurisdiction, Prepared for the North Carolina Bar Association Committee on Improving and Expediting the Administration of Justice in North Carolina* (Chapel Hill: Institute of Government, University of North Carolina, 1957), p. 1.

92. Southern Regional Council, *Racial Discrimination in the Southern Federal Courts* (Atlanta: Southern Regional Council, 1965); and see Cameron's dissent in *U.S.* v. *Wood*, 295 Fed. 772 (5th Cir. 1961).

93. Institute of Government, *Report on the Wilmington Police Department* (Chapel Hill: Institute of Government, University of North Carolina, 1972), p. 27.

94. Institute of Government, *Rural Law Enforcement in Union County, N.C.* (Chapel Hill: Institute of Government, University of North Carolina, 1970), p. 2.

95. Sanders, "Modern Forms of County Administration," p. 22.

96. "Home Rule," *American County Government* 33 (April 1968): 11.

97. Wager, ed., *County Government Across the Nation*, pp. 346-47, and North Carolina General Statute 153.4 and 153.5.

98. Wager, ed., *County Government Across the Nation*, p. 353.

99. Ira Sharkansky, *Regionalism in American Politics* (Indianapolis: Bobbs-Merrill Co., 1970), p. 98.

100. V. O. Key, quoted in Frederick M. Wirt, *The Politics of Southern Equality: Law and Social Change in a Mississippi County* (Chicago: Aldine Publishing Co., 1970), p. 312.

101. Jewell, *State Legislatures, Politics and Practice*, p. 48.

102. Citizens Conference on State Legislatures, "Legislatures Move to Improve Their Effectiveness," in *Research Memorandum No. 15* (Kansas City, Mo.: Citizens

Conference on State Legislatures, 1971), p. 7.

103. Leach, *American Federalism*, p. 120.

104. McConnell, *Private Power*, p. 184.

105. Ibid., p. 190.

106. See Sanford, *Storm Over the States*, chap. 16; and Committee for Economic Development, *Modernizing State Government* (New York: Committee for Economic Development, 1967).

107. Dye, *Politics in States and Communities*, p. 161.

108. Ibid., pp. 461-64.

109. "What programs the state spends money for and how much it spends along with the determination of priorities among programs and emphasis within programs are planning matters" (Lawrence Logan Durisch, "Southern Regional Planning and Development," in *American South in the 1960's*, ed. Leiserson, pp. 42-43).

110. Basil J. F. Mott, "State Planning," in *The State and the Poor*, ed. Richard E. Barringer and Samuel H. Beer (Cambridge, Mass.: Winthrop Publishers, 1970), p. 251.

111. Duane Lockard, *The Politics of State and Local Government*, 2d ed. (New York: Macmillan Co., 1969), pp. 359-60.

112. See Committee for Economic Development, *Modernizing State Government*, pp. 59-60; Sanford, *Storm Over the States*, p. 200.

113. Ball, *Report on Court Structure and Jurisdiction*, p. 4.

114. C. E. Hinsdale, *North Carolina's General Court of Justice* (Chapel Hill: Institute of Government, University of North Carolina, 1969), pp. 9-10.

115. North Carolina General Assembly, *Report of the Court's Commission to the North Carolina General Assembly* (Raleigh: North Carolina General Assembly, 1971), p. 8.

116. Agricultural Policy Institute, *Creating Opportunities for Tomorrow* (Raleigh: North Carolina State University, 1970), p. 12.

117. See David Lawrence, *Inter-local Cooperation in North Carolina Enabling Legislation* (Chapel Hill: Institute of Government, University of North Carolina, 1970), p. 6.

118. National Advisory Commission on Rural Poverty, *People Left Behind*, p. 150.

Chapter 6

1. A Standard Metropolitan Statistical Area (SMSA) is an "integrated economic and social unit with a recognized large population nucleus. To serve the statistical purposes for which metropolitan areas are defined, their parts must themselves be areas for which statistics are usually or often collected. Thus, each standard metropolitan statistical area must contain at least one city of at least 50,000 inhabitants. The standard metropolitan statistical area will then include the county of such a central city and adjacent counties that are found to be metropolitan in character and economically and socially integrated with the county or central city" (U.S. Bureau of the Budget, Office of Statistical Standards, *Standard Metropolitan Statistical Areas* [Washington, D.C.: Government Printing Office, 1967], pp. vii-viii). "SMSA" is used in this chapter interchangeably with metropolitan area. An SMSA is divided into a "central city" or "inner city," which is that city of 50,000 mentioned above in the definition, and a "suburban" or "outer ring," which is the remaining part of the county and any other "integrated" counties.

2. George H. Brown, "The Changing South" (Paper delivered at the International Conference on Population Priorities and Options for Commerce and Industry, University of North Carolina, Chapel Hill, N.C., 23 October 1970).

3. Joel L. Fleishman, "The Southern City: Northern Mistakes in Southern Settings," in *You Can't Eat Magnolias*, ed. H. Brandt Ayers and Thomas H. Naylor (New York: McGraw-Hill Book Co., 1972), pp. 169-94. Also see Lynn Smith, "The Emergence of Cities," in *The Urban South*, ed. Rupert B. Vance and Nicholas J. Demerath (Chapel Hill: University of North Carolina Press, 1954), pp. 24-37.

4. Leonard Reissman, "Urbanization in the South," in *The South in Continuity and Change*, ed. John C. McKinney and Edgar T. Thompson (Durham, N.C.: Duke University Press, 1965), p. 92.

5. U.S. Department of Commerce, Bureau of the Census, *Census of Population and Housing, 1970*, Final Reports, Series PHC(2) (1971), table 2.

6. Jerome P. Pickard, *Dimensions of Metropolitanism* (Washington, D.C.: Urban Land Institute, 1967), pp. 30-33.

7. Reissman, "Urbanization in the South," p. 93.

8. Karl E. Taeuber and Alma F. Taeuber, *Negroes in Cities: Residential Segregation and Neighborhood Change* (Chicago: Aldine Publishing Co., 1965), pp. 29-31, 36-37.

9. U.S. Department of Commerce, Bureau of the Census, and U.S. Department of Labor, Bureau of Labor Statistics, *The Social and Economic Status of Negroes in the United States, 1969*, Current Population Reports, Series P-23, no. 29, Bureau of Labor Statistics Report no. 375, p. 10.

10. Nicholas J. Demerath and Harlan W. Gilmore, "The Ecology of Southern Cities," in *Urban South*, ed. Vance and Demerath, pp. 156-57; Leo J. Schnore and Philip C. Evenson, "Segregation in Southern Cities," *American Journal of Sociology* 72 (1966): 58-60; Taeuber and Taeuber, *Negroes in Cities*, p. 43.

11. U.S. Department of Commerce, Bureau of the Census, and U.S. Department of Labor, Bureau of Labor Statistics, *The Social and Economic Status of Negroes in the United States, 1970*, Current Population Reports, Series P-23, no. 38, Bureau of Labor Statistics Report no. 394, p. 15, table 9.

12. Comparisons are made here between figures based on color and those based on race, and this will be done of necessity throughout the chapter. Very little distortion should result when the South is viewed as a whole, however, for according to 1970 figures, 96.6 percent of nonwhites in the region were Negro. For one state, Oklahoma, the distortion is extremely significant. There, because of the large Indian population, only 40.3 percent of nonwhites are Negro (U.S. Department of Commerce, Bureau of the Census, *Census of Population, 1970: General Population Characteristics*, Advance Reports, Series PC [V2]).

13. See Fleishman, "Southern City," pp. 169-94.

14. U.S. Department of Commerce, Bureau of the Census, *Census of Population and Housing, 1970*, table A.

15. John F. Kain, "Housing Segregation, Negro Employment and Metropolitan Decentralization," *Quarterly Journal of Economics* 82 (1968): 178; John F. Kain and Joseph J. Persky, "Alternatives to the Gilded Ghetto," *Public Interest* 14 (1969): 75-76; and Taeuber and Taeuber, *Negroes in Cities*, p. 78.

16. U.S. Department of Commerce, Bureau of the Census, *Social and Economic Characteristics of the Population in Metropolitan and Nonmetropolitan Areas: 1970 and 1960*, table E.

17. Chester Rapkin, "Price Discrimination Against Negroes in the Rented Housing Market," in *Essays in Urban Land Economics* (Los Angeles: Real Estate Research Program, University of California, 1966), pp. 533-45.

18. Davis McEntire, *Residence and Race* (Berkeley: University of California Press, 1960), p. 89.

19. *Hawkins* v. *Town of Shaw, Mississippi*, 437 F. 2d 1286 at 1288-90 (5th Cir. 1971).

20. National Commission on Urban Problems, *Building the American City* (Washington, D.C.: Government Printing Office, 1969), p. 13.

21. President's Committee on Urban Housing, *A Decent Home* (Washington, D.C.: Government Printing Office, 1969), p. 13.

22. Gunnar Myrdal, *An American Dilemma: The Negro Problem and Modern Democracy* (New York: Harper & Brothers, 1944), p. 618. For a different perspective, see Edward C. Banfield, *The Unheavenly City Revisited* (Boston: Little, Brown & Co., 1974).

23. *Swann* v. *Charlotte-Mecklenburg Board of Education*, 91 S. Ct. 1267 at 1283-84 (1971).

24. Kain, "Housing Segregation," pp. 178-79.

25. Jack Rosenthal, "Large Suburbs Overtaking Cities in the Number of Jobs Supplied," *New York Times*, 15 October 1972, p. 1.

26. Kain, "Housing Segregation," pp. 178-79; Kain and Persky, "Alternatives to the Gilded Ghetto," p. 77.

27. Dorothy K. Newman, "The Decentralization of Jobs," *Monthly Labor Review*, May 1967, p. 8, table 1.

28. Daniel R. Grant, "Urban Needs and State Response: Local Government Reorganization," in *The States and the Urban Crisis*, ed. Alan K. Campbell (Englewood Cliffs, N.J.: Prentice-Hall, 1970), p. 66.

29. John F. Kain, "The Distribution and Movement of Jobs and Industry," in *The Metropolitan Enigma: Inquiries into the Nature and Dimensions of America's "Urban Crisis,"* ed. James Q. Wilson (Cambridge, Mass.: Harvard University Press, 1968), pp. 3-4.

30. Dick Netzer, *Economics of the Property Tax* (Washington, D.C.: Brookings Institution, 1966), pp. 109-16; Dick Netzer, *Impact of the Property Tax: Its Economic Implications for Urban Problems; Research Report Supplied by the National Commission on Urban Problems to the Joint Economic Committee* (Washington, D.C.: Government Printing Office, 1968), pp. 22-30.

31. Paul Davidoff, Linda Davidoff, and Neil N. Gold, "Suburban Action: Advocate Planning for Open Society," *Journal of the American Institute of Planners* 36 (1970): 13; Paul Davidoff and Neil N. Gold, "Exclusionary Zoning," *Yale Review of Law and Social Action* 1 (1970): 57.

32. *Report of the National Advisory Commission on Civil Disorders* (New York: Bantam Books, 1968), p. 22.

33. H. Paul Friesema, "Black Control of Central Cities: The Hollow Prize," *Journal of the American Institute of Planners* 35 (1969): 75-79.

34. U.S. Department of Commerce, Bureau of the Census, *Statistical Abstract of the United States, 1970*, table 1094. Figures of the census South are for the eleven ex-Confederate states, Kentucky, Oklahoma, Maryland, Delaware, and the District of Columbia.

35. U.S. Department of Commerce, Bureau of the Census, and U.S. Department of Labor, Bureau of Labor Statistics, *Social and Economic Status of Negroes in the United States, 1970*, p. 27, table 18.

36. Rapkin, "Price Discrimination Against Negroes in the Rented Housing Market," pp. 335-39.

37. U.S. Department of Commerce, Bureau of the Census, *Census of Population and Housing, 1970*, table B.

38. Fleishman, "Southern City," p. 182.

39. National Commission on Urban Problems, *Building the American City*, p. 231; Dick Netzer, *Economics and Urban Problems: Diagnoses and Prescriptions* (New York: Basic Books, 1970), pp. 122-25.

40. National Committee on Urban Growth Policy, *The New City* (New York: Frederick A. Praeger, 1969), p. 36.

41. U.S. Department of Commerce, Bureau of the Census, "Rank by Population Size of Many U.S. Metro Areas Changed as a Result of 1970 Census," mimeographed news release (1971).

42. Also see Brett W. Hawkins and Thomas R. Dye, "Metropolitan 'Fragmentation,'" *Midwest Review of Public Administration* 4 (1970): 17-24.

43. U.S. Department of Commerce, Bureau of the Census, *Census of Governments: 1967*, vol. 1, *Governmental Organization*, table 1.

44. Jack Rosenthal, "The Outer City: U.S. in Suburban Turmoil," *New York Times*, 30 May 1971, p. 1.

45. Robert H. Connery and Richard H. Leach, "Southern Metropolis: Challenge to

the Government," in *The American South in the 1960's*, ed. Avery Leiserson (New York: Frederick A. Praeger, 1964), p. 66.

46. Grant, "Urban Needs and State Response," p. 61; National Commission on Urban Problems, *Building the American City*, pp. 326-28; Advisory Commission on Intergovernmental Relations, *Alternative Approaches to Governmental Reorganization in Metropolitan Areas* (Washington, D.C.: Government Printing Office, 1962), pp. 12-14.

47. Netzer, *Economics and Urban Problems*, pp. 175-81; Netzer, *Impact of the Property Tax*, pp. 37-38.

48. See Rudolf Heberle, "The Mainsprings of Southern Urbanization," in *Urban South*, ed. Vance and Demerath, pp. 8-9.

49. Ibid., pp. 9-11.

50. Lynn Smith, "The Emergence of Cities," in *Urban South*, ed. Vance and Demerath, pp. 24-37.

51. Otis D. Duncan, W. Richard Scott, Stanley Lieberson, Beverly Duncan, and Hal Winsborough, *Metropolis and Region* (Baltimore: Johns Hopkins University Press, 1960), p. 271.

52. Richard L. Forstall, "Economic Classification of Places over 10,000, 1960-63," in *The Municipal Year Book, 1967* (Chicago: International City Management Association, 1967), p. 45.

53. U.S. Department of Commerce, Bureau of the Census, *Statistical Abstract of the United States, 1970*, table 383.

54. Forstall, "Economic Classification of Places over 10,000," pp. 45-47.

55. See James Clotfelter, "The South and the Military Dollar," *New South* 25 (1970): 52-56. The South received much more than its share of military *base* spending.

56. U.S. Department of Commerce, Bureau of the Census, *Census of Population, 1970: Characteristics of the Population (VI)* (1973), pt. 1, sec. 1, p. 36, fig. 42.

57. C. Horace Hamilton, "Continuity and Change in Southern Migration," in *The South in Continuity and Change*, ed. John C. McKinney and Edgar T. Thompson (Durham, N.C.: Duke University Press, 1965), p. 55; William H. Nicholls, "The South as a Developing Area," in *American South in the 1960's*, ed. Leiserson, p. 34.

58. Charles Tilly, "Race and Migration to the American City," in *Metropolitan Enigma*, ed. Wilson, p. 142.

59. Demerath and Gilmore, "Ecology of Southern Cities," pp. 156-57; Schnore and Evenson, "Segregation in Southern Cities," pp. 58-60; Taeuber and Taeuber, *Negroes in Cities*, p. 5.

60. Schnore and Evenson, "Segregation in Southern Cities," pp. 64, 66.

61. Fleishman, "Southern City," p. 182.

62. U.S. Bureau of the Budget, Office of Statistical Standards, *Standard Metropolitan Statistical Areas*, pp. 4-43; Connery and Leach, "Southern Metropolis," p. 70; Joseph F. Zimmerman, "Metropolitan Reform in the U.S.: An Overview," *Public Administration Review* 30 (1970): 536.

63. Connery and Leach, "Southern Metropolis," p. 70.

64. *Brown v. Board of Education of Topeka, Kansas*, 347 U.S. 483 (1954).

65. *Swann v. Charlotte-Mecklenburg Board of Education*, 91 S. Ct. 1267 (1971).

66. "Spirit of Charlotte Sagged during the Controversial Year," *Charlotte Observer*, 3 January 1971, p. 2E.

67. "Concerned Parents Group Opposes Consolidation," *Charlotte Observer*, 5 March 1971, p. 1A.

68. *Hawkins v. Town of Shaw, Mississippi*, 437 F. 2d 1286 at 1288-90 (5th Cir. 1971).

69. *James v. Valtierra*, 91 S. Ct. 1331 (1971).

70. Robert E. Anderson, Jr., and Horace Barker, *Equal Housing Opportunities in the South: A Challenge* (Atlanta: Southern Regional Council, 1971), pp. 13-22.

71. Eunice Grier and George Grier, "Equality and Beyond: Housing Segregation in the Great Society," in *The Negro American*, ed. Talcott Parsons and Kenneth B. Clark

(Boston: Houghton Mifflin Co., 1966), pp. 525-54.

72. U.S. Commission on Civil Rights, *Racial Isolation in the Public Schools* (Washington, D.C.: Government Printing Office, 1967), p. 22.

73. National Commission on Urban Problems, *Building the American City*, p. 57.

74. U.S. Commission on Civil Rights, *Racial Isolation in the Public Schools*, pp. 23-24.

75. Ibid.

76. Robert B. Semple, Jr., "Nixon to Enforce Rights Measures," *New York Times*, 12 June 1971, pp. 1, 35; and Jack Rosenthal, "U.S. Sues Suburbs on Housing Bias," *New York Times*, 15 June 1971, pp. 1, 35.

77. National Commission on Urban Problems, *Building the American City*, p. 334.

78. Ibid.

79. Netzer, *Economics of the Property Tax*, pp. 108-9.

80. U.S. Department of Commerce, Bureau of the Census, *Census of Governments: 1967*, vol. 4, no. 5, *Compensation of Government Finances*, tables 48, 44.

81. U.S. Department of Commerce, Bureau of the Census, *U.S. Census of Population: 1960*, vol. 1, *Characteristics of the Population*, pt. 1, U.S. Summary, table N.

82. Richard L. Forstall, "Population Change in American Cities, 1960-65," in *The Municipal Year Book, 1966* (Chicago: International City Management Association, 1966), p. 41, table 4; John C. Bollens, "Metropolitan and Fringe Area Developments in 1966," in *The Municipal Year Book, 1967* (Chicago: International City Management Association, 1967), table II; John C. Bollens, "Metropolitan and Fringe Area Developments in 1967," in *The Municipal Year Book, 1968* (Chicago: International City Management Association, 1968), table II.

83. U.S. Department of Commerce, Bureau of the Census, *Social and Economic Characteristics of the Population in Metropolitan and Nonmetropolitan Areas: 1970 and 1960*, pp. 19-20, table 2.

84. U.S. Department of Commerce, Bureau of the Census, *Census of Population and Housing, 1970*, table B.

85. Connery and Leach, "Southern Metropolis," p. 70.

86. Ibid.; Grant, "Urban Needs and State Response," pp. 66-68.

87. Ky. Rev. Stat., sections 81, 100-81, 110; Miss. Code Ann., sections 3374-10 through 3374-14; General Statutes of N.C., section 160-453 to 160-454, especially 160-453.13-24; Tenn. Code Ann., sections 6-309-311; Code of Va., 15.1-1032-1041; Frank S. Sengstock, *Annexation: A Solution to the Metropolitan Area Problem* (Ann Arbor: University of Michigan, 1960), pp. 19-25.

88. Richard F. Babcock, *The Zoning Game* (Madison: University of Wisconsin Press, 1966), pp. 4, 134-38.

89. National Commission on Urban Problems, *Building the American City*, pp. 211-12.

90. Davidoff and Gold, "Exclusionary Zoning," p. 59.

91. *Baker* v. *Carr*, 369 U.S. 186 (1962).

92. Reissman, "Urbanization in the South," pp. 81-82, 85.

93. James Clotfelter and William R. Hamilton, "Beyond Race Politics," in *You Can't Eat Magnolias*, ed. Ayers and Naylor, pp. 136-59.

94. Reissman, "Urbanization in the South," pp. 83-86. Also see the issue on "Urbanization and Social Change in the South," *Journal of Social Issues* 22 (1966): 1-116.

95. Robert L. Lineberry and Edmund P. Fowler, "Reformism and Public Policy in Cities," *American Political Science Review* 61 (1967): 701-16. Also see John H. Kessel, "Governmental Structure and Political Environment," *American Political Science Review* 56 (1962): 615-20.

96. For example, see Resolution 23 on "Housing Opportunities" of resolutions adopted at the annual meeting of United Conference of Mayors, Philadelphia, 16 June 1971.

97. John H. Powell, Jr., "Corporate Relocation to Restrictive Suburbs," in *Open or Closed Suburbs: Corporate Location and the Urban Crisis* (White Plains, N.Y.: Subur-

ban Action Institute, 1971), pp. 33-34.

98. Anderson and Barker, *Equal Housing Opportunities in the South*, p. 3.

99. Advisory Commission on Intergovernmental Relations, *1970 Cumulative ACIR State Legislative Program* (Washington, D.C.: Government Printing Office, 1969), pp. 1-12.

100. See Council of State Governments, *The States and the Metropolitan Problem* (Chicago: Council of State Governments, 1956).

101. Grant, "Urban Needs and State Response," pp. 68, 72; Zimmerman, "Metropolitan Reform in the U.S.," pp. 532-33.

102. National Commission on Urban Problems, *Building the American City*, p. 340.

103. Committee for Economic Development, *Reshaping Government in Metropolitan Areas* (New York: Committee for Economic Development, 1970), chap. 4.

104. Babcock, *Zoning Game*, pp. 159-73; National Commission on Urban Problems, *Building the American City*, p. 242.

105. Advisory Commission on Intergovernmental Relations, *Urban and Rural America: Politics for Future Growth* (Washington, D.C., 1970), p. 162.

106. U.S. Department of Commerce, Bureau of the Census, "Rank by Population Size of Many U.S. Metro Areas Changed." Seven states presently have inter-Southern metropolitan areas.

107. Anthony Downs, "Alternative Forms of Future Urban Growth in the United States," *Journal of the American Institute of Planners* 36 (1970): 5-8.   108. Victor

108. Victor R. Fuchs, *Differentials in Hourly Earnings by Region and City Size, 1959*, Occasional Paper 101 (New York: National Bureau of Economic Research, Columbia University, 1967).

109. Anderson and Barker, "Equal Housing Opportunities in the South," pp. 13-17, 22-24.

110. John Kain, "Coping with Ghetto Unemployment," *Journal of the American Institute of Planners* 35 (1969): 82.

111. Powell, "Corporate Relocation to Restrictive Suburbs," pp. 2, 32.

112. Advisory Commission on Intergovernmental Relations, *1970 Cumulative ACIR State Legislative Program* (Washington, D.C.: Government Printing Office, 1969), no. 31-31-00, pp. 1-4.

113. Netzer, *Impact of the Property Tax*, pp. 13-22, 29-30.

114. National Committee on Urban Growth Policy, *New City*, p. 123; Netzer, *Economics and Urban Problems*, pp. 176-77, 179-81.

Chapter 7

1. U.S. Department of Agriculture, *Rurality, Poverty, and Health*, Agricultural Economics Report no. 172 (1970), p. 1.

2. Alabama, Senate Hearings, pt. III (1971).

3. F. Ray Marshall to Thomas H. Naylor, private correspondence in possession of the authors.

4. James Clotfelter, "The South and the Military Dollar," *New South* 25 (1970): 52-56.

5. Coleman, *Educational Opportunity*, 1:273.

6. Ralph McGill, *The South and the Southerner* (Boston: Little, Brown & Co., 1963), p. 163.

7. Hubert H. Humphrey, "A Plan for Breathing New Life into Rural America," *Los Angeles Times*, 26 September 1971.

8. James M. Pierce, *The Condition of Farm Workers and Small Farmers in 1970* (New York: National Sharecroppers Fund, 1971), p. 10.

9. U.S. Department of Agriculture, *Welfare Reform: Benefits and Incentives in Rural America* (1971), p. 13.

10. Pierce, *Condition of Farm Workers and Small Farmers in 1970*, p. 9.

11. A report by the U.S. Department of Agriculture's rural development service in 1973 found that the physician shortage is more acute in rural areas, people in rural areas have to travel longer distances to obtain health care, emergency health services are more deficient and work-related injuries are higher ("Rural Health Care is Lagging Far Behind," *Durham* [N.C.] *Morning Herald*, 23 July 1973, p. 58).

12. John Delafons, *Land Use Controls in the United States* (Cambridge, Mass.: Joint Center for Urban Studies, Massachusetts Institute of Technology and Harvard University, 1962), p. 16.

13. Ibid., p. 51.

14. U.S. Department of Agriculture, Economic Research Service, *Differential Assessment of Farmland Near Cities . . . Experience in Maryland Through 1965*, by Peter W. House (Washington, D.C.: Government Printing Office, 1967), p. iv.

15. John V. Van Sickle, *Planning for the South: An Inquiry into the Economics of Regionalism* (Nashville: Vanderbilt University Press, 1943), p. 118.

Index

A

Abortions, free of charge, 73-74
"Academic common market" plan, 168
Advisory Commission on Intergovernmental Relations, 62, 256
Agrarianism: problems in, 264-67;
  inputs to rural South, 268-71;
  influence of on economy, 271-72;
  influence of on education, 272;
  influence of on politics, 272-73;
  social factors of, 273; policy
  recommendations for, 274-77; and
  land-use planning, 278. *See also*
  Great Depression, the: strategies to
  bring South out of
Agricultural and Industrial Board of
  Mississippi, 54
Agricultural Stabilization and
  Conservation Service (ASCS), 270
Agriculture: decrease of employment
  in, 28-30; diminished importance
  of, 48; federal programs in, 270;
  prices in, 271. *See also* Agrarianism
Aid to Families with Dependent Chil-
  dren (AFDC), 274
Alston, Wallace M., Jr., 107
American Association of University
  Professors, 139
American Federation of Teachers, 140
American Philosophical Society, 131
Antebellum period, 13-19; social classes
  of, 16. *See also* Economic growth
Appalachian Regional Commission, 69,
  74, 277
Ashmore, Harry, 104
Askew, Governor Reubin, 196, 243, 283
Association of Educators, 92
Atlantic Coast Conference. *See* Colleges,
  intercollegiate athletics in public

B

Baker v. *Carr*, 185, 190, 193, 204, 244,
  251
Barnett, Governor Ross, 30, 43, 132
Basic Educational Opportunity Grant,
  150
Big Eight Conference. *See* Colleges,
  intercollegiate athletics in public
Blacks. *See* Colleges; Education, higher;
  Education, public; Racial discrimina-
  tion; South, the
Bouhuys, Arend, 52
Brown v. *Board of Education*, 83, 102
Bumpers, Governor Dale, 283
Burger, Chief Justice Warren, 103
Business and industry: expansion of
  ownership of, 64-66; policy
  recommendations for, 64-68
Busing, 92, 104, 126-27, 244
Byrd, Harry F., Sr., 182

C

Campus Facilities Associates, 113
Capital investments, 121; shortage of,
  37-38; supply of, 33-34. *See also*
  Industrialization, factors affecting
  extent of
Carnegie Commission on the Future of
  Higher Education, 134, 160, 165
Carter, Governor Jimmy, 283
Cash, W. J., 16
Chiles, Lawton, 212
Christian, Virgil, 38
Cities: definition of, 222; black popu-
  lation in, 225-26; residential segrega-
  tion in, 225-27; annexation in, 228,
  247, 249, 256, 261; black migration
  into, 229; urban sprawl in, 232;
  governmental units within, 233-34;

impact of federal legislation on, 244; policy recommendations for federal aid to, 253-54; public mass transportation in, 255-56; new incorporations in, 256; city-county consolidation in, 257; development around small existing, 259; suburban fringes of, 261-62

Citizens Conference on State Legislatures, 184, 185, 204, 213

Civil Right acts (1960s), 33, 42, 46, 52, 59, 64, 68, 112, 181, 192, 245, 254, 260

Civil War, 13, 16, 17, 18, 20-22, 31, 35, 42, 44, 45

Climate. See South, the: natural resources in

Clotfelter, James, 183

Coastal Plains Regional Commission, 69, 74, 277

Coleman, James, 79, 81. See also *Equality of Educational Opportunity*

College of William and Mary, 18, 136

Colleges: private, 153; financing of private, 153-54; church-related, 154-55; enrollment of church-related, 154; public, 155-59; financing of public, 155-57; aid to out-of-state students in public, 156; enrollment in public, 157-58; administration in public, 158; intercollegiate athletics in public, 158; accountability to students in public, 158-59; community, 159-61; social aspects of community, 159-60; curriculum in community, 160; location of community colleges, 160-61; blacks in community colleges, 161; predominantly black, 161-65; cycle of deprivation in black, 162-63; problems of predominantly black, 162-63; enrollment in predominantly black, 162, 163; interinstitutional cooperation with black, 164-65; financial needs of black, 165; reorientation of programs in land-grant, 276. See also Education, higher

Commercial institutions, contribution to personal income, 49-50

Commodity Credit Corporation, 277

Common-schools movement, 83

Connally, John, 183

Concerned Parents Association, 244

Conference for Education in the South, 83

Cooperation Extension Service (CES), 270

Corporate income tax: as instrument to control industrial growth, 71. See also Revenue

Corporate policy making, policy recommendations for, 69-70

Cotton, production of, 13-14

Counties: as administrative units, 187; problems in, 187-88; administration of, 209; funds allocated to, 209; policy decisions made in, 209; home rule in, 219; consolidation of, 220; state restrictions in, 220; interlocal cooperation in, 220-21; special districts in, 221

D

Dallas Alliance for Minority Enterprise, 65

Dallas League for the Advancement of Education, 105

Davis, Mayor Russell, 53

Delafons, John, 278

Democratic party: 68, 177, 178, 179, 182, 183, 185, 198, 199-201, 211, 283

Department of Agriculture, reorientation of, 279-80

Department of Health, Education, and Welfare, 104, 112

Department of Housing and Urban Development (HUD), 254, 255

Department of Rural Development, proposed, 65, 66

Depression, the. See Great Depression, the

Desegregation, 84, 102-3, 105; positive results, 103-4; federal executive branch influence on, 104. See also Education, public: federal-level policy decisions affecting

"Doctrine of White Supremacy," 22, 25

Draconic laws, 19

Duke University, 131, 173

Dye, Thomas, 178, 203

E

Early childhood development, policy recommendations for, 121

Economic Development Administration, 69, 277

Economic growth, retarded because of insufficient industrialization, 13-15

Economic institution: inputs into, 35-41; influence of external factors on, 41-42; effect of political institution on, 42-43; effect of social institution on, 43-45; effect of educational institution on, 45-46; influence of state policies on, 47, 48; summary of major policy recommendations on, 281

Economic problems. *See* South, the: economic problems in

Education, defined by Charles Silberman, 77

Education, higher: increasing cost of, 129-30; quality of graduate faculty in, 131; troubles in, 129-32; willingness of South to support, 130-31; factors contributing to the situation of, 131; and the predominantly black college, 131, 138; causes for plight of, 132; enrollment in, 132-34, 138, 140, 144; black enrollment in, 134, 138, 144; degree production in, 134; income of families of students in, 134; historical development of, 136-38; in 1940s, 137; in 1960s, 137; admissions selection in, 138; inputs into, 139-42; physical plants in, 139; student-faculty ratio in, 139; faculty in, 139-40; characteristics of faculty in, 139-40; organization of, 141; financing of, 141-42; constituency of, 142; philanthropy from foundations, 143; external factors influencing, 143-45; and the job market, 144; and the population trend, 144; faculty recruitment in, 145; student unrest and, 145; influence of economic institution on, 146-47; influence of political institution on, 147-49; influence of public education on, 149; influence of social institution on, 149; federal appropriations to, 150; state appropriations to; 150-51; university appropriations to, 151; admissions in, 151-52; intelligence tests in, 152; personnel policies in, 152; curriculum planning in, 152-53; graduate education in, 165-67; graduate enrollment in, 166; graduate programs in, 166-67; policy recommendations for, 167-76, 282; organization and structure in, 168; reduction of disciplinary isolationism in, 168; academic programs in, 169; selection of administrators in, 169; administration of, 169; criteria for resource allocation in, 170; formulation of goals in, 170; ability-to-pay principle, 171; alternative schemes for financing, 171-72; voucher plan in, 171-73; grants for, 172; guaranteed loans for, 172; open-door admissions policy in, 172; adult education in, 173; minority-group recruitment in, 173; student involvement in planning curriculum in, 173; intercollegiate sports in, 173; stu-

dent internships in, 174; loco parentis of students in, 174-75; counseling procedures in, 175; focus of toward the community, 175; emphasis on societal problem-solving, 175. *See also* Colleges

Education, public: in South, 18-19; development of in South, 82-84; inputs into, 84-98; instructional staff in, 84-88; pupil-teacher ratio in, 87; curriculum in, 88-89, 123-25; organization and structure in, 89; facilities in, 90-92; degree of integration in, 92-93, 126; characteristics of students in, 94-95; administration of, 93-94; financing of, 95-98; federal appropriations to, 96; state appropriations to, 96-97; per pupil expenditure in, 97; average annual salary of personnel in, 97-98; influence of social institution on, 104-5; business leaders' interest in, 104-5; influence of the institution of the family on, 106; influence of the economy on, 107-9; influence of politics on, 109-10; influence of higher education on, 110; policy decisions of school boards affecting, 110-11; state-level policy decisions affecting, 111-12; federal-level policy decisions affecting, 112; vocational education in, 115; adult education in, 116, 124; policy recommendations for, 119-28, 281-82; evaluating student performance in, 122

Educational accountability, principle of, 121

Educational attainment, measures of, 78-82

Educational inputs, influence of on educational outputs, 98-102

Educational process, federal courts' input into, 103-4

Educational television, 126

Education and technology, investments in, 34-35. *See also* Industrialization, factors affecting extent of

Education Commission of the States, 113

Elementary schools, in the South, 113-14

Emergency School Assistance Program, 114

Employment: antidiscrimination laws in, 68; suburbanization of, 227-28; problem of communication of opportunities in, 260-61. *See also* Manufacturing, employment in

Endowments. *See* Institutions, method of analysis of

Equality of Educational Opportunity,
81, 87-105 passim, 110, 111, 119, 121,
266-67, 272
"Equal terms," defined by Chief Justice
Earl Warren, 102
Executive Order on Equal Opportunity
in Housing (1962), 245
Expenditures: per capita, 64; per pupil,
120. *See also* Economic institution,
influence of external factors on
External factors. *See* Institutions, method
of analysis of

F
Family Assistance Program, 274
Family planning services, 73
Farm Bureau, 273
Farm price-support programs, elimina-
tion of, 279
Farmers. *See* Antebellum period, social
classes of
Farmers Home Administration (FHA),
270
Faubus, Orval, 43
Federal Education Act (1972), 171
Federal Farm Loan Act (1916), 280
Federal funds. *See* Revenue
Financial incentives, 68
Financial institutions, no serious problem
in future economic development in,
50-51
Floyd, Joe, 34
Flynt, Wayne, 107
Ford Foundation. *See* Education, higher:
philanthropy from foundations
Froman, Lewis A., Jr., 177
Full employment policy, 68
Funds, state and local: policy recom-
mendations for disbursement of, 72.
See also Revenue

G
Gallop poll, 84, 92
Georgia State University, 136
Goldwater, Barry, 200, 201
Goods and services, demand for, 32. *See
also* Industrialization, factors affecting
extent of
Government: state constitutions in, 189-
90; rewriting of state constitutions in,
212-13; "in the sunshine" law in, 215;
black employment in, 217; unified
court systems in, 218
Grady, Henry, 69
Grandfather clause, 180
Great Depression, the, 24-27, 41, 83;

strategies to bring South out of, 25-28
Guaranteed annual income, 71, 274

H
Harris poll, 7
Hawkins v. *Town of Shaw, Mississippi*,
244
Head Start Projects. *See* South, the:
kindergarten in
Health care delivery systems, 72-73
Healy, Timothy, 158
Heard, Alexander, 78, 131, 183
Heywood, Nathaniel, 14
Highway system. *See* Transportation
and communications systems
Hill, Samuel S., Jr., 107
Holshouser, Governor James E., Jr., 283
Holton, Governor Linwood, 217, 283
Home rule, definition of, 208-9
House Committee on Agriculture, 29, 30
Housing: discrimination in, 226; impact
of federal legislation on, 245-46;
federal resources and power to affect
patterns in, 255; federal subsidies for
low-cost, 255; local open-housing
ordinances in, 259-60; securing of by
corporations for employees, 261

I
Industrialization: factors affecting
extent of, 15-20; degree of improved
in South, 30; effect of on the environment, 51; textile industry in, 52-54;
racial descrimination in, 53; planning
of 54-55; economic policy recommendations for, 67-68
Input variables. *See* Institutions, method
of analysis of
Institutions: framework of analysis of,
4; method of analysis of, 7-9
Internal Revenue Service, 119
International trade, 66-67

J
James, A. C., 93
James v. *Valtierra*, 244
Jefferson, Thomas, 18
Jencks, Christopher, 119, 165; report
by, 119-20
Jewell, Malcolm E., 206

K
Kain, John M., 228
Kerner Commission, 229
Kerr, Clark, 130
Key, V. O., 209

King, Lonnie, Jr., 126
King, Martin Luther, 30
Korean War, 41
Ku Klux Klan, 30, 273

L
L. Q. C. Lamar Society, 54
Labor: supply of, 38-39; industrial, 55-59; wage differentials in, 55-56; and labor unions, 56-58; right-to-work laws, 58-59; minimum-wage laws, 59; racial discrimination in, 59
Land, zoning of, 278-279. *See also* South, the: natural resources in
Land-use planning, 278-79
Lander, Ernest, 18
Law enforcement: selection of judges in, 207, 218; size and effectiveness of, 207-8; public interest law firms in, 218-19; appointment of court officials in, 219; legal aid available to all, 219; racial composition in, 219; training centers for officers in, 219
Leach, Richard H., 214
Legislators, increase salary of, 213
Legislatures: state, 184-87; reappointment of, 185-86, 192-93, 203-4; campaigns for, 201-2; bills introduced in, 202-3; annual sessions of, 204, 213; governor's formal power in, 205, 206, 215, 216; governor's leadership ability in, 206-7; facilities in, 213; policy recommendations for, 213-17; research arm for, 213; ethics in, 214; gubernatorial self-succession in, 214; multimember districts' effect on, 213-14; reduce number of elective offices in, 214-15; governor's responsibility in, 216-17; departments of administration in, 217
Lewis, John, 191
Long, Governor Russell, 182

M
McCormick, Cyrus, 19
McFarlane, William F., 154, 155
McGovern, George, 283-84
Maddox, James, 88
Maddox, Governor Lester, 147
Marshall, Ray, 38, 267, 270, 272, 277
Management information systems. *See* State planning
Manpower: and employment, 68-70; training programs, 69
Manufacturing: earnings in, 31; employ-ment in, 31. *See also* South, the: manufacturing in
Median family income. *See* South, the
Meredith, James, 30
Meyerson, Martin, 170
Military defeat. *See* Civil War
Minimum level of health care, concept of, 72
Minimum-wage laws, 69
Morrill Land-Grant Act of 1862, 137
Morris, Willie, 105
Myrdal, Gunnar, 77, 226

N
NAACP, 126
National Academy of Science, 131
National Business League, 50, 65
National Commission on Urban Problems, 226, 246
National Education Association, 139
National Opinion Research Center, 81
National Science Foundation, 150
Naylor, Thomas H., 47
Negroes, education of, 83
New Deal, 25, 26, 83, 276
"New South," colonialism in, 22-24
Nicholls, William H., 12, 44-45, 197
Nixon, Richard, 104, 183, 199, 274; administration of, 246, 279
Noland, William E., 106
Nordheimer, Jon, 35
North Carolina Bar Association's Committee on Court Improvement, 207
North Carolina Department of Conservation and Development, 54
North Carolina Governor's Committee on State Government Reorganization, 186
North Carolina State University, 136
North, Douglass, 19

O
Odum, Howard, 74
Office of Economic Opportunity, 66
Out-migration. *See* Great Depression, the: strategies to bring the South out of
Output variables. *See* Institutions, method of analysis of
Ozark Regional Commission, 69-74, 277

P
Peabody Fund. *See* Education, higher: philanthropy from foundations
Per capita income. *See* South, the: per capita income in; United States, per capita personal income in

Perot, H. Ross, 41, 54
Personal income tax. *See* Revenue; South, the
Phi Beta Kappa, 18
Phillips, U. B., 180
Planning. *See* State planning
Planters. *See* Antebellum period, social classes of
Plessy v. *Ferguson*, 83, 192
Policy recommendations, 7; in the economy, 64-76; in public education, 119-28; in higher education, 167-76; in politics, 210-21; in urban development, 253-63; in rural development, 274-80; summary of major, 281-82; implementation of, 283-84
Political systems, inputs into, 189-94
Politics: ideological polarization in, 42; one-partyism in, 177-80; discrimination in, 180-81; electoral voting behavior in, 181-84; urban-rural balance in, 190-91; growth of black influence on, 191; influence of economic institution on, 194-96; influence of educational institution on, 196-97; influence of social institution on, 197; policy decisions in, 198-99; party structure in, 200, 211; primaries in, 200-201; governors' role in, 204-7; policy recommendations for, 210-21, 282; campaign cost and expenditure in, 211-12; nonprofessional political participation in, 212; voter organization in, 212; public opinion surveys in, 215; voice of small farmers in, 280
Pollution, national standards for purity of air and water, 256
Population: blacks in, 43-44; policies for state, 73
Poverty: definition of, 12; extent of in South, 12
Presecondary schools, nongradedness in, 125
Presidential Commission on Urban Growth and America's Future, 224
President's Advisory Council on Minority Business Enterprise, 49, 65
President's Commission on School Finance, 96
President's Commission on Urban Housing, 226
Principal, the black, 92-93
Property tax. *See* Revenue; South, the
Protectionist trade policy, 67
Public Affairs Research Council in Louisiana, 213

Public services, county responsibility for, 262

R

Race Relations Information Center, 92
Racial discrimination, 22, 25, 53, 207; in employment, 59; in housing, 225-26
Reed, John Shelton, 3
Republican party, 68, 179, 183, 185, 198, 199-201, 211, 283, 284
Resource, Conservation and Development Program, 277
Revenue, 60-63, 70, 71, 127-28, 262
Reynolds v. *Simms*, 185, 190, 193
Ribicoff, Abraham, 254
Riesman, David, 163, 165
Robertson, Willis, 182
Rockefeller Foundation. *See* Education, higher: philanthropy from foundations
Rogers, Will, 199
Romney, George, 246
Roosevelt, Franklin D., 10

S

Sales tax. *See* Revenue
Sanders, John, 208
Schauland, Horst, 47
Scholastic Aptitude Test, 163
Schools: secondary, 114-15; facilities and equipment in, 125; local district control of nonfinancial affairs, 127; city and county systems, 127; impact of federal legislation and desegregation, 105, 244. *See also* Education, public
Schultze, Charles L., 270, 279
Scott, Governor Robert, 166
"Segregation academies," 84, 95; Internal Revenue affect on, 119
Serrano v. *Priest*, 262
Sharkansky, Ira, 209
Silberman, Charles, 77
Singletary, Otis, 132
Skilled labor, 32-33. *See also* Industrialization, factors affecting extent of
Slaves. *See* Antebellum period, social classes of; South, the: slaves in
Small Business Administration, 65, 66
Smith, Howard, 182
Smith v. *Allright*, 180
South, the: regional focus on, 3-4; major problems of, 5; per capita income in, 10-11, 13; in 1920, 24; in 1940, 28; in 1960, 30; reasons for lag in per capita income in, 12-13; economic problems in, 12-20; slaves in, 14;

plantation system in, 14-15; manufacturing in, 20-22; democratic changes in between 1940 and 1960, 29-30; median family income between 1959 and 1969, 30; immigration to, 30-31; black employment in, 38-39; natural resources in, 39-40; management and entrepreneurship in, 40-41; worker alienation in, 58; desegregation in, 84; kindergarten in, 113; special education in, 116-18; private schools in, 118; special education in, 128; "brain drain" in, 131; degree of urbanization in, 222; substandard housing in, 229-31; natural resources in, 268-69; capital in, 269; human resources in, 269, 274-75

Southeastern Conference. *See* Colleges, intercollegiate athletics in public

Southern Association of Colleges and Schools, 119, 151

Southern courts, problems of, 207

Southerners, attitudes of skepticism toward institutions, 6-7

Southern Governors Conference, 217

Southern Growth Policies Board, 74, 259

Southern Regional Council, 255

Southern Regional Education Board, 147, 153, 166, 168; goals of, 134-36

Southern states, reliance of on property tax, 247

Southern subregions, identification of, 222-23

Southern whites, median family income of (1970), 12; in contrast to southern blacks, 12; concept of education in New South, 83-84

Southwest Conference. *See* Colleges, intercollegiate athletics in public

Speaker Ban Law (1963), 148

Standard Metropolitan Statistical Area (SMSA), 222, 225, 227, 233, 238, 240, 247, 256

State planning, 74; reorientation of departments, 75; policy recommendations for, 75-76

Swann v. *Charlotte-Mecklenburg Board of Education*, 103, 111, 227

T

Taft-Hartley Act, 58

Talmadge, Eugene, 132

Taxes. *See* Revenue

Teachers: demotion of black, 92; participation in policy making, 122;

teachers' aides, 122; teacher education programs, 123

Telephones. *See* Transportation and communications systems

Tennessee Valley Authority, 39-40

Tenure. *See* Education, higher: policy recommendations for

Texas Governor's Committee on Public School Education, 106

Textile industry. *See* Industrialization

Thurmond, Strom, 43

Timber. *See* South, the: natural resources in

Tindall, George, 178

Tocqueville, Alexis de, 77-78

Transportation and communications systems, 40

Trippitt, Frank, 203

U

Unionization, effect on industry of, 56-57

United States: median family income of (1960), 12; per capita personal income in, 11; in 1920, 24; in 1940, 28; personal income tax in, 61; zoning in, 249-50; welfare system in, 274

United States Commission on Civil Rights, 81, 104, 245

United States Department of Agriculture, 265, 270, 274, 277, 279

United States Labor Department, 69

United States Office of Education, 95

United States Supreme Court, decisions of, 42, 73, 84, 102-3, 105, 112, 126, 156, 180, 192, 193, 196, 244

Universities. *See* Colleges

University of North Carolina at Chapel Hill, 18, 131; graduate school of business, 41

University of Texas, 131

Urban development: inputs into, 241-52; influence of external factors on, 243-52; policy recommendations for, 253-63; state-level policy recommendations for, 256-63; modern approaches to planning and development, 263; summary of policy recommendations, 282

Urban growth: conurbation in, 224; history of, 236-40; from 1920 to 1950, 237; from 1950 to present, 237-40; and blacks, 240; influence of political institution on, 250-52; influence of social institution on, 252; influence of educational institution on, 252; national housing policy in, 254-55

Urban problems, impact of state legislation on, 246-47

V
Vietnam War, 41, 145
Vocational training, policy recommendations for, 120-21
Voter Education Project, 191
Voter turnout, factors influencing, 177-78
Voting Rights Act (1965), 192
Voucher system, in education, 128

W
Wagner, Paul M., 188
Wallace, Governor George, 30, 43, 57, 132, 198, 266, 284
Wall, John W., 47
Ware, Nathaniel A., 15,17
Warren, Earl, 102

Washington, Booker T., 126
Water resources. *See* South, the: natural resources in
Watson, Peter, 152
West, Governor John, 52, 217, 283
White Citizens Council, 30, 273
Williams, John Bell, 43
Wisdom, John Minor, 180
Woodward, C. Vann, 24
World War I, 22, 23, 41, 83
World War II, 22, 28, 41, 44, 62, 64, 83, 252; impact on the economy, 28-30
Wyly, Sam, 41

Y
Yarborough, Ralph, 183
Yeoman.*See* Antebellum period, social classes of